THE RAGIN' CAJUN

MEMOIR OF A LOUISIANA MAN

MERCER UNIVERSITY PRESS

Endowed by

TOM WATSON BROWN
and
THE WATSON-BROWN FOUNDATION, INC.

THE
RAGIN' CAJUN
MEMOIR OF A LOUISIANA MAN

DOUG KERSHAW
WITH
CATHIE PELLETIER

MERCER UNIVERSITY PRESS
Macon, Georgia

40 Years of Publishing Excellence, 1979–2019

MUP/ H978

© 2019 by Doug Kershaw and Cathie Pelletier
Published by Mercer University Press
1501 Mercer University Drive
Macon, Georgia 31207
All rights reserved

9 8 7 6 5 4 3 2 1

Books published by Mercer University Press are printed on acid-free paper
that meets the requirements of the American National Standard for
Information Sciences—Permanence of Paper for Printed Library Materials.

Printed and bound in the United States.

This book is set in Adobe Caslon Pro.

Cover/jacket design by Burt&Burt.

ALL PHOTOS used are from the personal collection of DOUG KERSHAW.

The artwork in this book was done by the late Floyd Sonnier, who helped select the
prints for us. They can be found at his gallery in Scott, Louisiana:
www.FloydSonnier.com.

ISBN   978-0-88146-716-1
Cataloging-in-Publication Data is available from the Library of Congress

To the memory of my parents,

Mama Rita and Daddy Jack,

My brothers,

Edward, Nelson, and Rusty,

My wife,

Pamela Marie,

And to my five sons, my grandchildren, and great-grandchildren.

Ragin Cajun

From the land of Bigmouth lunker bass
And Spanish moss he came
Shakin' up the civilized
Kershaw was his name

Dyed-in-the-wool and registered
Cajun as they come
First time he was seen in town
He puzzled people some

With swamp mud on his ankles
But talent to the bone
His mind was wrung, his songs were sung
He struggles on and on

He wrote of his Cajun country
And the world took a look or two
They saw that he really meant it
And wasn't just passing through

He'd fade and almost vanish
As changes came and went
Then he'd bounce back smiling, like:
"Hello world, I'm sent!"

He's been a long time coming
Thank God he has survived
Get ready for him this time world
My Cajun friend has arrived!

A poem originally written by Johnny Cash and used as liner notes on Doug Kershaw's 1969 LP *"The Cajun Way."* (Used with permission by Johnny Cash, 8/25/98).

CONTENTS

PREFACE

Lake Arthur, Louisiana

Some things you have to leave home to do. I had to travel a long way to make my mark in rock 'n' roll and in country music. But I never forgot how Cajun music got me there. Or that my Cajun heritage defined me. Other things draw you back home. I couldn't have started writing this book anywhere but in Southwest Louisiana. So, like the prodigal son, I went home to tell my story.

When I first started thinking about my life, about trying to make some sense out of it, I called up images I thought I'd lost, the sights, sounds, and smells of Louisiana. And of the Mermentau River where I was born. I thought about the secrets, too, because down in Louisiana secrets are thick as deerflies. And like a deerfly, those secrets can sometimes bite hard enough to draw blood.

When I went back to Lake Arthur, just miles from where I was born, the memories started to wash over me like the waters of the Mermentau. There was Mama Rita boiling rice on the banks of the river, and Daddy Jack heading across Lake Arthur to trap mink and muskrat. I remembered the first pair of shoes I owned, and the first pair I shined for pennies. I could hear all those *fais do-dos,* where we kids fell asleep listening to the fiddle and accordion, to loud laughter, and steady dancing. And, much too often, to fighting.

My memories aren't all happy ones. I still have dreams so scary I can't, or won't, remember what they were about. I suspect they're leftovers from the river days when we Cajuns lived on houseboats so far back in the swamps that the government didn't know we existed. Back when a lot of us were ashamed of our lack of worldly knowledge, of our Cajun French language, of our very roots. Back in the days before Cajuns were considered *trendy.*

The pull on my spirit was strong that first night. I slept very little. By 6 a.m., I was up brewing a pot of strong Louisiana coffee. With a cup in my hand, I walked down to the wharf and stood looking to the east, where the sun was already up and shining. Spanish moss hung in gray clumps from the cypress trees. Most people think Spanish moss kills the tree, but that's not true. The moss just needs a bit of support. A place to rest. Sometimes, that's all any of us need.

"Speak to me, Lake Arthur," I said.

As I stared out across the water, I began turning slowly, clockwise, until I was facing west. That's when I saw the most beautiful rainbow I'd ever seen. The end of it was pointing to the very place where I was born, Tiel Ridge. You won't find it on a map. It's just a spot along the river where Daddy Jack and Mama Rita tied our houseboat to a cypress tree, back in the swamps. I guess some folks will say it was a coincidence that the rainbow ended right where my life began. But I don't think so. I think it meant I'd come full circle to write down this story.

I stood looking out across that lake as if I was looking straight back into my past.

"Talk to me, Mama Rita," I said. "Talk to me, Daddy Jack. And, God, maybe you could talk to me a little too."

Then, hell, I just listened to what everybody had to say.

ACKNOWLEDGMENTS

Thank you to all the people whose names appear in this memoir, and who were a huge part of my life. And thank you to those musicians, singers, and songwriters who are still out there on the road, making the magic happen.

—*Doug Kershaw*

Thank you, Tom Viorikic, for always holding the fort.

Special thanks to the late Patsi Bale Cox, and to Shelley Liles McBurney, who traveled to Louisiana with us for research, hard work, and much fun. Carl E. Hileman, of Tamms, Illinois, who also made the trek to Louisiana with his camera, and to northern Maine.

A special thanks to the fine team at Mercer University Press for their patience and belief in this book, especially Marsha Luttrell.

LOUISIANA:
The artwork in this book was done by the late Floyd Sonnier, who helped select the prints for us. They can be found at his gallery in Scott, Louisiana: www.FloydSonnier.com. Also many thanks to Verlie and Tim Sonnier for their assistance.

Wade Falcon, for creating the index and for helping with local info.

And to all those Cajun friends and relatives: *Laisser le bon temps rouler!*

MAINE:
Janet T. Mills, for the hospitality and Kershaw event on North Haven island; the late Joan Pelletier St. Amant, for reading the manuscript; Colleen and Rick McLaughlin, in Millinocket; Allen Jackson, for the help during Doug's visit to Maine; Aaron Bernstein, for assisting with digital

photo files; The Inn of Acadia, in Madawaska, Jim, J J, and the Roy family and staff, for welcoming Doug to the inn. In memory of the late Louis A. Pelletier, Sr. for his love of Acadian fiddle and all things Kershaw; And thanks to Darrell McBreairty for help with photo files.

To all you Acadian cousins in Maine and Canada who were a great support.

TENNESSEE:
Randy and Melanie Ford, for reading the manuscript; Annie Mosher, for help with archives research; Nelson and Mariana Eddy; Edgar Rothschild; Brandi Nash; Heather Ward McDonald and Dan McDonald. And thanks to the late Jim Glaser for helping with Music City info from the 1960s.

And many thanks to the following folks for various tasks and friendship:

Larry Wells, and also Kathleen Woodruff Wickham, in Oxford, MS; Carol and Gary Vincent, in Clarksdale, MS; Kathleen Wallace King and Nicholas Lee Daniels, in Los Angeles; Zoran Popovic, in Hollywood; Rosemary Kingsland and Neil Jefferies, in Peasmarsh, England; Ken Onstad, in Minnesota; Jack and Cherie Page, in Massachusetts.

A special mention to Callahan Levi Flipo, and also Rita Shellard, both of Montreal.

In Romania, for the technical help, Emanuel, Carmen, and Eva Zeries.

PART 1

LIFE ON THE BAYOU

Back Porch Waltz

1

PILLAR TO POST

"They call my mama Rita and my daddy Jack . . ."
From "Louisiana Man"
By Doug Kershaw

Here's how I've heard the story told many times over the years.

Rita had been in pain most of the day when Jack finally came in off the Mermentau River. When he stepped inside the two-room houseboat, he realized that his young wife was about to give birth to their first child. Jack's sisters were doing their best to make Rita comfortable, but it was obvious things weren't going well. Jack didn't say much. He just climbed into the skiff and went downriver to get the local midwife, *la chasse femme*. She would charge him five dollars, cash money, for a birthing. That was a week's catch of fish for Jack Kershaw, but he had no choice.

It was a long, hard labor, and despite the midwife's efforts, the baby girl was just too big for Rita's small body. With one final push the baby was born, her neck twisted brutally to one side. That child, who would have been my oldest sibling, lived for six hours. My father was good at estimating the weight of his catch. He believed the baby weighed almost ten pounds. Rita had nothing to take to kill the pain. All she could do was lie there and wait for her first child to die. When it was over, Jack headed back out to run his fishing lines.

I will say this about my father. He was a hard worker and a good provider. When he was sober, he was even a good man.

Some days later, Rita got back into her usual routine. She rose each morning at 3 a.m., brewed coffee, and made *couche-couche*, or steamed cornmeal, for Jack. As soon as he ate his breakfast and headed out on the river again, Rita would open the box that held her few personal possessions. I suppose you could say it was her trousseau. Inside were the bundles of rags she'd stuffed with Spanish moss and fashioned into dolls. Then, with Jack off fishing, she'd climb up into the arms of a cypress tree and sing songs to her homemade babies.

Rita Kershaw had just turned thirteen years old.

They call my mama Rita and my daddy Jack.

The Lake Charles *American Press* once ran an article tracing the roots of the Kershaw and Broussard families. It spoke of the first Kershaw who came to Southwest Louisiana, an English doctor named John Nedham Kershaw, who was issued a cattle brand in 1824 in St. Mary Parish. So the first Kershaws were not Acadian exiles from Canada, as were most of the Louisiana Cajuns. They eventually ended up on the river and in the swamps, but they didn't start out there. As they say down in Louisiana, you get to be a Cajun by blood or by the ring. The Kershaws got there by the ring, by marrying into the Broussard family.

The first one of John's descendants to live on the Mermentau was Joseph Nedham Kershaw, who married Onesia Touchet. They lived at Cypress Island, between Grand Lake and Lake Arthur, and raised seven children. After Onesia died, Joseph married Olivia Plaisance and started a second family. By the time these two finished having children, there would be ten more. One of them was my father, Jack Kershaw, born on August 16, 1902, the man I would know as Daddy Jack.

The Kershaws might have started out as cattlemen, farmers, and slave owners with sizable properties, but by the time Daddy Jack was born, they had ended up in the swamps and bayous of Southwest Louisiana. And they were poor as church mice. I wish I knew how they went from landed gentry to swamp rats in just two generations, but I don't. The boys were taught young how to survive by catching fish, hunting ducks and geese, trapping minks, muskrats, and otters. And, of course, poling for alligators. That was a typical education for Cajun boys. Cajun girls were taught to cook, to sew, and have babies.

Part of the year Daddy Jack's family lived in a houseboat tied up along Lake Arthur. Other times they traveled up and down the Mermentau River. Like all Cajuns, the Kershaws loved to dance. Down in Louisiana, folks used to say that if you lived in the swamps, you would end up web-footed. But I knew a long time ago that wasn't true. If it were, there wouldn't have been so many good dancers! The Kershaws all drank a lot and they fought a lot too. They'd duke it out with each other or with some-one else. It didn't much matter. Keep in mind, they were from that gener-ation of men who worked long, hard days, from sunup until sundown. Fighting was entertainment, a release for all that pent-up emotion and frustration. To the Kershaws, fighting was almost an art form.

Mama Rita's grandfather was Nicholas Broussard. Family records say that Nicholas was seven feet tall. The Broussards were among the first tattered and tired band of Acadian refugees to walk upon bayou soil. As the years went by, folks along the river started saying that the whole Brous-sard family "could make a fiddle soar and an accordion dance." The sound of those fiddles is my first memory of Mama Rita's family.

Mama Rita. Looking out over Lake Arthur and thinking about my mother makes me smile, because there was no other woman like her. When she was born they threw away the pattern. She spoke three lan-guages—Cajun French, broken English, and Cuss. Mama Rita could em-barrass a sailor. She didn't have a shy bone in her body, and she would have told the president of the United States where to go just as easily as she would a bum on the street. That was my mother. Ask anyone who ever met her. And then ask them what they thought of her, and they will all say without any hesitation, "I loved that woman!" The old-timers will tell you that she was a good-looking woman, a proud woman, and a fearless woman. She stood her ground, always. And they'll agree that she was a champion cusser. The first Cajun French my wife, Pam, learned after we got married were swear words from Mama Rita. *Fils de putain,* or "son of a bitch," was Mama Rita's favorite cuss of all. As my old friend A. J. Ber-trand once said, "Everybody loved Mama Rita. Even when she called them a *fils de putain!*"

My mother was born in Creole, Louisiana, Cameron Parish, just after midnight on July 23, 1911, the second child of Albert Broussard and Ophelia Benoit Broussard. Albert and Ophelia already had a son, Paul, born three years earlier, but they were separated by the time Rita came along. Ophelia and Paul were staying with a cousin named Billy LaBove, whom Ophelia had asked to stand as godfather to Rita. Billy agreed on one condition: that Ophelia never let Albert Broussard see the baby girl. If she did, Billy threatened to throw both Ophelia and her children out. Why did Billy hate Albert Broussard so much? Mama Rita didn't know. That's another one of those swamp secrets. But hate him he did, and he stood by his word. In a letter she wrote years later, Mama Rita tried to make sense of it all. "My mother done nothing but go to a dance and showed me to my daddy," Rita wrote. "But Cousin Billy put us out, and that's when I made a miserable life going from pillar to post."

Albert Broussard did take his wife and children in for about a year before he, too, threw them out. I never learned the reason or what kind of trouble was brewing between husband and wife, but it was their children who suffered most. After her husband tossed her out, Ophelia kept Paul, but she turned her baby girl over to another couple to raise. That couple soon tired of parenting, and off the baby went to yet another home. Mama Rita was tossed back and forth several more times before landing with some Broussard cousins, where she lived until she was almost seven years old. Sometimes Ophelia also dropped off Paul for several months. But usually it was just Rita who got passed around. Albert and Ophelia eventually had three more daughters, Victoria, Viola, and Estelle. In the end they, too, got left behind.

When I consider the plight of those first Cajuns, my ancestors, I see an irony in how it compares to Mama Rita's own personal history. The Cajuns had come from France to Canada in the early 1600s and were known as Acadians. They founded Port Royal, Nova Scotia, and many other small villages in the provinces now known as New Brunswick, Prince Edward Island, and Newfoundland. In time Acadia, or *Acadie* as it was known in French, became a political football between France and England in the struggle for control in North America. The British eventually got permanent possession. Mind you, these Acadians were Catholics who spoke French. The British Empire saw this as a dangerous thing. They demanded that the Acadians swear loyalty to the Crown or be deported to other British colonies in North America. For their part, the Acadians would have preferred to remain neutral. They were good people who liked to fish, who grew crops in soil that was fertile and giving, and they loved their fiddles and dances. But the British set out to destroy their language, their religion, their very culture.

In 1755, the deportation began for all those Acadians who would not swear allegiance to England. The famous poem *Evangeline,* by Henry Wadsworth Longfellow, recreates this event. But it wasn't very poetic in real life. Many Acadians stayed on in Canada, some by hiding in the woods. Thousands of others, at least those who managed to stay alive, ended up in the harshest of conditions and scattered about the English colonies. About four thousand of these refugees, my own ancestors included, found themselves in the bayous and swamps of Louisiana. When I think of this today it's hard to believe. These were French-Canadians who had probably never even heard of an alligator, or ever dreamed the day would come when they'd see Spanish moss hanging from cypress trees. They must have been heartbroken, especially those first ones who could remember home so vividly—the cool, mild forests and rivers of eastern Canada. How did they adjust during that first long, hot summer, when the temperatures rose higher than they could ever imagine? But adjust they did. They endured.

I read recently that Acadian descendants who are still living in Canada and states like Maine tend to think of themselves in terms of the past, in terms of who they *were*, before the deportation. But we Cajuns are different. It's true that we still retain a lot of the old traits and customs. The fiddle is a fine example, as is our love of a good dance. And Cajun crafts still include spinning and weaving in the old tradition. But Cajuns—the word comes from *Acadians*—are now said to have a unique and independent culture. We tend to think of who we've *become*, instead of dwelling on who we *were*. I kind of like that. There's a fierce survival instinct at work there. Maybe that's how Mama Rita survived her own uprooted life going from *pillar to post*, as she called it.

Ophelia and Albert Broussard did give their children a home from time to time. But even when the family was together, they had little food and few comforts, the reason being that Albert was often without work. The Broussards didn't live off the river where you could trap or catch food. They lived on the lowlands that surrounded the Mermentau and Lake Arthur. Food was always scarce, and most of the time the family lived on boiled rice. Many of the local Cajuns worked in the rice fields, but I don't think Grandpa Broussard did much of anything. At least, he never seemed to have a paying job. He was a decent fiddle player, so maybe that's where he put his energy and care. But playing a fiddle wasn't considered much of a steady job in those days. Hell, even after Mama Rita saw me on national television shows, with folks such as Ed Sullivan, Dick Cavett, and Johnny Cash, she still pestered me to "give up that fiddle and get a steady job." So maybe Grandpa Albert just wasn't as lucky as I was. But that doesn't excuse him for not trying to feed and clothe his family.

Ophelia owned two dresses in those days. When her daughter turned five years old, she took one of the dresses and cut it down so that Rita would have something fit to wear to school. But there was no money for a coat or shoes or even any underwear. Sometimes Rita's feet were so cold by the time she got to school that she had to sit on them to warm them up. It must have been cold on her backside, too, since she had nothing on beneath that dress. Come to think of it, that might explain how she got to cussing early. I don't suppose waking each day to that kind of life was much fun. Mama Rita often told me that she rarely ate any breakfast. The first food she had during the normal school day was at lunch, when she walked home to eat boiled rice. But she did get a treat now and then, a raw sweet potato that she carried to school. That's hard times in anybody's book.

On top of everything else she lacked, Rita didn't have any school supplies for her classwork. This meant she always came to class unprepared. One day, the teacher got fed up and whipped her for this. So Rita solved the problem by stealing a pencil and paper from another child. That night, when she started to do her homework, Ophelia saw the pencil and paper and knew they were stolen. She cut a branch from a tree and thrashed her daughter all the way to the teacher's house, where she demanded that Rita confess to the crime. It was this display of bad temper that ended up putting Albert in jail. The teacher saw and heard enough to realize just how bad the living conditions must be at the Broussard home. She reported the situation to the principal, and the school filed neglect charges against the family. Albert was locked up for a couple of months which, of course, merely kept him from working what little he did.

With her husband in jail, Ophelia had to take in people's wash to keep the family going. Rita was now eight years old, and she helped her mother after school and on weekends. Paul was almost eleven, so he began playing his fiddle at *fais do-dos* on Saturday nights. When ten o'clock rolled around and everyone was drunk, Paul passed a hat for money. That way, he was able to pick up a couple of dollars from the crowd to help buy food for the next week. When Paul needed a backup musician, he realized that if he found one in the family, he wouldn't have to split those tips. That's why Rita learned to play the guitar at age eight. And while she never became an accomplished guitarist, Mama Rita had nonetheless inherited that Broussard flair for music. She also realized early on that music was a means of survival, a notion that she passed along to me.

Believe it or not, there was a splash of humor here and there among all this poverty. And Albert provided at least some of it. I didn't know my grandfather very well since he never visited us when I was growing up. For obvious reasons, Mama Rita didn't care much for him. Even so, she did have a funny story to tell about her father. I don't think Albert ever cracked a smile at home, but I'm told he could be funny as hell when he was with his friends. Now, there are a lot of wild stories that circulate in Cajun country, and a few of them actually happened. A Cajun will tell you tall tales whether you want to hear them or not. Like my friend Dallas Monceaux once said, "I better get on home. I've run out of the truth, and I'll have to start telling lies." But I believe this story is true, and here's why. Albert was mean as a snake to Mama Rita, so I don't think she'd make up a story that allowed her father to shine.

This is the tale of Grandpa Albert and the Parish Bully:

Louisiana doesn't have counties, the way other states do. It's the only state that uses a division called a "parish." As a young man, Albert Broussard used to fantasize about beating up on the parish bully. In those days every town and every parish had its bully, and Cameron Parish was no exception. Men from all over would come with one thing in mind, to beat the bully. Some managed, but most didn't. Albert knew he didn't have the nerve to just go up to the bully, face to face, and start a fight. But one night an opportunity presented itself, and Grandpa Albert rose to the occasion.

Albert was sitting in a local tavern when he happened to notice the bully sitting at the bar, crying in his beer. The man looked like he really had the blues. Albert knew who he was, so he walked on up to him.

"Hey, what's the matter?" Albert asked, acting real concerned. "You look like you just lost your best friend."

"Hell, Albert, none of these *fils de putains* around here wants to fight me anymore. I've done whipped them all," the bully whined.

That's when Albert came up with a plan, and when he did, a big smile spread across his face.

"Hell, that's no problem," Albert said. "I know how I can get you somebody to fight with."

"*Mais,* how?" the bully asked.

"Here's what we do," Albert said. "You and me, we go outside like we're mad at each other. You lay down on the ground, and I'll straddle you

9

and pretend we're fighting. The first one that comes to separate us, I'll let you up and you can fight with him."

"That's a great idea, Albert, let's go!"

So the two went outside and the bully got down just like Albert had suggested. Then Albert straddled him and beat the hell out of him.

Mama Rita loved to tell this story, and I do too. In fact, I even got a song out of it. In 1961, at a little bar in Nashville, I told the story to the great singer and songwriter Don Gibson. "Man, you should write a song about that," Don said. So I pulled out a pen, grabbed the guitar, and wrote "Cajun Joe, the Bully of the Bayou."

> *People still talks about Cajun Joe,*
> *Cajun Joe was the Bully of the Bayou*
> *He'd fight anything, a beast or man*
> *In bayou waters or on dry land,*
> *In bayou waters or on dry land.*

And so on.

If I could go back in time and talk to Grandpa Albert, I think I'd ask him why he didn't support his family, at least financially if not emotionally. I'd ask him how he felt about Mama Rita. Did he ever care for her at all? For any of his children? It sure didn't seem like it to Mama Rita. She told me many times that there is nothing as awful as growing up without love.

When Grandpa Albert finally got out of jail, the family was back together for a while. But it wasn't long before Ophelia couldn't take having all those children around and a husband to boot. So she dumped the kids on Grandpa Albert's parents, Ursilla and Nicholas Broussard Jr. Mama Rita was about eleven years old by this time, and if she thought she'd had no love before then, she quickly learned that things could always get worse. Here's what Mama Rita once wrote me in a letter about those days.

> *Mother said she couldn't do for us no more, and we had to go to Grandpa Broussard. I cried my eyes out that day. My little sister Viola cried so hard when Mother left that Gramma Ursilla put red pepper in her mouth to make her stop. I couldn't take it no more, Doug. I just hit Gramma as hard as I could. Then my daddy's sister, Aunt Matile, whipped me and said she wouldn't stop until I*

begged Gramma for forgiveness. I never did, and Aunt Matile finally took me away to her house to live. I think it was so I wouldn't see how bad the little ones got treated. I had to work hard at her house to pay my own way. In the mornings I'd feed the chickens, slop the hogs, and do my part of the housework before I could go to school. Then, as soon as I got home in the afternoon, I picked cotton until dark. I never did have any time to do my lessons, and I wanted to learn to read and write real bad.

It was a sad life. And it was about to get sadder.

It was around this time that Daddy Jack entered the picture, at least briefly, when Mama Rita was barely twelve years old. My mother often told me about the first time she ever laid eyes on my father. It was music that brought my parents together. One thing Jack Kershaw loved to do was play Cajun accordion. He was never a great musician, but since he could play well enough to make people want to dance, he often turned up at the houseboat dances. And that's where Jack Kershaw met Rita Broussard, the night he walked in with his accordion, ready to pump out a few tunes at some *fais do-do* where Rita and Paul were already playing.

I know this sounds like a great story about a family full of music makers, with the romantic twist of a young couple meeting and falling in love. But for Daddy Jack and Mama Rita, it was neither a simple tale nor a romantic one. As was the custom at a *fais do-do*, anyone who could play would get a turn. Mama Rita said that when Jack Kershaw came up to take a turn, he complimented Paul and his little sister on their playing. Now Jack didn't even know, or care to know, Rita's name. She was only twelve years old and he was already twenty-one, a grown man by anyone's standards. After he did a few tunes, Jack took his accordion and disappeared. That should have been the end of the story. But it wasn't.

Mama Rita had been twelve years old for six months when the world as she knew it changed forever. It was January 1924 when Albert's sister, Matile, sent for him. When he turned up at Aunt Matile's house, wondering what the hell was going on, she told him a whopper of a story. Maybe she just wanted to get rid of Rita, although I don't know why, since she was cheap labor. Maybe Aunt Matile really did believe what she told Albert that night. Or maybe she just ran out of the truth and had to start telling lies. Whatever the reason, Aunt Matile told Albert that Rita was pregnant. Albert went a little crazy, yelling and screaming like a man possessed. He beat Rita hard, demanding that she tell him the name of the man who had done it. Mama Rita later said that while she knew women got big stomachs and ended up with babies, she still didn't know how it happened. She had never been with a man before. Hell, she'd never even kissed a boy. But she did know the name of that fellow who loved to play the accordion. It was *Jack Kershaw*. And that's the name she finally cried out to her father that day.

"I had to do something, Doug, to get my daddy to stop," Mama Rita told me when I pressed her hard about the past. "If I didn't, I figured he'd beat me until I died."

What must twenty-one-year-old Jack Kershaw have thought when Albert Broussard came calling with the law? Albert had Jack put in jail and threatened to kill him when he got out unless he married his daughter. I guess Jack figured a child bride was better than jail because on January 31, 1924, Rita Broussard and Jack Kershaw got married. They never went on a honeymoon. That would have been a luxury in the swamps in those days. Besides, there was work to be done.

There's a Creole expression "married got teeth." It can bite you damn hard. The day after their wedding, Jack and Rita boarded the *Delta*, a passenger boat that chugged them over to Negro Island, which was actually known as Nigger Island back in those days. My grandfather Joseph Nedham Kershaw was waiting there in his skiff to take them on to the Kershaw houseboat. Daddy Jack's mother had died a couple years earlier, but his brother and two of his sisters were still at home. That two-room houseboat would have to house them all until Mama Rita and Daddy Jack could get a place of their own.

I wonder what went through Mama Rita's mind as she sat in that boat for the twelve miles it took to cross Grand Lake to Cypress Island, where the Kershaws had their houseboat tied up. That was one mile for every year she had lived. And I have to wonder what Daddy Jack thought about his shotgun wedding to a girl he'd never touched, a girl who was a virgin on their wedding day, but a girl everyone believed to be pregnant.

It wasn't the best way to start a marriage.

Mama Rita said that after they married, Daddy Jack had to finish raising her since she was still a kid. He would whip her if he felt she needed it. He even whipped her when she didn't need it, just so she wouldn't forget. That's how Daddy Jack explained it to Mama Rita. She was his wife, yet she was also a child he could punish.

But that child part didn't stop him from having sex with his wife.

2

HOUSEBOAT DAYS

"Got to make a livin', he's a Louisiana man."
From "Louisiana Man"
by Doug Kershaw

Daddy Jack might have been dangerous when he was drunk, but he was also a hard worker and a decent provider. Folks on the river considered him a good neighbor. In the summers he fished for catfish, and he also hunted alligator. During the winter months he trapped muskrat and mink. This was how he managed to support his new wife, his father, and a younger brother, Abel. Mama Rita soon learned that while life on the river was hard, there were also benefits. For the first time since she could remember, there was plenty of food to eat.

When my parents first got married, Daddy Jack couldn't afford to buy a motor for his skiff. In order to fish and trap, he had to use an oar to get up and down the river to Lake Arthur and Lake Misere. Once a week, a man named Wallace Rhodes passed through the fishing camps on a big boat to pick up each family's catch. He sold the fish at the market and returned the next week with the money. My mother told me that in all the years she knew him, Wallace Rhodes was never a penny short. Jack Kershaw would have known because, as I said earlier, he was a good judge of the weight of his catch. Maybe he couldn't read or write, but Daddy Jack could calculate how much money he was owed.

Thanks to that steady income from Wallace Rhodes each week, Daddy Jack finally bought a small boat with a Cushman motor. It wouldn't go very fast since the motor was only three horsepower, but it allowed him to expand his fishing operations. He added thirty more pounds of line and set two thousand new hooks in the water. Mama Rita went with her husband every day to run the motor while he set the lines. The two of them worked hard as hell, but times seemed good to the young couple.

Since Daddy Jack didn't believe in banks, he rolled up the money Wallace paid him each week and put the wad in a fruit jar. When he had enough saved, he bought the materials to build his own houseboat, eight feet wide and fourteen feet long. He had to buy a wood stove, but Daddy Jack made everything else. He built a table and chairs, a cabinet for groceries and dishes, shelves for folded clothes, and a bedstead. Mama Rita pulled Spanish moss from the cypress trees and stuffed it into sheets to make a double mattress. Despite the tragic delivery of their first child and a stillbirth the following year, Daddy Jack and Mama Rita planned on having a big family to support. And it even seemed like their new finances might permit it.

But unfortunately, when the couple moved to their new houseboat, they changed their "banking" habits as well. They began to save for an even larger boat by stashing rolls of dollar bills up in the rafters and keeping only enough money to survive in the trusty fruit jar. About a year later, when Mama Rita was pregnant for the third time, they began pulling their savings from the ceiling, only to discover that it had been so badly chewed by moths that it was unusable. It's a shame that Daddy Jack wasn't educated enough to know about banks and banking procedures.

It seemed like that one episode marked the beginning of a streak of bad luck. Until that time Daddy Jack and Mama Rita had been making a pretty decent living on the Mermentau. But their good fortune started to disintegrate, just like the pile of cash money had done. That winter they tried to relocate to Orange, Texas, about sixty miles away, to set traps in the marsh. They had no more than started off down river when the boat pulling the houseboat broke down. They waited for two days until a tugboat finally came along to tow them. But there must have been leaks in the houseboat. From a nearby barge, Mama Rita and Daddy Jack watched helplessly as their home began to sink as it floated along behind the tug. Soon, it disappeared beneath the surface of the water. They had lost their savings to the moths. But that day they lost everything to the river.

They rented a little camp out in the swamps for five dollars a month, and Daddy Jack began to set his traps. They didn't have much company out there other than alligators, mink, muskrat, mosquitoes, and deerflies. But at least their good luck came back to visit, that winter of 1927. Mama Rita often said that what started out to be one of their worst years ended up one of their best, there in that little camp. Trapping was good that season, and Daddy Jack caught mink and muskrat by the hundreds. Then, as spring came creeping back to the bayou, followed by summer, his haul of fish, crab, and crawfish was his biggest ever. Wildlife seemed too plentiful to be true. He and Rita dined on wild duck as often as not.

On March 15, 1927, two weeks before the trapping season would end, Mama Rita gave birth to their first son. They named him Edward Joseph Kershaw, but since everybody got nicknamed back in the swamps in those days, they called him "Ti Neg," meaning "Little Negro." I'm not sure how Edward ended up with this nickname, but I do know that we all meant it as an endearment!

As soon as Mama Rita could travel, they readied themselves for the trip back to their old spot on the Mermentau. Our neighbors, the Price family, bought the houseboat Daddy Jack had built. They paid him a hundred and fifty dollars and three pigs. A tornado destroyed it later, and that makes me very sad. I have almost nothing of my father, and I'd give anything to have that houseboat. He made it with his own hands.

The Mermentau River that had brought them such bad luck only a season ago now welcomed them home. It didn't take Daddy Jack many months of fishing until he had enough saved to buy a new houseboat, twelve feet wide and thirty feet long. He even had some money left over for furnishings. With this bigger houseboat came a bigger problem. Daddy Jack now needed a boat for towing it. So he bought a sixteen-footer with a more powerful motor. Like I said, Daddy Jack had his sins, but sloth wasn't one of them. Back on the river, he ran into a fellow named Martin Istre, who hired him to work at his fishing camp. Daddy Jack's job was taking out-of-state sportsmen on fishing expeditions. Mama Rita stayed behind and set the Kershaw lines. It's ironic how things finally ended. Daddy Jack really did want to provide for his family, and he worked day and night to do it. I now believe he loved us very much. If liquor hadn't been in the picture, I might have believed it even then.

Daddy Jack always headed into the swamp with his pole, looking for alligators. Poling for alligator isn't my idea of a good time. First you make a long pole and attach a hook to one end of it. Then you follow the gator's trail through the grass and marsh until you come to those holes in the side of the bank where the gators live. When you find one, you poke your pole down into that hole until you make the gator mad. When he comes out to clamp his jaws down hard on the pole, you hook him and pull him out fast.

If you don't kill him right away, he's gonna come after you. Some men used guns to shoot the gators. But Daddy Jack always favored hatchets. Even when a gator was shot, you still had to use a hatchet to sever its spine. If not, that powerful tail presented another kind of danger.

The next morning Rita would skin his catch, salt down the hides, roll them tight, and put them in a wooden barrel until they could get them to market. Since Cajuns wouldn't consider eating alligator, not even back in those hard times, Daddy Jack sold the meat to outsiders. One of his neighbors was Russell Gary, who stood tall at four feet, eleven inches. Russell was so short that when he farted the dust flew, but he was known as one of the best gator men who ever lived. He even liked the taste of gator. "I doan know why Cajuns doan like it," Russell said. "Them gator legs taste jus' like turtle."

Russell Gary used to work at the Lacassine Game Refuge, and he would get to telling stories about those days. He told me of the time Daddy Jack had been poaching mink on the refuge. According to Russell, my father didn't know he had a mink hanging out of his rubber knee boot. He was about to walk right past some of the overseers until Russell hurried over to stop him.

"*Mais,* Jack, you better check that boot," Russell said. "Unless that mink is just hitchin' a ride, you gonna be in trouble, yeah."

On July 20, 1930, Jack and Rita had another baby boy, Nelson Adam Kershaw, nicknamed Pu-toot until someone decided Pee Wee would be better. Now that the Kershaws were a family of four, Daddy Jack went looking for more work. He found it at a hunting camp owned by a fellow named Pete Buras. This camp worked much like the fishing expeditions, only the game was wild duck. Daddy Jack built duck blinds in the marsh and took groups of hunters out every morning. He'd get home by ten a.m. and go back out to run his own traps and lines. It was during this period that Mama Rita decided to start her own fishing operation, so she bought herself a skiff. She would set a big wooden washtub in the skiff and put Pee Wee on Edward's lap for safekeeping. Then she'd go out and run her own lines. The biggest problem the family faced in those days, according to Mama Rita, was the weekly journey to town for supplies. It was a fifteen-mile boat trip that took all day and cost them time and money.

Rita lost three more girls, at birth or soon thereafter, in the five and a half years after Pee Wee was born. I mentioned earlier that the swamp kept its secrets, and there's no better example of that than the relationship between Mama Rita and her sole female friend during those years, our neighbor, Mrs. Price. These days, when women get together, I'm sure they must talk about what's going on in their personal lives. And I would assume that those talks include problems with husbands. Maybe the times have just opened up more, but back then, out in the swamps, Mama Rita never once confided in Mrs. Price. She never talked about the babies she lost or the fear she had of her hot-tempered husband. Mrs. Price passed away years ago, but I went to visit her in Lake Arthur before she died. She told me that she and Mama Rita talked about cooking food for their families, about having enough flour sacks to make shirts for the children, about the week's catch, and about the best way to dry alligator hide. But their *real* problems, the kind that only the heart knows about, were left unspoken. That's one reason I'm glad I finally got Mama Rita to talk a little and to write down on paper for me the pain of her early life. Otherwise, I'd never have known. And the swamp would've kept those memories to itself.

On the morning of January 24, 1936, on a houseboat at Tiel Ridge, Louisiana, in Cameron Parish, yours truly was born, Douglas James Kershaw. I weighed about seven and a half pounds, which was small compared to my brothers. The midwife who attended my birth was known to everyone as Tante Pelagie. Mama Rita always said that I cried so damn much as a baby that she knew back then I'd grow up to become a singer. I guess I was just getting my vocal cords ready for the Big Time. To keep me quiet, She would give me a dried pod from a wild Kentucky coffee tree. When you shook the pod, you could hear the beans rattling inside—a natural toy. She'd string gator teeth on a piece of cord for us to cut our own teeth on. And she washed us kids with soap made from raccoon fat. There was a lot of recycling going on in the swamps.

Mama Rita and Daddy Jack asked Raoul Roy, a neighbor, to be my godfather. I can't even think of Raoul without remembering his little container of Vicks VapoRub. He carried it around with him everywhere he went and was constantly dabbing the Vicks into his eyes. Two years after I was born, on February 2, 1938, Mama Rita and Daddy Jack had one more child, Russell Lee, nicknamed Rusty, which rounded out the family to four healthy boys. It's strange to think that none of the girls born out there in the swamps, my sisters, managed to survive but that's the hand nature dealt.

By the time Rusty was born, Daddy Jack had bought a new and bigger houseboat, fourteen feet wide and thirty-six feet long. It had a kitchen and two bedrooms. Our bathroom was a little outhouse on the porch. Since Cajun French was our only language back then, we called it a *cabinette*, which is a pretty-sounding word for an outhouse. It was a one-holer, and that hole was over the open water. Needless to say, the Sears & Roebuck Catalog didn't last very long. When we ran out of catalog pages, we used rags. If an old shirt had outlived its usefulness, it ended up doing duty in the toilet. I do remember vividly the community rag that hung in the out-house until there wasn't a clean spot left on it. Now there's a smell I could do without remembering. We kept slop jars inside the houseboat for nighttime use. All in all, we felt that our lives and the way in which we lived them were as modern and good as anyone else's. But we had nothing to measure ourselves against. The social ruler didn't appear until we moved to town.

But that story comes later.

When you live on a houseboat, your life just sort of picks up and moves along with it. Wherever Daddy Jack worked his traps and his lines, that's where our lives would be tethered for a time. Sometimes we were rocked by violent storms or eaten alive by swamp mosquitoes. Moonless nights were so black you couldn't see your hand in front of your face. But there were good days, too, with a soothing yellow sun and plenty of fish biting at our lines. People hear the word "swamp" and they tend to think of a murky, dreary backwater. But the swamp in spring and summer is a busy place full of flowers and butterflies. The bald cypress trees are draped in vines and covered with moss. Swamp magnolias are blooming, along with morning glories and honeysuckle. Duckweed and waterlilies are eve-rywhere. Alligators bask on the banks, and turtles sleep on logs. Birds are abundant: egrets, pelicans, spoonbills, cranes, herons, and storks.

I remember summer evenings as a boy when I'd glance up and see a flock of storks headed home to their night roosts. Or a couple hundred pelicans, with their six-foot wingspan, cutting a wedge through the sky. At night, you could hear owls hoot from a mile away. Locusts and crickets kept up a steady racket, and so did the bullfrogs. There's an old saying in the swamps: *Quand la pluie tombe, ouaouarons chantent.* When the rain falls, the bullfrogs sing. And they sure did. One tree frog, or *grenouille,* we had in the swamp was the Bird-voiced tree frog, considered to make the most beautiful frog call in North America, an echoing whistle that sounds just like a bird. The swamp puts on a hell of a symphony. It's just hard to tell what's first chair.

I really think those days were probably the happiest my parents had as a married couple. The old-timers say it was the best time to live on the river too. They say that back then you could harvest enough food to live off the land. But nowadays the big oil and gas corporations own the land, and Cajuns can't even tie up their boats on the banks of the Mermentau without a permit.

"They came in and bought it all for about fifteen cents an acre," Russell Gary once told me. "Nowadays the big companies own the land, and you either work for them or you don't work at all."

I can't even imagine what Daddy Jack would have thought of the change. Somehow, I don't see him working for a giant corporation in any capacity. But then, men like Russell Gary, Dallas Monceaux, A. J. Bertrand, and Warren Price never dreamed they'd see that day either.

But it's here all right.

3

FAIS DO-DOS

"On a houseboat tied to a big tall tree,
a home for my mama and my papa and me."
From "Louisiana Man"
by Doug Kershaw

Chuk. Chuk. Chuk. I can still hear the sound of Daddy Jack's boat. His going-out boat, that is. He had two boats. The bigger boat, the one he used for pulling the houseboat to wherever the fish were biting, was called the *Muskrat*. The *Muskrat* was also used for fishing, trapping, hunting, and catching alligators—and bringing it all into town to sell. In other words, the *Muskrat* was Daddy Jack's working boat. On the *Muskrat* was a large wooden box filled with blocks of ice from the local ice houses. That's how he was able to refrigerate his catch. During the hot summer months, the kind we knew so well in Louisiana, Uncle Abel curled up on the ice box to sleep. It must have made a cool bed during those humid nights.

The boat that made the sound I remember so well was smaller and named the *Alice*. That was Daddy Jack's going-out boat. He took the *Alice* when he had to go to town, or visiting on the river, or to a *fais do-do*, those Cajun house dances I mentioned earlier. The *Alice* had a cab over the middle, and it was open in the back. It was powered by a one-cylinder Cushman engine, and that's what made the unusual sound. *Chuk. Chuk. Chuk.*

It's true that our memories are tied to our senses. When I remember the sound of that little one-cylinder engine, I can actually smell the *Alice,* as if she's right in front of me again. I can smell the odor of all those fish, and those dried animal hides. That's when my memory sweeps me back instantly to those *fais do-dos* and the pitch-black nights of coming home in the *Alice,* Daddy Jack steering us up the dark bayou, drunk as a Cajun skunk, the sounds of fiddle and accordion dying away behind us. But that was a long time ago, in those days when I still believed that someone, maybe even God, would come into those swamps and save our family. Someone strong enough to make things right in Daddy Jack's heart and mind. A kid knows a lot of things he isn't told, and I was no exception. Maybe that's why music became like a warm blanket that would wrap itself around me, protect me for just a little while.

That's what the sound of a fiddle can do. It can give you hope.

Fais do-do means "to make sleep," and that's what the Cajun mothers did to their children while music was playing and dancers were dancing. We children were separated from the music, all in one room with only a thin wall between us and the party. We would sleep on the bed in that one room. When bed space ran out, we had the pallets our parents put on the floor. When the mothers came in to look after us, they'd sing, in French, the lyrics to whatever song was playing in the outer room. Then they'd whisper, *"Fais do-do, ma ti bébé."* Go to sleep, my little baby.

So, for the women, a *fais do-do* meant eating, drinking, dancing, and putting babies to sleep. For the men, it was a night of eating, drinking, dancing, fighting, drinking, and more drinking. There was usually enough homemade wine and hard liquor to see a *fais do-do* through to the end. Considering the time I spent in these *fais do-do* rooms, from birth until I was seven years old, I must have heard every Cajun song ever composed. And that's why I never had to learn any of them when I started playing an instrument. It was as if I had been born with them already inside me, in my heart and in my mind. All I had to do was teach my hands and my vocal cords to bring to life what the rest of me already knew. To this day, you name a Cajun song and I can play it for you.

Sometimes, when the mood hits me, I'll take my fiddle out and close my eyes. Then I go back into my mind and let the music flow. When I slip back into time to recapture those fleeting, childhood moments, those sounds and colors of the *fais do-dos,* I feel light. There's no other word. *Light.* My mind drifts upward, almost leaving my physical body behind. For a second there, it's as if I've never been judged or criticized or hurt. It's as if I could never do anything wrong. What I feel is pure love. Then it's over, and I'm gone from that old time and place. I'm back in the "now" time. I don't dwell on the past. But I plug into it from time to time.

One of the most vivid memories I have of life on the river is a happy one. It goes back to a chilly morning in Southwest Louisiana, and me sitting on the bank of the Mermentau waiting for the sun to come up. I was only a few years old and I was with my big brothers, Edward and Pee Wee. I still remember how they were more excited than I had ever seen them. But all they would tell me was that it had to do with *Christmas,* and that Christmas had something to do with presents.

"Watch for the tugboat," they kept saying.

I didn't know anything about Christmas, or even what presents were. I know that's hard to fathom in these days of holiday abundance, but it's true. The biggest gifts our parents gave us back then was enough food to eat and clothes to wear. I might not have known about Santa Claus, but I was familiar with tugboats. After all, I was a kid born on the Mermentau. Not a day went by that I didn't see a tugboat or two, either pulling or pushing barges up and down the river. Those barges were mostly loaded with shells, the kind they used instead of gravel to pave roads. Or the boats might be filled with oil, gas, or chemicals. At night you could see their spotlights sweeping from one side of the river to the other and hear their fog horns. To a kid, they sounded like swamp monsters. The river is an exciting place at night.

But back to that first Christmas memory. Edward, Pee Wee, and I waited as the sun rose slowly over the trees. Sure enough, there came a tugboat around the bend. The minute I saw it, I knew it was no ordinary tugboat run. One man stood on the deck while three more men were on the barges. They were all throwing things overboard and into the river. I didn't know what was happening, but I knew it had to be something special. The *things* they were throwing into the water began to take on colors and shapes as the waves brought them closer to shore. One of the red objects finally reached me. I got down on my stomach, reached in, and grabbed it. It was a big red apple. Then the orange colors started to arrive and the yellows. We ran up and down the riverbank collecting apples, oranges, and bananas. We ate as much as we could, then carried the rest home to Mama Rita and Daddy Jack.

That was my first real Christmas.

The Kershaws never celebrated Christmas, not once in all the time I lived with Mama Rita. To tell you the truth, she wasn't much for celebrating *any* holiday. Not even our birthdays. I suppose her early upbringing had a lot to do with that. I don't know if Daddy Jack was brought up to celebrate Christmas, or any day for that matter. Somehow I doubt it. So we boys were thankful for that morning on the banks of the Mermentau. I later learned that the man responsible for this act of holiday kindness was an old tugboat captain. Apparently, he knew that the children of the Cajun families living on the river would have very little in the way of Christmas gifts. In our case, the apples, oranges, and bananas were the only way we knew that the world was having a holiday.

I have been given gifts in my life. But nothing quite compares to the happiness I felt that Christmas morning. No memory of my childhood has remained quite as beautiful, or as untarnished.

I have many memories of events that took place on the Mermentau River before we moved into town. But the course of time does funny things to memory. You think that something in childhood happened a certain way, and you believe it for years. Then, you get to reminiscing with older folks who recall that event better than you do. And you soon discover that you've changed the facts as the years fell away. Sometimes, it's for your own protection. I think that's the case with one memory I've lived with for most of my life, believing it true until I began writing this book. Not only that, I had told it many times on national television.

This is *my* story of Melton Monceaux Jr. and the Alligator:

The first person I remember knowing other than family was a boy my age who lived on the houseboat next to ours. His name was Melton Monceaux Jr. In my memory, Melton and I are playing alone near the river early one morning. This is not unusual, considering that the riverbank was our front yard in those days, our playground. I turn away from the river to pick up a stick I see on the ground. When I turn back around, Melton is gone. I call his name over and over, but he never answers. I run back to the Monceaux house and tell them that I can't find Melton. We look all that day and into the night, but Melton Monceaux Jr. is nowhere to be found. The next morning we see a large alligator floating on its back in the water. A very dead alligator. Daddy Jack and Melton Monceaux Sr. pull the gator up onto land and cut him open, dreading what they'll find. I watch as they pull Melton out of its belly, my first memory of a dead person.

Now, I have lived with this picture story in my mind for all these years. It's as real to me today as ever, but it's not what happened that morning on the riverbank. Dallas Monceaux, the boy's uncle, told me what really occurred. So this is the story of Melton's death, and it's told by someone who knew the facts.

I guess you could call it the story of Melton Monceaux Jr. and his Mama:

Melton's mother died soon after giving birth to him. In fact, she was dying when they put little Melton in her arms. His mama kissed him and held him to her breast. Then she handed the child to its grandmother. "You can have him now," Mrs. Monceaux whispered. "You can have him now, but I'll come back for him."

This was her deathbed vow, and everyone knew it.

When little Melton was two years old, he went to live with his Uncle Dallas, who intended to raise the boy as his own. This was a fairly common practice for the times, that a relative would raise a child in need of parenting. A lot of swamp kids were taken in by whoever could and would. Melton had a good home for the next couple of years with Dallas and his wife. On that fateful morning I just told you about, Dallas was out walking along the riverbank, getting ready to run some fishing lines. He noticed that little Melton was following him. "Go on back Junior," Dallas yelled.

Melton turned and started walking back to the house, as he was told. Thinking the boy would be fine, Dallas went on his way. It didn't take him long to run his lines and head back to the house himself. Dallas said he was about halfway back when he saw his nephew floating face down in the river. He jumped into the water and grabbed the boy up in his arms. It was too late. And this is where I come into the story. As it turned out, my brother Rusty and I were walking along the riverbank and happened upon the scene just as Dallas was pulling Melton from the water.

When I heard Dallas Monceaux tell the story, I realized that an alligator didn't get Melton at all. So how had my memory rewritten his death for all these years? The only answer I can come up with is that my own childhood fears of the alligators and snakes that lurked beneath the waters had shaped the event in my mind as a lesson. *This river can kill you, boy, so be careful.*

It's true. That river could be your friend one minute and take your life the next. Yet, it was my home. I had no choice but to live on it. Growing up, I didn't think much about the dangers of the swamp. Boys were expected to be tough as men. But I'll bet you that my young, subconscious mind wasn't nearly as tough. It was wary and watchful. It knew of all the pitfalls, from drowning in the Mermentau to being killed by alligators or bitten by one of the many poisonous snakes—a cottonmouth, also called a water moccasin, or a massasauga. Over time, my greatest fears of the environment found a voice in the life and death of Melton Monceaux Jr. I tell this story now, in its most genuine form, as a kind of memoriam to little Melton. It's my opportunity to pay respect to a boy who never had a chance to see the world as I did. And to Dallas Monceaux too. I'll never forget the pain I saw in Dallas's eyes when he relived the events of that day.

"You know, Doug, I could have saved him," Dallas told me, "if only I would have knowed that thing they teach you today. What you call it?"

"CPR," his daughter, Norma, answered him.

"Yes, that's it, CPR," Dallas said. "Melton still had a pulse when I found him. I could feel it beating." Then Dallas thought for a minute, and I could see tears form in his eyes. "But then again," he added, "you know his mama had vowed to come back for him."

We never went hungry back when we lived out on the Mermentau, at least not when Daddy Jack was still alive. We had wild game and fish to eat, and sometimes Daddy Jack had a pig or a cow. We also had some chickens. And every so often the Cajuns down on the river got together and butchered someone's cow or hog. There were about forty families living down there, and folks would take turns donating an animal to be killed. Everyone got together on a Sunday and used the *boucherie*, or slaughtering, as an excuse for a dance. Times might have been hard, but that didn't stop Cajuns from kicking up their feet at a dance every now and then. Or pulling out a fiddle. Slaughtering one animal at a time like that was also a practical answer to the problem of keeping meat fresh. Each family would take only as much meat as they could preserve and use before it spoiled. Sometimes they'd make all sorts of things. *Boudin* was sausage made with rice, pork, and seasonings. *Andouille* was sausage made with pork and garlic. And *tasso* was Cajun jerky used as seasoning for vegetables. But, more often than not, they just salted down most of the meat and cooked the rest for the party. People would eat, drink, and dance all night long.

I was always right there with Daddy Jack when he was skinning his muskrats and other catch. I thought I was trying to help, but I'm sure it was more like trying his patience. He did seem to have more patience with me than he had with Mama Rita and the other boys. At least Mama Rita always claimed I was Daddy Jack's favorite. For the first two years of my life he never spanked me once. This was astonishing for Jack Kershaw, since he was always spanking Ed and Pee Wee. But not me. He even called me his *ti gateau,* his little cake. That's why I was so surprised the first and only time he actually hit me. It happened after he'd spent a long, hard day in the swamps and was trying to fix a window on the houseboat. Every time he put down his knife, I'd grab it. He'd take it back and push me away.

"*Laisse ça tranquille, ti gateau,*" he'd say. Leave that alone, little cake. Of course I didn't leave it alone. It was a hell of a knife, and I wanted to hold it. Suddenly, something hit me on the side of my head. *Whack!* I thought it must be some giant swamp mosquito. I went running in circles, flapping my arms about my head. Mama Rita, who was watching from inside the houseboat, couldn't believe that Daddy Jack had actually hit me with his fishing hat.

"*Il a cassé la blanc d'oeuf dessus son ti gâteau!*" Mama Rita yelled to my brothers. He broke the frosting off his little cake!

Daddy Jack only hit me that one time as far as I can remember. But he came close another day. And it's a day I won't forget, since it was a fiddle that saved me.

For as long as I can remember there was a fiddle, guitar, and accordion on the houseboat. I was fascinated with these instruments. Pee Wee and Edward were old enough to play them, but no way did they want me messing with them. I was patient, however. If they made the mistake of leaving them lying around where I was tall enough to reach, I did just that. I started walking when I was only about nine months old, and I'm sure it was because of my yearning for those instruments. Especially *le vieux lons,* the fiddle. I got into plenty of trouble with my brothers over this, but it seemed like my Uncle Abel was always there to bail me out.

Uncle Abel was my *ange gardien,* my guardian angel. Even before I was walking, he built me a little rocking chair. Mama Rita always talked about how I loved to rock in that chair, back and forth, rocking sometimes for hours. Years later, I wrote a song called "My Uncle Abel," about how much we cherished him in our family. Uncle Abel was awfully proud of that song. I know he was always telling his friends about it.

My Uncle Abel took an old oak tree,
He made a little rocking chair for me.
Back and forth rocking all day long,
He'd see to it everybody left me alone.

When Uncle Abel saw how much trouble I was getting into because I wanted to play the fiddle, he decided to make me one. He took a cigar box and cut two holes in the top so that sound could come out. Then, somehow, he attached a neck he had whittled out of a piece of hardwood. He also whittled the tuning pegs and a bridge, then made a tailpiece out of a chunk of gator bone. The most creative part of all were the strings. For those, he took wires from window screens. This meant that my four strings were all the same gauge. Then Uncle Abel whittled me a bow from a tree branch. If you thought the strings were creative, listen to this. He put a tack on each end of the bow, and then borrowed some of Mama Rita's No. 50 white thread. He tied the thread around one tack and wound it back and forth from tack to tack until there was enough. Then he tied it to the other tack. That was my bow. I was barely three years old, but I had my own fiddle!

Uncle Abel knew the cigar-box fiddle wouldn't last long. But he figured it would keep me out of trouble for a time with Ed and Pee Wee. And especially Daddy Jack. What Uncle Abel didn't count on was my actually learning how to play anything on that fake fiddle. But I did. That's when I knew I had to play the real thing. And the day finally arrived when I stole the opportunity to do just that, when I was about five years old.

Since we didn't have a closet on the houseboat, Mama Rita hung our clothes in a chifforobe. The guitar was always kept under the bed, but the fiddle and accordion were put on top of this chifforobe. Daddy Jack assumed they'd be safe from my little hands up there. For a time, they were. But I was lying in wait like a baby gator, my beady eyes watching everything. One day, when Daddy Jack and my brothers left the house to check their fishing lines and Mama Rita was out checking her crab lines, I decided to strike. I pulled a regular chair up to the chifforobe, put my little rocker on top of it, and climbed on up to heaven. As soon as I had the fiddle in my hands, away I went, fiddling as long as I dared. It brought such a joy to me that I knew I had to keep doing it.

Usually, I could get the fiddle back on top of the chifforobe before anyone came home and caught me in the act. But one day, as I hurried to cover my tracks, the chair rocked, I rolled, and down I went. I picked up the fiddle and ran my hand over its back. To my horror, it had a tiny crack there. I scrambled to put things back in order, hoping that nobody would notice. Or praying that Ed or Pee Wee would think they had accidentally done it.

The next time one of my brothers took down the fiddle, that's the first thing he noticed. And he didn't think for a second that he had done it. I don't know which one busted me, but whoever it was made a beeline for Daddy Jack. That is when I almost got that second whipping. First, I've got to tell you that Daddy Jack's hat trick on the side of the head was only used for minor offenses. For major crimes he used his razor strap. When he saw the cracked fiddle, he didn't say a word. He didn't have to. He reached up and took his razor strap off the wall. I knew then I was in for it. With the strap in one hand and the fiddle and bow in the other, he pointed to the bedroom door. I followed him in, my head lowered, my lip trembling. He closed the door behind us, and then he looked at me for what seemed the longest time. I remember feeling some relief that he was sober that day, for when Daddy Jack wasn't drunk, he wasn't violent. So I didn't know if he was working up the courage to whip me or trying to think of a way not to. I kept looking at the razor strap and trying hard to stop shaking.

"Douglas," he said, finally.

That's when I *really* knew I was in for it. No *ti bébé,* and no *ti gateau.*

"Douglas," Daddy Jack said again. He spoke to me in French, of course, because Daddy Jack never did speak a word of English. "I tell you what. I'm gonna hand you this here fiddle and this here bow. If you can play a song on it, I won't whip you. But if you can't, your ass belongs to me."

That changed everything. My very own command performance. In an instant my hands stopped shaking as I took the fiddle and the bow from him. I tucked the fiddle under my chin and played three songs for Daddy Jack. The first one was a song I had learned on my cigar-box fiddle. I'm not certain of the song, but since Daddy Jack's favorite was "Fe Fe

Poncheaux," I would bet good money that's what I played. And the other two? Hell, I made them up right on the spot. Daddy Jack just sat back and smiled, a big grin. That's the day I learned how important it is to win over your audience.

It wouldn't be the last time music saved my Cajun ass. But it was the first.

By 1942 we had tied up the houseboat in Lowry. It wasn't a town, just an area on the Mermentau River where the Kershaws often tied up, especially in the winters. I was six years old that fall, so I started school right along with Edward and Pee Wee. This was at Live Oak School, a little one-room schoolhouse about seven miles from the houseboat. Some days we boys walked to school, along with the other children who lived on nearby houseboats. Sometimes we all hitched a ride in the back of a neighbor's truck. That truck was gray, I remember, and had a canvas shell over the back that protected us on rainy days. But sometimes Edward, Pee Wee, and I rode our horse, Old Blue, to school. Daddy Jack had just recently bought Old Blue, and since the houseboat was permanent for the time being, Old Blue lived onshore, along with three milk cows. However we managed to get to school, one thing is sure. We got ourselves there with no shoes on. It would be two more years before I owned my first pair of shoes.

It was at Live Oak School that I was introduced to the English language. My teacher was Mrs. Fanny Savoy, who taught grades one through eight. I don't know if she graded me that year, or if I was just "sitting in" so that I could begin learning English. I do know that it wasn't a good idea to let Mrs. Savoy catch you speaking French. She had a paddle big enough to get your attention. Because there is no *th* sound in the French language, a French-speaking person tends to substitute a hard *d* sound instead. *Them* becomes *dem* and *that* becomes *dat*. To teach us how to make the *th* sound, Mrs. Savoy would hold our tongues. Try to say something in *any* language when you have a mouthful of fingers. I don't want to imply that I wasn't an attentive student, but all I really remember about that first year, other than having my tongue held a lot, was the fate of Mrs. Savoy's paddle. As I said, the school consisted of just one room, but it had two doors. One day someone nailed Mrs. Savoy's paddle right across those two doors, from the inside. Along she came in a hurry, flung open the doors, and snapped her paddle in two. There weren't any tears shed over the paddle, not unless they came from Mrs. Savoy.

It was on the back of that old gray truck that I tried to speak my first words of English. We were on our way to school one cold morning, all of us bouncing around in the back of the truck. Frost had settled down over the bayou during the night, and now it covered the ground and glistened from tree branches. It was such a pretty sight in that early morning sun that I guess it brought out the poet in me. In French, frost is *gelée blanche*. But I guess this got lost in the translation. "*Ga lá bas!*" I said to the kids. Look there! They did, and so I took a deep breath and spoke my first words in English. "White jelly!" I said proudly. This drew a round of laughter from the back of the truck. So much for bayou poetry.

By then our lives had settled into something of a routine. The houseboat was tied up permanently in Lowry. There were still the *fais do-dos* and the *boucheries*. The mail boat chugged into the swamps once a week, bringing us proof that the world was still out there. Uncle Abel was always close by, as a guardian angel should be. Everything seemed to be moving along just fine.

I didn't know it yet, but the waters of the Mermentau were about to be riled. And they'd never be calm again.

4

COUP DE GRÂCE

"That Jack Kershaw.
You didn't want to make him mad, 'cause out come that knife."
–Dallas Monceaux, Lake Arthur, Louisiana

Around Lake Arthur they say that the Kershaw boys were so mean that if they couldn't find somebody else to fight, they'd fight each other. In fact, there's still some Kershaws in Texas who got there because Daddy Jack told one of his brothers to get out of Louisiana or die. I don't even know what these two fought about. I guess that's another of those secrets the swamp keeps to itself. Or maybe Daddy Jack was on another one of his *I'm-gonna-kill-you* drunks. I remember several of them very well. They always got underway at a *fais do-do,* and yet I have such good, safe memories of those dances. Again, maybe the music wrapped itself around me, made me *think* I was safe.

But one night that safety blanket was pulled away from me. We were on our way back up the bayou from a *fais do-do,* making our way home in the *Alice.* Over the constant noise of the *chuk-chuk-chuk,* I could hear Daddy Jack playing "Fe Fe Foncheaux" on his accordion. Rusty and I were curled up at the back of the boat, while Daddy Jack sat up front. I had my eyes closed, trying to fall asleep, but I knew what Daddy Jack looked like up there, piloting the boat with his foot so he could play the accordion with his hands. I'd seen it so many times before on our trips home. To this day I don't know what set him off that night, but suddenly all hell broke loose. Daddy Jack stopped playing and started cussing Mama Rita. She cussed back at him, and this was her big mistake.

"*Jetez ces ti bâtards dans la rivière!*" Daddy Jack shouted. Throw those little bastards in the river. He meant us. I'd never been so scared before.

"*Non, non!*" Mama Rita screamed. She started backing away from him and that did it. Daddy Jack picked up a pipe wrench and flung it, hitting her forehead. Blood was flying everywhere, and they were both swearing. Then Daddy Jack threw down his accordion and came charging to the back of the boat where Rusty and I were cowering. Mama Rita was all that stood between us and him, and she didn't look like she could put up much of a fight. Blood was streaming down her face from the cut on her forehead. Daddy Jack grabbed her arm and tried to pull her aside. I knew he wanted to get at Rusty and me. I could only pray that he was bluffing Mama Rita, that he wouldn't really throw us kids in the river. But I wasn't sure. Mama Rita held her ground, and finally Daddy Jack quieted down. It was almost like he couldn't remember why he was standing back there on our end of the boat. Or why his wife's head was bleeding. He staggered back to his job of steering us home. He was so drunk that I don't know how he even found the wheel. Maybe he just put the going-out boat on automatic pilot, for we went on up the black bayou that night—*chuk-chuk-chuk*—coming home from just another *fais do-do*.

Uncle Abel had lived with Mama Rita and Daddy Jack for most of his life. I think he felt more like a brother to Mama Rita than a brother-in-law. As I said, Daddy Jack had helped to raise his younger brother, and I'm sure Abel appreciated it. But that didn't stop him from standing up to Daddy Jack where we kids were concerned. As soon as he got big enough to hold his own, Uncle Abel came to our rescue many times. The last time he stepped in to help was on yet another one of Daddy Jack's *I'm-gonna-kill-you* drunks. I remember this like it was yesterday. Same old script, at least in the beginning. Again, we were coming back from a *fais do-do* down river when Daddy Jack, drunk to the gills, started in on Mama Rita.

"I'm gonna kill you!" he threatened her. "And I'll kill those little bastards, too!" This time, all four of us boys were on the boat. Daddy Jack was cussing and waving his shotgun around in the air. Once again, Mama Rita stood her ground, holding Pee Wee, Rusty, and me behind her. My brother Edward, who was barely sixteen years old, jumped in front of Daddy Jack.

"*Arrête ça!*" Edward shouted at Daddy Jack. Stop it! I couldn't imagine one of us kids telling Daddy Jack to stop anything. That act of defiance alone would probably have gotten Edward shot had it not been for Uncle Abel, who was piloting the boat. He just gunned the motor and hit the shoreline going as fast as the *Alice* could manage. Everybody flew forward, into a heap.

I can still feel Mama Rita lifting me up by my shirt, then dragging Rusty and me off the going-out boat toward the houseboat. There was a railing around the outer edge of the houseboat so that you could circle the living quarters. Mama Rita's idea was that if Daddy Jack tried to get to us, she'd just keep running round and round on that walkway to avoid him. Daddy Jack must have had lots of anger in him still, because he staggered to his feet and lit out after us. He was still screaming and waving his shotgun in the air. Mama Rita was pulling us behind her as she ran. It all seemed dreamlike to me. When I think of this episode, my heart still pounds as if it's going to jump from my chest, as if it's all still happening. Even today, as a grown man, I remember the fear of that night.

This is when Uncle Abel jumped from the *Alice* and ran to find a weapon. Here's where time has changed another memory of mine. I always thought Uncle Abel found a fence post that night and used it to protect us against Daddy Jack. I do know that he waited on the front porch of the houseboat for Daddy Jack to turn the corner. When he did, Uncle Abel let him have it across the face.

Dallas Monceaux remembered it differently. He said Abel got his rifle, and when he hit Daddy Jack with the barrel of it, the barrel actually bent from the force. *Whatever* hit him, Daddy Jack flew out into the yard, his head bent to one side, blood spewing everywhere. Even when he hit the ground, Uncle Abel kept his weapon gripped tightly in his hands. Abel Kershaw had seen his brother hurt and bleeding before, and yet like a cat with nine lives, come back to life and beat the hell out of his attacker. But on that night, Daddy Jack didn't move for so long that we thought Uncle Abel had killed him. We all stood frozen, staring down at him. When he let out a muffled groan, Mama Rita and Uncle Abel grabbed some rags and pressed them against the gash on the side of his head. It took a while, but they finally got the bleeding stopped. When Daddy Jack came to, he couldn't talk. That's when we realized his jaw was broken.

There weren't any doctors out where we lived in the swamps, but we knew Daddy Jack was tough. Hell, when he had a bad tooth he pulled it himself with a pair of pliers. But I'm sure that broken jaw must have hurt something awful. Mama Rita fed Daddy Jack liquids until he started feeling better. I always wondered if that blow caused any damage to my father's brain. He never did tell us he was sorry for what happened that night. If he *was* sorry, he was too proud or too stubborn to admit it. But he did have one question about that awful night, when he could finally talk again.

"*Mais,* Abel," he asked his younger brother, "why'd you hit me so hard?"

In the days following that incident, there was actually a peaceful lull in our lives. Daddy Jack was hurt too bad to go find any liquor. He didn't even seem that angry about getting whacked. But Uncle Abel knew that all it would take was a bottle of moonshine, and the jig would be up. So he decided to leave while the leaving was good.

"If I stay," he said to Mama Rita, "he'll either kill me or I'll kill him." No one cared to argue this point. Hell, we all knew it was true.

As soon as Uncle Abel saw that his brother was almost well, he left for Hackberry, Louisiana, a boomtown where he hoped to find work in the oil fields. Uncle Abel and Daddy Jack had three sisters living there— Ozite, Milian, and Rose. And a half-sister named Camellia. Uncle Abel even tried to get Mama Rita to leave, too. But, as afraid as she was of Daddy Jack, she was more afraid of what the world away from him might be like. She turned down the invitation, and Uncle Abel left alone that night. It was as if all hope went out the door with that man. I remember standing near the railing on the houseboat and staring down the bayou after him. I was hoping he'd change his mind and I'd hear the sound of his boat turning around. But it disappeared. All I heard were night birds, and frogs, and the gentle slap of water against the houseboat. Uncle Abel was gone. And he stayed gone, since he eventually found work as a shrimper in Hackberry. I'd lost my *ange gardien.*

Edward was now the only "man" left to look out for us. He was afraid Daddy Jack would kill us all as soon as he got well enough to get drunk and reminisce about what had happened. And when he did, Edward's name would rise to the top of the list. So, Edward kept begging Mama Rita to pack up and leave. She refused. Who knows what keeps a person tied to a hopeless life. Maybe it's love, maybe it's hate, maybe it's fear, or maybe it's a mixture of all three. But the day came that Daddy Jack got himself up and around and back out fishing on the river. That's when Edward finally said, "Mama, I gotta go, whether you and the boys come with me or not." So he followed Uncle Abel to Hackberry and found work in the oil fields. Mama Rita must have realized that with both Uncle Abel and Edward gone, there'd be no one to protect her or us younger kids. It would be just a matter of time before Daddy Jack went on another *I'm-gonna-kill-you* drunk.

On the night after Edward left home, Mama Rita waited until Daddy Jack took off to run an errand down river. When the *chuk-chuk-chuk* had died away in the distance, she quickly packed what few clothes we owned. Grandma Ophelia and Grandpa Albert had thrown in the towel years earlier and gotten a well-deserved divorce. Grandpa had remarried, a woman named Arise, and she was awfully kind to us kids the few times we visited. She was more a grandmother to us than Grandma Ophelia. But at least Grandma Ophelia had room for us, since she was living alone. Off we went to Bell City, about fifteen miles away. Someone must have driven us by car since Bell City is inland. All I really remember about that night was terror. I was so afraid that Daddy Jack would come back and catch us before we got away. *Chuk. Chuk. Chuk.* Or that he would follow us to Bell City. I don't think Mama Rita was afraid once she made it to Grandma Ophelia's door, because that meant she was back with her kin. Even though her immediate family had shown her little in the way of love, they were still her blood.

Russell Gary and Warren Price told me that for the next couple of weeks Daddy Jack wandered around out there in the swamp, sometimes mad as hell, sometimes depressed, and sometimes threatening to kill himself. Folks knew well enough to leave him alone. Better to let Jack Kershaw work out his demons by himself. Then, at 8 o'clock on Wednesday morning, June 30, 1943, my godfather, Raoul Roy, was tying up his boat when he heard a shotgun blast come from the direction of our houseboat. Raoul dropped what he was doing and ran as fast as he could to the houseboat. Daddy Jack teetered in the doorway, covered in blood, with half his face blown away. But he was still alive, and he was holding his twelve-gauge shotgun. Horrified, Raoul stopped dead in his tracks. And that's when Daddy Jack let out this wild cry, like a wounded animal might make. Raoul took off as fast as he could to try and find help. But he hadn't gotten far when he heard a second blast come from the houseboat. Some of the neighbors had rushed outside their own houseboats, wondering what the explosions had been.

"Jack has shot himself!" Raoul shouted. And those were the same words he told us when he finally got to Grandma Broussard's house in Bell City. We piled into his old car and he drove as fast as he could back to the houseboat. We found out later that my father shot himself twice. The second time, he had to point the gun upward at his chin and pull the trigger with his toe. It blew off the rest of his head.

There's no other way to say this. By the time we reached our houseboat, the chickens were pecking at Daddy Jack's brains. For as long as I live, it's a sight that I will never forget. Blood and brain were splattered on the wall behind the table where he always sat for his morning coffee. A half-full cup was sitting on the table, as if he'd just put it down. You could smell freshly roasted coffee beans, as well as the blood.

Daddy Jack never made much of a mark in the world, but he made front-page news the following day in the Jeff Davis *Parish News.*

MAN ENDS HIS LIFE
WITH 12 GAUGE GUN

Jack Kershaw, Despondent Over Domestic Troubles and Separated From Wife Blows Face Off

---

Cameron Fisherman's First Try Ineffectual So He Pumps Second Shot

Said to have become despondent over domestic affairs, Jack Kershaw, 40, a fisherman, ended his life by blowing away his whole face with a powerful 12-gauge power shotgun as he sat in his houseboat tied up at the Streator Plantation in Cameron Parish at 8 yesterday morning. Kershaw first tried suicide by firing a shot which blew away his jaw, but this did not prove fatal and he took up the weapon a second time to pump the load into his face, which ended his life and so mutilated his face that he was unrecognizable.

He is said to have been separated from his wife for two weeks and grieved over his domestic situation. Besides the wife, he is survived by four sons. The Cameron Parish coroner gave a verdict of suicide.

No one, not his friends, not his neighbors, and not the law, considered Daddy Jack's death to be anything but suicide. But I'm his son, and I'm not sure. I can still picture him sitting there every morning with that shotgun propped between his legs. It was such a dangerous habit. Russell Gary tells me Daddy Jack threatened to kill himself many times during the two weeks after Mama Rita took us boys and left him. But I'd heard him make those threats before. I want to believe it's possible that the first shot was an accident, a slip of fate that happened while Daddy Jack sat there sipping his morning coffee. There's a French expression, *coup de grâce,* which means, literally, *a stroke of mercy.* It's the final blow, or shot, that brings death to a sufferer. I picture Daddy Jack crawling to the doorway, wounded and hurt, and, like he would do for any injured animal, he put himself out of misery. *Coup de grâce.*

I don't know if that's how it happened. Maybe it's denial, but it's how I choose to deal with my father's last morning on the bayou.

They took Daddy Jack's body to the local funeral home, where they held a wake before the burial service at the Bell City Catholic Church. Mama Rita told us kids that his funeral, including the cypress wood casket, would cost $65. I've no idea where she found that kind of money, but she must have found it somewhere since there was a service for Daddy Jack. I walked into the room where people were standing around the casket. At seven years old, I felt pretty tiny. So many large things had happened, adult things over which I had no control, and it had shaken up my world. I made my way through the mourners and over to the casket. I have no memory of who lifted me up in their arms so I could pay my last respects to Daddy Jack. But when I looked down into that cypress box, I didn't see my father's face, handsome, rugged, smiling at me. *Ti gâteau. Laisse ça tranquille, ti bébé.* I saw a pillowcase stuffed with Spanish moss. On top of it was Daddy Jack's fishing hat. In those days, a funeral parlor back in the swamps did what worked best.

That was the last time I saw my father, that day I said goodbye.

There's so much that a person doesn't know while trying to live a life. It's not easy to sort through the good and the bad and survive at the same time. Daddy Jack didn't know he was an alcoholic. He didn't know alcoholism is a disease, a particularly vicious one that turned him into a drunk son-of-a-bitch.

And there was so much that a seven-year-old boy didn't know, especially during that Louisiana summer of 1943, the summer Daddy Jack died. For instance, I didn't know back then that Daddy Jack would pass his disease on to me. But he did. As I said, I'm his son. So I became a drunk son-of-a-bitch, too. A *fils de putain*.

I guess Daddy Jack left me something after all.

5

LAKE ARTHUR

*"When you live on the water, you spend your life
doing a lot of things you shouldn't have to do."*
–Mama Rita, *Newsweek*, 1974

Life on the river was impossible without Daddy Jack. Even though his *I'm-gonna-kill-you* drunks scared the daylights out of us, he was also our sole provider and protector. I don't know what Mama Rita was thinking during those two weeks we were holed up at Grandma Ophelia's house. Did she plan to take us and go back to the houseboat and Daddy Jack? It wouldn't matter now. Those two shots fired on that June morning put things in perspective mighty fast. After years on the river, Mama Rita had to move back to town.

Edward had come home from the Hackberry oil fields to attend the funeral. Knowing we had to have a place to live, he stayed long enough to pull the houseboat up to the town of Lake Arthur. But it was as if Daddy Jack's bad luck had followed us out of the swamps. The *Muskrat*, which pulled the houseboat from place to place, sank on the Mermentau. Mama Rita finally had to sell the *Alice*, and then the houseboat, too, for next to nothing. The truth is, we really didn't want the houseboat, considering what had happened in it. The family that bought it never bothered to wash Daddy Jack's blood off the ceiling or walls. The new owner eventually just towed it out to the swamps and used it for many years as a hunting camp. Fishermen and trappers slept there, a haven on those black nights they had to spend out in the swamps. A. J. Bertrand once told me he remembered lying on the mattress that was left there and staring up at that splotch of blood on the ceiling. Russell Gary, who probably knew Daddy Jack best, never would step a foot back inside. The Bible says that blood is an atonement for the soul. I hope that's true, and that my father has found peace, wherever he is.

It was a fearsome time for folks in Lake Arthur. Money was short and the war kept everybody depressed as hell. My small world had been shaken up, but the big world out there was getting shook up some too. The Allies were tearing up Europe, and thousands of Japanese-Americans had been interned in camps around the United States. Food rationing was in effect, and Americans were digging in, doing their share for the war effort. But those problems didn't seem to match the ones we Kershaws faced after Daddy Jack's death. Our life was already riddled with uncertainty and tragedy. So what if a war was being waged somewhere? At least that's how Mama Rita saw our predicament.

"What's a world war, more or less, gonna do?" Mama Rita said. "Is it gonna make our lives worse?"

This was optimistic of her, considering we were living in a chicken coop at the time. But that's what it had started out as, that little house in Lake Arthur. *Un caban à poule.* Mama Rita used the money from the sale of the two boats to buy it. It was just a little one-room coop on a plot of ground at 424 Commercial Street. The first thing we did was to make it livable. You could see daylight through cracks in the walls, so our main problem was keeping out the wind and rain. If you know anything at all about Louisiana, you know that rain is a common visitor. It leaked in through cracks in the walls and down from the roof. And it got a lot of help from the wind. Mama Rita put us boys to work. Pee Wee and I walked all over Lake Arthur, asking store owners for cardboard boxes. We toted them back to the little house, broke them apart, and tacked the pieces to the wall, as if it were paneling. When we painted it white, it looked as if we had legitimate walls.

"We got us a real house," Mama Rita said. She even seemed proud.

Hell, we were swamp kids. We believed her.

Mama Rita had brought a bed, table, two coal-oil lamps, a small kerosene stove, and a pot-bellied wood stove from the river, along with a few other household items. The coal-oil lamps gave us enough light at night that we could do household chores, or just stare in wonder at our new cardboard walls. The kerosene stove was for cooking, and the wood stove would heat the place when the weather grew colder. I'll always remember how I left a patch of my ass on that stove one winter. I'd just finished a sponge bath and was bending over to dry my legs and feet when I backed right up into it. You could hear me sizzle. I still have a scar on my lower left cheek. You might say it's a battle scar. There *was* a war going on at the time.

With the war came the nightly blackouts. A lot of our neighbors were afraid of them. But blackouts didn't worry us Kershaws. Out in the swamps we were used to such things. We just called them *nights* instead of *blackouts*. Darkness had been a part of our lives from birth. If there was no moon, once the coal-oil lamp was put out on the river, pitch-black was all we had. But at least we could afford it.

Sounds, however, were another thing. Unless you count Daddy Jack's drunks, the only loud noises we had in the swamps came from nature. Birds. Frogs. Animals hunting food. When you live in the heart of nature, you grow used to hearing gators bellow their grunts from across the bayou, which is what they did during mating season. You get used to the hoots of owls and the sounds of fish jumping. After a time, you don't notice these sounds at all. They become part of your existence. Considering this, imagine my hearing an air-raid siren for the first time, shrieking in the night. I tell you, I'd never even imagined such a frightening sound as that. At least the gators were in love. They had something to look forward to that was better than bombs falling.

Running a close second to air raids was the sound of church bells pealing out on Sunday mornings. Those bells were as alien to me as the air raids. We always said our prayers back in the swamps. They were in French, of course, since Mama Rita had taught us. We called it praying to the rosary, or *egrainer le chaplet*. Later, we learned to pray in English. But there were no churches on the bayou then. I always thought God could hear our prayers anyway, even if he did live in town. It took some time before the church bells didn't startle me.

During July and August we slept with the doors and windows open and prayed for a breeze. We didn't have screens on the windows, but that didn't matter. It was so hot that the mosquitoes refused to come inside anyway. We had an outhouse, a one-holer, but we kept a white ceramic pot for use during the night, a *pot de chambre*. Like *cabinette* for "outhouse," this sounds a little uptown for the item described. Also, I think you should have a *chamber* in order to have a *chamber* pot. Mostly, we called it "the slop jar," but it did have a lid. And, thank God, it had handles so I could carry it to the toilet and dump it. It stayed under the bed until someone needed it. That may also explain why the mosquitoes weren't too anxious to get inside.

Mama Rita slept in the one bed. Sometimes, she'd let Rusty crawl in with her since he was the youngest. Pee Wee and I slept on the floor. Surprisingly enough, it wasn't the one-room chicken coop, the intense heat, or even sleeping on the floor that bothered me most about town life. It was being off the river. Until we moved into Lake Arthur, I didn't realize how much I enjoyed the feel of our house rocking back and forth, and the sound of water slapping against it. You've heard it said that when sailors have been to sea a long time they have to get their shore legs back, in order to walk well again on dry land? That was me when I came off the river and into Lake Arthur. I had to get my shore legs.

The biggest problem we faced was money, hard cold cash, or the lack of it. With the war rationing going on, we had to have stamps to buy sugar and gasoline. Since we had no car, the gas rations weren't needed anyway. Sugar would have been nice, but you still had to have money to pay for it. Those ration stamps meant only that you were entitled to buy your ration of sugar. It didn't mean sugar was free. We had no money anyway. This posed a dilemma. We had seldom needed cash money on the river, but in town it was a necessity. When Daddy Jack was alive, he was able to barter for the things we needed. Every tugboat captain traveling the river knew Jack Kershaw. They knew they could always get fresh fish, wild duck or geese, even shrimp. Those captains were therefore ready and willing to trade Daddy Jack rice, beans, potatoes, and flour for his catch. Keep in mind that those goods came in *sacks,* which was an extra bonus since Mama Rita used them to make us shirts. Now, not only did we lack cash for rice and beans, we no longer had material for clothes.

Mama Rita turned to the parish for public assistance, but she was rejected. I can't imagine us not qualifying. Hell, if poor was an Olympics, we'd have been gold medalists. But for some reason the parish didn't agree. I remember being almost relieved when Mama Rita told us. Even at the age of seven I was embarrassed that we had to ask for charity. So, like many poor women have always done, Mama Rita started taking in washing and ironing, working from dawn to dusk. She earned about fifty cents a day. She'd take Rusty with her to pick up people's dirty clothes, carry the basket home, pump and heat the water to wash the clothes, and then hang them on a line. When they dried, she'd press them with an iron she had heated on the wood-burning stove. Even in the heat of summer that stove had to be burning, and it was up to Pee Wee and me to provide the wood. It was hard work for us boys, but it was even harder work for Mama Rita. Yet I never heard her complain. I don't know where or how she learned to look after her children. She sure as hell didn't get lessons from her own mother. I guess with Mama Rita it was instinct.

Pee Wee and I started school in Lake Arthur, that same year Daddy Jack died, in 1943. I skipped the second grade and went directly into the third so that I'd be with kids my own age. Rusty was still too young to go to school, so he stayed at home with Mama Rita. For the next three years, come rain or shine, Mama Rita brought Pee Wee and me our lunch at school. We called it dinner back then. It was usually some gravy poured over a little rice, or *couche-couche*, steamed corn meal. That rice and corn meal went a long way toward feeding the family.

As I said, Mama Rita cooked on a kerosene stove back then. She'd cook one meal a day, and that's what we would eat, morning, noon, and night. Sometimes, the food lasted over into the next day too. But leftovers were rare, and scraps didn't exist. If there happened to be some leftover rice the next morning, Mama Rita would reheat it and fry it up with eggs. It tasted really good too. Later, when we finally got natural gas, it took me a long time to get used to food that wasn't *á la kerosene*. Once in awhile Mama Rita would vary the menu and make corn bread instead of *couche-couche*, which gave a different texture to the same old taste. We couldn't afford real milk, so she'd get canned milk and dilute it with water.

Gone were the days when neighbors on the river gathered for a *bou-cherie*, that old communal hog butchering. If we got lucky and caught a fish or a neighbor gave us part of their catch, Mama Rita would either steam it on the stove with sauce *piquante* or fry it and pour the grease over rice. Unless someone gave us vegetables, we did without them that first year. It wasn't until the next summer that Mama Rita could plant a garden. But we did have a treat now and then to break the monotony of being poor. When Mama Rita finished with a can of Karo syrup she let us have the dregs. She called it rock candy.

Needless to say, our first year without Daddy Jack was *un enfant de chien*. A son of a bitch. I often use humor to deal with painful memories, especially of those early years. Sometimes it seems to soften the blow. So I joke about those lean times. "We were so poor," I tell people, "that Mama

Rita had to come to school every day and feed me Moon Pie and titty." But it wasn't so funny back then. I became obsessed with where the next meal was coming from, and to this day I will never take the last piece of anything from the table. I never want to be the cause of someone else going hungry.

But poverty didn't bother me as much as finding out that I was a Cajun, and realizing that for some folks, Cajun was a dirty word. Like many little *chaouis*, or coon-ass kids, I didn't know English when I started school in Lake Arthur. I had only spent that one year with Mrs. Savoy, at our school out on the river. And then, when her paddle was broken, well, I sort of lost my drive. Keep in mind that in Louisiana it was against the law to speak French then. Way back in 1898, the constitution of the state of Louisiana had said that French could be taught in those places where it was spoken as a main language. But then some folks in high places in the state Legislature decided this wasn't a good idea after all. So, the constitution of 1921 outlawed the speaking of French in the schools. Paddles were busy all over the Pelican State, wherever little Cajun kids were slipping up and speaking Cajun French. And that was easy to do when you consider that almost all of us had parents who couldn't speak a word of English.

With those paddlings, and tongue holdings, came a kind of humiliation and shame. After a time I began to feel that something was innately wrong with me and my "kind." A.J. Bertrand told me that he made a vow to himself years ago that he would never allow his children to speak Cajun French. He was only trying to spare them the embarrassment he once felt. He lived to regret that decision. It cost his kids a part of their heritage. My own boys don't speak Cajun French either, I'm sorry to say. So they've lost a piece of their heritage too.

But some things take time to sort out in our hearts. I was well into my adult life before I started to swell with pride when I spoke of my Cajun roots. As a child, I didn't even understand what a *Cajun* was, or how we differed from whites, blacks, or anyone else. I remember the day I first started questioning my Cajun background. It happened while I was walking around Lake Arthur with some boys. Soon I needed to use the bathroom, and this led to my first encounter with a public restroom. They were really just two small outhouses, located back off the street a bit. So off I go to use the restroom. But then I saw the signs on the doors. One said *Whites* and the other said *Coloreds*. Remember that I couldn't read much English yet, so one of the boys had to explain it to me. *Whites* meant people with white skin. *Coloreds* meant Negroes.

"*Mais!* There's no door for us *chaouis?*" I asked him. He just shrugged and pointed to the door marked *Whites*. I don't really think he knew either. I always used the *Whites* restroom after that, but I still wasn't sure it was the correct one.

It was a long time before I found out that *Cajun* refers to a culture and its dialect. *My* culture, and *my* dialect. This race business was very confusing to a little Cajun boy fresh out of the swamps. I used to hear people talk about Cajuns being part black, part Indian, part this, and part that. The truth is, most careless people back then called Cajuns *coon-asses* or *chaoui*, which translates to "raccoon." And they called black people "niggers." I didn't quite grasp that terms like those were derogatory. As I mentioned earlier, there was even a Nigger Island located close to Tiel Ridge, which they've now changed to Negro Island on Louisiana maps. This was the island where Grandpa Kershaw was waiting in his skiff for Daddy Jack and Mama Rita, the day after their marriage. In fact, I didn't even know which of those terms fit *me*, since that hot Louisiana sun had charred me a deep brown. Blacks didn't look very different from me. So I didn't know that I wasn't "mixed" until I was twenty years old. That was in 1956, when Rusty and I moved to Wheeling, West Virginia, to play on the Jamboree. When winter started setting in, my skin started getting lighter and lighter. "Hey, look at this!" I said to Rusty. "I'm losing my nigger!"

A helluva way to put it, but I didn't know any better.

I realize that many Cajuns today consider *coon-ass* a derisive term, and I can understand why. But I'll tell you how I feel about it. I got over it. Just like I got over those early feelings of inferiority about being Cajun in the first place. It's just a damn word, and I'm not going to let it affect me or hurt me in the least. Why should I? I know who I am, and I'm proud of me. A word can't change that, nor can it change what people think of me. I even have a little fun with it on stage. "I know some of you folks call us Cajuns *coonasses*," I tell my audiences. "But you should hear what WE call YOU." It makes people laugh and, hell, maybe it even makes them think about the words they choose, and if they're the best ones.

I may even have Cherokee blood in me, from some grandma on Daddy Jack's side. At least I always heard that while I was growing up. I haven't checked yet, but I hope it's true. Whether we have a little black, a little red, a little yellow, or a little white, it won't hurt us any. It just keeps us interesting. And besides, down in Southwest Louisiana, poverty was colorblind in those early days.

What I remember most about those first years off the river is not that we were often hungry, or that Mama Rita earned only fifty cents a day. I remember the cowboy movies, and that Mama Rita somehow found a way to give me nine cents every Saturday, the cost of a ticket at the Lake Arthur movie theater. It was also the cost of a loaf of bread in those days, so it was a big sacrifice. That had to be the best nine cents my mother ever invested in me, because it introduced me to a world where men could be heroes. They took care of people. I'd watch Tex Ritter in *Old Chisholm Trail* and Roy Rogers in *King of the Cowboys*. Sure, Tex and Roy shot at a few bad guys. But they didn't strike women or threaten to harm their kids. And the *fais do-dos* Roy and Tex went to always had happy endings.

I can remember sitting there wide-eyed in that darkened theater, wishing that I was a cowboy riding along that dusty Chisholm Trail, all the way from San Antonio to Abilene, Kansas. Wishing I was a grown-up man who could take care of things. Wishing that I could be a hero to *somebody*. So I came home one afternoon from a cowboy movie and I made Mama Rita a promise.

"Mama Rita, I'm gonna take care of you for the rest of your life," I told her.

"*C'est bon, cher*," Mama Rita said. That's good, dear.

So I started looking for ways to earn money.

6

SHINE?

In the evening, and in the shadows,
I'll be waiting in Louisiana,
And when I hear your sweet voice,
I'll rejoice, I'm so happy
And I'm saving all my kisses for you.

—"Jolie Blon," traditional Cajun song.

A year after moving out of the swamps and into Lake Arthur, I found a way to keep my promise to Mama Rita. And it was all thanks to three black boys. Every weekend I'd see these boys out shining shoes around town. It looked like pretty steady work to me. So I started saving the nine cents Mama Rita was giving me for the cowboy movie. This meant I'd have to put Tex and Roy on hold for a time, until the big bucks started to pour in. First, I asked Pee Wee to build me a shoeshine box, which he did. When I had enough money, I bought a shoe brush and two cans of shoe polish, one black and one brown. It took me five long weeks to get up the investment cash since the polish cost me ten cents a can, and the brush was a quarter.

I didn't tell Mama Rita what I was doing until I was ready for my last item, a shoeshine rag. I had noticed that the black kids used only one rag, one side for brown polish, the other side for black. So I asked Mama Rita if she'd sew one up for me. She took the material from an old pair of bib overalls that were worn out, and made me a shoeshine rag.

I was eight and a half years old, but I was ready to take on the world.

All week long I thought of nothing else. I was so anxious for Saturday to come so I could start making my fortune that I couldn't sit still. Finally Mama Rita had had enough.

"*Mais,* Doug," she said. "*Dansers comme un dinde la cendre chaude!*" You're dancing like a turkey in hot ashes.

When Friday night finally arrived, I got out the shoeshine box and took inventory. I had to be sure everything was there. Over and over again I inspected the items. Two cans of shoe polish, one shine rag, and one shoe brush. I was ready. The next morning I hoisted the shoeshine box onto my shoulder, and off I went to my first day of work. I had to walk about a mile before I got to the busiest section of town. I was within two blocks of the corner I'd picked as my work station when those three black kids jumped out in front of me. I figured they were businessmen, just like me, so I assumed they wanted to talk shop. *They* saw *me* as the competition.

"You better not be goin' to town with that shoeshine box, you little white bastard," one of them warned. I must have looked confused. A second boy pointed a finger in my face.

"Whites ain't allowed to shine shoes in Lake Arthur," he informed me. "Just coloreds." I was familiar with the "this town ain't big enough for the both of us" philosophy, thanks to all those cowboy movies. But this I didn't understand.

Nonetheless, there were three of them, so I saw no purpose in arguing the point.

"That's fine with me," I said. Then I turned and walked back down the street, as if I were headed home. When I got far enough away, I cut through someone's yard and headed toward the center of town. I didn't want to fight. Sometimes, at school, Pee Wee would talk me into fighting one of the bigger boys. But before they had a chance to hurt me bad, my teacher would always come along and break it up. I had come to depend on that teacher. And since she was nowhere around, I sat down on a heavily traveled corner to wait for my first customer. He showed up about an hour later.

"*Tu veux je shine tes souliers? S'il vous plâit?*" I asked. Do you want me to shine your shoes. Please? He took me up on my offer, and I went to work. I wish I knew the man's name because he represented my first real job. I shined his shoes until you could see all of Lake Arthur in them. When I finished, he nodded, flipped me a dime, and walked off. Easy as that. I was still staring down at the dime in the palm of my hand when my competition ambushed me again. Same three black boys. Only this time they were really mad. One grabbed the dime out of my hand and shoved it into his pocket. The other two kicked my ass *and* my shoeshine box all the way down the street and out of town. A helluva way to ride off into the sunset. And no one had turned up to save me, not my teacher, not Roy, not Tex, not even Gabby Hayes.

But I wasn't going to give up on this hero stuff because I remembered what that dime had felt like in my hand, cool and slick. I could almost feel it shine. There's an old Cajun saying, *Lache pas la patate.* Don't let go of the potato. Hang right in there, in other words. And that's what I intended to do. I kept right on trying to get a foothold in the shoeshine business, so to speak. But the next two Saturday mornings that I turned up to work, the boys didn't even give me time to get a customer before they chased me off my corner and out of town. It was a sad spectacle. To tell you the truth, I had begun to take those ass-kickings personally. So I decided that if I was going to make it as a shoeshine boy, I would have to come up with a damn good plan. It was time to circle the wagons.

On the fourth Saturday, I left the house before sunup. This time, I was carrying something besides my shoeshine box. I had my fiddle with me. Kind of like those guns the cowboys toted. I had long since graduated from the cigar-box fiddle. I don't know what happened to it. I wish I had it today, but I suspect it ended up in the trash. Pee Wee had managed to get himself a new fiddle by this time, and he had given me his old one. So, I "rode" into town long before the competition arrived and picked a spot in front of the Red & White Café. I figured lots of people must come to the Red & White for breakfast. Sure enough, before long I saw a few people headed up the street.

I opened the wooden case and took out my fiddle. I tucked it under my chin and waited for the folks to get closer. I didn't know who they were, only that they must be Cajuns because Lake Arthur was mostly Cajun. When they got within earshot, I laid into "Jolie Blon" and played it like I never had before. "Jolie Blon" is so damn pretty it can stop you in your tracks, even if you're hungry. I hooked them. The same way Daddy Jack would throw out his fishing lines, I hooked them. Then I reeled them in. The crowd grew, and the bigger it got, the harder I played. Hell, I played up a storm. Out of the corner of my eye, I saw the three black kids around the corner. I could tell by their faces they were stunned. But there I was, in the safety of the circled wagons.

The next thing I did turned out to be the most important lesson I ever learned, at least where my professional life was concerned. When I finished "Jolie Blon," I put the fiddle back in its open case, simple as that. Let's face it. There's nothing quite so sweet as an encore. And that's what the crowd wanted. So I came up with a good business slogan, right on the spot.

"Let me shine your shoes for a dime," I offered, "And I'll play you a song for free."

They not only paid me for a shine, most of them gave me quarters, and two of them even gave me a dollar. Man oh man, it's a helluva feeling to make money with just talent on your side.

The lesson I learned that day has helped me survive all my life. It seemed pretty damn simple. I could work for a song shining shoes, or I could let the song work for me and make some good money. All I had to do was entertain the crowd as well as I could. Then, if I got out of town fast enough, nobody could kick my ass.

This would come in handy, years later, when I ended up in Nashville.

By the time I got home that night it was 10 o'clock and way past dark. I was so covered with brown and black shoe polish that all Mama Rita could see was my eyes. But I had earned $10.20 that day, so those eyes must have shone with pride. I reached into my pockets and dug out all those quarters and dimes, and a couple dollar bills. I tossed them on the table in front of Mama Rita. She was as stunned as I had imagined on my walk home. Together, we laughed and danced and I think she cried a little. It's a wonder we didn't knock down the chicken coop. We ate beans for a whole week, and what a treat that was for the family. I was sure we'd hit the big times for good.

The black kids left me alone once I staked out my spot in front of the Red & White Café. There were enough dirty shoes in town for all of us, and I guess they figured I wasn't worth an ass-kicking every Saturday morning. I even came to be friendly with my competition. Our house bordered the black section of town, and sometimes the four of us walked home together after a hard day's work. It wasn't that the shoeshine business was without pitfalls. I met with some obstacles. I remember one time how I was running low on black shoe polish, right in the middle of a busy day. I had to think fast. Zenis Lacombe owned a service station next door to the Red & White. So I raced over to the service station and got some black grease from Zenis. I mixed that in with what was left of the shoe polish and went back to work shining shoes. All day long I kept praying, "Please, God, don't let anyone light a match near their shoes."

A Thibodeaux couple owned the Red & White Café back then. I remember they had a daughter named Theresa, who was my age. I never saw the Thibodeaux family again, not after I moved away from Lake Arthur. But I'll never forget them. Every day that I shined shoes on the sidewalk out front, I would peer in through the café window, just to get a glimpse of their world. I wanted for the Kershaws what I saw inside the Red & White Café. Plenty of food. Neat, clean tablecloths. Paper napkins. Shiny forks and knives. There was an order in how things were done. There seemed to be a safety in that world, and that was the key to it all. Although I couldn't put it into words back then, every day I was learning what my future could hold. I was learning to want more than what little I had, or to at least dream about it. So the Thibodeaux family helped give a small boy a push in the right direction.

For the next two years I went to school on weekdays. Weekends, I played music and shined shoes in front of the Red & White. I still couldn't believe that I was being paid money to do something that I loved so much as fiddling. The shoeshine part was tougher, but it meant dimes hitting the palm of my hand. When it got too dark to see a shoe in front of my face, I'd pack up and go on home to supper, my shoeshine box in one hand, my fiddle case in the other. I was as tired and dirty as a kid could get, and it's a wonder I didn't fall asleep at the table. But as soon as supper was over, never fail, someone would pull out a guitar or a fiddle. Then someone else would pick up an accordion. Soon, the little room was filled to the rafters with music. That was my favorite part of the day, those times after supper with just Mama Rita and us boys. Pee Wee played guitar, fiddle, and accordion. Rusty was still little then, so mostly he just listened and watched. But sometimes he tried to play, too. I suppose this was a great way for him to learn.

Uncle Abel came to visit every now and then from the Hackberry oil fields. He'd bring along his accordion and sit in with us. And Edward came home once in a while to see how we were doing. He had learned to play accordion at a very young age, so he'd join in, too. Mama Rita played guitar and fiddle. I used to get a kick out of how she played melodies on the fiddle with just her index finger. "Because I forgot, me, how to use the other three," she'd say, repeating the pronoun. Many French-speaking people who are not so accustomed to English do this. It's the nature of the language itself. During these nightly sessions we all took turns singing, but mostly Mama Rita was the vocalist. This was her way of teaching us the words to all those old Cajun French songs. I can still hear her singing the words to "Jolie Blon," or *pretty blonde*, in French and English.

Quoi Ta fai? Tu ma quité, pour t'en aller.
What did you do? You left me, to go away.

Jolie blon, Cajun angel,
Let me tell you once again that I love you.

When I sing some of these same old songs today, they carry me back to those nights at 424 Commercial Street and the little chicken coop house. I don't know what everyone else was thinking, but I missed Daddy Jack at times like that. During the days that had passed since his death, we all tried not to speak of him. There was still so much pain in what had happened that morning on the bayou. We tried not to speak of it, but his memory followed me wherever I went. For a long time I was mad at Daddy Jack. He seemed to be in a place where he didn't have to worry about food to eat or clothes to wear. He had left us with the short end of the stick. But through my anger, I missed him. I missed the good things about him. And on those evenings when I played my fiddle, along with Mama Rita and my brothers, I could almost feel Daddy Jack's spirit in the room with us, his accordion pumping out "Fe Fe Foncheaux."

There was a lot of learning to be done in those first years off the river. It would be a long time before I forgave my father for that morning on the houseboat. But I know for certain I wouldn't have made it through those hard years without my fiddle. It didn't just make money to feed my body. It fed my soul, too. I might have lost my father, but I had found music there at my side. I could count on it on it hard times.

Life trudged on. School, music, and shoeshine. Shoeshine, music, and school. And then, one day when I was around nine years old, I discovered something that stunned me. Cajun music wasn't the only kind of music in the world! This discovery came after I left my spot in front of the Red & White Café and moved my business over to another café called the Sea Breeze. I needed fresh customers who would sometimes give a dollar bill to hear a Cajun boy play the fiddle. And most folks around the Red & White had grown accustomed to my talents. What the Sea Breeze had that the Red & White didn't was a jukebox. In my book, the invention of the jukebox is right next to the invention of the wheel.

Up until that time my only musical influences were the Cajun fiddlers and accordion players who came through town to play in the clubs around Lake Arthur. Mama Rita loved to listen to them, so she'd take us boys right along with her to the bars. When I got to playing in clubs myself, at the age of nine, I got to hear people like Nathan Abshire and Iry Lejeune. Iry Lejeune played Cajun accordion and sang with more feeling than anyone I had ever heard. It was as if he had the souls of Hank Williams and Ray Charles all rolled into one. Iry was no purist. He listened to blues *and* country, and he let those styles seep into his own music.

Iry had also spent a lot of time with his accordion-playing cousin, Angelas Lejeune, who recorded back in the 1920s. And he had done his homework on Amédé Ardoin, the great black accordion player who also recorded in the twenties and thirties. This is how Iry picked up his soulful presentation and his diverse influences. We owe a big debt to Iry Lejeune for popularizing Cajun music back in the 1940s and 1950s. It was a tragic loss when he was killed accidentally in his prime. Iry and fiddle player J.B. Fuselier were on their way home from a show at the Green Wing Club in Eunice, Louisiana, on October 8, 1955, when a tire blew on their car. Iry got out to watch J.B. fix it, and the two were struck by a passing automobile. J.B. was badly hurt, but Iry Lejeune died on the spot. All of Southwest Louisiana mourned the loss of this great legend. And so did I, since it was from performers like Iry Lejeune that I realized music could be a profession, not just something to entertain my friends at a *fais do-do*.

But not until I discovered that jukebox at the Sea Breeze Café did I understand all the elements that went into Iry's music. I had just begun to shine my first pair of shoes in my new location when my life changed for good. I even remember the customer's name, a fellow named Mr. Tauzin.

I was at work on his left shoe when I heard music playing. And it was a music I'd never heard before.

I stopped working and listened.

"*Qu'avez-vous?*" Mr. Tauzin said when he saw me sitting there, just staring at the café. What's the matter with you?

"Who's in there playing that music?" I asked. Mr. Tauzin laughed.

"That's Glenn Miller," he told me. "But he's not in there, Doug. It's just a record that somebody played on the jukebox." I honestly think my mouth dropped open.

"*Vraiment?*" I asked. Really? Mr. Tauzin nodded.

"It's called 'In the Mood.' It's a great song, ain't it?"

"*Oui, c'est bon,*" I whispered. Yes, it's good. Man, oh man, it sure was. I was barely able to catch my breath. That's how beautiful that sound was to my ears.

Keep in mind that we had no record player in our house while I was growing up. Hell, we didn't even own a radio until I was fourteen years old. So I'd never heard songs sung in English before. Since "In the Mood" was an instrumental, I thought maybe this was some new Cajun group from over in Jennings or Big Mamou. Wherever they lived, they sure kicked ass. Then I heard the next record. Ernest Tubb was singing "Walkin' the Floor Over You." I couldn't believe that this man was singing a fine song in the very language my teachers were shoving down my throat. That is the damn truth. Ernest Tubb was a better reason for me to learn English than a thousand ass-paddlings.

And Ernest never once held my tongue.

I started listening to the jukebox very carefully after that. I noticed that most of the songs were in English, songs like "Sentimental Journey" and "Faded Love." They were in English and, *mon dieu,* those songs were pretty! Then one day I heard the best version of "Jolie Blon" in Cajun French that I'd ever heard. I stepped inside the Sea Breeze and stood there, staring at the jukebox as it sang to me. I finally got up the courage to ask someone who the singer was. It was Harry Choates, and he was also playing the fiddle. *How strange music really is,* I remember thinking. *So many different sounds.*

I also took notice that day of how the jukebox didn't care one bit what the language was. It just went ahead and sang its heart out. No prejudice there, especially in those days before the music industry had a chance to brainwash the consumer. That's part of the reason I've had a love affair with the jukebox to this day. A jukebox was then the purest form of artist-to-consumer communication ever invented. A customer drops money in and immediately hears a favorite song. Nowadays, with the internet, everything is at our fingertips. But the jukebox had the first "downloadable" music.

On the night of August 14, 1945, the end of World War II hit Southwest Louisiana like a bomb. All at once Lake Arthur went crazy. The lights of town blinked off and on. Church bells rang out. Air-raid sirens shrieked nonstop. Cars tooted their horns. Foghorns sounded out on the river. People raced through the streets, screaming for folks to wake up. I'd never heard so much noise! I jumped out of bed and ran outside. I was scared to the bone and trembling all over. I knew it had to be a tornado close by. Or maybe it was the end of the world. There had always been talk by the adults of whether or not the Japanese would drop bombs on the mainland, the way they did at Pearl Harbor. If it wasn't a tornado, I was sure the bombs were finally arriving. It was *finis* for the Kershaws. The chicken coop was not exactly a bomb shelter.

Mama Rita tried to calm us down, but I could tell she didn't know what the hell was going on either. Then someone went running past our house, shouting.

"Japan has surrendered! It's over! The war is over!"

Those words meant a lot of things to us and to the country. They meant men and women were coming home. They meant more money in everyone's pocket. They meant more food and spirits once again. In Southwest Louisiana our somber mood was quickly replaced with a sense of Mardi Gras, a pure *joie de vivre* as celebrations began. Now, all people wanted to do was eat, screw, and fight. But, most important for the Kershaws, those Cajuns wanted to dance!

Laisser le bon temps rouler. Let the good times roll!

7

THE BUCKET OF BLOOD

"Step aside, good people, so I can show this pig out!"
—Albert Broussard,
Proprietor, the Bucket of Blood

One of our neighbors back then was Zenis Lacombe, whose house sat behind ours, facing the other way. Zenis owned a service station and auto repair shop, just next door to the Red & White Café. This was where I went for grease when I got low on black shoe polish. Pee Wee had been playing music with Zenis but had already left to join Amédé Breaux and his band. So after several months of listening to me fiddle in front of the Red & White, Zenis invited me to come to the musical gatherings at his house. Since I was always working on Sundays, I didn't know that Zenis's family and friends always gathered at the Lacombe house to play music. I also didn't know that my neighbor was a fairly well-known Cajun accordion player. I'd been missing out on a lot of musical jams by shining shoes.

Being self-employed, I took the next Sunday off. I was nine years old and scared half to death. But I was also thrilled that these accomplished musicians accepted me as an equal. I even felt I belonged with them as we played the afternoon away. Finally somebody, some music-loving soul, said the magic words. "*Mais*, Zenis, you and the boy are good enough for the Bucket of Blood."

That same night Zenis went to talk with the owner of the big dance hall that sat on the road leading out of Lake Arthur. It was called *le Bucket de Sangre*, or the Bucket of Blood. Strangely enough, the Bucket of Blood was owned by a little man with the same name as my grandpa, Albert Broussard. As far as we could tell, the club owner was no relation to Mama Rita. But he was pretty famous around the state, considering that the Bucket of Blood was the wildest place in Southwest Louisiana. It wasn't considered a good night at the Bucket unless there were at least three fights and a knifing. Still, Albert Broussard threw the worst troublemakers out the front door. He would come dragging some drunken *couillon* behind him, some crazy *nut* who had started a fight. But he always tried to show a bit of courtesy to his other customers at the same time. He'd gesture for the crowd of dancers to part and let him through.

"Step aside, good people!" Albert would shout, "so I can show this pig out!"

Mr. Broussard agreed to let us audition the next Saturday night. If his crowd liked us, we could come back every Saturday night. And he'd even pay us. Just the chance to audition for the Bucket was enough incentive to put a band together. Mama Rita would play guitar. Zenis's wife, Marie, would play drums. I would play fiddle, of course, and also do vocals. And Zenis Lacombe would play the instrument he was known for, the accordion. All that week we rehearsed whenever we could, which was tough since Zenis had his gas station to run, I had my after-school job in front of the Red & White, and Mama Rita was still taking in washing. But, come Saturday night, we were ready for our audition. We piled into Zenis's car and drove over to Albert Broussard's club.

At the Bucket of Blood all the musicians walked through a door at the back of the stage and then stepped up onto the stage itself. I was too tiny to make that step, so an adult had to lift me up. I still didn't own a pair of shoes at this time, even though I'd shined hundreds of them. Shoes didn't come into my life until later, after I started playing in clubs full time and could afford to buy a pair. So I played barefoot at the Bucket of Blood, my little ass sitting on an upside-down beer crate. Who needed shoes if you had a fiddle? I was ready for that audition in my bare feet. And what a Saturday night it was. All those Cajuns danced until the sweat poured off them. And they drank rivers of booze. Albert Broussard only had to show a few pigs to the door that night, since even the troublemakers loved us. I had to be careful not to step on broken glass, but our little makeshift band got the gig. Our careers were launched.

In those days, in the clubs of Southwest Louisiana, if someone didn't like the way you played "Jolie Blon," they didn't hesitate to let you know by throwing a bottle. And there weren't just bottles flying in these rowdy places. People flew too. Sometimes folks would get so drunk that they'd forget and throw a bottle to let you know they *loved* your playing. It was a no-win situation. Some club owners cared enough about the band that they enclosed the stage area with chicken wire to protect the musicians from serious head injuries. The Bucket of Blood, rowdiest of the rowdy clubs, still hadn't done this. But shortly after we began playing there, chicken wire went up around the stage area as if by magic. I suspect Mr. Broussard didn't want to explain to a judge why his nine-year-old band member had a concussion, especially since I wasn't old enough to work where alcohol was being served in the first place. From then on, bottles *and* people bounced off the chicken wire. We kept on playing, smiles on our faces, and pretended not to notice.

I don't know what Zenis made each Saturday night, but he gave Mama Rita and me each ten dollars. That first time he paid us, after a long, sweaty night, I looked up at Mama Rita's face. She was pretty impressed with her own ten-dollar bill.

"We're never gonna beg for anything again," I said to her, and she smiled. I could almost see the relief on her face.

The Kershaws were in high cotton.

But the cotton never got so high that I gave up my day job. I kept right on shining shoes. I just quit early on Saturday nights. I was working a grueling schedule. I went to school five days a week, shined shoes and fiddled all day Saturday, then played music for four hours at the Bucket of Blood every Saturday night. Come Sunday morning, I was back shining shoes in front of the Sea Breeze, bright and early, rain or shine. I never thought much about it or ever considered complaining to Mama Rita. In my mind, it didn't matter *who* worked for the money, as long as we were all eating. Daddy Jack had been a good provider when he was alive and sober. And that's all I wanted to be.

Now that our ragtag band had a place of employment, we needed a name for ourselves. Back in the 1940s and the early 1950s, all Cajun bands were usually named after the town where the musicians lived, the club where they played, or for the band leader. You'd often see the word "Boys" or "Playboys" tacked onto the end of the name, just for good measure. We had bands like Nathan Abshire & the Pine Grove Boys, who were named after a nightclub. There was Aldus Roger & the Lafayette Playboys, named after the town of Lafayette. Some bands were more inventive, like the great Lawrence Walker & the Wandering Aces.

Zenis Lacombe's initial idea for our own band name came from my "stage clothes." It was the sight of my oversized white shirt, one I had borrowed from Pee Wee, that set Zenis off the first time.

"That's it!" he shouted when I walked into his house.

"What's it?" his wife, Marie, asked.

"The name of the band! Zenis Lacombe & the White Shirt Band!" Then he ran back into his bedroom to put on a white shirt.

It wasn't what I would call an inventive name, certainly not on the level of Lawrence Walker's Wandering Aces. Nor was it practical. Marie pointed out that neither she nor Mama Rita had a white shirt. And I reminded Zenis that I could only wear my white shirt when Pee Wee wasn't wearing it. My typical outfit in those days was a pair of bib overalls with no shirt at all, much less a white one. Once Zenis realized that he was the only one who'd be wearing a white shirt on a regular basis, he finally agreed to think of something else. But try as he may, Zenis couldn't come up with anything that stuck. As the days wore on, we remained an unnamed band. And Zenis wasn't happy about it.

My greatest fear was worse than us remaining nameless. I was certain that one day, when we were least expecting it, Zenis's eyes would suddenly shine and he would shout, "I've got it! We'll be Zenis Lacombe & the Bloody Buckets!"

But we had already left the Bucket behind when a name for our band finally fell onto Zenis's head and stuck there. We had been hired to play a dance at the Pine Grove Club in Evangeline, about fifteen miles away. As we drove through Jennings on Highway 26, Zenis spotted the Seven-Up bottling company.

"*Mais,* that's the name of the band!" Zenis shouted, pointing at the sign.

And that's how we became known as Zenis Lacombe & the Seven-Up Playboys.

Even though two of us were *girls*.

I immediately started thinking up ideas that would set our band apart from everyone else's. After all, this kind of strategy had worked well for me in the shoeshine business. So I kept my eyes and ears open to what other bands were doing. I received my first good lesson in strategy when I saw Will Kegley play fiddle with Nathan Abshire & the Pinegrove Boys.

Now I'd seen a lot of good fiddle players by then, even at my young age. But the first time I saw Will Kegley, he just blew me away. Will could bring an entire crowd to its feet with his fiddle tricks. Sometimes he'd play fiddle sitting down in a chair, which was an unusual sight. Often, in the middle of a song, he'd put the fiddle behind his head and keep right on playing. Or he'd take the bow and slip it under his right leg and play that way.

I noticed that all eyes were on Will Kegley when he did that trick fiddling.

"I can do that too," I told myself.

I started practicing standing up, sitting down, dancing, playing behind my head, and even between my legs, which was not an easy thing for a short-legged nine-year-old to achieve on a full-size fiddle. I soon found out that I loved to do everything except sit down when I was playing. Sitting down meant sitting *still*, and I had too much energy for that. I wanted to move all I could on stage, even as a kid.

Being a cute little boy has its advantages, especially when you're doing fiddle tricks. Soon all eyes were on *me* at our dances, which was exactly as I'd planned it. But then something happened that I hadn't anticipated. I started getting all the tips. Hell, that was a trick I could learn to live with. Before long I was making more money on tips than Zenis was paying me. It couldn't have happened at a better time, either, because Mama Rita wanted to quit the band. She was worried about leaving Rusty home alone since he was only seven or eight years old at that time. Trouble was, we had always needed that extra money she brought in. But now that I was making so much in tips, I could more than carry her share all by myself. That's when Mama Rita decided it was time to say goodbye to the Seven-up Playboys. She figured I was in good hands with Zenis and Marie, so she gave Zenis her notice one Saturday night and left the band. A guitar player named Ernest Dyson took her place.

Unfortunately, Zenis thought *he* needed the extra money too. It all came to a head one night while we were playing at Sweeney Hebert's club in Cameron. I was having one helluva good night. The shrimp boats had just come in that afternoon, up from the Gulf of Mexico. They were loaded down with tons of shrimp, so everybody had money for the kid fiddler. I raked in about forty bucks in tips with my antics. I had visions of Mama Rita cooking up crawfish pie or a fine shrimp gumbo. Every seafood I could think of was swimming through my head! I was even thinking that I could take the whole family to eat at the Red & White Café. After the dance, Zenis pulled me aside. I guess my success had been gnawing at him for some time. He hadn't said anything before, but that night *le merde a voler*, I guess you could say. The shit flew.

"Son, you gonna have to give me half them tips," Zenis said, his tone stern. "You playin' in *my* band, you know."

That put a damper on my good feeling, no doubt about it. Funny how someone can pull your good time away from you, if you let them. Once again, I was just an ignorant little Cajun boy and not some big screen movie cowboy. Then, in a flash, I got mad as hell. I got mad at the fact that I had practiced and worked to earn this extra money, and now somebody wanted to take it from me. This was a turning point in my life and a damn big one. I didn't want to be rude to Zenis, but from somewhere down inside, maybe from something I inherited from Daddy Jack, I pulled out a different answer than Zenis had expected.

"*Pas d'affairé, Zenis!*" I told him. Nothing doing. Then I stuffed the forty dollars in my pocket, tucked my fiddle under my arm, and I ran out the door.

It just so happened that Cameron was where my Aunt Anna lived. She had married Duprée Kershaw, a brother to Daddy Jack. When he died young of pneumonia, she married a man from Cameron named Sidney Naquin. We had always stayed friendly with Aunt Anna, even after her remarriage. So when I ran out of Sweeney Hebert's club, I headed straight for Aunt Anna's house. Although I didn't know it at the time, Zenis went straight to Sweeney and told him that he'd fired me.

"Tell you what," Zenis said. "I'm not gonna let that little bastard talk to me like that, Sweeney. I'll just get somebody else on fiddle."

Sweeney Hebert and his family had been awfully kind to me. It didn't take Mr. Hebert long to reply to Zenis. For the second time in one night, Zenis Lacombe got an answer he didn't like.

"No, Zenis, I'll tell *you* what," Sweeney replied. "If Doug's not on stage with you tomorrow night, don't even bother to set up."

Next morning, bright and early, I looked out the window and saw Zenis Lacombe making his way up to Aunt Anna's front door. Zenis knocked a few times before I came outside to hear what he had to say.

"You can come back, Doug," Zenis said. He looked like someone had pissed in his gumbo. "And you can keep your tip money."

"*C'est convenu,* Zenis?" I asked. It's agreed? Zenis nodded.

"*C'est convenu.*"

"Then we got a deal, Zenis," I said. From that day on Zenis Lacombe treated me fair and square. But there it was again, that good old Cajun philosophy. *Lache pas la patate.* Don't let go of the potato. Especially if somebody's trying to grab it out of your hand.

8

THE CONTINENTAL PLAYBOYS

"Pooh Ya!"
—Ozide Kegley,
playing drums, Club Avalon

By 1947 we were doing pretty good. Pee Wee was still playing fiddle with Amédé Breaux, and I was still shining shoes and playing with Zenis Lacombe's Seven-Up Playboys. We were not only eating well, we even had some savings. It was a far cry from 1943, when Daddy Jack died and the *Muskrat* sank in the river. I thought things were going along just fine when, out of the blue, Mama Rita sold the little house and its lot in Lake Arthur. With the money she got from the sale, she bought us another house in Jennings, about ten miles inland. The move was actually a good one for Pee Wee. Since Amédé Breaux lived in Crowley, on the other side of Jennings, the move brought my brother ten miles closer to his band leader. I always suspected that this had something to do with Mama Rita's uprooting us in the first place. But I never asked, and no one ever explained.

For me, that move to Jennings had an upside and a downside. The downside was obvious. I lost my shoe shine spot in front of the Sea Breeze Café. And now Zenis and the Seven-Up Playboys had to drive to Jennings to pick me up for each gig. I'd get all dressed up and wait on the porch for Zenis's car to appear at the end of the street. After a few weeks of this, I could recognize its headlights from all the other cars in Jennings. Eventually I didn't even have to see the car. I could tell it was Zenis from the reflection of his lights the instant they shone on the house across the street. That was my cue to pick up my fiddle case and head on down to the curb.

The upside of the move had a lot of fine points. The house Mama Rita bought, on the corner of West Division and Anna Street, had two rooms. That meant the bedroom was no longer in the kitchen, and neither was the slop jar. What a nice change, to be able to smell roasting coffee beans without the lingering odor of the *pot de chambre!* We had an outhouse, but the slop jar was still our only indoor toilet facility. But at least it was away from the kitchen now. That didn't mean I liked carrying it to the outhouse to dump any better than I did back in Lake Arthur. That's the thing about a slop jar. Like the jukebox, it ain't prejudiced. The slop jar will smell like a slop jar no matter where you live. I'm pretty sure that if the Queen of England had one at Buckingham Palace, it wouldn't smell a bit better than ours did back at the chicken coop in Southwest Louisiana.

I guess the finest points about the move to Jennings lay in things closer to my heart. I was growing into my adolescent years, and my needs were changing. I wanted to look like the man I believed I'd become. It was in Jennings that I started smoking at the tender age of eleven. I had been lighting cigarettes for Mama Rita for a few years by this time and stealing a puff or two before I handed them over to her. Now it was time to carry my own pack. It was also in Jennings that I got my first set of wheels, a Western Flyer bicycle. Jennings was where I heard the best Cajun musicians I'd ever heard in my life. And Jennings was where I first fell in love with a girl.

I fell for the Western Flyer first. It was more a necessity than a luxury since I was walking to school at the time. Kids who lived five miles or more from the schoolhouse got to ride the bus. As luck had it, we lived three miles away. That meant I was walking six miles a day for my three Rs. Hell, that's two miles per R. I mostly brown-bagged lunch, but sometimes I ran home to eat. I had to get there, eat, and get back in an hour. I must've burned up what little food I ate. There was a bright moment in the journey, however, because on the way to school we passed a lot of pecan trees. We'd pick fast and furious, stuffing them into our pockets. Our hands would be black with pecan dust. It wasn't until first recess that we got a chance to wash up. But those nuts helped round out the day's lunch.

Since going to school meant more walking and running than reading and arithmetic, it soon began to take a toll on me. I was just a kid, after all, and yet I was playing in bars until one or two in the mornings. That's when I came up with a better plan for myself and Rusty. Rusty went to Central school, which was a lot closer to the house than mine, but he had to walk too. So I made Mama Rita another deal.

"If you let me use some of the money I make at dances to buy a bike," I told her, "I'll ride Rusty to school on it."

Put that way, Mama Rita soon saw the logic in it and agreed. I guess you could say that the bicycle was to me what the houseboat was to Daddy Jack. It gave me a real taste of freedom. I could just pick up and go to where the action was. Of course, with freedom comes responsibility. Thinking back on those rides to school, I'm forced to make this observation. Whoever first said *he ain't heavy, he's my brother* was full of shit. Rusty rode on the handlebars and *I* did the pedaling. I'd strap our books on the back and away we'd go. And thus began a long history of Rusty and Doug being a team, and the first of many times our relationship got a little too heavy. But that's getting ahead of my story, because long before there was a Rusty and Doug, there was a Pee Wee and Doug.

Our lives went onward in our new town, with music filling up the biggest part. I guess my reputation as a fiddle player had spread around the area, because as soon as we got settled in Jennings, I started getting offers. For the next couple of years I managed to stay pretty busy. Pee Wee had gotten married in 1948, although he was barely eighteen. He and his wife, Georgia, built a house on Anna Street just across from ours and settled down to married life. But in 1949, Pee Wee had a falling out with Amédé Breaux. At this time, I was playing steadily with Shuk Richard and Marie Falcon. That's when Pee Wee came up with the idea that we should form a band together. After all, we were brothers. On top of that, I was ready to move on. The shoeshine business had whetted my desire for independence. I liked being my own boss.

But then again, so did Pee Wee.

There was a club in Lake Arthur, the Blue Goose, where Mama Rita went to dance. It was owned by a man named Crip Cormier. Even after Mama Rita gained a lot of weight, she was still a very pretty woman. And she was light on her feet. I know because I used to dance with her all the time. She loved dancing more than almost anything, and so did Crip Cormier. Crip also loved the ladies. And as we were noticing more and more, our mother loved the men. Before we knew what was happening, Mama Rita asked Crip to move in with us.

66

"*Mais,* why not?" she said. "We got us two rooms now." Maybe love had been the real reason Mama Rita sold the one-room chicken coop.

Crip's real name was Aldus, but since he'd been born with a deformed left hand, everyone called him Crip. He didn't seem to mind the nickname, or his hand, which was smaller than the right one and turned in at the wrist. When Crip heard Pee Wee and me talking about how we needed a drummer, he offered to play drums for us.

"You can play drums, Crip?" Pee Wee asked, and he nodded. I wasn't really surprised, since most of the Cajuns I knew in those days could play an instrument. I guess Crip thought it just wasn't worth mentioning. We never even auditioned him. Hell, we never even *questioned* him. We just took him at his word. That first night Crip joined the band, I was amazed at how he played. He held the drum stick in that smaller left hand and played a shuffle rhythm on the snare drum, and a 4/4 beat on the bass drum while a cigarette burned in his mouth the whole time. He wasn't the world's greatest drummer, but he was good enough. Added to that he was a damn good man. And that's all that mattered.

Once we had Crip in the group, we hired a guitar player, Jake Mier, and called ourselves the Continental Playboys, after the Continental nightclub that sat on the outskirts of Jennings. Pee Wee and I might have been brothers, but I got my first clue as to who the real leader of the band was the night of our first gig. Pee Wee had supplied the drum for the band. When he pulled it out of its case, it had our name printed across the side. *Pee Wee Kershaw & His Continentals.* There wasn't enough room to write the word *Playboy,* so he just added an "s" to *Continental* and let it go at that.

Even missing a word, it was a pretty big clue.

By this time Pee Wee had bought himself a car, a used 1936 Ford Sedan, shiny black, with four convenient doors for loading equipment. Every Saturday night the band would pile into Pee Wee's Ford, fighting for room among the drums, amplifiers, guitars, fiddles and accordions, and head out to whatever club had booked us. We paid for the upkeep of the Ford from the money we made playing clubs. Back in those first days of the Continental Playboys, we were taking in forty or fifty dollars a night. Pee Wee and I paid the other two musicians first, and then we split the rest of the money three ways. One-third went to Pee Wee, a third went to his car, and a third went to me, which meant Mama Rita got it since I was still handing over my paycheck to her.

Ironically, our first stint as a house band wasn't at the Continental Club in Jennings, our namesake, but at the Club Avalon, a popular nightspot in Basile, about twenty miles to the north. The owner of the club was a man named Quincy Davis, and that's who we auditioned for. Quincy obviously liked what he heard, because Pee Wee & His Continental Playboys got the Sunday afternoon slot, 3 to 7 p.m. This was a great opportunity for our band, since the Avalon was one of the most popular clubs in Louisiana. All the finest Cajun musicians were known to play there at one time or another in their careers. It wasn't long before Pee Wee & His Continental Playboys built up a loyal following. But for me the real thrill of working at the Club Avalon was the fact that I was able to hear one of my favorite Cajun bands every week, Nathan Abshire & the Pinegrove Boys. My musical education was growing.

Nathan and his band were the Sunday night headliners. They'd had a regional radio hit, "Pine Grove Blues" also known as "Ma Negresse." They were so popular that Quincy Davis hired school buses to shuttle people to and from Club Avalon to hear them play. Nathan Abshire fans, and music lovers in general, were charged a dollar to ride the bus from Evangeline, Opelousas, Eunice, Kinder, Oberlin, Jennings, and other towns. Since I was still a learning kid, anxious to hear all the good music I could, I'd hang around the club after our own show each Sunday afternoon and listen to Nathan and his Pinegrove Boys. And since I was there without Mama Rita, I was able to indulge in a little more than music. Even at thirteen years old, I could always count on somebody to slip me a drink.

Everyone knew that Nathan Abshire couldn't be beat when it came to singing, playing Cajun accordion, smoking, and drinking. That was a reputation he had earned, by God, so he deserved it. I hoped to get a reputation like that too, one day, and the Club Avalon was a good place to begin. I also liked the reputation Nathan Abshire had for hiring only the best musicians he could find for his band. He had Atlas Fruge on lap steel guitar. As far as I know, Atlas's rhythmic sound and style of playing has been copied by every steel guitar player who ever played in a Cajun band. And, of course, Nathan had Will Kegley, the fiddler with all the tricks. As I said, I'd always been impressed with Will Kegley's fiddling, but it wasn't until I listened to him on a regular basis that I realized just how good the man really was. It was the rhythm that Will played on fiddle that made Nathan Abshire's accordion sound so amazing.

Will Kegley's sister Ozide played the drums in Nathan's band. She may not have been the best drummer in Southwest Louisiana, but she was one of the most flamboyant. I'll never forget the first time I ever saw Ozide Kegley play a show at the Avalon. She was pounding on the drums and throwing back whiskey as fast as Nathan did. As I said, Nathan was no amateur drinker. Then, along about midnight, Ozide threw her hands up into the air, still holding those drumsticks. "Pooh ya!" she screamed. Then, she went right on with the song, never missing a beat. I turned to a fellow standing next to me and asked him if that was a part of the song.

"*Mais,* no," he said. "Ozide gets so drunk by midnight, she pees in her pants. But she keeps right on playing."

"Why does she yell *pooh ya?*" I asked.

"Just to let everyone know she don't give a damn."

By the end of the night, a small stream of Ozide's pee would be running over to the edge of the bandstand and down onto the floor. The philosophy was simple enough. When you gotta go, you gotta go.

Ozide Kegley wasn't the only excitement the Nathan Abshire band had to offer a naive kid like Doug Kershaw. My hormones had started to speak to me about that time, and I was doing my best to listen to them. They seemed to be talking a lot about girls, and girls were from a different world. One Sunday night I asked a young lady to dance. I don't recall her name. I just know that Nathan and his band were playing. Suddenly, I heard the most beautiful female voice singing. It was the voice of an angel, the kind of voice you will probably hear just before you die.

"Excuse me," I said to my dancing partner. I knew it was rude, but hormones have no manners. I left her standing in the middle of the dance floor while I made my way to the bandstand. No wonder the voice had sounded like an angel. It was coming *from* an angel. There she stood, singing "When My Sweet Love Ain't Around," by Hank Williams. When the song was over, Nathan Abshire stepped up to the mike.

"Let's give Ti Frances a big hand," he said.

Hell, I was ready to give Little Frances both of my hands. As it was, I clapped until my palms hurt. Ti Frances was beautiful. She was so beautiful that my knees felt like wet rags. That's how I knew it must be love.

Nothing had done that to my knees before, not even those ass-kickings from the black kids back in Lake Arthur. And it wasn't like I hadn't gotten around a bit since my houseboat days in the swamp. As I said, even at thirteen I was already drinking a few beers and sipping whiskey and wine. And I'd smoked a lot of Camel cigarettes. But never before had I felt so intoxicated. It was *coup de foudre,* no doubt about it. Love at first sight.

I started asking around and learned that the angel's full name was Frances Courville. Like me, she was only thirteen years old. That didn't stop me, though, since thirteen was a year older than Mama Rita was when she married Daddy Jack. But I didn't want to get married. Hell, no. I wanted to *dance.* So I forced myself to walk up to Ti Frances when she came off the stage, and that was no easy feat. Unless I'm on stage with a fiddle and a microphone—or as I would find out years later, unless I'm high on drugs—I'm a pretty shy guy. And I was especially shy back then. But shy or not, I was a dancing fool. Slow dancing was never my style because it's too damn *slow* for someone with my energy. If I asked Ti Frances to slow dance, I might step on that angel's foot. I waited for a fast song, a good jitterbug. Granted, it would have been better to impress Little Frances with my music, as a lot of male artists are known to do with the female sex. I was no exception, but that night I wasn't on stage. I had to bank on the jitterbug.

Little Frances said *oui.*

So there we were, jitterbugging and sweating all over the dance floor. I was just starting to wish I knew how to slow dance, so I could get closer to her, when up walks a guy named Robert, the biggest, toughest country boy I'd ever seen. He might easily have been kin to Albert Broussard's old friend, Cajun Joe, the Bully of the Bayou.

"*Ti Frances elle est mon fille,*" he said. Little Frances is my girl.

Like Ozide Kegley when she peed in her pants, I never missed a beat.

"Not for long," I said.

Love had made me brave.

Every chance I could find over the next few weeks, I pursued Little Frances. I sought her out at the Club Avalon every Sunday where she performed with the Pinegrove Boys. I sat next to her when possible. And I danced with her every chance I got. I found out that a male friend of mine named Shirley Bertrand was her cousin. I talked him into taking me to her house a few times. I even got her to come watch the Continental Playboys on Sunday afternoons. I felt I was ready for her. I had learned Will Kegley's fiddle tricks and even had my own up my sleeve. All this time, however, tension was silently growing between Big Robert and me.

Thinking back, I might have won Little Frances away from him that hot summer had I not tripped myself up with a bottle of wine. It all started when I heard that the Club Avalon's weekly jitterbug contest would reward the winning couple with two one-dollar bills. My friend and I had been wanting to buy a bottle of wine, but between us we couldn't come up with three dollars. Keep in mind, Mama Rita got every cent I earned, and she doled it out to me in dribs and drabs. We got to thinking that if I jitter-bugged with *two* girls instead of one, it would mean three dollars in prize money. I figured I could handle two girls on the dance floor. Like I said, I was a jitterbugging fool. Then, all I had to do was slick-talk the girls out of their share.

Sure enough, I found two good female jitterbuggers, and we won the contest. I talked them into giving me their dollars, sweet friends that they were. Now we two boys had our own bottle of wine, and before long we were buzzing. This was when Robert decided to make his move. Usually, I wouldn't be stupid enough to fight someone so damn big. Hell, I was bound to lose. But being all wined up as I was, I guess Robert looked smaller. And I must have felt bigger. So out we went to the parking lot. There's no way to put this gently. Robert beat the *merde* out of me. My friends had to scrape me off the ground. Little Frances broke my heart, and Big Robert broke my nose. Love hurts.

What I should have learned from that night is to never get crazy drunk again. But I didn't. Instead, I did what most songwriters do when they get their hearts broken. I wrote a song about Little Frances, "When Will I Learn To Stop Loving You." It turned out to be the first one I ever recorded, when I was fifteen years old. It was on a 78 rpm, and I still have a copy of it to this day.

When will I learn to stop loving you?
When will I learn that we're through?
Each night in my sleep
I see your lovely face
I hear you say sweet words
Time can't erase.

And so on. Ain't love a bitch?

71

Speaking of love and hardship, Crip Cormier and Mama Rita eventually threw in the towel when it came to their own love life. I was never told the reason. I do know that Crip went on to marry a woman named Ruby, so maybe she was the cause. But I can't say for sure. This meant Mama Rita would have to find herself another man. But it was a greater tragedy for the Continental Playboys, since we had to find another drummer. Before the lovebirds split up, however, we got a job playing three nights a week in Port Neches, Texas, about seventy miles away. And I got a Crip Cormier story that I'll cherish forever.

Port Neches was too far for us to drive from Jennings, so we rented a small aluminum trailer over there for a short time. I guess the biggest excitement we ever had as the Continental Playboys happened in Port Neches and involved Crip Cormier. Crip had become a father figure to Pee Wee and me. We looked up to him. One night we got back from the show during a helluva thunderstorm. Crip had to take a pee. As with every place I had lived so far, this aluminum trailer had no bathroom facilities. So Crip unbuttoned his pants, whipped out his equipment, and let fly a stream of pee against the side of the trailer. Right about then the sky lit up with lightning. It didn't actually hit the trailer, but it hit close enough to send a jolt of electricity off the aluminum, up the stream of pee, and into Crip's pecker. Pee Wee and I stood there, soaking wet from the rain, our mouths open in horror while Crip peed and screamed in pain, peed and screamed. When he finally finished and the connection was broken, he shook himself off. He glanced over at us as he zipped his pants.

"Boys, that felt good," Crip said.

By God, there was a performer.

9

DREAMING HARD

10 + 10 + 10 = WIN!
—The Doug Kershaw Formula for Success

I won't say that hearing thousands of fans applaud your music is like a jolt of lightning hitting your privates. But I will say that when you hear that applause, you know what it feels like to have electricity pass through your body. You tingle. Applause feels damn good. I wanted to be a star since the first time I picked up my cigar-box fiddle and played songs on the banks of the Mermentau River. Later, when I played that command performance for Daddy Jack, I knew what it was like to hold someone's attention with my music. That was my first adrenalin rush. But I wouldn't know what a star actually was until I watched Tex Ritter ride across the silver screen. By the time my fiddling drew a crowd in front of the Red & White Café, my fate was sealed. I got the message and, to quote Crip Cormier, "Boys, that felt good."

Adrenalin is a powerful, addictive drug. I knew from the time I was a little kid that if I wanted more of it, I'd better stick to music, not get what is known as a "real" job. So unless you count my days as a fiddle-playing shoeshine boy and my two years in the army, I've only worked a day job once. And that was enough to convince me that making music was a lot more fun than the kind of work Daddy Jack did every day.

This is the story of Doug and the Shrimp Boat:

It all started when a letter arrived one day in the spring of 1952. My Aunt Anna was writing to ask Mama Rita if she wanted to come work for her, at her laundry business in Cameron. Aunt Anna could make Custer's last stand sound like a *fais do-do*. Not only would Mama Rita's job come with a two-room apartment and our own outhouse, there was even more good news. *Sidney can get Doug a job on a shrimp boat.* If I had known then what I came to know later, I'd have grabbed my fiddle and run back to the swamps. Mama Rita still believed that I should get a "real" job. I was sixteen and wanted to spend my life in music. But it was hard to argue with Mama Rita.

There was one big issue to think about if we moved to Cameron. I would have to drop out of school, since it was impossible to work full time on a shrimp boat *and* do homework. But school didn't interest me anyway. World history was keeping me awake when I needed to sleep after playing past midnight at some club. I was anxious to meet life head-on, and Mama Rita herself was itching for a move. Dropping out of school seemed intriguing to me. Much of the money that kept us going had come from music, or my "fake job." But that didn't seem to occur to us. I would please my mother. She was certain I would find respectability in shrimp. I gave in. Goodbye, World History.

In truth, I had thought back to all that tip money the shrimpers used to throw at me, at Sweeney Hebert's club, when I did my trick fiddling. Shrimpers were some of the richest customers I'd ever seen. I figured, "Hell, why not?" My plan was to shrimp all week, but still play on the weekends with the Continental Playboys. In a couple of years I'd be a millionaire. So, on April 29, 1952, we packed up and off we went to Cameron, about fifty miles from Jennings. Cameron sits just below Calcasieu Lake and just atop the Gulf of Mexico. It was a damn good place to go into the shrimp business, and I was ready.

As promised, Uncle Sidney got me a job aboard one of the boats. He picked me up at 3 a.m. that first morning, and we headed out on a three-day run into the Gulf of Mexico. I thought I was used to rocking, thanks to those days when the houseboat would rock like a gentle cradle. But that shrimp boat was a cradle from hell. I was seasick right from the start, and I stayed seasick for most of the trip. Seasick and exhausted. The captain cooked meals of rice and whatever shrimp or fish we caught. I couldn't eat a damn thing because I couldn't hold food in my stomach. The captain had never seen the likes of me before, and he said so. But I had never seen the likes of him either. "How can a man do this for a living?" I kept thinking as I wobbled to the rail and puked overboard. *Peeing* overboard required an even greater skill since I had to hold the rail with my free hand. Maybe Ozide Kegley could have done this with style, but Doug Kershaw sure as hell couldn't. I even wet my pants before that trip was over. And I was too damn sick to yell, "Pooh ya!"

The captain took pity on me and suggested that I lie down for a spell. "What a nice man," I thought, not realizing that this is the worse thing a human can possibly do when seasick. Within seconds I scrambled to my feet and bolted for the railing, which seemed to amuse the captain even more. I can't say I puked my guts out because I had already done that. Hell of a nice guy, the captain. I do believe he considered me the entertainment for those three days at sea.

There's an insane work ethic aboard a shrimp boat. A shrimper works twenty-four hours around the clock and naps here and there only if he must. I've never before or after done such hard work. God bless the men who work on shrimp boats. God bless every one. If I had known what they go through to make their money, I would have thrown those tips back at them. I spent three solid days vomiting, tossing nets overboard, vomiting, hauling nets back in, vomiting, and then dumping the catch onto the deck. You might say that the job the captain trusted to me was that of a special- ist. I was to separate the crab and shrimp from the snakes, sharks, starfish and stingrays. I would discover later that knowing how to separate the sharks and snakes would be good training for the music business. But it was still hell on a young fiddle player's hands. I swear I thought of jumping overboard and swimming back to Cameron. That's how bad it got. We were about thirty miles out to sea, but drowning seemed like a rest com- pared to shrimping.

By the end of that three-day run my hands were so swollen from the iodine in all those shrimp that they were twice their size. And they were full of little pin-pricks from the sharp spines that catfish have along their backs. As we pulled into the bay at Cameron and prepared to dock, I stood looking down at the two misshapen things attached to the end of my arms and was certain I'd never play fiddle again. Since shrimpers are paid by the pound, the job now was to unload the shrimp onto a large scale, weigh them, and then carry them over to a conveyor belt. Not me. No sir. I hopped off that shrimp boat before it completely docked. I didn't even stick around long enough to collect my check. I went home and nursed my hands. I swore to God that if the swelling ever went away I would play my fiddle again and get my ass back in school. And I'd never let anyone—this meant Mama Rita—lure me away from music again.

I went back to Jennings after that shrimping disaster, carrying with me the hard-earned knowledge of what I really was: a musician.

I've worked for myself ever since.

Mama Rita soon quit her own job in Cameron and followed me home to Jennings. By this time Rusty had joined the Continental Playboys, so Mama Rita went back to being self-employed as banker for her two sons. This is where the money part of the Continental Playboys got a bit complicated. After Rusty joined the band we had only one other non-Kershaw musician to pay. The rest of the money was now split four ways. Rusty got a share, I got a share, Pee Wee got a share, and the 1936 Ford coupe got a share. That old arrangement had worked fine when we were kids making just enough money to get by. But later, when we started making damn good money—and getting sponsors and doing radio and TV shows—the split stayed the same. Now, I've never claimed to be a mathematician, but even a little swamp rat like me knew something was wrong. I couldn't see any more wear and tear on that Ford on a five-hundred-dollar night than on a fifty-dollar night. The Ford was making as much money as I was, and I had yet to hear it sing a song or play an instrument. For what the Kershaws were paid, Mama Rita got my share and Rusty's, and Pee Wee and the Ford got the rest.

I went to Mama Rita and told her I wanted my own car. I didn't have a clue whether we had enough money for a down payment, since I was strictly on allowance.

"*Mais,* Doug, why you need a car, *cher?*" Mama Rita asked.

"So I don't have to bum rides to school," I said. This was true. I was bumming rides from Jessie Stutes, who was a year ahead of me in school and who would later play steel guitar in a band with me. Jessie was madly in love with a girl named Mary Ann, and while I appreciated the ride, I felt like a third wheel. I also knew that owning a car might lessen the problem I had with paying the Ford a sideman's wages. But I didn't get into that with Mama Rita.

"Other guys in the eleventh grade have a car," I added. "And yet I'm the only one who works all the time." It was true. School was taking a helluva toll on my energy too. Thank God for Mr. Blanchard, who taught the Future Farmers of America class. Mr. Blanchard always let me sleep in FFA. Maybe he thought in my case it stood for Future Fuckups of America. It didn't matter to me. I just needed some shut-eye.

My argument seemed to break Mama Rita a little.

"And I'm embarrassed to be pedaling a bicycle at my age," I added. "I'm just wearing out my legs to give my ass a ride."

"*Tu me dis pas,*" Mama Rita said. You don't say. She thought that over. "All right, *cher.* You go look for a car. You find one you like, you let me know."

So I went shopping down at the used car lot. Right out in front, waiting for me to come by and rescue it, was a 1946 maroon Ford Coupe. Man, what a gorgeous piece of steel! Unfortunately, it had a price tag of seven hundred dollars. I went home and told Mama Rita, who promptly hit the ceiling.

"Seven hundred dollars! You think I got money up my rear end, *cher?*"

I had no idea *where* Mama Rita banked her money. I just knew that some of it was mine. I finally talked her into coming with me to take a look at the Ford. The two of us walked down to the car lot where Mama Rita inspected the coupe from every angle. She turned to the salesman.

"We gonna take this Ford," she told him.

I couldn't believe my ears!

"How you wanting to finance that, Mrs. Kershaw?" the salesman asked. He had no idea he was talking to a woman who had lost all her money to moths and then to the Mermentau River. How did Mama Rita plan to finance the car? Good question.

"Finance?" She almost spit the word back at him. "*On merde moi, pas!*" she answered. "Don't shit me!" Then she reached down into her bra, which was a 46 DD, and rummaged around between her bosoms. She pulled out a wad of money big enough to choke an alligator! She quickly counted out seven hundred dollars, then deposited the rest back into her bra. Now I knew where *the bank* was. It never bothered me that Mama Rita was spending my money in the first place. I loved the hell out of that woman for buying me a car. When I got behind the wheel of that 1946 maroon Ford Coupe, I was certain I looked as cool and slick as any movie star. Too bad Little Frances wasn't around to witness the sight.

Maybe it was the experience of working on that shrimp boat, but I started to get serious as an undertaker about my music that year. And I started thinking about how to make the Continental Playboys a better band. Cajun music was big in our area, but after those years of listening to the jukebox at the Sea Breeze, and to other people's radios, I knew that country music, sung in English, was more commercial. A band could probably enlarge its audience a lot if it didn't stick to just Cajun French songs. Most of the folks around Lake Arthur and Jennings wanted to listen to Cajun music, but there were others who wanted a mix. World War II had seen to that. Boys coming back home from wherever they had spent the war years brought with them a lot of the things they'd discovered in the larger world. And one of those things was a love for different kinds of music. I'd sit at my desk, in whatever class I had at the time, and I'd stare out the window at nothing at all. That's when I did my serious dreaming about the Continental Playboys, about being a star, and about how I could pull it off.

I might have been daydreaming in school, but outside the classroom I was paying attention to the business end of the music. I wanted to understand about bookings, how you got them, and who was getting jobs at which clubs. I wanted to know which bands were most popular with audiences. It also occurred to me that the Continental Playboys were limited by performing in the same sixty-mile radius every week. That started me off on a new dream, one that saw us playing shows all the way to Oklahoma and Arkansas. Maybe even Tennessee. Keep in mind, I'd barely been out of Southwest Louisiana, except for those gigs across the border in Texas, and my three days in hell aboard that shrimp boat.

I concentrated on my old friend, the jukebox. I got to thinking about the mix of music I heard on it. And I started asking myself questions. When people played the jukebox, did they mostly play fast or slow songs? Did they play country or Cajun rhythm and blues? I would sit for hours in the local cafes with a pen and a piece of paper, doing my homework. I finally came up with a formula that I was certain would make me a star, a star capable of playing anywhere, not just in swamp country.

10+10+10 = WIN!

I decided that the band should learn thirty songs, but we should mix up the genres. We'd learn 10 Cajun French songs, 10 hillbilly songs in English, and then we'd add 10 rhythm and blues songs. Since we already knew every Cajun French song, the first 10 were taken care of. Country music was still called hillbilly music back then, and we'd been listening to a lot of great songs by Ernest Tubb and Hank Williams. Rock-a-billy was also popular, so we could mix in a little of that too. That took care of the second 10. As far as rhythm and blues went, there were a lot of good songs that were popular at that time, songs by Fats Domino like "I'm Walking," and "Blueberry Hill." And Ray Charles had had some big hits, including "I've Got A Woman." Then, just for the hell of it, we'd learn some straight blues, something by Lightnin' Hopkins. That would take care of the last 10, and the formula would be complete. I figured we were surviving on the Cajun music, and I was thankful for that. But we had to do more than just survive if we wanted to become stars. We had to grow.

Something else had been happening at this time, and it fed my hunger to become a star. I'd been picking up my guitar and writing songs in English. *English!* And no one was holding my tongue or hitting me with a paddle to get me to do it. I was turning toward a new language now, and I knew a hell of a lot more words by this time than *white jelly*! With this new formula, and new outlook, came a new confidence. I was tired of hiding the songs I'd been writing in a dresser drawer. I was ready for people to hear them. I knew success wasn't going to come easy, but I didn't care. Hell, from the day I was born nothing in my life had been easy. I was willing to work my butt off as long as I never had to go back to throwing snakes off the deck of a shrimp boat.

God bless every shrimper who ever lived.

I was willing to dream harder than I ever had in my life to make big things happen for me and the Continental Playboys. I wanted to be a star. Looking back on this period of my life, one of the things I regret most is that I wasn't able to concentrate on music *and* school. Back then I really liked history, math, and science. But I was sixteen. I had discovered girls and jukeboxes. When you mix music with hormones, how can the Roman Empire compete with that? That may even be why it fell.

10

NIGHTCLUB ROW

*"My picture's in the paper, my name's on the radio
I've even had an offer to go on a TV show."*
—From "The Country Singer"
by Doug Kershaw.

"Maybe you shouldn't take a whole one the first time."
–Rufus Thibodeaux,
handing me my first magic pill.

By 1953, we had Pee Wee playing accordion, me on fiddle, Rusty on guitar and drums, and Jessie Stutes as the first in a succession of steel guitar players. It irritated me that Pee Wee had appointed himself band leader. But there was no getting around the fact that he was five and a half years older than me. That made him the adult in the group, the one who dealt with club owners, with bookings, and with counting out the money. In effect, Pee Wee was the father figure of the band—and a tough father at that. Man, he was critical of me. Sometimes, I felt incapable of doing *anything* right. I don't think Pee Wee's heavy-handed manner ever really bothered Rusty. He was the baby of the family, the good-natured, quiet one who wore his Captain Marvel T-shirt on stage and seemed like he was just along for the ride.

It's very hard for me to talk about my brothers. I loved them both fiercely, but at times I resented the hell out of them. I guess you could say I'm a typical sibling in that respect. To understand the underlying dynamics in the Continental Playboys, you'd have to go back in time to when we were just kids. That's when Pee Wee would entertain himself by making Rusty and me fight each other. He'd stand there and yell at us to keep punching, even when we were both in tears and wanting to quit.

"Fin!" he'd yell at Rusty. "Keep in there, Fin!" That was Pee Wee's nickname for our little brother. Or, if he saw I was beginning to tire, that I wanted to stop, he'd shout at me the same way. "Keep in there, Doug!"

I suppose it was just kid stuff. Game playing. Trouble is, I was always too damn busy playing fiddle to play games. I was too busy trying to make a living. But as far as *real* kid games go, I was pretty good at marbles because I was a good lagger. The way you get to be a lagger is this: You draw a line in the dirt and everyone tries to shoot his marble right to the line. Whoever is closest to the line is the lagger, or the first shooter. It's like getting to break in a game of pool. You have a lot more targets to shoot at. The problem with the Continental Playboys was that I never had a chance at being the lagger. Pee Wee had first shot every time. And I was still too young and naive to draw a line in the dirt.

Even though there was tension growing in the band, bigger things were ahead for the Continental Playboys, thanks to radio. And it was thanks to Clovis Bailey that the radio came to town in the first place. Lafayette and Lake Charles both had stations that broadcast Cajun music, but those stations were forty miles away from Jennings. Clovis had the foresight to start his own station, KJEF, which began broadcasting at 500 watts. Since the Playboys had been practicing hard, we felt we were good enough to do a weekly show on KJEF. By this time Clovis had graduated to 1,000 watts and was broadcasting the show from the Bruce Theater. It was Clovis Bailey who reminded me not long before he died that the Continental Playboys had won a KJEF contest. I'd forgotten about it.

KJEF was holding a contest for a fifteen-minute spot on Saturday afternoons, which was considered prime time for live music shows. Hell, no one listened to the radio on Saturday *nights*. They were all out dancing in the local clubs, listening to bands play music. So winning that spot would be the good news. The bad news was that the spot would still cost the winner thirty dollars.

"Even if we win," I told the others, "we can't afford to pay that kind of money each week." Pee Wee agreed.

"We'll need sponsors," he said. So the Continental Playboys entered the contest and won. We had the radio spot, so now came the harder job of finding those sponsors. Pee Wee went around Jennings scouting out possibilities. I can't remember who all came on board, but I know that Traux Service Station was one sponsor. I think they put up ten dollars each week. And I believe that some of the local clubs we played for were the other sponsors. What I do remember is that we boys were convinced that someone important would hear our fifteen-minute show on that little Jennings, Louisiana, radio station. They'd hear us, and they'd make us big stars. It wasn't impossible, either. That's how many record men found talent back in those days, by driving around the country scouting it out. Somebody on a white horse could ride into Southwest Louisiana at any given time. I never doubted this.

As it happened, our man on the white horse was already in town. Bee Monceaux, who lived a few doors down from us in Jennings, worked for the local Bewley Mills Flour and Feed distributor, which was headquartered in Fort Worth, Texas. Every now and then the company sent executives out into the field to advise the various distributors on their operations. One day, a Bewley Mills marketing guy with the unlikely name of B. B. Raspberry showed up in Jennings to talk about increasing sales. As luck would have it, Bee Monceaux was loading bags of flour in the warehouse when he overheard his boss talking sales strategies with Mr. Raspberry. The more Bee listened, the more he realized that B. B. Raspberry wasn't a typical marketing executive. He was also a musician who played bass fiddle with several Texas Western Swing bands. And he was a staunch advocate of using music to help sell flour and feed. He told Bee Monceaux's boss that Bewley Mills was having great success in Texas by sponsoring radio shows featuring bands like the Chuck Wagon Gang and the Texas Dough Boys. If those shows were working in Texas, he said, why wouldn't they work in Southwest Louisiana? It was this part of the conversation that prompted Bee Monceaux to walk up to Mr. Raspberry and make a suggestion.

"Sir, why don't you talk to the Kershaw boys?"

"They any good?" Mr. Raspberry asked. He went on to explain that the band his company picked would also be expected to do a radio show for Bewley Mills as well as make personal appearances promoting Bewley Mills Flour and Feed.

"They're *real* good," Bee Monceaux assured him.

"All right," said B. B. Raspberry, "I'll give 'em a call."

"They don't have a telephone," Bee Monceaux said.

The damn telephone. It was one invention I'd even prayed for, but it wasn't one of Mama Rita's priorities. "You wanna talk to someone, *cher,*" she would say, "you go to their house and you talk right to their face."

So, Bee Monceaux sent Mr. Raspberry over to Anna Street to find us in the flesh.

I'll never forget the day. I was in the front yard pushing a lawn mower with dull blades back and forth, chewing up grass on Mama Rita's front lawn. I saw this car with a Texas license plate pull up and park. I stopped mowing and just stood there, watching and waiting. Pretty soon a man wearing a nice suit and tie got out and strolled across the lawn toward me. I can still remember his words to me that day.

"I'm B. B. Raspberry," he said. "I'm from Fort Worth, Texas, and I work for Bewley Mills. We make feed and flour, and I'm here to talk to the Kershaw boys. Are you one of them?"

"Yes sir," I told him. "I'm Doug Kershaw. What can I do for you?" I was still in the dark as to why a complete stranger from Fort Worth, Texas, would be looking for the Kershaws. He asked if he could come inside and talk a bit, so I dropped the old push mower and we went in and sat down at the kitchen table, where it was cool from the heat of the day. Mama Rita made up a pot of her strong coffee while Mr. Raspberry explained why he'd come to Anna Street looking for us. I couldn't believe my ears. If we got the job, we'd travel all over the state, playing rodeos, fairs, and festivals.

Mr. Raspberry didn't mince words. He wanted to know two things. "Are you interested?" and "When can I hear you play?" Was I interested? Is a pig interested in a mud puddle? Hell, yes, I was interested. And as far as I was concerned, Mr. Raspberry could hear us play as soon as I could round up the other guys.

"Let's you and me go across the street to Pee Wee's house," I said to the man in the fancy suit and tie. "If he agrees, and I'm sure he will, we can set up our instruments at his house tonight. Then you can hear us." My heart felt like it was going to pound out of my chest I was so excited. Before we got to Pee Wee's, I thought of something.

"Mr. Raspberry, you don't want just Cajun music, do you?" I asked.

"No," he said. "I'll want some hillbilly music too."

"Rhythm and blues?"

"Sure," he said.

What a break. I could try out my formula of 10+10+10=WIN.

So I introduced the Bewley Mills man to Pee Wee, who listened closely as Mr. Raspberry talked. Pee Wee knew I was excited because I kept interrupting.

"*Ferme ta bouche,* Doug!" Pee Wee finally said. Shut your mouth.

Pee Wee knew from experience that if I was this excited, he'd have to agree to the offer. And he did. We decided to get everyone together for an audition that evening. Pee Wee didn't have a phone either, so when B. B. left to go eat supper, I ran the two blocks to Jessie Stutes's house. Rusty happened to be there, so I dragged both Rusty and Jessie back to Pee Wee's place and we quickly started setting up the equipment. Pee Wee went into the bathroom and found a Kotex pad belonging to his wife. He taped it on the back drum head to muffle the sound of the foot pedal banging away. When I saw this, I was reminded of how Rusty and I were paying for use of the Ford coupe.

"I hope that Kotex is working for free," I whispered to Rusty.

When we were all set up, I threw a curve into the audition by announcing that we needed some hillbilly songs.

"I got a pile of them," I added. "*En Anglais.*" In English.

Then I confessed that I had also written down the lyrics to songs I'd been hearing on the radio so that I could learn them in private. I pulled out a bunch of pages and showed the guys. Carl Smith had just had a smash hit with "Hey, Joe!" penned by Boudleaux and Felice Bryant. It was a great hillbilly song, so we decided to learn it before B. B. Raspberry finished his supper.

"I hope the hell he orders dessert," I told the guys.

We were so involved in working up the song that we didn't hear the car with the Texas license plate drive up. Nor did we hear B. B. Raspberry knock on the door. I don't know how long he stood out there, listening through the screen, but all of a sudden we heard the sound of a bass fiddle. We looked up and there stood Mr. Raspberry, playing his fiddle right along with us on Pee Wee's porch. And he was doing pretty good, too, so we finished the song that way. Mr. Raspberry did the Bob Wills signature yell, a high, clear "*Ah ha!*" as he smiled in through the screen at us. I don't know if he could tell that this English song was new to us or not. If he did, he didn't let on.

"I got me a band," is all B. B. Raspberry said.

My heart rose up at the news, and then it sank with the follow-up.

"Now all I've got to do," Mr. Raspberry added, "is convince my boss in Fort Worth that you're the boys for the job."

Up until then I'd assumed that B.B. Raspberry was the man making the decisions. Not so, it seemed. We still had to pass another test. B.B. saw the look on my face and understood.

"Don't worry, Doug," he said. "I've got a foolproof idea."

B. B. went down to KJEF the very next morning and met with Clovis Bailey. His idea was simple. He asked Clovis if we could do a half-hour show that Saturday afternoon so that he could tape it. Then, he would present that tape to his boss at Bewley Mills. Clovis agreed, and Pee Wee & the Continental Playboys did the show on KJEF. When we finished, B. B. went on the air with a request to the listeners.

"If you like Pee Wee Kershaw and the Continental Playboys," he said in a very professional voice, "and if you want to hear them on the radio every week, then write a letter to Clovis Bailey at KJEF in Jennings, Louisiana."

A few days later Clovis called B.B. at the boarding house where he was staying.

"Hell, B. B.," Clovis said. "You better bring a truck over here to carry all this mail away. I got letters stacked all over the damn station."

That turned out to be something of an overstatement, but nonetheless B. B. brought a big mailbag of letters over and dumped them on Mama Rita's kitchen floor. We all sat down on the floor and started opening the mail. In letter after letter our listeners asked and even *demanded* that the Continental Playboys remain on KJEF. It made my damn heart warm, especially since I knew Mama Rita didn't write well enough to have done it herself. These were legitimate fans! Out of about five hundred responses, only six people weren't enthusiastic about our music. Mr. Raspberry, Pee Wee, Rusty, Jessie Stutes and I sat there with that pile of letters, reading aloud the most complimentary lines as Mama Rita listened. It was applause on paper, that's what it was. But it still came packed with a lot of adrenalin.

When we finished, B. B. Raspberry stuffed all the letters back into the mailbag and headed for Fort Worth, Texas. He drove straight through the night and was waiting for Mr. Bowers when the Bewley Mills president arrived at his office the next morning. Just as he'd done in Mama

Rita's kitchen, B. B. dumped the letters out on the floor. Then he scooped some up and placed them on the desk in front of Mr. Bowers, along with the tape of us singing.

"Listen and read," he said.

Mr. Bowers read only two or three of the letters before he looked up.

"I guess you better play me that tape," he said. So B. B. threaded the reel-to-reel into Mr. Bowers' machine and sat back to wait. He told me later that his boss never said a word, just sat there reading and smiling for the whole thirty minutes that the tape played.

"Well, B. B.," Mr. Bowers said in that slow Texas drawl. "I don't know why that wouldn't sell flour."

With those few words we became the Bewley Gang. We were on our way to radio stardom, at least in Southwest Louisiana. For a while we even lived a double life. Some nights, when we played around Jennings, we were still billed as Pee Wee Kershaw and the Continental Playboys. At least that was the name still painted on the drum set, minus the Playboys.

The first thing I did when we got the radio show was to order a telephone. Next thing I did was buy myself the biggest, baddest amplifier I could find. It was so big, in fact, that we couldn't get it into the car, so I had to continue using the little one. But I didn't care. At least I knew that I *owned* a fancy amp back at the house. I guess it all comes around to staring through the window of the Red & White Café, to being poor and knowing it. You start to think you need stuff you don't need, and it always has to be BIG STUFF. A few years go by and then you come to understand that what you had in the first place, the small stuff, wasn't all that bad. It's kind of like that 1946 maroon Ford coupe of mine. Once the freshness of it wore off, I'd look at it and pray for a bigger car, or a better car, or certainly a newer car.

Now I'd give anything for a 1946 Ford coupe.

The radio show was our line to the world of bookings, which meant more shows and better money. And it happened quickly once we were sponsored by such a well-known company. Besides playing at the Bewley Mills distribution centers, we played anywhere they'd pay us. Even for hog callings. We rode on the backs of flatbed trucks for any parade that wanted us. We played at parish fairs and festivals. We started hearing from venues where we couldn't have gotten arrested a few weeks earlier. Dozens of club owners began calling the radio station, and I was proud that Clovis Bailey could say, "You can telephone Doug Kershaw at home." Playing those big festivals taught me a lesson about holding an audience's attention. And it was as good as the lesson of Will Kegley's fiddle tricks. Crowds milling around are a tough audience since there's a lot of other activity to distract them. So I spent hours perfecting songs that I considered crowd-grabbers.

Some years before he died, B. B. Raspberry telephoned me at my hotel suite in Las Vegas, where I was doing a show. He wanted to talk about the old days, reminisce about those times when he'd grab his fiddle and join us on stage.

"Remember our old crowd-grabbing trick?" B. B. wondered. I sure did. If the audience got restless and started to drift off towards the Ferris wheel or the food booths, B. B. would look over at me. "Hit it, Doug!" he'd say. And I'd tear into "Orange Blossom Special." There must be some magic in that song because it always worked.

Between "Orange Blossom Special," Cajun music, hillbilly songs, and rhythm and blues, our radio show got to be one of the most popular in the region. Bewley Mills was moving feed and flour like crazy. Then, one day B. B. Raspberry got a telephone call from Mr. Bowers.

"Bewley Mills is gonna sponsor a show on KPLC-TV in Lake Charles," Mr. Bowers said. "Think the Bewley Gang will agree?" Agree? Shit, I'd have fought an army of parish bullies to get my face on television. I knew in my bones, way back then, that television was special. It made stars quickly.

I was so nervous for that first television show that the only thing I remember is carrying our instruments into the television studio in Lake Charles. The rest is just a blur. Since it was a live show we knew we had to get it right the first time. But, hell, we did a live show every night on stage. But we were nervous as long-tailed cats in a room full of rocking chairs. Luckily, as had happened at KJEF, the listeners responded immediately and positively. KPLC and Bewley Mills said we were on our way. Who were we to argue with that? We'd made it out of the swamps, all the way to the Bucket of Blood, then the Club Avalon, and KJEF radio. Now we were starring on our own KPLC-TV show.

It's a funny thing, stardom, no matter what magnitude. People immediately turn a blind eye to a lot of things. You can be the biggest bastard in the crowd, for instance, and they'll forgive you. Another thing I noticed is that you don't even have to be Gregory Peck handsome. Before I went on television I was just another gangly kid with a big nose and big ears. Once people thought I was a *star,* hell, I guess my nose and ears must have shrunk. Or maybe it was just that my head got bigger. Whatever it was, that little bit of regional fame got me to thinking I was awful *purty.* In fact, I was so *purty* I started to draw flies—and not the kind with wings. Before long I had relatives I'd never heard of and friends I'd never met. I also had folks buzzing around me who said they'd make me rich and famous. Ah, the magic of television. It's just a damn box, with all kinds of electrical signals being sent to it. But it would play the biggest role of all in my career. I didn't know it yet, but that television magic would bring me to Nightclub Row, where I learned to fuse styles together and develop a sound that I hoped was like nobody else's.

In Southwest Louisiana the hottest places to play were the clubs along Highway 90 between Lake Charles and Sulphur, a strip called Nightclub Row. It was a musical gumbo along that highway, with everyone making their own roux. You could go from club to club and hear a different kind of music: Cajun, R&B, hillbilly, traditional blues, and what would later be called zydeco. It was the land of Oz to a young and hungry musician like me. Nightclub Row was known for the best music, the best gambling, and the best whoring in that part of the state. Thank God I was too young to gamble. There were clubs like the Silver Star, the Loma Linda, and the Moulin Rouge, and in those clubs some of my musical contemporaries played every week. Once we got the television show we received an offer to play the Silver Star on a regular basis.

The Moulin Rouge had three unique acts that rotated shows. There were Jimmy Newman, Clifton Chenier, and Cookie & the Cupcakes. Usually, at least two of the acts would play every night, and sometimes all three did. The place would be packed with dancers and drinkers, and sometimes the music went on until dawn. But if you went to the Silver Star, from 9 p.m. to 1 a.m. the only entertainment was the Bewley Gang show, and we packed the place too.

One of our fans was a young singer from over in Vidor, Texas, a guy named George Jones. We had a mutual admiration society going. George was rooting for us to get something happening, and we were rooting for him. I was happy when George recorded one of his own songs, "Why Baby

Why," on Starday Records and thrilled when it hit top 5 on the national charts. Then, one summer night, George came into the club all excited. He actually ran across the dance floor. "Doug!" he shouted. "Guess what! Webb Pierce cut my song. Ain't that great?" As it turned out, Webb covered "Why Baby Why" as a duet with Red Sovine, and it stayed at No. 1 in *Billboard* for a month, establishing George Jones as a solid new songwriter. Well, we all know how things worked out for the Possum. He became a worldwide music legend. But every time I think back to Nightclub Row, that's one of the memories that stands out, the night when George Jones shared his good news with me.

George was just one of the great singers I admired back then. Another was Hank Thompson. You can look far and wide, but you won't find many country artists any better than Hank. I love Western swing, and I think Hank Thompson's Brazos Valley Boys rivaled even the great Bob Wills in that department. Every time I heard him on the radio singing songs such as "Wild Side of Life" and "Wake Up, Irene," I wished more and more that I could hear him in person. That's when I cooked up an idea. When I told the other band members about it, they all agreed to go along. So I approached Hampton Fusilier, who was the owner of the Silver Star. Our proposition was simple. If Mr. Fusilier would bring in Hank and the Brazos Valley Boys and reserve the Bewley Gang a table right down front, we'd play the Silver Star two nights free of charge.

"You don't even have to introduce us to Hank," I told Mr. Fusilier. "We just want that table by the stage." Hampton Fusilier didn't hesitate.

"You got a deal, Doug," he said. What a guy. And I don't mean to be sarcastic by saying that, either. For him to consider two nights of the Bewley Gang worth one Hank Thompson, well, it made us proud.

The night of Hank's show finally arrived. We were sitting down front, just like Mr. Fusilier had promised. After the show, Hank Thompson came off the stage and walked over to the table to shake our hands.

"Hampton Fusilier told me you boys gave up two nights' pay to see my show," he said. "I just wanted to tell you how much that means to me." Bless Mr. Fusilier's heart. That night I not only got to hear one of country music's biggest stars, I got to meet him, too, right there on the Highway 90 strip. The biggest thrill of all, though, was that I ended up getting to play music with Hank. Several times after that, when he was playing shows without his band, Hank asked us to back him up.

Jimmy Newman played at the Moulin Rouge long before he added the "C," for Cajun, to his name. When I was done playing the dance at the Silver Star, I'd drop by the Moulin Rouge to listen to Jimmy. Sometimes Rufus Thibodeaux, his fiddle player, would let me sit in. Rufus was another fiddler whose league I wanted to be in. He was a couple of years older than me and from the Lake Charles area. He could play Cajun and country with ease, switching effortlessly from "Jolie Blon" to "Cry, Cry, Darling."

I loved to hear Rufus Thibodeaux play Bob Wills-flavored Western swing, and that brings me to another person I saw as a standard. Bob Wills. When he played his fiddle soft and sweet, the whole crowd would hush until you could hear a guitar pick drop. Bob Wills knew how to sell himself to a crowd. I believe he knew what I came to learn. You can be the best musician or vocalist on the planet. But if you don't embrace your audience, if you don't get them to believe in you too, you might as well stay home and sing to the birds.

Clifton Chenier also played at the Moulin Rouge, and when I could manage it, I was there. It was quite an experience to stand by the bandstand and listen to a black man play those same Cajun French songs that I did. Music was bringing us all together. Clifton wasn't the first black man to become well-known for playing Cajun music. That title might go to Amédé Ardoin, the man I mentioned earlier. But Clifton was the first black man *I* ever saw playing those songs. He was also one of the first to play Cajun songs on a piano-style accordion instead of on the smaller, button-style Diatonic accordion that everyone else played.

I should mention here that some scholars believe German immigrants who settled in Louisiana introduced the accordion into Cajun music in the late 1800s. The fiddle is the granddaddy of Cajun instruments, having come down from Canada with our Acadian ancestors. But those first accordions didn't tune well with the Cajun fiddle. It wasn't until the 1920s that the Monarch and Sterling Diatonic accordions were made, and these were the ones that were widely absorbed into our music.

Clifton Chenier is also the man who popularized, if not invented, zydeco music by fusing Cajun songs with R&B and Creole rhythms. There are several theories about where the name zydeco came from, but most musical historians believe it derives from *Les Haricots Sont Pas Sales*, an old song that used to be played at Creole house dances. The snap beans aren't salted, a likely reference to hard times. When the Creoles and Cajuns, with their thick French and English accents, pronounced *les haricots* (lez-ah-ree-ko) it often sounded a little like the word *zydeco*. Zydeco is usually more up-tempo, more Caribbean in nature, and more rhythmic, whereas Cajun music is melody-driven, with more waltzes and two-steps. In many cases, the song is the same, the arrangements are different. Zydeco and Cajun music have been described as neighbors and, like all good neighbors, they may have differences. But they also tend to borrow from each other.

Clifton Chenier went on to see a lot of success in his lifetime, but he never forgot his roots, or how that early music got him where he was. That's how I feel about my own Cajun roots. We have that in common. Clifton even won a Grammy in 1983.

This is where we differ.

Where's *my* Grammy?

Other performers who followed in Clifton's footsteps were colorful artists such as Queen Ida, who was my secret love. She wasn't there on Nightclub Row when I was, but I have to mention her. Years later, Queen Ida would take zydeco music to a whole new audience and popularize it further. She's a hell of a musician. Imagine playing an accordion when you have boobs! Especially a push-pull Diatonic accordion. Hell, it hurts *me*, and I'm flat-chested.

And last, but certainly not least, Cookie & the Cupcakes were playing at the Moulin Rouge while the Bewley Gang was over at the Silver Star Club. Cookie was really Huey Thierry, a local boy from Jennings. He was one of the hottest performers around. His hit song "Mathilda" is still considered the purest of any swamp pop recording. Cookie was a Little Richard before there even *was* a Little Richard, and he took Southern blues toward rock 'n' roll long before that art form reared its head in Memphis.

So, needless to say, I went to school by watching and listening to all the folks who came, who saw, and who conquered Nightclub Row. All those different musical styles simmered around me, expanding what I did and how I approached my performances. When I needed to, I'd dip into that gumbo pot just like everyone else. Trouble is, I was tired all the time. Hell, I was playing music all night long. During the day, I was trying to finish high school and write new songs. And I'd just met a guy named J. D. Miller, a writer and record producer, who was using me on sessions. By this time my skinny ass was dragging. I noticed that Rufus Thibodeaux had more energy than anybody around. It took my brother Rusty to show me where he got it. Rusty kept telling me that "tired" was an easy thing to fix, and that Rufus had the cure. He finally took me over to the Moulin Rouge and Rufus gave me one of his magic pills.

"Maybe you shouldn't take a whole one the first time," Rufus suggested. So I took his advice. I cut the pill in two, swallowed half, and slipped the other piece into my pocket for a rainy day. Then I went on stage to fiddle. Before long every hair on my head stood on end, and my eyes didn't close for four days. I don't remember how many songs I wrote during that period of time but it was a bunch. I even came up with a theory too. The Doug Kershaw Wasted Time Theory. As I saw it, human beings were wasting far too much time by sleeping. I got a pencil and paper and figured it all out. If I slept eight hours a night, I would lose twenty years by the time I was sixty! No way in hell was I going to do that. Life was too short as it was.

When I came down from the first half of the pill, I reached into my pocket for the other half. Damned if it wasn't already gone.

Laissez les bons temps rouler! Let the good times roll.

The year 1954 would be a milestone in the lives of many of us on Nightclub Row. When I think back to it, I don't really remember it as the year I took my first magic pill, although it was. I think, instead, to how the musical pot was not just simmering any more. It was beginning to boil over.

Jimmy C. Newman had a big hit with "Cry, Cry, Darling."

Clifton Chenier and Cookie & the Cupcakes got big recording deals.

The Bewley Gang turned into Rusty & Doug, and we got our first record deal.

But in 1954, the whole world seemed to be changing, not just the action on Nightclub Row. It was changing and it would never be the same again.

Bill Haley released "Rock Around The Clock."

Elvis Presley signed a contract with Sun Records.

Rock 'n' roll was right around the corner.

Hell, we'd been rocking around the clock on Nightclub Row for years.

11

NOWHERE TO SOMEWHERE

"I feel obligated to look out for young musicians like Doug."
—J. D. Miller, Crowley, Louisiana

As I said before, I'd been doing my musical homework. I found out that there were three record labels down in Southwest Louisiana. In Lake Charles there was Khoury Records, owned by George Khoury. There was also Goldband, owned by Eddie Shuler. And over in Crowley, the rice capital of America, there was Feature Records, owned by J. D. Miller. Khoury and Shuler concentrated on Cajun French recording artists such as Iry Lejune and Nathan Abshire, as well as a style of music they called "swamp pop." J. D. Miller, on the other hand, concentrated on rhythm and blues and country records. Everybody I talked to said that all three of these record men, George, Eddie and J. D, were crooks. You've heard about the law firm called Dewey, Cheatham & Howe? That could have been these three. But as far as I could see everybody was a crook to somebody. And I knew that the way out of nowhere to somewhere ain't easy the first time. Sometimes not even the second or the third times.

I think about this often, about how you can lose your way on the road from nowhere to somewhere. You start down the wrong path or you get bad directions. Sometimes, you let another traveler drag you along with him, and before you know it, you're headed in the opposite direction from *somewhere*. Hell, you're on a line drive right back to *nowhere*. In any case, you've only got yourself and experience to blame. So get back on the bus and remember that a lot of things in life aren't fair. A few years ago, a journalist asked me what I considered the key to success. I didn't hesitate.

"A positive attitude," I told him. "No doubt about it." Sometimes it's hard to do, but you gotta hang onto a good attitude as if your life depends on it.

Soon after we got the television show, J. D. Miller came driving up to our house on Anna Street to offer me a job as a session player on one of his recordings. Man, what an opportunity. We went into the house so I could tell Mama Rita about my good fortune. I offered J. D. a chair in the little front room. Mama Rita was in the kitchen, so I stood in the doorway between the two rooms to talk to her. She folded her arms across her big bosoms as she listened. I fell all over myself telling her what an important man J. D. Miller was. Of course, J. D. could hear every word I was saying. He fidgeted a bit on his chair as he waited for me to finish.

"J. D. wants me to go over to Crowley," I said to Mama Rita. "He wants me to play fiddle on a recording session." I could hardly contain my excitement. When I'd said my piece, Mama Rita leaned forward and peered into the other room at J. D.

"*Sa voix pas la merde*," Mama Rita said. He's not worth a shit. I thought I'd die right there of embarrassment, but I didn't realize it was about to get worse. "Everybody knows J. D. Miller is a crook," Mama Rita added. J. D.'s face turned red as a boiled crawfish. Then his eyes narrowed as he squinted at Mama Rita.

I saw the road from nowhere to somewhere come to an abrupt end. My own mother had just ruined my career. Maybe even the rest of my life. There went my opportunity to make a record, even if I was just a session player. There went an old dream, torn to shreds by my own mother. I started talking as fast as I could.

"You don't know that," I told her. Then I turned to J. D. His eyes had all but disappeared by this time. "Mama Rita's been listening to too gossip," I said and hoped I was right about that. But still, I wasn't gonna let a little thing like J. D. Miller's being a crook stand in the way of my recording career. Who knows why J. D. didn't walk out on us? Instead, he rose from his chair and joined me in trying to convince Mama Rita that he was a honest man. This was somewhat like an alligator telling a mink he's a vegetarian. But J. D. became downright eloquent as he talked. Shit, he even had *me* believing him.

"I feel obligated to look out for young musicians like Doug," J. D. explained. All he wanted to do, he added, was to work with me on my music. Open some big, heavy doors for the poor kid from the swamps. He was downright fatherly. And maybe that's why he won me over, at least in the beginning. I'd grown weary of Pee Wee's criticisms, and this protective concern felt good. I could get used to it.

Of course, I found out later that being slick was part of being J. D. Miller. I suspect J. D. was slick on the day he was born. He just slid out and hit the ground running, looking for some sucker kid like me. But I'll be damned if he wasn't slick enough to get past Mama Rita. She sighed. She unfolded her big arms. She gave us both another good look.

"*Mais, okay, va tête dure,*" she said. Go, hardhead. Then she added, "But don't come crying to me."

J. D. smiled as he shook Mama Rita's hand. And that's how I headed out from nowhere on the *Snow Job Train,* otherwise known as the J. D. Miller Express. To get aboard this train you could buy a ticket for a song, your song or J. D.'s song. It didn't matter to him. After all, he was the conductor *and* the engineer.

J. D.'s method of operation was simple. His artists either recorded one of his songs or they recorded one of their own. If they recorded one of their own, they had to let J. D. put his name on it as co-writer. Did he ever contribute to those songs? I don't know about the other writers, but in my case, J. D. sometimes added his name without adding a single word. Other times he threw in a word or two, just to make it look legit. Maybe it even helped his conscience a little. I do know he was capable of writing a good song. He'd done it. So, when it came my turn to record with J. D. Miller, I knew all about his train, and I was willing to pay his price for the ticket. And because of that, I guess J. D. wasn't a crook. And I wasn't a dumbass. We were what you call "music business associates."

The first record I played session fiddle on was for a guy named Joey Gills. When I first saw Joey, I thought he was Hank Williams, alive and in the flesh. He looked like Hank, dressed like Hank, and even sang like Hank. He had all of Hank's mannerisms down too. So, standing in that studio and playing on Joey's record was a ghostly experience. Until I heard Hank Jr. sing his dad's songs years later, I never heard anyone come as close to the man as Joey Gills did that day. It was like playing for Hank Williams himself, so I played my butt off.

And I kept right on playing it off for J. D. Miller. I'd do the television show, go out and fulfill the tour dates with the Bewley Gang, then head for Crowley to play on J. D.'s records. My grades suffered badly since I ended up skipping school about half the time. But in among all those countless nights of playing in clubs to earn money, I managed to finish high school, the first one of Mama Rita's sons to do so. And I think I even learned a few things for my troubles. A trade school had opened up next to the high school, and it was offering college business courses. High school students were encouraged to take some of the classes, so I signed up for accounting and typing for my last two years of high school. I knew accounting would come in handy in a music business career. It did, too, in the end. I was able to account for how much money I lost and how much was stolen from me in various ways. As for typing, I probably knew I'd be better off typing all those song lyrics, rather than scribbling them on paper.

In 1954, I was ready to graduate from high school. I didn't go to either my senior prom or to the commencement ceremony because I was playing fiddle on both nights. I suppose I could've taken off if I had really wanted to, but music and making a living were always my priorities. Not that I didn't have my eye on a lot of pretty local girls. I did. I'd watch them while they were dancing to our music. But it always took me all night long to get up the nerve to ask one out. By that time, she would have left the club and gone home. So I hadn't invited any girl to my senior prom. Still, I wanted to at least remember the occasion, so I bought myself a nifty suit from the Sears & Roebuck Catalog. It was a grayish color and cost me about twenty-five bucks. I looked good in it, I must say. Mama Rita thought so too. She looked me up and down.

"It's nice, Doug," Mama Rita said. "Now you can go to funerals." I didn't go to a funeral. Instead, I went to school and had my picture taken in my prom suit, just as all the other seniors did. Then I took off my new suit and headed out to whatever club we were playing that night. I never wore it again. But I still have the picture.

I can't say I was working for J. D. Miller for free. Sometimes J. D. ordered in hamburgers, courtesy of his record label. But I figured I was getting him in my debt, that sooner or later I'd cash in when he asked me to make my own record. When I finally brought it up, J. D. hemmed and hawed.

"Well, I guess so, Doug," he said. Then he added that I should record under the name of the Bewley Gang, for obvious promotional reasons. I knew he was only doing it to keep me on the staff as the unpaid fiddler, but I didn't care. I was finally going to make a record! You might call this screwed without being kissed. We went into the studio like it was the back seat of that 1946 Ford Coupe. But there I was, singing my very first record. And guess what the A side was. "When Will I Learn?," the sorrowful love ballad that I'd written for Little Frances. I should have dedicated it to J. D. Miller, now that I think of the title. The flip side was another song I'd written called "My Heart Is Broken." They were the only songs J. D. didn't put his name on as co-writer. I would soon find out why.

I sang the first song in the key of A, but somehow the pressing plant speeded it up to the key of B-flat. I have no idea to this day if J. D. had anything to do with that. But "When Will I Learn" sounded like it was being sung by Alvin the Chipmunk, not Kershaw the Cajun. J. D. had five hundred 78 rpm records pressed up, gave me ten of them, and then dumped the other four hundred and ninety in a corner of the storeroom. I think it's safe to say that he had no intention of recording me again. He was just finally paying me for the session work. When I asked about this, he kindly explained the situation to me.

"You're not much of a singer or a songwriter, Doug," he said. "But you're a helluva fiddle player, so you can hang around the studio and play on my records."

It turned out that I was more determined and less dumb than J. D. thought. To me, it was just another swamp I had to cross to get to solid ground. So I put my back to the wall and started writing more songs. I knew I had to hone my writing skills in the same way as I'd done my vocals, by working on them all the time. But what I didn't count on was another broken heart. Now, *that* will sharpen your skills to a fine point faster than anything.

It started when the Bewley Gang was playing several shows in Lacassine. The club, appropriately named the Lacassine Club, had a bandstand with a low ceiling and a decorative picket fence along the front. There were three booths right up against the fence, and that's where a girl named Shirley English sat each night to hear the show. One night, Shirley brought along one of her friends, Ruby Monceaux, from nearby Welsh, Louisiana. I took one look at Ruby and was smitten right down to my toes. Shirley's mother and brother usually came to hear the show, too. So, every time we took a break, I slid down off the bandstand and went over to talk to Shirley's family, just to get close to Ruby Monceaux. When Ruby told me she worked at the movie theater in Welsh, I let it be known that I loved movies.

From then on I was at the Welsh movie theater every evening I wasn't playing a show. Ruby finally decided to take me home to meet her parents. To my great surprise, her father was Melton Monceaux, the father of Junior, the little boy who had drowned all those years ago. Ruby was Melton's child by his second wife, which meant she was Junior's half sister. Small world, ain't it? Nothing ever happened physically between Ruby and me, just a little kissing. But after a few months of going around together, I took it for granted that we were an item. I was so sure that she loved me too that I planned to ask her to marry me. It never occurred to me that she might have other plans. I was one of the Bewley Gang. Girls smiled up at me every night from the dance floor. My very presence sold bags of flour all over Southwest Louisiana. What female could say no to that?

With matrimony on my mind, I stopped by Ruby's house one night to talk to her. She wasn't home, and I soon discovered that Ruby had matrimony on *her* mind, too.

"She's out with her fiancé," Mrs. Monceaux said. Her fiancé? Hell, I didn't even know she had a boyfriend. Or if she did, I thought it was *me*.

"Does this mean she's getting married?" Love can make you dumb. Ruby's mother nodded.

"*Oui, c'est vrai*," she answered. Yes, that's right.

Kissed again without being screwed.

And that's what happened. Ruby Monceaux got married. The oddest things float through your brain at times like that. I remember thinking, *Shit, she didn't even invite me to the wedding.* Guess she thought I'd stand up and shout "Pooh ya!" when the preacher asked if anyone had reason to object. That's when I got mad as hell. How dare she marry someone else and not invite me to the wedding? So I sat down with my guitar and started picking out some chords. I wrote down these words:

No, no it's not so, I wasn't invited to go.
Why try to lie, the truth still shows,
And the love in my heart still glows.

It wasn't *War and Peace,* but it was a breakthrough career moment. Somehow, with that one song, I saw how you could turn personal emotions into a commercial product. This was more than just writing down sad lines and singing them. These lyrics could mean something to almost anyone who heard them, especially if they'd ever known heartbreak. They could relate. That's one of the most important things you must learn about songwriting: how to turn a personal moment into a universal one. But I also picked up a bad habit right then, too, a pattern I didn't lose for years to come. I'd find a girl I liked, and then I'd do my damnedest to make her like me back. When it seemed that she did, I'd turn around and treat her so awful that she'd leave me with another broken heart. Plus three or four new songs about how heartbroken I was.

Harlan Howard, one of Nashville's best songwriters, usually got three hit songs out of every marriage and three out of every divorce. But it must have taken a toll on him because he told Willie Nelson that he'd decided not to get married any more. "I'm just gonna find me a woman I can't stand and buy her a house," Harlan said. My apologies to the wonderful Jan Howard for repeating the joke. I learned there's a better way to tap into one's creativity by just working hard at it. But that's how it started for me. I had lost Ruby and gained a song. As I finished writing the last words, I heard Rusty singing in the next room, harmonizing with me. *Man,* I thought, *that sounds great. If I get to record this, I'll have Rusty sing harmony.*

I persuaded Rusty to come with me and we headed over to see J. D. Miller, at M & S Music in Crowley. One thing about J. D. Miller is that he could pick a hit song. Rusty and I had barely finished singing "No, No, It's Not So" before J. D. had his name on it as co-writer. That meant he really liked it. I should have been mad as hell. But I was getting another shot at making a record, so I let it pass. If nothing else, I knew this meant the song would be published by the company that handled all of J. D.'s songs, the mighty Acuff-Rose up in Nashville, a music publishing conglomerate that had been founded by Roy Acuff and Fred Rose. We rounded up Pee Wee and a couple of the local studio musicians, and we went to work. By the time we finished recording "No, No, It's Not So," J. D. had written a song for the B side called "It's Better To Be A Has-Been Than A Never-Was." This just happened to be a line he had "borrowed" from Rusty.

This time when J. D. pressed up the five hundred 78s, he actually put them in the mail to radio stations. The song was an immediate hit all through Louisiana and Texas, reaching a far wider audience than ever before. As great as it felt to hear my voice on the radio, the real thrill was when I first heard the song on a jukebox. Remember, I've always had a love affair with the jukebox. I'll never forget the sensation as I dropped a nickel into the slot, listened as it clunked its way down the tube, and then pushed the buttons for my own song. I can even tell you where it was. It was the Silver Star Club out on Highway 90, between Lake Charles and Sulphur, Louisiana. Rusty and I were playing there at the time so I brought the owner, Mr. Fusilier, a copy of the record. He put it on, right at the top of the list. "No, No, It's Not So" was A-1. The flip side was A-2. Mr. Fusilier let Rusty and me play the record ten times for free. After that we had to put up our own money. I almost wore out my index finger that day, punching buttons on the jukebox at the Silver Star. It's a memory that will live in my heart forever.

What wasn't so thrilling for me was the moment when I first saw the record label.

"No, No, It's Not So"
(Miller-Kershaw)
Rusty & Doug
With String Band Accompaniment

I'll be damned if that didn't hurt worse than getting dumped by Ruby. I'd gotten used to the idea of J. D. being cowriter, but I hadn't actually thought of my taking second billing on a song I'd written about my broken heart. He'd never even met Ruby. Added to this, I was singing lead and Rusty harmony. I guess someone decided switching the names would sound better, maybe even me. Once we had a regional hit, J. D. started writing songs like mad for us to demo. Then he'd take them to Nashville to play for Acuff-Rose in the hopes that they'd get them cut. Acuff-Rose wasn't just a publishing company. They also had their own label at this time, Hickory Records. I knew J. D. was just pitching the songs, that he wasn't pitching Rusty and me as artists. Nonetheless, I kept on trying to write another hit for Rusty & Doug. Meanwhile, I stayed on the roster at J. D.'s company as an unpaid session singer and fiddle player.

J. D. Miller had already found songwriting success in 1952 when Kitty Wells recorded "It Wasn't God Who Made Honky Tonk Angels." At least I *assume* J. D. wrote it. His name is on it. This song was what was known as an "answer song," written in response to Hank Thompson's "Wild Side Of Life." Kitty Wells was hot at that time, and she took the song all the way to No. 1. So, J. D. was more than anxious to write a follow-up hit. When Kitty and Red Foley had a 1954 hit with "One By One," J. D. sat down and wrote another song, the title of which now escapes me. What J. D. really wanted was to get a good recording of the song, in the hopes that Red and Kitty would then cover it. So he called me up and explained that he wanted me to record the song with a sensational new female singer named Little Sunshine. J. D. was hot about this girl. He said I'd go nuts when I heard her. I figured I'd better write a song for us to record if she was *that* good. So I wrote "Nothing Matters, Dear, As Long As I Have You."

I headed out to the studio that day, anxious to hear this new talent, anxious to pitch her my new song, and anxious to record with her. I walked in and who do I see standing at the microphone? The very first girl I'd ever written a song about, my first true love, Frances! Before I said a word, I looked around the room to see if Big Robert had come with her, since it's difficult to sing through a broken nose. Ti Frances and I said our hellos, and then we got straight to the job at hand. We recorded J. D.'s song and my song, and that's the last I ever saw of her. Nothing ever came of the recordings either, although something came of my song "Nothing Matters, Dear, As Long As I Have You." Years later, I was browsing through a record bin and noticed an interesting release on Bear Family Records in Germany. It was titled *The Legendary Jay Miller Sessions*. It contained the demos we sang to pitch J. D.'s songs to Hickory Records. On it was the recording of me and Little Sunshine singing "Nothing Matters, Dear, As Long As I Have You." Only thing was, my name was nowhere on it as writer. I have never received a penny for this song, not as writer or artist. Here's what the liner notes said about that particular cut. "A nice country item with fine steel guitar, swinging country boogie piano and a great piano solo from Doug Kershaw. Little Sunshine's name is forgotten, but Jay Miller recalled that she was from Eunice."

Screwed without being kissed *or* given cab fare!

Sometimes I wonder if I wasn't trying to write myself out of any chance at solo stardom since I kept penning songs with Rusty's harmonies in mind. Ironically, the song that got us our shot in Nashville was written for a trio performance. During our concerts I had been singing covers of two popular tunes, "Good Night Sweetheart," and "(Oh Baby Mine) I Get So Lonely." Johnny and Jack had a country hit with the latter song in 1954, and the Statler Brothers in 1983. If you remember how the Statlers did it, you'll know how important the bass part is to the overall song. I used to call my high school friend John Earl Richard to the stage to sing that part, and the audiences went wild when he hit the bass notes. But music wasn't John Earl's dream then, and he wasn't always available.

Then J. D. Miller reminded me of Wiley Barkdull, the guy who played piano on "No, No, It's Not So." Wiley was a helluva bass singer who wanted to record for Feature Records. J. D. didn't know quite what to do with him. But when I listened to a demo Wiley had done—his soft, low voice just rattled the speakers—I knew immediately what to do with Wiley Barkdull. We hired him to play piano and sing bass. What I didn't know was who the hell his boss was. Was it Pee Wee and the Continental Playboys? The Bewley Gang? Or Rusty & Doug? But the first time I heard Wiley hit one low note on "Be Nobody's Darling But Mine," it vibrated my bones. I knew we had a winning sound. Since it was getting harder and harder for John Earl to make every show, Wiley stepped in on "Good Night Sweetheart" and "Oh Baby Mine." I was so inspired that I wrote a song especially for the three of us called "So Lovely Baby."

J. D. was pretty excited when we recorded it. He said he was releasing it on Feature as soon as he returned from one of his song-pitching trips to Acuff-Rose in Nashville. Hearing this, I made a snap decision that changed my entire life. I asked J. D. if I could accompany him to Nashville, since I'd never been to Tennessee. The truth was, while I did want to see Tennessee in general and Nashville in particular, I had a gut feeling that I should be at this meeting. Since my songs were being published by these people up at Acuff-Rose, I wanted to know more about how the business worked, and especially how J. D. Miller fit into it all. J. D. just shrugged.

"I don't see any reason you shouldn't come," he said.

Sometime in the late fall of 1954, J. D. and I drove to Nashville, the farthest I'd ever been from Southwest Louisiana, over six hundred and fifty miles of two-lane highway. And I loved every inch of it, sitting up in the front seat of J. D. Miller's big, white Cadillac. We pulled up in front of Acuff-Rose and we *both* went into Wesley Rose's office. It was nothing fancy, just a small, informal work space. J. D. introduced me to Wesley. I remember thinking, *Hell, this man doesn't look like a big music business executive. He looks like an accountant.* I found out later that Wesley actually did have a degree in accounting and took care of the Acuff-Rose books. There were several other executives in the office and J. D. introduced me to them as well. Then, with no further mention of me, he played all his new songs. The men talked music all through the listening session, and I think J. D. forgot I was even there. When the last song finished playing, he asked Wesley if he wanted to hear a new song he'd written. He had called it "So Lovely Baby."

"I'm gonna release it on a couple of Louisiana boys," J. D. said. There was no mention of me as either the writer or the artist. I just sat there, not saying a word, but getting a better understanding of how J. D. Miller fit into this business in Nashville.

"Fire away," Wesley said.

J. D. pulled the master tape out of his briefcase and put it on Wesley's reel-to-reel. The first thing you heard on that record was my fiddle, and damn it sounded good. Wesley must have thought so, too, because he took the pipe out of his mouth and sat back in his chair. As he listened to that three-part harmony, he looked over at the other men in the room. A grin spread across his face. *Damn*, I thought. *This is Nashville and I got me a hit!* Or at least I might have had a hit if "So Lovely Baby" was on Hickory Records and not on Feature. Then fate stepped in. Right about the time the tape was ending, the machine stretched it so badly it was worthless. J. D. Miller jumped up from his chair.

"Shit, Wesley!" he shouted. "That's the only copy I got!"

Wesley Rose sat puffing on his pipe, not a bit riled or worried, that grin still on his face. He glanced over at his colleagues, then back at J. D. Then he took the pipe out of his mouth.

"I'll record those boys on Hickory Records," Wesley announced. "Who are they?"

J. D. seemed dazed. He looked over at me, and I was grinning like a possum. Then he glanced around at the other men in the room. They were all smiling like possums. J. D. had no choice but to join in.

"That's one of them boys right there, Wesley," he said. "Doug Kershaw. It's him singing lead, and that's his brother Rusty singing tenor."

"Who's the bass singer?" Wesley asked.

"A guy named Wiley Barkdull," J. D. answered.

"I'll take him too," Wesley said. "Bring the boys up in a couple of weeks and we'll cut the record." He stood up behind his desk, an obvious signal to the rest of us that the meeting was over, so we stood too. Wesley Rose started to leave the room when he suddenly stopped, his hand on the door knob. He looked back at J. D. Miller.

"J. D.," Wesley Rose said, "you've written yourself another hit."

J. D. didn't look at me, nor did he utter a single word. Neither did I. I wanted a contract with Hickory Records more than I wanted a fight with J. D. So we drove back to Southwest Louisiana, where I wrote my butt off. My plan was to get more of my own songs on that first session with Hickory Records. But J. D. had other ideas. When the band got together to begin rehearsing, he made an announcement.

"We'll do 'So Lovely Baby,'" he said. We already knew this since Wesley Rose himself wanted that song. "And we'll do three of my songs," J. D. added.

We worked around the clock on those sessions. In fact, you might say J. D. worked the pants off us, because at one point we were so hot from recording in that little studio of his that Rusty and I took off our trousers. There we were, singing in our underwear. We demoed all four songs. In May 1955, the whole band headed up to Nashville. Pee Wee's Ford Fairlane kept its nose to the rear end of J. D. Miller's Cadillac all the way. In the car with Pee Wee was Rusty, Wiley Barkdull, and Louis Forett, who had joined us as steel player. I rode in the Caddy where I could keep a close eye on J. D. Miller. Thinking back to those days when air-conditioning was still a dream away, it must have been a long drive. I remember we kept the car windows rolled down a bit so that cool air could drift in. What a damned exciting time in a young musician's life. And that excitement grew the closer we got to Nashville, Tennessee. Hell, we'd be playing for a major record label this time, Hickory Records, even though none of us had a clue about how sessions in Nashville worked.

When we walked into the studio, Wesley Rose saw that we had our instruments with us.

"Put down your instruments, boys," he said. "I've got the best musicians in town for this record."

Louis Forett did get to play steel, and Wiley Barkdull played piano. As it turned out, it was the three Kershaw boys who got eighty-sixed. Chet Atkins played guitar instead of Rusty. Since Wesley didn't want drums, that left Pee Wee out. And Tommy Jackson played fiddle instead of me. By the time it was over, I was just thankful they were letting Rusty and me sing. J. D. played the demos we'd recorded so the session players could learn the songs. I watched in astonishment as each musician jotted down a series of numbers, then turned around and played the songs as if they were reading sheet music. I'd never heard of the Nashville number system before, and I couldn't believe that those numbers over the lyrics were enough that these men could play a song after hearing it just once. But play they did, especially this guitar player named Chet Atkins. Man, what a picker.

The first song we recorded was "So Lovely Baby," and it turned out pretty good. It was not the way I heard it in my head, mind you, but good anyway. Then we moved to a song J. D. had written. It was titled "Why Cry For You," a real hillbilly tune that featured my funky fiddle playing. For the first time that day, I saw these musicians falter. Tommy Jackson started to frown. Wesley Rose put a halt to the session and said, "Tommy, play the fiddle exactly as it's played on the demo."

"Hell, Wesley," Tommy said. "I've forgotten how to play that bad!"

Now I can laugh at this today, but back then I was a pissed off Cajun.

Tommy tried the part a couple of more times, and each time it sounded worse. Wesley finally turned to me.

"Doug," he asked, "can you copy the fiddler on the demo?"

"Mr. Rose," I said. "That fiddler is *me*."

"Well, why didn't you say so in the first place?" Wesley asked. "Get your fiddle and come on over here." I shot a look at Tommy Jackson, who didn't look back. I got the fiddle and kicked off the song. I sang while I played, just like I always did, and that stunned some of those session guys. Few fiddle players ever do that.

Tommy Jackson packed up his fiddle and went home.

I didn't let his remark bother me. I could hear that he was a damn good musician. He knew how to play the way Tommy Jackson played. Besides, I was a nineteen-year-old kid with a record deal and a hit song, at least according to Wesley Rose. And his prediction was close, since "So Lovely Baby" went to No. 14 in the nation. I was on my way from nowhere to somewhere.

First Nashville Lesson. In all the years that have passed since that day in the studio, I have never, *ever,* let anyone else play the fiddle parts on my records. And I never will.

PART 2

LEAVING HOME

Cypress Breeze

12

JENNINGS, TO WHEELING, TO NASHVILLE

*"The Opry of 1957 represents the highest quality of entertainment
since I have been with the show."*
—Roy Acuff, Nashville *Banner*, 1957

I was so thrilled about having a hit that I did another stupid thing. I gave away an even bigger share of my songwriting. I'd always resented the fact that J. D. Miller was getting a part of my songs. But I really got mad when I learned that Wesley Rose thought it was J. D. who was doing the writing, and that he was just sharing the money with me. In other words, J. D. was representing me to Wesley Rose as some kind of Cajun charity case. Hell, I'd have gone back to shining shoes rather than accept charity from J. D. Miller. But while I was mad about the fifty-fifty split, I still couldn't figure out any way to get out of it. Then it hit me. I approached Rusty with an idea.

"I'll put your name on each of my songs," I told him. "That way the share will be split three ways." As I saw it, that would leave the Kershaws with two-thirds and J. D. with one-third. What this new split meant was that I would no longer get half of the royalties. But at least more money would go to the Kershaw family. I got just what I asked for. On "Look Around," our second record, the writers were listed as J. D. Miller and Rusty & Doug. Not only would I get less money, but now I had *third* billing. If I'd been out on Daddy Jack's boat right about then, instead of hearing *chuk-chuk-chuk* ringing in my ears, I'd have heard *chump-chump-chump*. That's how I felt. But at least I *wanted* to give Rusty a share. I couldn't say the same about J. D. Miller.

Looking back on those days, I now believe that I was pulling Rusty deeper and deeper into my own personal dreams, whether he wanted them or not. I had never asked my brother what his own dreams were or if I was included in them. If I *had* asked and if he had been honest, I'm sure he would have said "no." But I didn't realize this until a few years later, when the US Army split up the brotherly duo of Rusty & Doug. After that happened, I quit giving away part of my writing unless there was a reason. One time, I gave Jimmy C. Newman fifty percent of a song called "Pirogue." But that was because Jimmy gave me the idea for the song, about a guy traveling down the river in a pirogue to see his girlfriend. I recorded it for RCA with Rusty and again as a solo artist on *Spanish Moss,* my second Warner Bros. album. So Jimmy deserved that for the inspiration.

But another time, I just really and truly messed up. And it would concern "Louisiana Man," my biggest song of all. I know I said earlier that you gotta make mistakes, deal the blows, and then go on with a positive attitude. But this one was tough. This dealt with a song about Mama Rita and Daddy Jack and my childhood on a houseboat in the swamps of Louisiana. I'll make no bones about it. It broke my heart. But that's the story of Doug Needing Money to Bail Rusty out of Jail. That story comes later.

Even though I made a few business mistakes, 1955 was a good year. We had a television show on KPLC-TV, a record contract with Hickory Records, and "Look Around" was shaping up to be our second hit. In the midst of all this, we were invited to play on the Grand Ole Opry. I learned fast that a hit record and an association with a powerful company such as Acuff-Rose meant everything in Nashville. I'm sure that the reason we were invited to play the Opry right away was because Roy Acuff wanted to promote his own writers. That was fine with me.

Just as our first television show had been nothing but a blur for me, so was that first appearance on the stage of the Grand Ole Opry. Too much adrenalin pumping, I guess. The Opry was still at the old Ryman Auditorium, down at Broadway and Fourth. I do know that Rusty, Wiley, and I piled into somebody's car—I can't remember if it was mine or J. D. Miller's—and we drove from Jennings to Nashville. It was only the third time we watched those same six hundred and fifty miles of white line disappear beneath the front bumper of the car. I remember more of the emotional side of that night, how people like Roy Acuff and Bill Monroe were so kind to us. We sang "So Lovely Baby," and the audience loved us. The spirit of the place itself was so strong that I could almost feel it seeping down out of the rafters and up through the boards of the floor. I kept thinking of how Hank Williams had sung "Your Cheatin' Heart" on that very stage to twenty-six encores. How can you not feel an energy like that?

110

Still reeling from the Opry, we went back to Nightclub Row. By then we were making so much more money that I talked Mama Rita into letting me trade the Ford coupe for a new 1955 DeSoto. It was a pretty blue, with fins on the back and a push-button gear shift. The cars were getting newer, but the career still seemed to be hovering in one place, and that was nightclubs. I don't want to leave the impression that I hated working clubs. After all, they were our bread-and-butter gigs. And Nightclub Row was still my classroom when it came to music school. But people patronize clubs to drink and to dance. It usually doesn't matter how good the band is as long as they can dance to the music. From a musician's standpoint, however, it gets boring when you play just for dancers, hour after hour, night after night. Boredom and Kershaw still don't mix. The bottom line was that I wanted to play where people came to hear good music—nothing more, nothing less.

By the late 1940s country music was getting popular everywhere, expanding far beyond the rural South. Around 1950, according to *Billboard*, there were 650 radio stations that had live country music at various times during the day, like the Bewley Gang Show, on KJEF in Jennings, Louisiana. I guess with all the interest in country music, some stations decided to try their hand at an even bigger market, and they began to follow the example of WSM's Grand Ole Opry. Some of these big event type shows were Shreveport's "Louisiana Hayride," Los Angeles's "Town Hall Party," and the "World's Original Jamboree" on WWVA in Wheeling, West Virginia.

The Bewley Gang had tried to play the Hayride back in 1953. We auditioned for the show's manager, Horace Logan, and got turned down flat. But a hit record and a big outfit like Acuff-Rose can turn things around for you. The minute Horace got wind that Rusty & Doug, the Kershaw boys, were on Hickory Records, he started booking us and telling people that we were regulars. That was Wesley Rose's clout. It reached all the way from Nashville. The Hayride was sometimes referred to as the Opry's farm team, since people usually worked there until the Opry beckoned. Faron Young and Webb Pierce started out there, as did Johnny and Jack, Kitty Wells, and Hank Williams himself. When we started playing the Hayride it was a wild and exciting place. Our fellow performers were the likes of Johnny Cash and Elvis Presley. I still remember the first time I was standing in a room backstage and Elvis Presley strolled in. It was like a bolt of electricity hit that place. Like the time poor Crip Cormier peed against the aluminum trailer. Presley was definitely the Hillbilly Cat. No doubt about it. And that boy could sing too.

The Hayride was broadcast over station KWKH in Shreveport, so we had the broad public exposure of a radio show. But we also got to experience what it meant to have hundreds of music lovers there just to hear you play. After the show, we'd head back to Nightclub Row and become a bar band again. It got to be a grind. Then, on a trip to Nashville in 1956, I managed to talk to Wesley Rose. I explained how unhappy I was about the deal I'd struck with J. D. Miller. Now I'm sure Wesley didn't want to jump in the middle of a fight between two of his writers, so he came up with an idea. Rusty and I should leave Louisiana.

"I can get you steady work on the Wheeling Jamboree in West Virginia," Wesley said. "Stoney Cooper is up there. I think he'll look out for you."

I jumped on that idea like a cajun cop on a beignet.

Wesley called Stoney, who set up everything with Paul Myers, the manager of the Jamboree. We faced one problem and that was the Bewley Gang. As I said, Pee Wee had married a few years earlier and he and his wife now had two kids. Pee Wee wanted to stay put in Southwest Louisiana where there was still a measure of security. He knew that between the television show and Nightclub Row, he could always feed his family. Rusty and I hung around Lake Charles just long enough to help Pee Wee audition band members to take our places. Now it truly was Pee Wee Kershaw's band, for better or worse.

In May 1956, I drove away from the little house on Anna Street and headed for Wheeling, West Virginia. I was behind the wheel of my 1955 blue DeSoto, with a hundred dollars in my pocket and brother Rusty in the passenger seat. Mama Rita didn't say much about two of her sons leaving home, but I knew she wasn't happy. After all, in those days of travel Wheeling was a long way off. But I knew in my bones that leaving Southwest Louisiana was the only way to get off the J. D. Miller Express. I pulled the DeSoto out onto Highway 90 and pushed the pedal down. We flew through Crowley, the rice capital of America and home of J. D. Miller. From then on, it was clear sailing to New Orleans, where we turned due north to Memphis, then on to Nashville, where I stopped to talk again with Wesley Rose. We slept that night at the York Motel, across the street from Acuff-Rose. The next evening, we were in Wheeling. We rented a room by the week at the Wheeling Hotel, in the heart of downtown, and fell into bed, exhausted. A new chapter of our lives was about to begin. I just didn't know then how big and crazy the whole book would be. All I could think of was that I was soon to become part of the World's Original Jamboree, on WWVA, in Wheeling, West Virginia.

The program was broadcast from the historic old Capitol Theater, on a 50,000-watt clear channel AM signal, to the biggest country music audience east of the Mississippi. It was at the Jamboree that I really learned how to be an entertainer, thanks to the tutelage of Stoney Cooper. Born to musical families themselves, Stoney and his wife, Wilma Lee, had been playing and recording music for years before they settled down at the Wheeling Jamboree. They soon became one of the most popular acts. They were also honest and caring folks, so having them in the Kershaw corner was a big plus. I remember one day, not long after we got to Wheeling, that I was watching Wilma Lee and Stoney's portion of the show. They brought out a guest entertainer who did everything he could to steal the show from the Coopers. But Stoney didn't seem ruffled at all. He just heaped praise on the fellow. Afterward, I asked him about it.

"If somebody tries to steal your thunder, Doug, just sell them to the crowd," Stoney said. "If you convince the audience how great this person is, you'll seem like a courteous host. And you'll look smart for having asked that person to appear in the first place. Trust me. It works." I never forgot that, whether it came to introducing my own band or a guest on one of my shows.

That brings me to Stoney's daughter, Carolee Cooper. Carolee had one of the most beautiful voices I ever heard, and I couldn't understand why Stoney wasn't recording her.

"She's not ready," Stoney explained in that thick West Virginia drawl of his. "I don't want to pigeonhole her into our sound, to typecast her. She either needs to wait a while or have someone else record her."

I didn't waste any time offering my services, and I even wrote a song I thought would fit her voice perfectly. I called it "Going Down the Road." On our next Hickory session, Rusty & Doug had a singing partner named Carolee Cooper.

"Beautiful," Stoney said when he heard his daughter's work. And he was right. It was beautiful. Carolee went on to form the Carolee Singers, and they became mainstays on the Opry, singing with a lot of people, including her mother, Wilma Lee. Stoney Cooper passed away in 1977 after twenty years on the Grand Ole Opry. It was a big loss for country music and for the people who loved him.

There were many great artists on the Jamboree when Rusty and I came to Wheeling. In addition to Wilma Lee and Stoney, there were Doc and Chickie Williams, the Osborne Brothers, and Dusty Owens, who had hired Buddy Spicher to play fiddle. I remember Dusty Owens well, mainly because of Buddy Spicher. Buddy's wife at the time was Donna Darlene, who sang with the show. While my brother Rusty had met and married Vesta Muster, a local girl, shortly after we moved to Wheeling, I was still single. Single enough that I noticed how pretty Buddy Spicher's wife was.

Donna Darlene Spicher would later become my first wife.

All of the acts on the Jamboree played other dates to supplement their incomes, traveling to shows in Pennsylvania, New York, or New Jersey during the week, then back to play the Jamboree on Saturday night. Bookings were easy because the Jamboree gave its acts such great visibility throughout the Northeast. I learned a lot of tricks from Stoney, like how to book a show in one place on a Thursday night, then an afternoon job the following day farther on down the road, to a Friday night show a little closer to Wheeling. The idea was not to let too many miles and meals go by without a show. One of the strangest places we played on our weekly route was from the roof of the concession stand at a drive-in movie theater. The mosquitoes and bugs almost drove us crazy. The audience sat in their cars, but they had a very distinct code to let us know what they thought. It was short honks if they liked us, long honks if they wanted an encore, and long honks and flashing headlights for a standing ovation. No honks at all meant they hated our guts. We got a standing ovation. It was just another step toward Madison Square Garden.

Ever since Rusty and I left Louisiana I'd been feeling guilty, as if I'd deserted Mama Rita and Pee Wee. I felt especially bad about Mama Rita, since I'd been looking out for her since I was eight years old. Then one day a letter arrived from Pee Wee. Bewley Mills had canceled the television show. Pee Wee and Mr. Raspberry had tried to keep it going, but Bewley Mills decided it wasn't the same without Rusty and me. I felt lower than a snake's belly in a wagon rut. That's when I came up with another one of my famous ideas. Pee Wee could join us on the Jamboree. He could bring his wife and two kids to Wheeling to live. Hell, he could bring Mama Rita, too. And while he was at it, he might as well bring A. C. Billeaud to play steel and Sonny Odon to play guitar. Rusty also played guitar, but Sonny wanted to come along, so why the hell not? There was just one obstacle. Pee Wee played accordion, fiddle, and drums. We didn't use an accordion, I played fiddle, and the Jamboree didn't allow drums.

Musical dilema.

When December rolled around, I told Pee Wee to pack up Mama Rita and his family and come to Wheeling anyway. I'd try to find a solution, and at least we could all spend Christmas together. I didn't say a word to any of the Jamboree officials, including Paul Myers or Hardrock Gunter. Instead, I went out looking for a house to rent so that the Kershaw family would have a roof over our heads, a roof big enough to include Sonny Odon and A. C. Billeaud. Then I waited for the entourage to arrive. Not long after Pee Wee and company rolled into Wheeling, he and I went over to the Jamboree and started setting up his drums for the show that night. Paul Myers immediately ran out onto the stage.

"Doug!" he yelled. "What the hell are you doing?"

"Getting ready for the show tonight," I said, all casual.

"I can see that, damn you," Paul said. "But you know I can't let you use drums. Even the Opry don't use drums."

Pee Wee stood listening. And at that moment I wasn't even mad at him for all the times he made me fight with Rusty while he watched.

"Then just tell the audience you won't let us play," I said, "because we need drums on our show."

"I won't do that," Paul said. He was getting madder.

"Then we won't play," I told him. I walked offstage, leaving Pee Wee standing there holding a drum. I saw Hardrock Gunter go over to Paul and say a few words. Gunter, who had had country boogie releases, was a disc jockey as well as one of the emcees for the Jamboree. He didn't have a barrelful of clout, but he had a pretty big bucket. I think Hardrock was on our side about the drums, so maybe what he said to Paul helped. I know Paul Myers then hurried over to stop me from leaving.

"Aw, what the hell, Doug," he said. "Go ahead and set up the damn drums."

115

So the Kershaws became a little piece of history at the Wheeling Jamboree.

It was the beginning of a new era in country music. Pee Wee was a damn fine drummer, and when we finished our first song, with those drums pounding out the rhythm, the audience went crazy clapping. If they'd been in cars they'd have honked their horns and flashed their lights. Chalk it up to a bunch of stubborn Cajuns. But the truth is that rock 'n' roll was breathing hard down country's neck, and our kind of music was sorely needed. So I think it's fair to say that we indirectly helped to bring drums to the Grand Ole Opry, too. Years later I read in the book *Country Roots* that Rusty & Doug were credited with the Opry's finally allowing rockabilly music on its stage. That makes this Louisiana man very proud.

I was always thinking big for the Kershaws. After all, those were the Eisenhower years, when America was thinking big about itself because bigger meant better. There was no finer example of this than the design of cars rolling off the assembly line each year. I fell in with the rest of America and traded the 1955 DeSoto for a 1957 Chrysler with big fins. They pointed at the sky like church steeples. Then I had a rack custom-built for the car that would hold our equipment, with a canvas snap-down top. My arrangement about the car, however, was very different than the old days. I decided that the band would make the monthly car payment, as well as pay for gas and any breakdowns. But the rest of the money would be divided equally among us. In other words, the 1957 Chrysler wouldn't be as well paid as the 1936 Ford.

Since Martha White Flour was sponsoring us at this time—they also sponsored Flatt and Scruggs—we had a sign painted on both door panels of the Chrysler.

MARTHA WHITE FLOUR
featuring
RUSTY & DOUG

We also had our own TV show in Wheeling by this time, a half-hour spot every Saturday called the *Rusty & Doug Show*, also sponsored by Martha White. Since we were making records as Rusty & Doug by this time, it seemed natural to use that name. I don't know how Pee Wee felt about this because he never mentioned it. I guess we'd come a long way from our days as Pee Wee and the Continental Playboys.

Before Pee Wee got his own place to live, we all managed to survive in one house for a few months. Mama Rita and Georgia, Pee Wee's wife, cooked for the whole damn tribe of us, even the sidemen. But Mama Rita didn't like Wheeling one bit.

"It's too damn cold here, *cher*," she said. "I gonna freeze my ass off."

I knew she would hate the change in climate. When Rusty and I had first arrived, back in the spring of the year, we almost froze to death too. Hell, we'd all grown up in the high humidity and heat of Southwest Louisiana. To us, West Virginia might as well have been Siberia. Keep in mind, Wheeling is in the northern panhandle of the state, only sixty miles south of Pittsburgh. For most of May I wore two pairs of pants at one time, and that was my entire wardrobe. But Mama Rita had arrived in Wheeling in the heart of December.

"I gonna freeze my ass first, *cher,* and then I gonna freeze my tits," she said.

But we would stay in Wheeling until the next October. And the cold weather would at least keep Mama Rita's mind off banking. Since she didn't have to worry about rent or groceries any more, and since I'd been on my own for awhile, she apparently decided it was time to let Doug handle his own money. I'm not so sure that was wise.

Here's how Rusty & Doug ended up the youngest duo to join the Grand Ole Opry. The year 1957 started out with a bang when we played a great New Year's bash in Richmond, Virginia. I remember one of the other artists was Marty Robbins. Dee Kilpatrick was in the audience that night, scouting Rusty & Doug for the Grand Ole Opry. Dee had replaced Jim Denny the year before, when Mr. Denny refused to give up his own businesses to stay on as Opry manager. Jim Denny is the guy who told Elvis not to give up his day job after Presley played the Opry. He had founded a publishing company with Carl Smith and Webb Pierce, and WSM decided that was a conflict of interest. In 1956, Jim Denny left, taking Webb and Carl with him. His departure even caused Minnie Pearl to leave for a time.

Dee Kilpatrick, who was employed by Mercury Records, was a big critic of the Grand Ole Opry back then. It was Dee's opinion that the Opry didn't have enough teenagers in the audience, and he set out to change that. Since Dee considered rock 'n' roll the devil's music, he was always walking a fine line when he scouted acts. There were three he approved of: Rusty & Doug, the Everly Brothers, and Johnny Cash. Since our debut appearance back in 1955, we had been playing the Opry every chance we could get. So, in October 1957, we gave up our TV show in Wheeling, packed up everything we owned, and moved to Nashville. Since Mama Rita still had all her body parts and vital organs intact, despite what the cold weather had done to them, she came with us.

Back home in Louisiana one of the worst hurricanes of the century had ripped through places like Cameron, leaving hundreds dead and more homeless. But Southwest Louisiana seemed a long way off as the Kershaw entourage pulled into Nashville and quickly rented a house that would hold us all. We didn't exactly put down roots, but we settled in for a time. A month later, in November 1957, we signed on as official Opry members. We were Rusty & Doug, and we had Pee Wee with us on guitar.

Those were exciting times for us. The Opry was counting on the rockabilly acts to bring in new fans, and we did that. Porter Wagoner, Stonewall Jackson, and Ferlin Husky also joined the Opry in 1957. Nashville itself was a simmering pot back in the late 1950s. It even seemed a lot like Nightclub Row, back on Highway 90. For instance, it was in 1957 that Ernest Tubb had a little too much to drink, grabbed his pistol, went over to *Billboard* magazine, and took a shot at Bill Williams, the office manager. It seems Ernest had received a death threat over the telephone and, for some reason known only to him, he held *Billboard* responsible. Hell, I've felt like taking a few shots at *Billboard* magazine myself. Nonetheless, the Texas Troubadour was arrested and charged with public drunkenness. So it seemed to me that Nashville might have the same wild underbelly as Southwest Louisiana. Imagine the Bucket of Blood sitting in the Bible Belt.

There was another great thing about that New Year's bash in 1957. Marty Robbins ended up being a good friend, and he ranked up there with Johnny Cash as far as his loyalty and willingness to help newcomers along. Talented too. What a voice. People thought he was singing just for them. Like many of us, Marty was doing a lot of pop songs at that time. We all knew that if we wanted to compete with rock 'n' roll, we had no choice. With Marty singing songs such as "A White Sport Coat And A Pink Carnation," Rusty & Doug were looking hard at the pop market for potential hits.

We found one when we covered Jill Corey's pop release of the Melvin Ensley song, "Love Me To Pieces." When that release rose to No. 14 in the country, it got us into a whole new level of exposure. Dick Clark called Wesley Rose and invited Rusty & Doug to appear on his popular show, *American Bandstand.* The national visibility helped put our version on pop charts in markets such as New York, Chicago, and a few others. I always knew that our television show in Louisiana had made us appear stars, whether we were or not. But until the appearance on *American Bandstand,* I never really grasped the importance of television. You can get all the radio play in the world, but it will never do what even medium television exposure can do.

So there we were, a couple of Cajun kids sitting on top of the world. We were hobnobbing with the likes of Marty Robbins and appearing on Dick Clark's famous television show. At eighteen and twenty-one years old, Rusty and Doug Kershaw were also the youngest duo on the Grand Ole Opry.

That great feeling didn't last very long.

The draft board had come calling.

What did the US Army want with *me?*

They already had *Elvis.*

13

UNCLE SAM'S *FAIS DO-DO*

*"So you're that skinny-assed star from Nashville.
Well, I got news for you, son. I'm the only star around here."*

—Sergeant Anastas, US Army,
Camp Chaffee, 1958

Going into the army hadn't even been on the list of things I might do one day. As a matter of fact, it was not something I had ever wanted to do. And it was the last thing Wesley Rose wanted me to do. Rusty & Doug were on a roll by this time. Wesley was acting as our manager, as well as our record producer and publisher. That meant the stakes were high. Acuff-Rose had put a lot of money into promoting us because they saw in Rusty & Doug a chance to reach into the rockabilly market. That's where teenagers were starting to spend their dollars. And it was obvious that Nashville could compete in this market considering that "Bye Bye Love" by the Everly Brothers had just stayed at No. 1 for seven weeks. The town had to diversify a little, that's all.

I got my draft notice on January 24, 1958, my twenty-second birthday. A helluva present. I felt like crying. This hurt me a lot more than Little Frances or Ruby ever had. But even back then I understood that success waits for no one. Not even Elvis. I just didn't know how I'd fare being out of the limelight. Some reporter had asked Elvis what he'd do if rock 'n' roll died while he was in the army. Elvis said, "I guess I'll starve." We all knew Elvis wouldn't starve. But I was worried about Doug Kershaw, whether rock 'n' roll lasted or not. I talked over the whole thing with Wesley Rose, as well as with Joe Lucas, who was Acuff-Rose's vice president and a man who had become a trusted friend. Wesley Rose had influence with a lot of important people, but Uncle Sam wasn't one of them. What a mess. I mean, America wasn't at war with anyone. Korea was over and Vietnam was still just a spot on the map. But Uncle Sam needed some warm bodies to fill those empty uniforms. *Whose* body didn't much matter.

I could refuse to show up. I could keep working until they came and dragged my body out from under the bed, or wherever I was hiding. But we also knew that wouldn't work. Shit, I wasn't cut out to be a draft dodger. I hadn't even been able to dodge Big Robert that night he beat the crap out of me. And then there was the problem of Rusty. The army was sure to come looking for my little brother in a couple of years. Then *he* would be the one missing in action and our career would suffer all over again. We decided the best solution was for Rusty and me to volunteer together. Our prayer was that we'd both flunk our physicals. But we knew that was unlikely.

If we both passed, there was at least a flicker of hope that we'd be able to skip work classification school and go directly to Atlanta, Georgia, to the Third Army Headquarters, Fort McPherson, where we'd be assigned to Special Services. Special Services had a band made up of soldiers who had musical backgrounds. This band performed on radio shows and at fairs and rodeos. The idea was that young men in the audience would hear the performance and it would be so intoxicating that they would run down to the recruiting office and sign up for the United States Army. This band wasn't sponsored by Martha White. It was sponsored by Uncle Sam.

Faron Young, another Louisiana boy, had done his army time in the Special Services Band. Faron replaced Eddie Fisher as the army's recruiting star, and this allowed him to keep touring and having hit records. He was on such a roll that he even married the master sergeant's daughter. When the recruiting officer told us we could replace Faron Young, whose tour of duty was up, that was enough to convince Rusty and me. It even convinced Wesley Rose, especially since the promise included that the Kershaw brothers could stay together. So we signed up.

I'll say this for the US Army. They did give us a deferment until we could make arrangements for the band. I felt terrible about leaving Pee Wee behind, but there was nothing I could do. At twenty-seven, Pee Wee was past the age of desirability for the military. I pulled things together for him as best I could by fulfilling several concert dates and doing a recording session. That left me time to allow the finance company to repossess my 1957 Chrysler. In my mind, I saw myself coming out of the army as a rock 'n' roller. That's where the real money was. It was in the army that Elvis had gone from his country, blues, and gospel roots toward rock 'n' roll. I had even made a conscious decision about it by this time. I had just about stopped playing my fiddle on our records. Instead, I played it around the house, those times when I was lonesome for its sound. Even though I brought a fiddle to the *fais do-do* given by Uncle Sam, the instrument I planned on using most was my guitar.

If Rusty and I thought it was hard leaving Mama Rita when we moved off to West Virginia, we were in for another shock. Being in the army left us feeling akin to orphans. It was different when we were in Wheeling, playing music and having a good time. At least we could call home anytime until Mama Rita finally joined us. Not so in the army. I won't say we were mama's boys, but we had spent a good part of our lives within cuss range. I can still hear Mama Rita scolding Rusty and me for hanging onto her skirts when we were little boys.

"What's the matter with you two?" she'd ask. "You afraid your Mama Rita gonna fart and you won't smell it?" Or sometimes she'd say, "Get out from under my skirts. You tryin' to go back where you come from?"

If it had meant staying out of the army, I might have tried it.

Eventually, the duo of Rusty & Doug was on a DC-3 headed through the clouds for Fort Smith, Arkansas, airfare compliments of Uncle Sam. I tell you, we felt pretty special to be flown by the United States Army like that. I figured the perks had already started to pour in. After all, we *were* recording stars from Nashville. Then, when we landed, we were told that the army had sent a bus to carry us soldiers from the airport to Fort Smith. And that ride, too, had been quite relaxing. I put my feet up on the seat in front of me and stretched my legs out a bit.

"Our own bus," I said to Rusty. The only people I knew of back then who had their own personal bus were Faron Young and Webb Pierce. "Shit, this ain't too bad."

As the bus pulled up in front of the barracks, I was wondering why we hadn't enlisted earlier. That's when Rusty leaned forward in his seat and pointed toward the building.

"Who's that?" he asked.

I undid my legs and sat up to take a look. A uniformed man was standing out front, all serious, like he was waiting for a hearse or something. He looked like a cypress tree in a shirt. I knew he had to have a neck somewhere. I just couldn't see one.

"I think that's the sergeant who welcomes us," I told Rusty. We stepped off the bus into a big puddle of reality. Maybe I had a look of too much confidence on my face. All I know is that this sergeant homed in on me like I'd been the only soldier on the bus. I would learn later he was Sergeant Anastas, whom we nicknamed "Sergeant Nasty."

"So you're that skinny-assed star from Nashville," he said, his face about an inch from mine, spit flying. "Well, I got news for you, son. I'm the only star around here. And I can be downright demanding. Now get in the prone position and give me fifty push-ups!"

When you drop to the prone position, on all fours, you look a lot like a gator. I'd had better welcomes. I knew right then I could kiss any special treatment goodbye.

Basic training was the hardest physical thing I'd done since my days on that shrimp boat. But, unlike the shrimpers, soldiers aren't allowed to puke when the going gets shaky. And the army business seemed awful shaky to me. Even more shaky than the music business. As far as I could tell, it was just a lot of push-ups, marching, running, kitchen duty, latrine duty, and getting yelled at in general. But things started to lighten up when my instructor, Sergeant Lee Brown, approached Rusty and me and asked if we wanted to entertain at the NCO club.

"Hell, yes," we said in harmony. I was itching to play music again. Maybe throw back a few beers. And I had heard a rumor that the NCO club was air-conditioned. So the Kershaw brothers went down to the club and did our show. We must have gone over well with those noncommissioned guys because they invited us back, again and again. But it was not to last.

Here's the story of How Rusty Kershaw Got Out of the Army.

After Rusty and I had been marching and pushing up and running around in circles and getting yelled at regularly, it was time for our written tests. Man, oh man, if only I had known then what I know now. If I'd been smarter, I promise you, I'd have been dumber. But I've always seen everything as a challenge, so I wanted to do well on this test too. I kept working on the problems and rereading the questions to make sure I understood them. They had put us all in little cubicles so that we couldn't copy off each other's work. But every now and then I'd turn and glance back at Rusty. I could just see his head, nothing more. It seemed to me that he was just sitting there, staring at his paper. Once in awhile he'd glance up at me, shake his head, and mouth the words, "I don't know the answers."

The upshot of it all was that Rusty flunked his test. He flunked brilliantly, and they sent him back to Nashville with an honorable discharge. So much for Uncle Sam's promise that he wouldn't break us up. I hated to see Rusty go, but he did have a wife back home. The short of it was that the US Army had broken up the duo of Rusty & Doug yet again. But the *Doug* part continued to play solo at the NCO club during the rest of basic training and for the next six weeks that I spent there at clerical school. There I was, in the damned army without Rusty, screwing up my career for seventy-five dollars a month. Less tax. And then, I sent half of *that* home to Mama Rita.

Rusty was such a great guitarist that he found some session work when he got back to Tennessee. Chet Atkins, God bless him, helped out by giving Rusty a lot of studio work. But even Chet couldn't keep my brother solvent, and that's because Rusty never paid any attention to the business part of music, to getting himself booked for sessions or for road work. "All I want is to play guitar," he had often told me. It's understandable. Most musicians want to concentrate on their instrument. So unless the job dropped into his lap, Rusty probably didn't get it.

More importantly, Nashville had become a big temptation to Russell Lee Kershaw. Amphetamines were beginning to walk the streets in broad daylight, like hookers looking for a john. Among many songwriters and musicians, pill-popping had become more than a Saturday night wild party. It was soon woven into the fabric of the job as well as the pastime. Rusty was quick to catch up. He loved hanging out with that creative crowd more than anything in the world. If they were doing pills, he would be doing them too. I was no different, but Uncle Sam was looking out for me. No one was looking out for Rusty.

Wesley Rose, Joe Lucas, and I had been keeping in touch via the wonders of the telephone. It wasn't long before I noticed something restrained in Wesley Rose's voice every time he mentioned Rusty. He didn't seem to want to talk much about him. When he did say something, it was always vague. This went on for several months, this hinting that something was wrong. Eventually, there was no mention of Rusty at all from Wesley

Rose. I don't know if Wesley or Joe or anyone had ever tried talking to Rusty about the fact that there were problems. I sure didn't try. I was finding out that the army had just as many pill-poppers as the music business. And just like Rusty, I jumped in head first.

I've always had an addictive personality, but once the army got me I went a step further. I started hitting the bottle. Maybe it was because of Daddy Jack's drinking that I had never been much of a boozer before. A magic pill every now and then, sure, just to keep me going and to make life interesting. But the minute I found myself in an environment where I didn't want to be, it seemed I needed more than one pill at a time to make me forget. Two pills became three. Soon I was taking any kind of pill I could find. I'd wash them down with a drink. Between buying liquor and pills and sending Mama Rita money each week, I found myself in dire financial straits. Liquor wasn't so expensive, considering I could buy it at the PX on the base. But pills could only be found on the black market, and they sure as hell weren't cheap. I was kept quite busy trying to find ways to enlarge my medicine cabinet.

Damn good thing the country wasn't at war.

Here's how I see it. If I leave this world broke, so be it. That's how I came in. But I was still in the world and I had a money problem. In those early years, Mama Rita had always held tight to the purse strings. Once those dollars went down between her bosoms, it would take an emergency and an oil drill to get them out. Looking back, my mother did the right thing. At least she used that money to buy food and pay for things around the house. That's why I didn't mind sending her half of the seventy-five bucks a month the army was paying me. If I hadn't, I would have spent that money on pills and booze anyway. I had a clear choice. Quit the pills or find another way to pay for them. I decided to look for extra work.

That's how a lot of addicts are. They'll double the load just to pay for their habits. As soon as I left Fort Chafee and got stationed in Atlanta, I asked the sergeant about local bands that might be playing in the area.

"I'd like to find some extra work on my nights off," I explained.

"Son," he told me, "being in the Third Army Special Services Band is a privilege. You can't play off post."

That privilege put a crimp in my plans. And so did the next thing I heard about my little brother. Not long after I was told I couldn't work off base, I got a call from my old friend Joe Lucas. Joe asked me to come meet him in Atlanta on my first furlough. I was glad I'd be seeing him because I wanted to tell him about my situation. I needed extra money, and I wanted out of the Special Services. I couldn't see how my being in the Third Army Band was helping the career of Rusty & Doug. But before I could start complaining about my own state of affairs, Joe dropped a bomb.

"Rusty is really messing up," he told me. "Wesley's had a meeting about him at Hickory Records. You need to get him out of Nashville if you two expect to have a career by the time you leave the army."

The statement was so firm and so frightening that I didn't ask for details. Joe thought we should contact Pee Wee and see if he could persuade Rusty to come home. After I went into the army, Pee Wee had played drums for Jim Reeves for a time. He was now back in Louisiana. Joe and I found a pay telephone and he called Pee Wee. I stood outside the booth, listening as Joe dumped the same news on Pee Wee that he'd just dumped on me. Looking back on it, it was Rusty's life. If he wanted to mess it up, who were we to stop him?

These days, with the lessons time has taught me, I'd do it all differently. I'd tell Joe to talk to Rusty himself and let Rusty make his own decisions. This was the biggest problem facing the team of Rusty & Doug. *Doug* had always made the decisions, right or wrong, and *Rusty* always went along with them. He never seemed to have an opinion, never appeared to care one way or the other. "I just want to play guitar." Maybe it was connected to Daddy Jack and that June morning that my godfather rushed us from Bell City back to the houseboat where our father lay dead. Rusty was there, too, four years and four months old. Maybe he was waiting for a father to turn up one day and guide him. I know now that my being in charge all the time was a disservice to Rusty.

When I shuffled Rusty's problem over to Pee Wee, I did him a disservice, too. And Pee Wee only worsened the situation. Instead of telling Rusty the truth, that Acuff-Rose was unhappy with his actions, Pee Wee lied to him. He told him that Mama Rita was sick and that Rusty was needed back home in Louisiana. Pronto. So Rusty and his wife, Vesta, packed up and hightailed it for Jennings. Thinking Mama Rita was dying, Rusty didn't even bother to phone ahead. It must have been a long six hundred and fifty miles. When he pulled up into the yard, Mama Rita was working in her garden.

"What the hell you doin' home?" she asked. "Somebody die?"

I don't know what Rusty thought at that moment, but it had been a miserable way for Pee Wee to handle the situation. Yet how could I criticize? I was the one who had stood outside the phone booth in Atlanta as Joe Lucas dumped the problem on Pee Wee.

Back in my own world as I waited for word from Louisiana, I transferred out of Special Services and got a position as a postal clerk at the base hospital. Once I got bored with that, I applied for and got a job as an eye-ear-nose and throat doctor's assistant. This is the truth. I actually liked that job, one of the few things about the army that held any interest for me. I learned how to give hearing evaluation tests and how to give an eye examination. It wasn't bad work, but I had gone from shining shoes on people's feet to the other end of the body. Plus, once I was out of the Special Services, I could look for extra work in Atlanta wherever a musician might be needed to sit in with a band.

When Rusty learned that Pee Wee had lied to him, he moved to Atlanta to work with me. Luck was with us the night we ran into Pete Drake in a nightclub there. Pete had one hell of a fine band, the Sons of the South, and he himself played the best steel guitar I'd ever heard. Pete Drake would later go on to become one of Nashville's biggest legends. But at that time he had a radio show on WLWA in Atlanta, and he and the Sons of the South played around town a lot. Pete gave Rusty and me work, helping us out like he would other guys struggling to earn a living as writers and artists, guys like Roger Miller, Joe South, and Jerry Reed.

I was still interested in becoming a rock 'n' roll singer at that time. But one night, not long before I was due to get out of the army, something happened that snapped me right back to my Louisiana roots. I'd been sitting on my bunk, practicing some rock rifts on my guitar and thinking I was pretty fine. Nobody in the whole barracks was paying any attention to me. Everybody and his dog fooled around on a rock guitar. Out of boredom and maybe feeling homesick, I pulled out my fiddle and played an old Cajun tune. At first I just hummed along, but then I started singing in French. One by one, the men in the barracks stopped what they were doing and drifted over to my bunk. They were spellbound. I played another Cajun song and then another—those sad, mournful songs that carry the Cajun spirit back to the days when we went from pillar to post. Those Iry

Lejuene kind of songs. Then I played a *fais do-do* tune, a wild, Will Kegley fiddle-style. As my fellow soldiers applauded, I realized something important. What had gotten me this far and what could keep me going was my unique Cajun roots and my Cajun fiddle.

It's a funny world we live in. Those fat cats in Nashville thought they had it all figured out. They considered the fiddle a hillbilly instrument. I was now determined to prove them wrong. When my ass finally got out of the army, I would have a renewed love for Cajun music. That, and a brand new drug habit.

14

PILLS, PUNCH LINES, AND PROMISES

"Kershaw, you got yourself a monster. Better name it."
—Bob Moore, about "Louisiana Man"

When I got back to Nashville in 1960, it didn't take long to learn I wasn't the only songwriter moonlighting in the pharmaceutical business. *Pills. Amphetamines.* Trade names include Benzedrine, Dexedrine, Methedrine, Obedrine. Their street names were prettier and more poetic. They were bennies, speed, meth, old yellers, L.A. turnarounds, speckled birds, black beauties. I'm not sure who named some of these drugs, but they didn't have to put a lot of thought into it. Old Yellers, for instance, were little yellow pills the size of aspirins. They had *Simco* written on them, the name of the company that manufactured them. L.A. Turnarounds were powerful enough that you could take one in Music City, jump into your car, drive like a wild man to Los Angeles, then turn around and drive back to Nashville without a lick of sleep. Thus the name. Since they were a black capsule we also called them Black Beauties. Speckled Birds were a deep reddish-maroon, speckled on one side and white on the other. They were larger than Old Yellers, thicker, and were layered with some sort of time-release tranquilizer to help fight off the wilder effects and keep your feet a little closer to the ground. I suspect it got its nickname out of reverence to the old Southern hymn first made famous by Roy Acuff, "The Great Speckled Bird."

Just about everybody I knew and hung out with back then, all those musicians and songwriters, had their amphetamine of choice. And while I tried all of the above and more at one time or other, my favorite was Old Yellers. You could take one and get high as hell, but after four or five hours you could come down enough to get some sleep. L.A. Turnarounds were just too powerful for my liking. Who the hell wanted to drive to L.A., turn around, and drive back? Jack Kerouac and Neal Cassidy maybe, but they didn't write songs. I mean, you should at least do a show and get paid for it before you start back. With Old Yellers, I seemed to have a bit more control over my antics, and God knows I needed it.

In that place and time, in that world of songwriting, drugs, and booze, there was no one that I liked hanging out with, singing songs with, and popping pills with more than Roger Miller. He'll live on in my memory as one of the most entertaining, unique, and brilliant people I've ever known. Roger had gotten out of the army just as I was going in. We two had a lot more in common than just pill-popping. Since Roger had come from heavy-duty poverty he saw music as a way out, and so did I. Roger was a fiddle player, and so was I. Roger had been stationed at Fort McPherson and had played music in Pete Drake's band down at Katherine Jackson's Ballroom in Atlanta. So had I. And Roger was such a left-of-center, wild-eyed country boy that people sometimes didn't know how to take him in those early years. This was true of me too. Hell, we were damn near born on the same day, me on January 24, 1936, and Roger on January 2, 1936. He was more than a friend, no doubt about it. Roger Miller was my soul brother.

While Roger and I were on the same wavelength, we were rarely on anyone else's. At least not in those drug days. For example, we'd say or write something that made perfect sense to us but that was nonsense to anyone else. People would look at us and think we were crazy. We'd look at each other and know we were! That's why we became such close friends. Even when months and years went by without a contact, I'd run into Roger on the road or in some Nashville bar, and it was as if I'd seen him just the day before. He always had something funny to say. He used to tell people that as soon as he became rich he was "going home to pave the farm." Bill Anderson has a funny story about the night Roger had been up partying until dawn. When he saw the sun rising, Roger said, "Oh, oh, here comes God with his brights on." I have to tell you just one more Roger Miller story. Roger was the only white kid at his school in Oklahoma, his other classmates being all Native Americans. "Every time we had a school dance," Roger would say "it rained for a month." Becoming close friends with Roger Miller was one of the high points of my life.

After I got out of the army, I wasn't just partying and hanging out with guys like Roger. I was also writing songs and trying to get Rusty and Doug back on track. I finally got us booked on the Opry and even found us some road work. We were both as broke as anyone can get. Poor Mama Rita was feeling such a financial crunch herself that during the last months I was in the army she got married. Usually when Mama Rita wanted a boyfriend, she put her teeth in and found one. But this time she decided she needed a husband. I don't want to take anything away from her marriage to Gabe Hebert. She'd known him most of her life and considered him a good friend. But I do believe that she saw marriage the same as I saw music. It was a means to survive. Gabe Hebert was a good guy, but he was never anything like a father figure, not like Crip Cormier had been. The biggest problem Gabe had was a double dose of Cajun. He had a nose twice as big as mine.

I came out of the army really wanting to sharpen my writing skills, so I hit all the pickin' parties with a vengeance. Nowadays a Nashville pickin' party might be held for a few hours an evening at one of the local clubs. When the show is over, guitars go into cases and pickers go home. But in 1960, a pickin' party could mean hanging out at somebody's apartment or motel room for days, popping pills, drinking whiskey, and writing songs. Not all of those songs were worth a damn, but we had a distinction between a "pickin' party song" and a "real song." The pickin' party song might be an inside joke or just drivel of one sort or another. But if a songwriter happened to be brokenhearted or lonesome, he was more likely to write a real song.

I wrote my signature song at the one and only pickin' party I hosted at my little apartment, located across from Acuff-Rose. It was a bona fide dump, but we were used to drifting in and out of dumps back then. Roger was broke. Willie Nelson was broke. Hell, back then God was probably broke. Well, maybe not Harlan Howard, who had already written some big hits by that time. One picker who lived in the same building that I did was a young guy named John Ramistella, a.k.a Johnny Rivers. A New Yorker by birth, Johnny moved with his parents to Baton Rouge when he was still a baby, so we count him as a Louisiana boy, despite his East Coast beginnings. Audrey Williams, Hank's widow, had brought Johnny to town to try to get his career started, and she introduced me to him. No one knew at the time that Johnny would go on to such a major and successful career, but we all knew he certainly had the talent. All he needed was some solid luck, which he obviously found once he'd moved away from that run-down building full of pickers and dreams.

I walked into my own bit of good timing one night in the summer of 1960, when a bunch of us got together at my place to start writing and doping. It might have been that night—or the next day or the next. A party like that always felt like one very long day. But at some point, after I'd written six songs, I got thinking about my first home back in Louisiana. Mama Rita and Daddy Jack. The houseboat days. The gators and the muskrats. The old bayou itself. So I went back into the bedroom, away from the drugs and the din, and picked out a melody on my guitar. It had a folksy sound to it and I immediately wrote these words:

> *At birth Mom and Papa called their little boy Ned,*
> *raised him on the banks of a riverbed.*
> *Houseboat tied to a big tall tree,*
> *a home for my papa and my mama and me.*

Time stood still as my childhood came alive on the page in front of me. I could almost smell the coffee beans roasting and the steamed *couche-couche*, as Mama Rita and Daddy Jack got ready for another day on the bayou.

> *The clock strikes three, Papa jumps to his feet,*
> *already Mama's cooking Papa something to eat.*
> *At half past Papa he's ready to go,*
> *he jumps in his pirogue headed down the bayou.*
>
> *He's got fishing lines strung across the Louisiana River,*
> *got to catch a big fish for us to eat.*
> *Setting traps in the swamps catching anything he can,*
> *he's gotta make a livin' he's a Louisiana man.*
> *Gotta make a livin' he's a Louisiana man.*

I was a small boy again but in a grown man's body. I was pilled out of my head, and a long way from Tiel Ridge, Louisiana. But that's where my heart and mind had gone at that moment. Back home.

He's got muskrat hides hanging by the dozen,
even got a lady mink, a muskrat's cousin.
Got them out dryin' in the hot, hot sun,
tomorrow Papa's gonna turn them into mon.

They call my mama Rita and my daddy Jack,
little baby brother on the floor that's Mack.
Bren and Lin are the family twins,
big brother, Ed, is on the bayou fishin'.

On the river floats Papa's great big boat,
that's how my papa goes into town.
It takes him every bit of a night and a day
to even reach a place where the people stay.

I could almost hear the sound of Daddy Jack's going-out boat. *Chuk-chuk-chuk.* Funny, but there I was writing about a man I'd known and loved for such a short time. I must have been missing a father all those years because the words poured out of me that day like I'd been waiting to write them all my life.

I can hardly wait until tomorrow comes around,
that's the day my papa takes the furs to town.
Papa promised me that I could go,
he'd even let me see a cowboy show.

I saw the cowboys and Indians for the first time then,
I told my papa gotta go again.
Papa said 'Son, we've got lines to run,
we'll come back again, first there's work to be done.'

I know I used to take trips to town with Daddy Jack now and then, in the *Muskrat,* on those times when he sold his furs. I doubt he ever took me to see a cowboy movie. Still, in the words of my song, father and son had done that. It was wishful thinking.

He's got fishing lines strung across the Louisiana River,
got to catch a big fish for us to eat.
Setting traps in the swamps catching anything he can,
he's gotta make a livin' he's a Louisiana man.
Gotta make a livin' he's a Louisiana man.

When I finished it, I knew exactly what I had done. I'd written a hit song. It was my tribute to Jack Kershaw. I remember, vividly, coming out of the room and sitting on an old broken-down couch, next to the great bass player, Bob Moore.

"Bob," I said. "I don't have a title for this yet, but you know what? It ain't no pickin' party song." And that's the first time I played the song for someone else to hear. Bob Moore sat there listening, shaking his head, smiling. When I finished singing, he looked up at me.

"Kershaw," he said, "you got yourself a monster. Better name it."

I thought about that for a few seconds. Then I wrote *Louisiana Man* across the top of the page. I must have looked like death warmed over by this time. I'd been up for days and I was high on pills. God only knows what I was wearing for clothes. And I'm sure I hadn't bothered to shave or comb my hair. But I was so excited that I ran across the street to Acuff-Rose. That's how I knew it was daytime, when I saw that Johnny Redlidge, the engineer, was in the studio. Johnny was Wesley Rose's brother-in-law.

"I gotta demo a song I just wrote," I told Johnny. I must have looked pretty desperate because Johnny put a tape on the machine. In no time I had put down a guitar vocal.

Things seldom turn around fast though. "Louisiana Man" sat on Wesley's desk at Acuff-Rose for weeks, waiting for somebody to cut it. Truth is, it never entered my mind that some other artist would want to cut a song about growing up on a houseboat in Louisiana, with parents named Daddy Jack and Mama Rita. It sure seemed logical that Rusty and I should sing it.

I wouldn't have to think about that until later. In the meantime, I decided that Rusty and I would move back to Wheeling, West Virginia, out of necessity. Rusty was doing a lot of drugs, mostly pills and marijuana. I was popping pills and slugging back whiskey. I knew this drugging and drinking would be the end of us, and it wasn't going to stop unless we got out of Nashville. I couldn't slow down if I was constantly around drugs, and I figured Rusty was in the same boat. But we had no wheels. You'll remember that my last car, the Chrysler with the big fins, was repossessed when I went into the army. I figured we were going to have to walk to Wheeling.

By this time Dee Kilpatrick had left the Opry and opened a booking agency for Acuff-Rose. Since we needed an automobile to get us out of Dodge, I called Dee, and Dee called a car dealer he knew. They tracked down a brand-new Oldsmobile Ninety-eight somewhere out of state and had it brought to Nashville. Dee arranged the financing for me, too, with no money down. I was at the Acuff-Rose office on Franklin Road when the car dealer rolled up behind the wheel of my new Olds. Man, ain't show business great? Repossessed one minute, back on the road the next.

Of course, that still gave us no traveling money, so I approached Pee Wee for a loan. Pee Wee had just sold his house down in Louisiana and moved back to Nashville, so I figured he could float Rusty and me a few hundred to get us settled. After we got something going at the Jamboree and on the road, we'd send for him. There are some moments in life that you never quite get over, and what happened next is one of them in mine. I asked Pee Wee for help. He hemmed and hawed and finally pulled a twenty-dollar bill out of his pocket and handed it to me. It was just enough to insult me and to get us as far as Cambridge, Ohio. That's where Rusty and I ran out of money *and* gas. Luckily, we had a friend living up there.

Sonny Oden was the guitar player who had left Louisiana to come play for us in Wheeling. He had married the daughter of a Cambridge nightclub owner and was playing in his father-in-law's house band. I made Sonny a deal. Rusty and I would sing in his father-in-law's club every night for a week. In return, we would be given a place to stay, food to eat, and enough money to get us on to Wheeling. That amounted to about a hundred bucks. I'd made better wages as a kid shining shoes on the streets of Lake Arthur. But I had no choice.

When Rusty and I finally got to Wheeling, we checked into what I kindly called the Hotel Fleabag. The management was kind enough to let us move in on credit, and soon we were performing again at the Jamboree. Later on, Rusty's wife and kids came to join him, so he moved out of our cruddy hotel room and into his own place. I was really alone for the first time that I could ever recall, and it felt strange. I had always been in a house full to the rafters with people. Even in the army there were other soldiers everywhere you stepped. And, unlike my brothers, I was still single. Up to that point in time, I'd never even had a serious relationship. That was soon to change, however.

I can't remember who called who, but before I knew it I was on the phone to Donna Darlene, the singer who had been Buddy Spicher's wife. Only now she wasn't Buddy's wife anymore. And she wasn't in Wheeling. She was out in Vegas, singing in one of the lounges with Abby Neil and the Ranch Girls. During one of those long phone calls we agreed that Donna Darlene should come to Wheeling to see me. And that's what she did. When she finally flew in to the local airport, I was damn happy to see her. Before that day was over she had moved into my hotel room. I'm not really sure why that happened. Or how it happened so fast. There had been nothing going on between us before, other than a slight friendship. And while I was tired of a life of one-night stands, I have to be honest and admit that my one-night stands had been few and far between. I was not your regular Romeo. I often found myself as tongue-tied around girls as I'd been when I first laid eyes on Little Frances. Plus, between drugs and music, I had precious little time for women, except to window shop. So I happily let Donna Darlene Spicher move in.

We played house for several months while Rusty and I did the Jamboree on weekends. During the week, he and I headed out to supermarket openings and concession stands at drive-in movies. It wasn't what I'd dreamed of, I can tell you that. Then one day I got a call from Wesley Rose. He sounded as excited as I'd ever heard him before. Don Gibson had listened to "Louisiana Man" and wanted to record it. Don Gibson? Don Gibson had had some of the hottest hits in country music, songs such as "Oh Lonesome Me" and "I Can't Stop Loving You." Any songwriter as broke as I was should have jumped at that chance.

"No deal," I told Wesley. "I want Rusty and Doug to cut it."

Wesley mulled that over a bit and finally agreed. He booked the studio, and the Kershaw brothers headed back to Nashville.

The next part of the story is one of those tricks of fate that happen to us all. And it happened in *my* favor this time. Rusty had heard "Louisiana Man" before, but he'd never said whether he liked it or not. On that trip to Nashville, I finally found out what he thought of my tribute to our Daddy Jack.

"I don't like it," Rusty said.

"What?" I asked. I couldn't believe it. I knew for a fact it was the best damn song I'd ever written. It was a damn good song *period.* I was proud of it. I felt that the lyrics brought to life a part of the country that most folks knew little about, the swamps and bayous of Southwest Louisiana. Not a lot of songs were talking about houseboats and muskrat hides. But more importantly, it was about us, the Kershaws, our way of life back when we were children with our parents.

"I just don't like it," Rusty said again. His words stung, no doubt about it. But they gave me the brilliant idea to finally stop putting his name on my songs. Especially *that* song. I hadn't signed the publishing contract yet, but I did as soon as I got back to Nashville. For the first time ever, Doug Kershaw was the only name listed as writer.

The second thing that happened that would prove important to the song's future was a quirk of fate. I learned that Pete Drake had also moved to Nashville and was trying to get established as a session musician. I wanted Pete to play on "Louisiana Man," and I told Wesley so.

"Hire him," Wesley said.

The next important element was Wesley Rose himself. He suggested that we give the song a "Cajun feel" instead of the folk-ballad arrangement I'd given it. The man who did the arranging for Hickory Records was Boudleaux Bryant, one of Acuff-Rose's biggest songwriters and the real "music man" on Hickory's sessions. So we had a great team with Wesley as producer and Boudleaux as arranger. I sat down with Pete Drake and worked out the steel part so that he'd play steel like I was playing Cajun fiddle. Keep in mind, many of the Nashville recordings in the early 1960s were also influenced by the emergence of rock 'n' roll. Owen Bradley was over at Decca making a rock star out of Brenda Lee. The Everly Brothers had signed a million-dollar contract with Warner Bros. Records. A lot of people in Nashville were trying to expand the music. So with Pete Drake, Wesley Rose, Boudleaux Bryant, and me all mixed in together, "Louisiana Man" was a blend of country, Cajun, and rock 'n' roll. I feel damn proud when I hear people refer to it as a "classic."

A funny thing happened before the session. Boudleaux was such a great song guy. He and his wife, Felice, had written too many hits to count, including "Rocky Top," and many that had helped make the Everly Brothers famous, such as "Bye, Bye, Love," and "Wake Up Little Susie." Boudleaux was always willing to help other writers and take no credit for it whatsoever. Throughout my time at Acuff-Rose, I could always count on Boudleaux for no-strings mentoring. Before the session started, he called me aside.

"Doug," he whispered. "Did you realize that one of your bridges is shorter than the other?" I admitted to him that I didn't realize it.

"But it sounds fine to me anyway," I told him. Boudleaux just smiled.

"It's fine then, Doug," he said. "I just wanted to make sure you knew." That was Boudleaux. He'd never say something like that aloud in a room where everyone would hear it, just to make himself look good. He'd pull a person aside and give them a quiet tip. That's the mark of a good man, not just a professional one. We left the bridges the way I'd written them during that crazy pickin' party spree months earlier. Hickory released the song to radio in February 1961. Within two weeks it had caught on all across the country. Rusty & Doug were back in business. Even more surprising was the fact that the song was getting pop and rock air play. Who said the fiddle and steel couldn't go pop?

A hit song does wonders. We started getting more and more offers to play bigger and bigger concerts, including package shows. One of those tours took us on a seven-day run through Texas, and it gave me one of my favorite Roger Miller stories. By this time I'd lost my Oldsmobile Ninety-eight—it was also repossessed, or as the French might say, *repris possession*. I had now slipped down the ladder a couple of rungs to a used Ford Falcon. It seemed cars kept going through my hands like shit through a goose, but Roger didn't own a car at all at this point. He was even worse off, and that's why he was riding with Rusty and me. We had just done a show in San Antonio for A. V. Bamford at KBER radio station. A.V. not only ran the station, he promoted package shows all over Texas, Louisiana, Arizona, and New Mexico. Our fellow performers on this particular show in San Antonio were Ray Price and Faron Young. Ray and Faron had their own transportation. I don't remember what those two were driving, but I know it wasn't a beat-up gray Falcon. When we finished the San Antonio show, we headed west to El Paso, where A. V. Bamford had also booked us.

This is the story of Roger Miller and the Bag of Dope.

I was behind the wheel and high on Dexedrine. I had the little Ford Falcon cranked up to seventy-five miles an hour on that straight Texas road. About halfway between San Antonio and El Paso, Roger whipped out a bag of marijuana and rolled a joint for him and Rusty. I was never a big fan of marijuana. Pills got me high, but marijuana got me paranoid. I'd do pills by the handful—red ones, white ones, green ones, striped ones—but smoking marijuana scared me. Maybe it had to do with the fact that people went to prison in Texas for smoking dope. You could get drunk as a heartbroken sailor and not have to worry. But those funny cigarettes spelled j-a-i-l in the Lone Star State. So when I saw the joint and the two of them lighting up, I damn near drove the Falcon off the road. They started passing it back and forth like it was the Olympic torch.

"Get rid of that!" I told them. The open bag was lying in Roger's lap. "No way am I going to jail for shit I ain't even doing myself."

"You gotta be kidding," Rusty said. I guess he figured I had plenty of Dexedrines on me at the time. What was wrong with a bag of grass? Having it in their own personal belongings was bad enough. If we got searched, it was theirs. Having an open bag in a fast-moving gray Falcon filled with gray smoke as *they* passed a joint involved the driver.

"Are you really serious, man?" Roger asked.

"Damn serious," I said. "Get rid of it." I wasn't prepared for what happened next. Before I could add anything, such as "put it in your suitcase," Roger grabbed the bag of dope. He stuck his hand out the car window and scattered the whole bag to the West Texas winds.

All I had meant was put it away.

As Roger Miller often said, when they made him, they "smoked the mold."

Rusty looked like he was about to cry. He stared in the rearview mirror a long time, reminiscing over what might have been. Roger didn't say another word about his bag of dope. It wasn't until years later when we were both stars and playing on stage at Lake Tahoe that Roger leaned over and whispered in my ear.

"Hey, Kershaw, know what?" he asked. "There's some fine dope growing along a highway in Texas, and nobody knows how it got there." What could I do but smile?

Remember this. All Roger Miller stories had a punch line. It's just that sometimes he waited years to deliver it.

With all the commotion surrounding the new boost to our career, Rusty and I felt obligated to leave Wheeling and move back to Nashville. About this time, during the summer of 1961, a promoter offered us a show in California, a state I'd yet to get high in. We were on our way to this California gig when I decided that we might as well stop off in Louisiana. I figured it was time to take my new girlfriend home to meet Mama Rita. There must have been something romantic hanging on the humid air in Jennings, because it was there that Donna Darlene suggested we make our arrangement legal. I guess she caught me when I was high or happy—or both. And since Mama Rita hadn't told me to throw this new girlfriend into the Mermentau, I took it as a good sign.

"All right," I said to Donna Darlene. "Let's get married!"

We found a justice of the peace in Jennings and I asked him to marry us. We held the wedding at his house and it was a grand affair, a wedding fit for a big record star, with goats and chickens wandering among the wedding guests. In the middle of our vows, a rooster strutted over and relieved himself on my boot. I guess he knew something I didn't. I looked down at that little wad of rooster crap. *This is a shitty thing I'm doing*, I thought. But it was too late. It was a good punch line when you think about it. And it was the first of many punch lines from my marriage. There's a saying in Louisiana that rain or tears at a wedding means bad luck. In that case, it should have been raining buckets and I should have been crying like a baby. At least it would have washed away the rooster shit.

After the California trip my new bride and I headed back to Nashville, where I bought a house in the suburb of Madison, just north of the city. That's where the two of us started down the road to married life. In all honesty, I guess Donna Darlene started down that road. Rusty and I were on another road at the time, the one that led to the next show. And the next. And the next. Like most entertainers, I was gone so much that I was just a shadow husband. I was home long enough during the next few years, however, to father two boys. Doug Jr., my firstborn, came into the world on January 5, 1962, in Madison, Tennessee. He happened to be born at a Seventh-day Adventist hospital, and we learned too late that they do not believe in inducing labor. Donna Darlene had a very long and painful delivery as a result, but Doug Jr., was born healthy. So there I was, a father at last. All my life I had been ready and willing to take on responsibility when it came to my mother and my brothers. But I discovered that being a father was the sweetest responsibility I had yet been given in my life. I wanted, and intended, to be a damn good one.

On the career front, however, things weren't going so well with Hickory Records. I owed everything to Wesley Rose, there was no doubt about it. And I sure as hell enjoyed working with him and the other guys there— Boudleaux Bryant, Joe Lucas, and fellow songwriters like Johnny Rivers. But Hickory Records was still an independent label. The longer I was in the business, the more I understood that comparing an independent label (no matter who owned it) to a major label was like comparing the county fair to the state fair. The county fair is nice. It's got bright lights and a Ferris wheel. It's even got some cotton candy. But it sure as hell ain't the state fair.

Every time we played a town where the deejay hadn't heard from our record promoters and the local record store wasn't stocked with Rusty & Doug records, I felt that difference. I'd walk into a store and see the bins piled high with product from Decca, RCA, Capitol, and Columbia. Maybe they had a few Hickory recordings and maybe not. It made my job twice as difficult. I was trying to phone ahead to learn if our songs were being played on the radio. And to ask if the record company had stocked the record store. This was in addition to contacting local promoters and venues about how the show was being promoted. We were reminded of the need for change every time we turned around. Out there on the road in package shows, it became painfully obvious that a Faron Young record on Capitol or a Jim Reeves record on RCA was being distributed and promoted far better than any record on the Hickory label. And yet the thought of leaving our home base was almost too frightening and painful to consider.

Money and drugs, or the combination of the two, were another problem. We were making a bit of money, but not enough to support two families. Rusty and I didn't help our finances any by taking pills or buying booze and an endless stream of cigarettes. And Rusty always seemed to have marijuana to smoke when he felt like it. But, as any artist will tell you, when you're the star coming to a venue, there's always a crowd of smiling faces standing around backstage, folks just aching to reach out to you, their hands full of drugs or a drink. It's all for free just because you're a star. Oddly enough, the pills never did seem to present a problem for our performances. Being high just meant higher energy, and I was all for that. But with every mile we traveled, I saw success slipping through our fingers. The road shows couldn't take the place of solid radio exposure. We were in danger of becoming what Rusty had handed Jay Miller as a hook line. We were *has-beens* before we ever *had been*. But we kept beating the rug just the same. We put out single after single, yet we never found a national follow-up hit for "Louisiana Man" and "Diggy Liggy Lo."

In 1963, we finally left Hickory and went over to RCA Victor. Our old Opry pal Chet Atkins was over there, and he'd always been a good friend and supporter. We signed on with RCA to record with Chet Atkins. We had high hopes, but when all was said and done, Chet was probably just doing us a favor. That's the kind of man he was. As 1963 drew to a close, the duo of Rusty & Doug seemed to have a future. That's all any entertainer can ask for.

Speaking of futures, I was about to become a father again. My second boy was born on December 9, 1963, at Vanderbilt Hospital in Nashville. Hospital officials refused to let Donna Darlene and me take the new baby home, since we still hadn't decided on a name for him. According to their rules and regulations, there had to be a name on the birth certificate. I had just signed with RCA Victor, and that sounded like a damn good name to me. *Victor.* So we named the baby Victor Conrad, the latter being the name of Donna Darlene's father. Good thing I wasn't still on Hickory Records. I'd have a son named Hickory Kershaw.

Now I was the father of two boys, just as Daddy Jack had once been father to four. I was certain that I could avoid the mistakes in raising my own children that Daddy Jack had made with his. I would embrace only Jack Kershaw's best qualities. I was sure of it. But we think a lot of things when we're young, when the biggest mistakes of our lives are still lurking up the road. I thought I'd be a great father. I was dead wrong. It wouldn't be the last time.

Up until this time Roger Miller had had just one top-ten hit, "When Two Worlds Collide." That was soon to change. One night very early in

1964, I rolled into Nashville a day sooner than I'd expected thanks to a canceled gig. I also rolled smack-dab into another Roger Miller story. I just didn't know it at the time. It was about 3 in the morning when I pulled into our garage and closed the door. In the kitchen I ate a doughnut and drank a glass of milk before I headed to bed. I was dead on my feet. Suddenly, I heard someone knocking on the front door. I went to answer it and there was Roger, standing on my steps like he was selling Bibles or something. The minute he saw me, he got all excited.

"Doug!" he said. "I've just recorded a new album!" Now if this had happened between two schoolteachers who had to get up early and go to work or two accountants, it wouldn't go down. But it was a scene between two songwriters, two buddies, two wild entertainers. Not only that, to hear that Roger Miller had just recorded a new album put the energy right back into me.

"Well, hell, come in and play it!" I said. Donna Darlene, hearing the racket, got up and came out of the bedroom to join us. So Roger Miller played us his entire album, which included "Dang Me." The rest is musical history, of course. "Dang Me" was soon released, and it would stay at No. 1 on the charts for six long weeks. It would also be the smash hit that would define Roger Miller as a major star. On that night in 1964, Donna Darlene and I sat there on the sofa and were thunderstruck by the quality of Roger's album. What a major talent this man was.

"Roger," I said, "you're gonna be a big star." I knew that "Dang Me" alone could do it. When Roger was ready to go, I walked him to the door. That's when he told me that he was leaving Nashville. That very night. I looked out to the street and, sure enough, his old car was packed to the roof with everything he owned.

"I'm heading to Los Angeles," Roger said. He was ready to make his fortune, but the only problem was he didn't have much money. The album that would make him rich still hadn't been released. He was between fame and a hard place. I checked my pockets and gave him all I had. Ironically, it was only twenty dollars, the same amount Pee Wee had given Rusty and me the time we were trying to get our asses to Wheeling. I guess all us Kershaw boys—and Roger Miller, too—would have been better off with Mama Rita stuffing our paychecks down between her big bosoms. There wasn't a banker among us.

I won't tell you now the punch line of The Night Roger Miller Played Me His New Album. That will come later. Roger always took his time in delivering the ending. And so will I.

In the meantime, as the rest of 1964 loomed heavy on the horizon, punch lines were the least of my worries. Trouble was on its way, like one of those hurricanes that move in fast and unmerciful in Southwest Louisiana, uprooting everyone and everything in its path. Good old-fashioned trouble was about to rear its ugly head in both of my marriages, the one to Donna Darlene and the one to Rusty Kershaw.

I just didn't see it coming.

15

TROUBLE

"I've always been in tune with trouble, and I heard its
music that night loud and clear. It sounded a lot like the steady
rattle of a snake."

—Doug Kershaw

RCA had released a few of our singles by this time, "Cajun Stripper," "My Uncle Abel," "Pirogue," and "Malinda." Rusty & Doug kept on hitting the top of the regional charts, but we couldn't seem to break through nationally.

Lesson #1 about major record labels. If you're not a priority act, forget it. Go mow the lawn. Do something useful with your life.

Lesson #1 about staying married. Pay attention. Maybe even mow the lawn once in a while. That way you can see if someone's hiding in the tall grass.

While I was struggling on the road, my marriage to Donna Darlene was falling apart back in Nashville. If I could figure out why people get married without thinking it through, I'd hang up a shingle and start shrinking heads for a few hundred bucks an hour. I wasn't ready for marriage, and I guess Donna Darlene wasn't ready for it either.

Down in Southwest Louisiana we have a ritual we call "jumping the broom." This is when the bride and groom jump over a broomstick to symbolize their wedding vows to each other. That insane act alone should be enough to alert a naive person. But I had jumped the broom and sure enough, the day came when I had to sweep up my mistake. Looking back on it, I thought of Donna Darlene as a pretty girl with a pretty voice. She was someone who helped me not feel so alone. But I never thought about what she might be like for the long haul. Or what I'd be like, for that matter. I can say this. She married me knowing that I was fooling around with pills and would continue to do so. I married her not knowing a lot of things. We weren't Ward and June Cleaver.

To tell the damn truth, I didn't pay much attention to what was going on with my wife in Nashville. When I was out on the road, I figured she was taking care of the boys, the house, and all those other wife expectations men had back in the early 1960s. I suppose I had them too. But remember, I was raised by Mama Rita. Mama Rita would have made Gloria Steinem run for cover. Looking back on it now, I know that Donna Darlene had one major expectation of me as husband, and it didn't fall into the *take-out-the-trash* category. She hoped I would be a boost to her own career ambitions. But I wasn't. Hell, I was too busy trying to stay on the lily pad myself. I was in no position to give anyone else's career a boost. You need jumper cables for that, and I was about to receive a *Dear John* letter from Chet Atkins and RCA. I'm not kidding. I got a letter.

Sometime in 1965, Chet Atkins had his cohort Bob Ferguson write a letter informing me that Rusty & Doug were being dropped. Knowing Chet, I'm sure he didn't like this part of his job one little bit. But there ain't nothing quite like struggling to get on a major label only to be dropped from it. It's a longer, more painful fall. But Rusty & Doug were still being booked at a lot of clubs, so we dusted ourselves off and kept on making a living in music. I don't exactly remember when I first started hearing rumors about my wife being unfaithful, but I do know the one that broke up my marriage.

This is the story of Donna Darlene and Shot Jackson.

I was on the road with Rusty, doing a show down in Little Rock, and I'd been trying all day to get Donna Darlene on the phone back home in Nashville. No answer. All day long. When she finally came home long enough to pick up the telephone, I asked her where she'd been. She told me she'd been someplace in Nashville, a shop or something. I asked her how she got over there since we had just the one car and I was using it on this road trip.

"Shot Jackson loaned me his car," Donna Darlene said. I thought about this. *Shot Jackson.* I knew Shot from my Opry days. But shit, I didn't know him well enough that I felt comfortable about his giving my wife a car to sport around town in while I was on the road. *Shot Jackson loaned Donna Darlene his car?* Shot was a well-known and well-liked guy in the music community. He was an earlier generation from me, about fifteen years older. He had started out playing steel and dobro with Cousin Wilber Westbrook and later with the Bailes Brothers. He'd recorded albums on Pacemaker and Specialty Records. At the time he was letting my wife borrow his automobile he was employed by Roy Acuff as a part of his Smokey Mountain Boys. And he'd just designed an electronic pedal steel guitar with Buddy Emmons, another steel-playing great. Shot and Buddy were marketing the instrument under the name Sho-Bud. I was actually better acquainted and friendlier with Buddy Emmons than with Shot Jackson. But I sure as hell *knew* Shot, and for some reason he had found it in his heart to let Donna Darlene drive his car while I was in Little Rock.

Figure that one out.

Did I mention that Shot had also designed a wife and kids?

He was as married as my wife.

I did my best on the telephone that day to get Donna Darlene to take the car back to Shot. But she informed me in no uncertain terms that she would do as she pleased, whenever she pleased, and with anybody she pleased. I hung up and just lay there on the bed, thinking. I knew Shot wasn't starting up a car-rental service, so I finally figured it out. His automobile wasn't the only thing he was letting my wife use. I started asking hard questions of our mutual friends. They said the affair had been going on for quite a while by the time I learned of it. We had some hell-raisers over her new boyfriend, Donna Darlene and I did. They were heated arguments, no doubt about that. Me yelling. Her yelling. Both of us yelling in harmony. Donna Darlene was no shrinking violet. She could hold her own in any fight. But it never came to violence, as she later claimed in court. I might be a *fils du putain* when I think it's necessary, but I don't beat up on women.

Mama Rita would've kicked the shit out of me if I had.

Donna Darlene and I did have one particularly bad fight. Speaking of our *heated* arguments, she threw an electric iron at me, just missing my head, and I slapped the side of her face. I'm not proud of that. It happened in the midst of a fight over her affair with Shot, at a time when I felt about as hurt and humiliated as a man can. I wish we had never had that fight, but we did. I slapped her once, and it never happened again. But that's not what she told the judge later on in divorce court.

So I took a few more pills, got a little drunker, and wrote myself a song that I titled, "Hardly Anymore."

You won't let me love you, hardly anymore.
And you won't let me kiss you, hardly anymore.
And you won't let me show you just how much I care,
No, you won't let me love you, hardly anymore.

Guess I couldn't think of anything to rhyme with "iron."

Did I ever think of beating up Shot Jackson? An old friend once asked me that question. "Beat him up?" I said. "Hell, I wanted to kill him." And I did, too, at least when I first found out about his affair with my wife. But then I remembered the advice Daddy Jack gave his own brother. "Get out of Louisiana or die." I figured the best thing to do was to leave town. Let tempers cool down a bit. I didn't want to end up in jail over Shot Jackson bunking down with my wife.

"You know what?" I said to Rusty. "We gotta get out of Nashville. Let's move to Texas." So late in 1965, Rusty and I headed first to San Antonio and then on to Houston. And that's how two more Kershaws moved to Texas, at least for a time.

I figured that eventually Donna Darlene and I would work it out so I'd be able to see the boys when I came to Nashville to record. But her next move was to pack up Doug Jr. and Victor and move in with Shot Jackson. By this time Shot had gotten himself a fast divorce from his own wife. I didn't care one way or the other about losing my wife. Well, that's not exactly true. I had no doubt that Donna Darlene saw Shot Jackson as a man with jumper cables, someone in a position to help restart her singing career. But I was still embarrassed as hell that guys all over Nashville knew that Shot had taken my wife and kids away from me. The public part was the humiliation of it all. The private part was the pain of losing my two sons.

In a big nutshell, RCA dropped me, my marriage fell apart, and my relationship with Rusty was going straight to hell in a handbasket. I guess Rusty and I really started to grow apart while I was in the army, and it didn't get any better when I got out. I have to say that I was carrying the load for both of us. I was the one doing the hustling, the bookings, and the songwriting. I don't know which was worse, listening to Pee Wee give

148

me orders back in the 1950s or listening to me give Rusty orders in the 1960s. But Rusty didn't *want* any part of the decision-making process, not like I did. And maybe one reason for that was that he was too busy hanging out with his crowd. And a bad crowd it was. A dumb crowd too. The guys I hung out with were doing drugs, but at least we paid attention to where we were and tried to stay a step ahead of the law. Rusty seemed willing to jump right into the law's lap. He'd do drugs anywhere and with anybody. It didn't matter if he knew them or even if he trusted them. Looking back now, it's easy to see that he must have felt his own pain from those swamp days on the houseboat, Daddy Jack's suicide, and that long stretch of poverty we had to go through as a family without a father. If I had known back then how to help Rusty—hell, if I'd known how to help *me*—we'd have all been better off. But I didn't. Those were the days when no one had even heard of a self-help talk show.

It was difficult to stay put in Texas knowing my boys were living in Shot Jackson's home, as if he were their father. Once, I even talked a friend of ours, Glen Holder, into driving me from Houston back to Nashville so that I could see the kids. We had met Glen in Houston at one of our shows. A pipelines welder by day, he was a big Rusty & Doug fan by night, and he often came to hear us when he could. I bet Glen Holder never dreamed he'd end up driving the Kershaw brothers around while our social lives fell apart. But that's almost what happened. Good thing he had a car.

Glen drove me from Houston to Nashville for my big Sho-Down at Sho-Bud. We covered the eight hundred miles without a break, tires on tar except for gas-ups and restroom stops. Glen finally pulled the car up in front of the sign that said Sho-Bud, across from Ernest Tubb's Record Shop down on Broadway. That was the street Glen Campbell made famous in "Rhinestone Cowboy." I got out and went inside while Glen waited in the car. Sure enough, there was Donna Darlene, and she had Doug Jr. with her.

"You can't see the boys, Doug," she said. I didn't say anything. I just reached down and took Doug Jr. by the hand. I walked out of the store with him following along beside me. Donna Darlene starting screaming her head off, and that's when Shot appeared outside. He was with a couple of his own sons, boys in their late teens, maybe early twenties, but big enough to be support for their daddy.

"Just try to get Donna Darlene and the boys back," Shot said to me. "I got Roy Acuff on my side." It sounded like one of those cowboy movies I used to watch as a kid back in Lake Arthur. Shot might have said Roy *Rogers* instead of Acuff. What he meant, of course, was that he had money and power behind him. Roy Acuff was, as I said earlier, half partner of the extraordinarily successful Acuff-Rose, my music publisher. Acuff-Rose had published all of my songs up to that point. And Acuff-Rose owned Hickory Records, the label Rusty & Doug had recorded for.

Hearing him say that, I should have jumped on Shot right there. But I didn't. I had to think of my kids, of what all this fighting was doing to them. It wasn't easy to get in the car and drive back to Texas. But we did, Glen and I. Tires on tar.

It was after we'd left San Antonio and moved to Houston, in the summer of 1966, that the whole she-bang finally unraveled for Rusty & Doug. I remember we were booked to play the Big D Jamboree in Dallas. By this time, the gray Ford Falcon had flown the coop. The bank had taken it back. Rusty and I had each gotten Ford station wagons after that, but those had also been repossessed. It was good ole Glen Holder, the pipelines welder, who drove Rusty and me to Dallas. We went on stage that night and I did a real sweat-flying, fiddling kind of show. Afterward, it was still early, so Rusty and I decided to drop by a local party we'd been told about. Now I knew for a fact that the guy who would be our party host was a Dallas drug dealer. I trusted him about as much as Mama Rita trusted J. D. Miller. But like two fools and still high on the adrenalin rush of the show we'd just done, Rusty and I went to a drug dealer's party. Doesn't that sound like a catastrophe waiting to happen? But this is the trap that a lot of entertainers fall into. You go on stage and perform for an hour or even two, all those cheering fans, the music going right into your bones. Then you come off the stage and suddenly it's all over. But you're not ready for it to be over, so you follow the high, as if it's a bright balloon floating just ahead of you. You find a party somewhere, anywhere. You take some pills, you smoke some pot, you drink some booze. You follow that adrenalin rush until your body won't do anything else but crash. That's when the balloon finally bursts.

First thing we did when we got to the party was find us each a stash. Rusty bought some marijuana, and I bought some pills. Once I had those pills in my pocket I wanted to hit the road. I had taken a quick look around the house and it was obvious that these guys were into some serious shit. It wouldn't be until years later, when I saw the famous bar scene in the movie *Star Wars,* that I'd ever seen a group of faces like that. I mean, they were heavy drug users. I've always been in tune with trouble, and I heard it coming that night loud and clear. It sounded a lot like the steady rattle of a snake.

"Let's hit the road while we still can," I whispered to Rusty. He blew me off, but I kept on pestering him. "Come on, Rusty, let's get back to Houston." He wouldn't listen. I gave him an ultimatum. "You can leave with me right now or you can find your own way home." Rusty just waved me away, as if to say he didn't give a shit. So I hit him in the stomach. I really did. Remember, I was as drunk and as high as he was. I just happened to have enough sense left to know we should get out of there. Guess what Rusty did when I hit him. He laughed, a big hearty laugh. It got the attention of all the serious dopers, mutants, and full-time thugs in the room. They probably thought it was rude of me to punch my brother in the stomach that way. Worse yet, I was spoiling the party. I knew it was time to cut and run.

It was late, but Glen and I got into his car and drove all night.

"We'll have to come for him tomorrow," I said, and Glen nodded.

To keep my mind off Rusty, I listened to the radio as the white line on the highway ate up all those vast Texas miles. My little Gibson guitar rode in the back seat, where Rusty should have been. Morning had broken bright and clear over Houston when we finally arrived at the apartment Rusty and I had rented. I was as tired as a man who's just driven two hundred and fifty miles late at night, after a kick-ass show and a drug party should be. I'd no more than dragged that little Gibson guitar into the apartment and stood it up in the corner when the phone rang. It was Billy Deaton, the guy who booked shows for Rusty and me. He was also our manager, and he was calling me from his office in San Antonio.

"Doug," he said, "you got some big trouble son."

In other words, *Houston, we've got a problem.*

I knew it was Rusty. And I knew Rusty was no John Glenn.

This wouldn't be a happy landing.

It wasn't.

"Rusty's been busted for drugs," Billy went on. "He's in a Dallas jail."

I should have seen it coming. I should have dragged his ass kicking and screaming right out of that house and thrown him into the back seat of the car, next to the Gibson.

"Between the bail and the legal fees," Billy added, "it's gonna cost eighteen hundred dollars to get him out."

"Shit, Billy," I said. "I don't have eighteen hundred dollars. And neither does Rusty."

I didn't know what to do, but I figured Louisiana would be the best place to start planning. I'm not clear all these years later how I got to Louisiana. I think I caught a bus. I might have flown, but if I did it would have been on the wings of a bad check. I probably took a Greyhound. I was hoping against hope that Mama Rita might have some money. But she didn't, and neither did Pee Wee. Money was tight. I thought my next best bet would be Nashville, namely Acuff-Rose. I felt in my heart, however, that my chances of getting any more advances from my publisher were slim. The Kershaw brothers were no longer anybody's fair-haired Cajuns. I still had to try. I probably took another bus on to Nashville. If I flew, it would have been on the wings of another bad check. All I really know is that I went to Nashville and got the answer I had expected all along. A flat no. I don't even blame Acuff-Rose. *I* wouldn't have loaned money to Rusty & Doug Kershaw then either. And I sure as hell wouldn't have taken one of our checks.

But those were desperate times and, as the saying goes, they required desperate measures. I must have had some bad checks left, because I left Nashville and flew to San Antonio. I had to talk to Billy Deaton. I told him the truth. I could probably walk on water easier than I could raise the bail money for Russell Lee Kershaw.

"You're gonna have to come up with it somewhere Doug," Billy said. "You don't want your brother to stay in that jail." He waited a beat. "Do you?" he added.

You know this kind of guy. He'll tell you your mama shouldn't be in one of those cheaper caskets that worms can penetrate. He'll ask you, "You don't want your mama in a cheap casket, do you? Better to buy the Super-Duper Copper Deluxe model, and I just happen to have one for sale."

You know the kind.

"Well, what the hell can I do?" I asked. I felt a panic coming on. "I don't own anything I can sell."

152

There was a short silence. I think this is what is generally known as a *pregnant pause*. That's when someone is fucking with you.

"I'll buy half the BMI performance royalties for your song," Billy finally said, his words measured. "And half the mechanicals. For eighteen hundred dollars." I knew right away what song he meant. "Louisiana Man." Mechanical royalties is the fee paid to a songwriter every time someone produces a record of their song. He wanted that and half the writing credit. I was dumbstruck. Even though I'd written almost all of my songs by myself, "Louisiana Man" was the first one that finally had just my name on it. I could shout to the world that it was mine and mine alone. I had to think of some other way.

"Maybe, Billy, I could borrow the money from you?" I asked.

"No, that's too much of a gamble for me to take," Billy answered.

I sat there trying to think of what I could do. In the end, I didn't have any other alternative. So I agreed. Billy had the papers drawn up faster than a deerfly can bite your ass. I signed them. I should have used my own blood as ink. Billy Deaton and I drove from San Antonio to Dallas with the eighteen hundred dollars and sprung Rusty from jail. Then Billy brought us back to San Antonio. I had decided by this time to just let the apartment in Houston go. I'd get back there when my life straightened out enough to allow it. As it turned out, that was a year later. The manager had sold everything I'd left behind—clothes, furniture, dishes, you name it. I can't say I blame him, but I wish he'd have held onto all those song-books of mine. They were filled with original song lyrics. But he sold those, too.

When court time rolled around that Texan judge sentenced Russell Lee Kershaw to two years of probation, with the provision that he not leave the Lone Star State during that time. But here's what I got out of it.

"Louisiana Man"
written by
Billy Deaton and Doug Kershaw

I swear to God.

Billy Deaton wouldn't know a swamp from a beach, yet there's his name on my autobiographical song. It's even *first*, given the nature of the alphabet. Billy Deaton's name on a song about Daddy Jack stringing his fishing lines on the river. A song about Mama Rita. A song about our houseboat tied up to a cypress tree. There's something wrong with that picture. But there I was, looking square at it. I was living a life apart from my boys. I was broke. I was about to be divorced. I was without a record label. And I was even without a singing partner, unless I wanted to waltz across Texas for the next two years with Rusty. Instead, I danced again with the devil.

"Billy," I said, "I need to get some money so I can get back to Nashville." Billy didn't even pause this time. I guess he saved his foreplay for the first time he screwed somebody. And that's how I sold Billy Deaton the second half of the mechanicals to "Louisiana Man." For six hundred dollars.

Got to make a livin' he's a Louisiana man.

I went over to Billy Deaton's office and got the money. My plan was to go to the airport and get out of there as fast as I could. Rusty didn't want me to leave, but I had no choice. He was confined to Texas for the next two years. And he and I were confined to a career that wasn't going anywhere. I gave him half of the six hundred dollars. I felt that made us even, with each of us starting out clean. Since Rusty couldn't leave the state, Glen Holder got him a job as a welder's helper on the pipelines.

With my half of the six hundred dollars, I took a cab from Billy Deaton's office to the airport—for some reason the little bastard didn't even drive me—and I bought myself a one-way plane ticket to Nashville. I had nothing but the clothes on my back and a Gibson guitar, minus its case. I had left my fiddle in Louisiana when I went there to see if Mama Rita had any money. The guitar meant more to me at that period of time than my fiddle, considering I was still three years away from being the "Ragin' Cajun." But with my guitar I could write songs.

As a last resort, Rusty even had me paged at the airport. He told me again that he wished I would change my mind. I told him again that I couldn't do it.

"No one's to blame for this Rusty," I said. "Not you. Not me." Then, the Gibson guitar and I boarded the plane. I looked down as we lifted up off the ground over San Antonio, Texas. Considering that some pretty impressive guys named Davy Crockett and Jim Bowie had gotten their own asses whipped in San Antonio, at the Alamo, I guess I shouldn't have felt so bad that Billy Deaton had whipped mine. It would be many years before the Billy Deaton story worked itself to an end. But that's later. In the meantime, I had a new life to build for myself. By the time the plane approached Berry Field in Nashville, I had done my share of soul-searching. I had grown up with people everywhere I stepped. I had spent my childhood with a family of brothers all crammed onto one houseboat, or in one tiny chicken coop or in one small house. Now I was at center stage, and I was standing all alone.

As far as my next personal move, I had to wait and see if the winds of change would blow Donna Darlene's way and she'd let me see my boys again. As far as my next career move I would, for the first time in my life, be just Doug Kershaw. It was time. The truth is that I didn't *want* to be Rusty & Doug anymore, but I also didn't know how to be a solo act. Ever since I'd been a kid, I was a part of something bigger when it came to my music, whether it be a band or a duo. Even in the army I had always performed with Rusty or with band leaders such as Pete Drake. This is an amazing thing, but for years after Rusty and I split, I'd subconsciously turn and look for him on stage. That's kind of like what happens when someone has an arm or a leg amputated. You keep feeling it there, even though it's long gone.

As the wheels of the plane touched down in Music City, I wondered how the gods that be would view me now. The solo Cajun. But I was certain that if a new career were to rise from the ashes, it would have to happen in Nashville, right where the fire had gone out. If I was going to sink this time, it would be in my own houseboat. Even if Billy Deaton's name was on one side.

16

FROM THE FRYING PAN INTO *LA MERDE*

"Chief, I got the answer to your problem.
You need to start wearing a mask like them professional wrestlers."

—Webb Pierce, drunk, and giving me career advice.
Nashville, 1968

Now that I was back in Nashville, I had to find myself a home. And with my limited funds, "home" meant a seedy room in a seedier motel on Gallatin Road, not far from Acuff-Rose. I can't remember if the rates were hourly, but it struck me as that kind of place. I settled in, unpacked my suitcase, stood my little Gibson guitar up in the corner, and took stock of my situation. The first thing I did was to phone Donna Darlene and ask about the boys. She hung up on me. I swear every time that happened I could see that pile of rooster shit on the tip of my boot. It seemed to be growing bigger every day. I decided I should get my bearings before I went after a solo recording contract. The best way for me to do that would be to concentrate on my songwriting. I was still a part of Acuff-Rose, even if the relationship was strained when Rusty and I left Hickory Records and Donna Darlene moved in with Shot Jackson. Once again, I started hanging out around Nashville, winding up at pickin' parties and writing songs.

A new writer named Kris Kristofferson had just hit town. He and I ended up running in some of the same circles. While he waited to catch a break in the music business, Kris was working as a janitor at Columbia Studios, sweeping the floors and emptying ashtrays. We all knew that Kris Kristofferson was about to knock Nashville on its ass with his poetry set to music. It was hard *not* to know. He was just too good, too original. Kris and I used to hang out at a little tavern near Music Row, drinking a few beers, shooting the shit about the music business, and complaining about how we couldn't seem to grab that brass ring. Kris had been a Rhodes

Scholar, an army officer, and an English professor, and yet he never once flaunted his intelligence. I decided the least I could do was return the favor. Whenever I was around Kris Kristofferson, I was careful not to flaunt my ignorance.

Kris was always ready to give a boost to someone else's career, even when he had no damn clout to do it. I remember one time that involved me. Even though I was still signed with Acuff-Rose as a songwriter, I was also an artist without a record label. Logic told me that the best way to get back on the Ferris wheel as an artist would be to record some new material and pitch it to perspective labels. Back in those days there weren't a lot of recording studios in town to choose from. But there were some, and when the labels weren't using them to record their artists, any poor fool could rent one if they had the money. With a writer's advance I got from Acuff-Rose, I booked my own session at Columbia Studios. The first musician I hired was Charlie McCoy, still known as one of the world's best harmonica players. Charlie then picked the other musicians. In all, I recorded four songs during that session. It ended up costing me eighteen hundred dollars, every penny of the advance and then some. So when it came time to get tape copies—the studio charged a few dollars for each copy made—I had no money left. I had paid for a session that I couldn't listen to because I couldn't afford to buy tape copies.

Since Kristofferson knew I needed those tapes to get myself a recording deal, he set a plan in motion. Remember, Kris was then the janitor at Columbia Studios, the man with all the shiny keys.

"I'll get you some tape copies, Kershaw," he assured me.

Kris waited until after midnight one night, when even the mice had left the building, before he pulled out his keys and unlocked the control room. His plan was a good one. But once he got inside the room he discovered that the equipment was also locked up. Apparently Columbia Studios trusted no one. Kris left empty-handed but he had tried, and he could have lost his job if he'd been caught. You know, I never did get a copy of that session. A few years later, I re-recorded one of the songs I'd written, "Louisiana Sun," on an album for Warner Bros. And I recorded that song again for Huey Meaux at a session down in Louisiana. "Louisiana Sun" was later released on a CD called *The Crazy Cajun Recordings* by Edsel, a company in the United Kingdom. Some things just take time.

But that was Kris Kristofferson, the friend. Kris, the writer, had an even bigger impact on Nashville's creative community. His songs were a great inspiration to me, as they were to so many of the writers who sat around night after night and listened to them. "For the Good Times." "Me and Bobby McGee." "Sunday Morning Coming Down." Man, the titles just go on and on. Pure classics.

Another person who inspired me back then was Boots Randolf. Whenever I'd get to feeling depressed or worried about where my career wasn't going to in a hurry, I'd head down to Printers Alley in Nashville. I'd order a cold beer and just sit back and listen to Boots play his saxophone. He was so damn good that in no time I'd feel like running back to the shithole and writing a happy song. I was always fascinated by the fact that—this is according to my ears only—Boots was playing sax the same way I played fiddle, with the same phrases and slides. I mentioned this to him one night.

"Well," Boots said. "That's probably because I learned to play sax listening to my grandpa play fiddle!"

In the music business it sometimes looks like you're just bumming around. And in some ways maybe that's what I was doing while I waited for something to break. But in another way I was back in the classroom. Once I'd gone to school on men like Will Kegley and Rufus Thibideaux. Now I was going to school on writers like Kris Kristofferson and musicians like Boots Randolph. It was a hell of a class, but I was anxious to graduate.

When I finally did get something going again it came out of left field. Early in 1966, Columbia Records called to ask if I'd work on an album with Del Wood, the Opry's ragtime piano player. I'd already met Del in my own Opry days with Rusty & Doug. Born and raised in Nashville, Del Wood's real name was Adelaide Hendricks. She had had a huge pop and country hit in 1951, a song called "Down Yonder." Even though she never again had a single on the charts, she was still considered the Opry's premier female instrumentalist until her death in 1989. When Del decided she wanted a swamp flavor added to one of her albums, the label thought I was just the Cajun to help her do it. I immediately went to work writing songs and then teaching them to Del. She and I worked off and on like this for several weeks. Del finally asked me to come to the Opry, where she planned to do one of my songs, "Cajun Stripper." She said she needed moral support to help her switch from ragtime to swamp rag. I couldn't miss out on that, but I damn well should have, considering how it would affect my life for many years to come.

Del did an instrumental of the song that night and never hit a wrong note. The audience loved it. Since my job of providing moral support was over, I spent the rest of the evening talking to the other performers, fans, managers, publicists, label executives, song publishers, all those people who tend to mill around backstage at the Opry. Among that crowd was a woman named Elsie Griffin, a widow in her late forties who happened to be Del Wood's dressmaker. Most people were impressed with Elsie's talent as a seamstress and designer, and I was one of them. So Elsie Griffin and I struck up a conversation. I soon found that she was very easy to talk to. She told me that her husband had died not long before, leaving her alone to raise four children, three of them still living at home. Since I was missing my two sons at the time, it felt good to hear someone else speak of their children.

When Del Wood was ready to leave the Opry that night, Elsie and I said our goodbyes. *Nice to meet you.* That kind of thing. And then Del and I went back to her house to work on some more material. Over the next few weeks, while Del and I wrapped up our recording sessions, I saw a lot of Elsie Griffin. I liked her more every time I was around her. I don't mean romantically, but in a familiar, comfortable way. Everyone at the Opry seemed to like her too. I suppose Elsie saw in me a lost soul who needed saving. Even better, she didn't mind listening to my woes about Donna Darlene and the boys. Del had already told her about my sorry living arrangements at the motel and how I was certain I'd be thrown out when the first of each month came around. Elsie didn't seem to think any less of me because of my financial situation, and that alone made her pleasant to be around.

Maybe that's why I called her up when I did. It was Father's Day 1966. I was sitting there by myself at the motel, half drunk and whole high. I was feeling pretty damn sorry for myself. I knew that if I called Donna Darlene and asked to speak to the boys, she'd hang up on me. So I picked up the telephone and called Elsie Griffin.

"I hope you don't mind me calling you at home," I said. I was trying hard not to slur my words. "It's Father's Day, and I don't have my kids with me."

"Well, honey, I got my kids here and they don't have a father to celebrate with," Elsie said quickly. "You come right on over here and have dinner with us."

"I don't have a car," I admitted.

"I'll come over and pick you up," she said.

And that's how I jumped from the frying pan into the *merde*.

I don't know what Elsie was looking for that particular day. Nor could I honestly tell you what I was looking for. I can tell you that I don't think it was romance. Not even for Elsie. I think she wanted company on Father's Day, and I just wanted a shoulder to cry on. Sometimes, as the song says, a shoulder is just a soft place to fall. Other times, it's like hitting a brick wall. For *both* occupants of the car. It was a nice Father's Day dinner. The kids were pleasant to me and the house was comfortable. Elsie and I talked into the night about the transition I was going through in my quest to get a solo career started, about songwriting, the music business itself. And we talked about her life, about the Opry, and the fashion design work she did for several of the stars who performed there. But there was no hint of anything except a friendly interest on either of our parts. Elsie drove me back to my ratty motel room.

"I need to have you over for dinner more often," she said when she took a look around the room. That was fine with me since she was also a good cook. But that ended it. We simply said goodnight.

It was about a month later that Elsie invited me back to dinner. This is when she showed me a little room at the back of her house.

"It's yours, Doug, rent-free if you want it," she said. "It's got a private entrance so you can come and go as you like." She also explained that I could use the kitchen anytime I wanted. I could watch television in the living room anytime I wanted. And I could eat supper with her and the family anytime I wanted. I didn't hesitate a second. Would anyone in my position? Elsie Griffin's offer meant a lot to me during those lean days. I had a place to live where I could start getting back on my feet. And it was a safe haven, too, where I could write without waiting for that knock on the door by the motel manager, telling me I had to pay up or move my ass out. Now I had a caring landlady, a woman who cooked me nice suppers, nursed my hangovers, and even fed my ego. More importantly, a woman who knew what I was going through because of losing my kids. Elsie understood and she sympathized. What more could a man want?

You guessed it. I had a mama again, one who didn't cuss.

I knew that was part of it. I felt cared for and protected. Elsie didn't even make me hand over my paychecks when I got them, like Mama Rita. That's not to say I didn't start paying my way as soon as I could because I did. But of course the relationship was complicated by the fact that Elsie *wasn't* my mother. She was a healthy, middle-aged woman. I lived in Elsie's house about six months before we ended up in bed together. I think this is when the guilt began to work on me. Even as a child I was the one bringing in the money, and now here I was depending on this woman's help. But I was still too wild, too naive, too unsettled in my life and career to realize what guilt can do.

A bigger issue was keeping me occupied, too, since Donna Darlene still wouldn't let me see my boys. I finally felt a breaking point. One night, after I'd been living at Elsie's for a few months, I decided I would visit Doug Jr. and Victor, no matter what. So I drove Elsie's car over to Shot Jackson's house trailer, where I knew Donna Darlene and the boys were living. I didn't give a damn what Shot might say. I just went up to the door and knocked. That's when Shot came outside and pulled a pistol on me. He pointed it at my head. Hell of a line, ain't it? *Shot pulled a pistol.* Maybe that's how he got his nickname. Donna Darlene appeared behind him, looking at me like I was the man from the IRS or something worse.

"You know, folks," I said. "I wish I could afford to buy a gun. At least it'd be a fair fight." But that was my anger talking. I never wanted to put myself in a position where I might have to use violence on someone else. If Donna Darlene wasn't worth going to jail over, neither was Shot Jackson. And then Doug Jr. and Victor were both there that day. They were just kids, and they didn't need to witness this fight between their father and their mother's boyfriend. So I didn't buy a gun and have it out with Shot. As it turned out, I never even owned a gun until Mama Rita died and I inherited her old shotgun. I didn't know it at the time, but thanks to that little scene at Shot's house trailer it would be a couple of years before I'd see my sons again.

But I didn't have long to ponder my sad state of affairs when Donna Darlene got my full attention again. Truth is, I never saw her next move coming. But it did.

This is the story of How Donna Darlene Filed for Divorce.

I had been back in Nashville for about a year by this time, living comfortably at Elsie's, when Donna's lawyer called to inform me that his client was filing for divorce. He added that I needn't bother coming to court because my goose was already cooked. Cajun style.

"I'm coming anyway," I told him. "I like to be present while I'm being screwed."

Screwed wasn't the word for it by the time it was over. Donna Darlene claimed that I'd been beating her. Not only did she testify to this, she got a girlfriend to come in and repeat the stories, word for word. I watched the judge's face as I listened to tales of how I beat up my wife. *Damn*, I thought, *if that judge believes even half of this shit, he's gonna think I'm some kind of bastard!*

He *did* think I was some kind of bastard.

"Is Mr. Kershaw in the court?" is what he asked. But he was thinking, *Is the bastard here?* I held up my hand anyway.

"Are you represented by counsel?" he wondered.

I admitted I wasn't. The judge then told me to come to the witness stand and be sworn in anyway. I walked to the front of the courtroom, placed my hand on their big Bible, and swore to tell the truth, the whole truth, and nothing but the truth. But no one in the courtroom that day was really interested in the truth. After I took the oath, I didn't get a chance to say anything. The judge was too busy telling me what a *fils de putain* I was. He explained that I was a miserable excuse for a husband, and that I was going to be paying Donna Darlene twenty-percent of my income for a very long time.

"As far as the minor children are concerned, Mr. Kershaw," he concluded, "the mother has full custody."

I knew right then what this meant. If Donna Darlene had full custody, I would *never* be allowed to see my boys! The room went spinning around. I could pay the child support, but I couldn't visit my sons. I couldn't hold my sons. I couldn't sing songs to my sons. I couldn't teach them a few words of Cajun French, just so they'd know a little something of their heritage. Mama Rita's heritage. Daddy Jack's heritage. I had lost my children in a matter of minutes in front of a complete stranger who held my entire family's destiny in his hands. I remember walking out of that courtroom in a blur. *How did this happen?* I kept asking myself. *My wife is shacking up with Shot Jackson, but I'm the bastard in this deal.*

There are no words to express how I felt over losing my boys. In many ways I didn't even know them. At the time of the divorce Doug Jr., was about four years old and Victor was only about a year. As I said, I wasn't a *Leave It to Beaver* kind of father, what with being out on the road so much. And, yes, I had that reputation for popping pills and boozing with my musician friends. I don't think I could have been Ward Cleaver even if I'd tried. This was 1966. I didn't have years of hindsight on my side, and it wasn't easy coming to terms with how my life was unfolding. I even thought about kidnaping the kids, hiding them deep in the swamps of Southwest Louisiana where no one would ever find us. But I knew I couldn't do that to them. Donna Darlene could say what she wanted about me, but she couldn't change the fact that I loved my children. Yet, that day in court, I lost those boys for a long, long time. I can't say that I hated my former wife. I didn't. But I will say again what I said before. *She was no June Cleaver.*

I went headfirst into my music after that dismal day in court. And if I drank booze or popped a few pills, so be it. At least that's how I saw it. *Keep ahead of the pain, boy, any way you can.* It's not a philosophy you can live by forever, but it kept me above water at a time when I needed it. This is when I made the acquaintance of another person I would rely upon heavily for the next ten years. This was Dr. Landon B. Snapp, a man who was well known in the music community as "the pill doctor." Dr. Snapp kept me running long and hard on Didrex, an amphetamine that was supposed to be used as a diet pill. With Snapp's number in my address book I would never be out of pills again, and that was important for me to know. Dr. Snapp would figure even more heavily in my life later on, but I'll cover that unfortunate incident when I get to it. First, there was Elsie.

I was now well-stocked with all the pills I would ever need to keep the pain at a distance—I thought I'd lost my sons forever—but I still felt guilt over Elsie Griffin. Here I was living with her when I knew in my heart I didn't love her. At least not the way a man loves the woman in his life. And that guilt got me so twisted up that when Elsie said we ought to get married, I figured marriage might be the answer, at least if *she* wanted it. After all, I was living in her home. Maybe in the back of my mind I even had an ulterior motive. If I married a stable woman, a respected member of the community, maybe I could get visitation rights, be allowed to see my boys again. So, with marriage in mind, Elsie and I packed up and headed for Louisiana. It was time for my girlfriend, who would be fifty years old on her next birthday, to meet her future mother-in-law, who was then fifty-seven.

When I introduced them, Mama Rita narrowed her eyes and looked first at Elsie and then at me. She didn't say anything until Elsie left to go to the store.

"*Mais*, Doug, you gonna have to push her up the aisle in a wheelbarrow," Mama Rita said. "She old enough to be your *ma-mère*." This was certainly not true. Elsie wasn't old enough to be my *grandmother*. Mama Rita was just pissed off that I was marrying someone almost as old as she was. I can't say I blame her, but I didn't let her disapproval stop me. Elsie Griffin and I were married that summer of 1968. The wedding took place right back at the scene of my first marital mistake in Jennings, Louisiana. This time there was no rooster to shit on the end of my boot, but there should have been. We were married by Judge Hershell Knight, an old friend of mine, a man I'd gone to school with back in those early days. I was thirty-two years old this time around. I was determined to at least work at the relationship. Elsie and I both tried. And then just Elsie tried. She *was* a good woman. Hell, she didn't even complain about my partying all night with drunk songwriters, all of us playing guitars and writing songs until dawn. At least she never said anything. But my mind was on other things than being a good husband, no doubt about it. I had a career to rebuild and I'll be honest. I cared more about *that* than my marriage.

I must say this. Elsie helped in the transition I made from a duo to a solo act. She may not have understood the intricacies of the music business, but she *was* a designer. She understood image-making, and we both knew I needed an image to replace that of Rusty & Doug. Being a solo act was proving to be far more difficult than I'd thought, and a large part of the problem was my mind-set. I couldn't get used to the fact that whatever I now did was my own success or failure. Before that, it was always Rusty & Doug. *A hit record? Great! That's Rusty & Doug.* We'd been compared to the Everlys before we split up. Hell, I recently read a magazine article that said Buddy Holly had studied our early work on Hickory Records. We were called trend-setters on both the Wheeling Jamboree and the

Opry. *Rusty & Doug.* As if those two people were inseparable. That's why, I suppose, we were also both known for the Dallas drug bust, even though I was the one who went home before the shit hit the fan. Well, what can I say? I'd had my share of wild nights on the town and *didn't* get caught.

But, alone, I had no image. I was not without professional advice, though. I remember one night when Webb Pierce and I ended up sitting on the floor of Elsie's living room after a long night of hell-raising all over Nashville. Webb was shit-faced drunk and I was far from sober. We were both flat on our asses, which was a good thing. At least that way we couldn't fall down and hurt ourselves or break any lamps. I'd been agonizing about my career, even thinking that maybe I should change my name and start over from scratch. Webb took a long pull off his bottle of Chivas Regal as he thought about this.

"Chief," Webb said. "I think I got it." His face was all lit up with inspiration.

"What?" I asked.

"The answer to your image problem," Webb said. I leaned in close to listen. Hell, Webb Pierce was a big, *big* star. If he had an answer to my image problem, I wanted to hear it.

"What should I do, Webb?" I asked, waiting.

Webb took another long drink of Chivas before he answered.

"You need to start wearing a mask, like them professional wrestlers," Webb said. "Call yourself 'Mister X' or 'Mystery Man.' You know, something to get the excitement going around town." Drunk as I was, I passed.

"I don't think so, Webb," I said. Then I took my own turn at the bottle. "You got any other ideas?"

Webb Pierce was right about one thing. Image is damn important. I took one look around and knew that if I wanted to fit in, I'd have to become more contemporary. As Bob Dylan was singing on the airwaves, the times they were a-changin'. We were smack-dab in the middle of a cultural revolution, the amazing and unpredictable 1960s. This Cajun fiddle player needed to get a foot in the door. That's when Elsie came up with a great idea. She began working on new stage clothes for me, suits that were in tune with the British rock movement. Ruffled shirts. Bell-bottoms. Velveteen. All of a sudden I not only fit in, I was cutting edge. You didn't see anyone else in Nashville wearing velvet bell-bottoms, I can assure you. That's what having an image will do for you. You'll stand out like a fox in a henhouse.

By 1968, I knew I had to get back to some serious performing. I figured the place to start was Printers Alley, which was Nashville's answer to Bourbon Street down in New Orleans. Like I said, Boots Randolf played in Printers Alley, along with many other great talents who were no longer on a record label. This drew the music-business crowd to those cobblestone streets, to the numerous nightclubs and strip joints. If I was going to interest someone in my solo act, Printers Alley was the place to do it. Of course, it was also a double-edged sword. If I was playing in the Alley, the industry folks would know exactly why I was there. I was looking for a break. But I decided to write it off as yet another one of life's humbling experiences and go for it.

Besides, I *needed* a break. Bad.

So I called up Dottie O'Brien, a booking agent friend of mine, and asked if she could book me for a regular gig at a place called the Black Poodle.

"I want to play six nights a week at a hundred dollars a night," I told Dottie. She got on the phone and cut the deal with the owner of the Black Poodle. I was back in business but earning a pittance compared to when Rusty & Doug were hot. At the end of each week I'd pay Dottie her ten percent and then pay the band scale. If there was anything left, I'd buy a round of drinks for the house. If we had an extra guy sit in and there was no money left, I'd charge a round. It ended up costing me money to play in Printers Alley.

After weeks of this, I was beginning to think that the Black Poodle was a red herring, at least where my career was concerned. I feared that instead of getting a recording deal, I'd end up playing in the Alley forever. Maybe I'd even die down there, an old man with a fiddle in his hands wearing purple bell-bottoms. Some good Samaritan would finally cart my dead ass out to make room for the next poor bastard down on his luck. But, slowly, something interesting began to happen. I started to build a following with both the fans and the industry. The press was watching too. Thanks to Elsie's velvet suits, everyone seemed to like my new "Edwardian" image. And they even seemed to love the songs I'd been working on over the past few years. People were starting to pay attention again. This time they were talking about *Doug Kershaw*, not *Rusty & Doug*. For the first time in my life I was becoming known as a solo act. I decided it was time to get serious about a record deal, so I called one of Nashville's biggest moguls, Buddy Killen. Before my relationship with Killen was over, I'd long for that mask Webb Pierce thought would be good for my image.

BLASTOFF

"That's not just my song! That's my life, goddammit!"
—Doug Kershaw, O'Hare Airport bar,
November 1969

Show business is funny. You can be so full of bad luck that it drips off you like poison. Then, something will happen overnight that kick-starts a series of good events, a domino effect that turns things around for you. The dominos started toppling in my direction in 1968, about the time I decided the songs I'd been writing were good enough to get me a solo deal. As fate would have it, I ran into Buddy Killen at the Nashville airport. I felt certain that if Buddy listened to my new songs, he'd want to produce me.

"Sure," Buddy said as he shook my hand. "Stop over at the office sometime, Doug."

The "office" he spoke of was at Tree International, a music publishing entity that was just that year adding thirteen overseas offices and becoming truly international. It was every bit as powerful as the mighty Acuff-Rose, and as the company's executive vice president, Buddy Killen was one of Nashville's most important men. I figured the team of Killen & Kershaw would be perfect since we both came from the same place, the one known as *abject poverty*. I'd left the swamps of Louisiana behind, and Buddy had left the Alabama cotton fields. He initially came to Nashville to play bass for Opry stars Jam Up & Honey, and he had gone on the road with artists such as Jim Reeves, Ray Price, Moon Mullican, and Hank Williams. Buddy wasn't making good money then. In fact, the bank had once repossessed his car. I figured Buddy and I had poor in common.

The best move Buddy Killen ever made was in 1953, when he hooked up with Jack Stapp, right around the time Jack founded Tree International. It so happens Jack had signed up Mae Axton, a great songwriter who had just written a song called "Heartbreak Hotel." You get the picture. Elvis's recording of that song put Tree International on the map. Buddy started out in the company as a talent scout and song plugger, and he did such a good job for Tree that Jack Stapp made him a partner in 1957. Buddy would later sign up two new writers for the company, Roger Miller and Dolly Parton. Tree International was growing by leaps and bounds. The company was getting its overseas offices up and running. And it was in the process of buying Pamper Music, which was home to the Willie Nelson and Hank Cochran catalogs. If Buddy Killen couldn't get me a record deal, neither could God.

My gig at the Black Poodle proved to be another one of those tumbling dominoes. Good events were put into motion when CBS decided to do a television documentary on country music, beginning with a piece on Mel Tillis. So the network sent a news crew headed by Hughes Rudd, a journalist known for his folksy style, down to Nashville to do the filming. The producers happened to stop by the Black Poodle one night for a little rest and relaxation. When they saw my show, they decided to include me in the film. I guess they liked the footage they shot, because when the documentary aired, I got the lion's share of screen time. It brought me to the attention of Warner Bros. Records.

Shortly after, I got a call from Andy Wickham at the label, who wanted to talk to me about signing with Warner Bros. I thought it would be a good idea if Buddy Killen attended that meeting, so I foolishly took Andy Wickham over to Buddy's big, fancy office. Here's why it was a foolish move. Andy Wickham had come prepared to make me a record deal and to negotiate the advance. And that's what he started to do until Buddy Killen took charge of the meeting. The minute Andy mentioned "advance," Buddy shook his head. He waved his hand, as if the concept of money was a shameful idea.

"Andy, we don't need anything up front," Buddy said.

We?

I was afraid I might feel pee running down my leg right then. Hell, yes, I needed something up front! I was playing at the Black Poodle, for Christ's sake, and rarely coming out with any money at the week's end. Buddy Killen, on the other hand, was a partner in one of the biggest money machines in Nashville. A Warner Bros. advance probably didn't mean shit to him. But it did to me. It turned out to be an interesting year for me,

1968 did. I ended up with a new producer, a new publisher, a new record deal, and no pot to piss in.

It's hard to know just what to say about my relationship with Buddy Killen. We made a lot of records together over the next ten years, but it was always a head-banging experience. Thank God I had Dr. Snapp keeping me well-stocked with amphetamines all that time. Killen once said publicly that I was the most difficult artist he ever worked with in all his years in the music business. He's worked with a boatload of them, too, so I almost consider that a compliment. Buddy Killen also went on the record to say, and I quote, "Doug Kershaw had a helluva talent and an innate wisdom, but an untamed spirit that kept him out of control most of the time." He failed to mention the Chivas and the pills.

Buddy also talked about the fact that his engineer, Ernie Winfrey, used to beg him not to leave the two of us alone in the studio after the session. It's true that I often kept him up all night listening to playbacks. Ernie knew there had to be a handful of chemicals that were keeping me that wired, something more than Chivas. He had a lot of patience. In fact, Ernie says one of his favorite memories of me in those wild days was my aluminum "briefcase." I had had it custom-made for my needs. On the outside it looked like a regular briefcase. Inside, it was all foam padding with the outline of a Chivas Regal bottle cut into it. That way, I could pop a bottle in there and know it wouldn't get broken.

But I gotta say this, dammit. The reason I kept Ernie Winfrey up all night listening to playbacks is that Buddy Killen never did understand my music. He kept trying to make a hillbilly out of a Cajun. I never could figure out why Buddy kept pushing me toward country when Warner Bros. had stipulated that they wanted to emphasize the Cajun sound. Sure, I wanted to appeal to the country audiences out there, but I also wanted to keep my heritage out in front. I had spent a lot of years thinking there was something wrong with being Cajun. But after I wrote "Louisiana Man," I found a pride I didn't know existed. I wasn't eager to let go of it. Not for Buddy Killen, or anyone else for that matter.

What I noticed was this: Buddy liked my Cajun songs enough to sign me to his publishing company, Tree International, which was Acuff-Rose's competitor.

What I wished was this: That if Buddy didn't relate to the Cajun side of my music, he would have said so from the beginning. After all, the album I was working on was titled *The Cajun Way*. That was a fairly substantial clue about the direction I wanted to go.

What I figure is this: If a producer can't work with an artist's vision, either resign from the job or get the hell out of the way and let the artist create that vision. Hindsight's a helluva thing. It's even free.

Since Warner Bros. didn't have a country division at the time, they marketed me as a kind of free agent. It was the single best thing they could have done for me. Some of my albums sold nearly a half-million units back then, and that was with very little radio airplay. For five years Warner floated my albums between rock, country, and folk. I'm grateful for that since it helped expose my work to a huge number of people with different musical tastes. But the *real* exposure that helped me sell records with little or no radio play was right around the corner.

In May 1969, when I was about half done recording *The Cajun Way*, I got a phone call from Scull Shulmann, a colorful character from Printers Alley. Back in those days, Scull was well-known to Nashville musicians, since he owned about half of the clubs in Printers Alley. He was as generous as they come, always giving songwriters and artists a free meal or a few beers when times were tough. But on this day Scull was calling on behalf of a man who didn't need a free meal or a free beer. *Johnny Cash*. It seems that Johnny was launching a new variety show on ABC television and he wanted *me* to audition for the network people.

"Come down and play a special show for them at the Black Poodle," Scull said. "I think they're gonna love you, Kershaw."

Within a couple of hours I'd rounded up the band and we were on stage auditioning for Johnny Cash and June Carter. After the show, I went over and talked to John. It turned out that another falling domino had led Johnny Cash to me. The Hughes Rudd special had caused a lot of excitement in Music City, so the *Nashville Banner* ran a big article on me and my music. When Johnny Cash read it, he decided that Doug Kershaw might fit the bill for his new show. The day after my audition, John came to me with a proposition. I could have my choice of appearing on the show's premiere night, or I could sign on as a regular for the season. You might think that someone as broke as I was would sign on for all the shows he could get. But I knew what my answer would be the minute I learned who else would be on the premiere. The other guests were Bob Dylan, Joni Mitchell, Fannie Flagg, and the Statler Brothers.

Bob Dylan and Johnny Cash on the same show? In 1969? The viewing audience would be huge. Bob Dylan had been in semiretirement since 1966 following a bad motorcycle accident. The crash had happened about a week after he released "I Want You," his fifth single on Columbia Records. Columbia went ahead and released one more single in 1966, "Just Like A Woman," and then Dylan was silent on the airwaves. "Lay Lady Lay" wouldn't be released until late summer of 1969, so I figured Dylan fans were probably starving for just a glimpse of him. The opportunity of appearing with him on the Johnny Cash premiere was one I wasn't going to miss. It was the big leagues, no doubt about it.

"John," I said. "I'll take the premiere."

After listening to my show, the producers at ABC decided which songs I should do. "Diggy Diggy Lo" and "Louisiana Man." At the time, Buddy Killen and I hadn't planned on putting those two songs on *The Cajun Way*. But the fact that they'd be heard on national television by an enormous viewing audience changed all that. We quickly added them to the album.

My biggest memory of that show happened before showtime. Since the premiere was to be filmed at the Ryman Auditorium, I had gotten myself a room at a downtown hotel. That way, I would have a place to go between rehearsal and the actual filming. When I arrived at the Ryman that day I noticed that Johnny Cash was in his usual black shirt and slacks. I personally was wearing one of my signature velvet suits, which was dark purple. As it so happens, Bob Dylan had also chosen to wear black for the show: black jacket, black shirt, black pants, black boots. He looked like a typical folk singer, so I didn't think anything of it.

Nervous energy before a show can kill you if you let it. I always pace or pick up an instrument and start jamming with another musician. It was backstage at the Ryman during rehearsal that I got to see a caring side of Bob Dylan. He and I had been jamming for some time when he suddenly put down his guitar and pulled me aside.

"Doug, what do you think of my outfit?" Dylan asked. "Do I look all right?"

We sounded like two girls in a high school bathroom.

"You look fine," I said. I was a bit surprised that he was even concerned. I mean, to this day the guy is a major star, a true icon. We went back to jamming, but before long Dylan put his guitar down and pulled me aside again.

"I don't think I'm dressed right for this show," he said. "But I didn't bring anything else. You got any extra stage clothes?"

Did Doug Kershaw have any extra stage clothes?

Elsie had brought enough clothes to fill a big trunk. They were spread out all over the hotel room I had rented for the occasion.

"Would you like to come look through my stuff?" I asked.

Schoolgirls.

Off we went to my hotel room. Come to find out, he didn't think it was right to be wearing all black since John was, and that was John's signature look. And he feared he was underdressed for the special itself. I waited as Bob Dylan tried on one of my velvet suits after another. It would have been comical if he hadn't been truly concerned. Dylan isn't a big man by any stretch of the imagination. But back then I was so skinny you could mistake me for a vine hanging off a cypress tree. None of my pants fit him. Looking back that was lucky for him. Can you imagine what America would have thought if we'd both shown up in velvet, Edwardian suits? He pulled a light-colored shirt on over his black tee-shirt.

We walked back to the Ryman and did the show. I can speak for all who watched the premiere of the *Johnny Cash Show* that night that Bob Dylan didn't need to worry about how he was dressed. When he and John played and sang "Girl from the North Country," the performance was captivating. There's no way to calculate how much critical acclaim and massive exposure that one show brought to my career. Just being on television with someone like Johnny Cash got people to pay attention. Add to the mix Bob Dylan, Joni Mitchell, and Fannie Flagg. Most television sets in America were tuned in. When the show finished, I had my regular gig in Printers Alley. I had obviously started popping pills and washing them down with Chivas by the time I went on stage at the Black Poodle. There's another part to that extraordinary night I just don't remember. I can thank *Rolling Stone* for writing it down for me.

"Later, Cash, Dylan and June Carter went down to the Black Poodle down in Printers Alley to see Doug Kershaw, the Cajun fiddler who also played

on the Cash show. To what must have been Dylan's delight, the attention was primarily on Cash. Joni Mitchell and Graham Nash were there, too. Kershaw really ripped loose on the first set and passed the mike around at the table when he did 'Orange Blossom Special.' A little later, Cash and his wife took to the stage with Kershaw backing them on his fiddle. I have never heard happier music. Dylan sat quiet and smiling through the set. The people who happened to be in the club when this began were stunned."

That's the big downside of too many pills: what is lost in the wake.

As I look back on my career, it's easy to see that the *Johnny Cash Show* was the big turning point. If someone had asked me back in the Rusty & Doug days if I was a star, I think I'd have said yes. And I would have been a naive fool. After appearing on Cash's show and seeing what followed, I realized what stardom was all about. I'd only been preparing for it.

What a year 1969 turned out to be. Man landed on the moon and Doug Kershaw landed on national television. I didn't see how it could feel any different. Right after that ABC premiere, Johnny Cash sent his manager to negotiate a deal with me to perform on some upcoming shows. Negotiate? Hell, I'd already signed with Warner Bros. for free, thanks to Buddy Killen. Besides, I'd have gone on the road with Cash for pocket change. But that wasn't how Johnny did business. So I went from playing Printers Alley for six hundred dollars a week to the Hollywood Bowl and Madison Square Garden for thousands.

I had always wanted to get away from playing clubs where people gathered mainly to talk, dance, and drink. There's a part of that atmosphere that's fun and exciting, and nobody knows that better than me because I love to do it myself. But the feeling of being on stage, playing to people who come to hear the music, is something else. I had experienced it when I did the Opry and similar venues. But I had never before felt the energy that poured off those crowds that Cash attracted. Thousands of fans were there to simply absorb his music. It was unbelievable. When I tried to thank Johnny, he just waved it aside.

"Kershaw," he said, "you added a lot to the TV shows and to the road show. I did it for myself too." This reminded me of Stoney Cooper's philosophy.

Johnny helped so many people in the business that it would be foolish to try to name them. But I was there when he decided to give Kris Kristofferson a break at the Newport Folk Festival.

"Doug, what do you think about me having Kris sing some songs?" John asked. I said it sounded like a damn good idea to me. Even though Kris was signed to Monument Records, he hadn't had huge exposure as an artist until Cash put him out in front of his audience, just as he'd done for me. That was the kind of man Johnny Cash was.

I wasn't feeling like such a big star on the home front. The more I was away from Elsie, the more I knew what a tragic mistake the marriage had been. My old pipe dream that being married might help me gain custody of my sons hadn't panned out. Donna Darlene still wouldn't allow me to visit Doug Jr., and Victor. As time went by, I could tell the boys even lost interest in seeing me.

Here was the scenario. I'd come in from the road, drop off my clothes to be washed, then head out for a night of drinking and carousing around Nashville with my pals. Sometimes I'd even invite the drunken crowd over to our place since Elsie never complained about this. At least she never complained to me. I think she may have been a little starstruck with the people I hung out with. Many times Kris Kristofferson's wife called my house looking for her husband. That's when Elsie had to admit that not only hadn't she seen *Kris,* she hadn't even seen *me.* Looking back on it, there's no doubt that Elsie and I used each other. As I said earlier, she was lonely too. She was trying to raise her children and she wanted companionship. It's just too damn bad that the companion she picked was in a period of turmoil and loaded down with all the pill prescriptions he would ever need. I still have such mixed emotions about that time in my life.

On the other hand, I treated Elsie with respect when I was with her. I was good to her kids. And from the very beginning I paid rent, which was necessary since her parents originally owned the house. They had died, and Elsie's siblings let her stay on. I think it always bothered her a little that she was still dependent on her family. But once I got out on the road with Johnny Cash and once I got some big royalty checks coming in, I gave Elsie the money to buy the house outright. It meant a lot to her. And as I said, I liked Elsie. I respected her. I appreciated her. But I never loved her. What I loved was the crowds, the applause, the stardom, the chemicals. As I saw it, drugs and rock 'n' roll were all that mattered.

And more and more I was moving into the rock world. In late 1969, I appeared on Hugh Hefner's weekly television show *Playboy After Dark*. I did a couple tunes, then chatted with Hefner and comedian Louie Nye, who was also a guest. I had been asked before the taping if I would mind playing my fiddle on a song with another performer, a newcomer named Tina Turner who was turning heads all over the country. I didn't mind at all. Of course, Ike and the band were there, but I don't remember seeing Ike Turner. How could you forget Tina once you've seen her dance? She sang "Honky Tonk Woman" and I played my fiddle.

It was later that same year that I agreed to close the Toronto Rock Festival. I put together a helluva band to go with me, knowing that it was going to be a major music event. I asked Charlie Daniels to come along as a band member, and he said he'd be happy to. Charlie had had an incredible year. He had just played on Bob Dylan's landmark *Nashville Skyline* album, produced the Youngbloods' *Elephant Mountain*, and was getting set to sign his own deal with Capitol. He was that successful, and yet he agreed to back me up. We kept hearing rumors at the festival that John Lennon might appear, but nobody knew for sure if the talk was grounded in fact or high hopes. I was backstage half-listening to some of the bands playing the show when the promoter brought the word that Lennon had arrived.

"And he plans on playing!" the promoter added. I thought he might pass out, he was so damn excited. But this was John Lennon's first appearance since the Beatles had split up, so I guess the promoter had a good reason for gushing. I just assumed that a former Beatle would close the show instead of me, but I was told that Lennon had no intention of grabbing my closing slot. I was stunned.

"No way am I gonna close for John Lennon," I told the promoter, who looked as if he might go into a coma just hearing this new information. But I meant it. It wasn't that I was afraid of following John Lennon, even though I knew he was like a god to the audience. It was out of respect for Lennon, for the Beatles, for the history. When John himself came and talked to me about it, I explained my position. He didn't say much, but I could tell he understood. At least he agreed to close.

After I finished my portion of the show, Charlie Daniels and I found a good spot on the sidelines so we could watch Lennon perform. We had come in late, but the guy was electrifying. He had just started singing "Money (That's What I Want)." So much pure, natural talent. He had thrown together a quick band with the likes of famed guitarist Eric Clapton, drummer Alan White, and bass player Klaus Voorman, calling it the Plastic Ono Band. Then everything became confusing. I could hear the audience whispering and giggling, and some fans were pointing. That's when I noticed something on the stage between Clapton and Lennon. It seemed to be a white sheet, all bunched up. At first I thought that somebody had forgotten to remove a pile of drum covers, but the thing was *moving*. It humped its way around on the stage. We were so distracted by it that we couldn't concentrate on the music.

"What the hell *is* that?" I whispered to Charlie. He hunched his shoulders.

"Damned if I know," he said. We tried to listen to John's song, but the sheet seemed to be getting more energetic. "What *is* it?" I whispered again. It was impossible not to stare. When it quit moving, I wondered if what was under it had died. Lennon finished the song. The blanket then stood up, and Yoko appeared from beneath it. She stepped up to the microphone to sing a duet with her husband, her part being a kind of wail. Charlie Daniels and I almost died. We weren't even making any musical judgments. I left that to Eric Clapton, who just kept playing his guitar and trying not to acknowledge what was going down. It was just the damnedest thing we ever saw. *That was Yoko Ono moving around under that damn sheet,* I kept thinking. Talk about a show-stealing scene.

I'm told they call it performance art?

I'm sure they do.

As 1969 drew to a close, things were going very well for me. *The Cajun Way* was already out on Warner Bros. and getting great reviews. I was playing big shows all over the country, sometimes with Cash, but more often as the headliner. Television had come courting me big time. I was hot, no doubt about it. On a larger scale, the hottest thing to happen for this country had already taken place that July, and the event made head-lines around the world. Neil Armstrong had been blasted to the moon and actually walked upon its surface. *One small step for man, one giant leap for mankind.*

Talk about a road trip. Now that's performance art!

On November 14, 1969, Apollo 12 was launched, carrying Pete Con-rad, Richard Gordon, and Alan Bean. This mission would be the first to try and pinpoint an actual landing spot on the surface of the moon, a hell of a feat. For several days all the major networks were carrying the moon shots live. We were stretching our horizons and boundaries, changing our world as we knew it. You could almost feel excitement in the air. And it was a *good* excitement, too, one that would balance all the bad news we were hearing about Vietnam, about American boys dying in the rice pad-dies over there. What a hell of a time that was for this country. There was so much turmoil and so much grief.

That same November, amid the excitement of Apollo 12, I found myself alone at Chicago's O'Hare Airport. I was on my way to Los Angeles to meet up with my band for some show. All over the terminal I could hear television sets blaring out from bars, mixed with the excited chatter of the drinkers. This would be only our second moon landing. The astronauts would not only make it, they would touch down six hundred and sixty feet from their target, an amazing achievement. They became true American heroes. Nowadays, even the space shuttle going up doesn't draw a serious crowd. It should, but it doesn't. Back then a space launch was a big deal, long discussions and scientific explanations. Maybe that's why I thought I was imagining it when I heard "Louisiana Man" coming from the racket of one bar. I walked on by. As I passed the door to the next bar it was obvious. I looked in and saw people crowded around, staring up at yet an-other television set. Then I heard it for certain. *They call my mama Rita and my daddy Jack.*

Damned if my song wasn't being broadcast back from space before Apollo 12 landed. I had to think about it. Cajuns had been kicked around for a long time. I had felt like a second-class citizen for most of my life. It had taken me years to come to terms with the stigma of my upbringing, at least enough to write about it in a song. Now, my life story was being told from space during one of our country's proudest moments.

He's got to make a livin' he's a Louisiana man.

Got to make a livin' he's a Louisiana Man.

The song ended. I looked around that little bar, at the faces peering up at our astronauts. There they were, floating like gray and white ghosts in their tiny capsule, a quarter of a million miles from home. I learned later that Pete Conrad had chosen a cassette of songs to take into space with him. "Louisiana Man" was one of them. I wondered what Daddy Jack might have thought, had he lived to hear the song I'd written about him. People in that bar—and all of America—were already listening to the next song, but I wanted to grab hold of everyone's collar, one at a time. I wanted to shake them and shout in their ears, "That's not just a song, goddammit! That's my *life!*" I took my fiddle case and went on down the concourse to my departure gate. I had to get to Los Angeles and my next show.

Above is my great-grandfather Nicolas Broussard, and his son, Savin, who was blind. Folks along the river said the Broussards could make a fiddle soar and an accordion dance. Below left, my paternal grandfather Joseph Needham Kershaw, and his daughter, Althèan Conner. Below right is Grandpa Albert Broussard, Mama Rita's father. I wrote "Cajun Joe, the Bully of the Bayou" about him.

These are typical family houseboats, ca. 1940. Folks up and down the river would gather to eat, visit, and drink. By nightfall, the houseboat would be packed and a *fais do-do* in full swing.

My father, a young Jack Kershaw.
He's the "Daddy Jack," in my song "Louisiana Man."

That's me and little brother Rusty, ages three and five. We never owned a pair of shoes until we left the swamps and moved into town. We also couldn't speak English.

This painting of Mama Rita and Daddy Jack was done
by my mother-in-law from an old photograph.

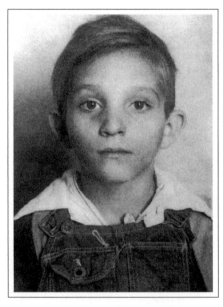

Me at age seven, shortly after Daddy Jack died.

My parents with my little brother, Rusty.

Mama Rita and her sons, Rusty, me, Pee Wee, and Ed, after we left the Mermentau River and moved into town. It doesn't look like any of us felt like smiling around that time.

In 1947, Mama Rita sold the "chicken-coop" we were living in and moved us to this house in Jennings.

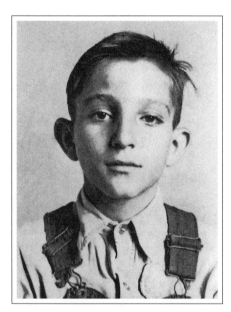

That's me after I became a shoe shine entrepreneur
on the street outside the Red & White Café.

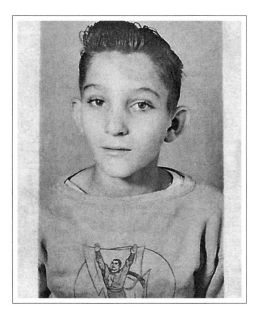

My second grade photo. I had been playing in nightclubs
for over two years by then. My t-shirt is proof I
was still hoping a hero would rescue me.

By age thirteen I had learned to be a cool musician.
I had also learned to smile again.

Pee Wee & His Continentals, in 1948. Above, from left to
right are J. W. Pelsia, Aldous Cormier, Rusty, me, and Pee Wee
Kershaw. We were supposed to be the "Continental Playboys," but
there was no room for that last word on the drum. So we became
the "Continentals." Below, that's me, Rusty, Pee Wee, and Jessie
Stutes on guitar.

Me with the "family twins," my brother Ed's daughters. I would later mention Bren and Lin in my song "Louisiana Man."

The Bewley Gang, ca. 1954. Wiley Barkdull is at the microphone. I'm at the piano, Pee Wee is on drums, and Rusty is on guitar. That's Louis Forett on steel, and B.B. Raspberry is in the back on the stand-up bass. This was the live television show we did for KPLC-TV in Lake Charles.

We did recording sessions for J.D. Miller, in Crowley. I can't say J.D. didn't pay his musicians. Now and then he ordered us hamburgers. It was so hot in that studio that we often peeled down to our underwear. Above, Wiley Barkdull on guitar, Rufous Thibodeaux on fiddle, Rusty, me, and I don't recognize who is at far right. I hope he survived that session. Below, Rusty and I are wearing the fancy shirts that Mama Rita made. This was 1953.

My first professional stage photo, taken in Jennings when I was eighteen.

Wheeling, 1957. Above, Martha White Flour sponsored us. I was proud of my new Chrysler. We were rolling in style. Pee Wee and Bob Metz are in the front seat, and I'm in the back. Below left, Rusty and me. Same coats, same cigarettes. Below right, notice the publicity photo behind us as we cut my birthday cake.

In 1957, the duo of Rusty & Doug became the youngest members thus far to join the Grand Ole Opry. The Opry was still at the Ryman Auditorium, down at Broadway and Fourth. The first time we ever performed there, it was an emotional night for me. Many of my musical heroes had stood on that stage. I remember we sang "So Lovely Baby." I kept thinking of how Hank Williams had sung "Your Cheatin' Heart" on that same spot to twenty-six encores.

I couldn't understand why the U.S. Army wanted *me* when they already had Elvis. Below, I won an award for Best Vocalist. During my time with Uncle Sam, I discovered a renewed love of Cajun music, and a brand-new love for pills.

In 1969, Johnny Cash approached me with an offer. I could be on the premiere of the *Johnny Cash Show*, or be a weekly regular. When I heard that Bob Dylan would be on the premiere, I knew what my answer would be. Above with John and below with the incomparable Joni Mitchell. John Cash helped the careers of a lot of musicians.

This was taken during rehearsal in the legendary Ryman Auditorium for the premiere of the *Johnny Cash Show*, in June of 1969. America hadn't seen much of Bob Dylan since a motorcycle accident three years earlier. I knew they would tune in for just a glimpse of him, and I was right. Millions watched that night. As for me, I saw a very caring and respectful side to Bob Dylan.

Offers to do national television shows just kept on coming, and I kept on accepting them. Above, with Dick Cavett in 1970, one of America's top talk show hosts. Below, earlier that same year, John Wayne invited me to take part in his NBC special which was a tribute to America.

After appearing on the premiere of the *Johnny Cash Show* bookings rolled in from everywhere, from Hugh Hefner's *After Dark,* to *The Flip Wilson Show.* Here I am (above) at the Newport Folk Festival, in 1969, with Arlo Guthrie. That festival was rich with talent: James Taylor, Ritchie Havens, Joni Mitchell, Jerry Jeff Walker, Pete Seeger, and many others. I played the Newport Jazz Festival, too. I wasn't just hot, folks. I was on fire. Below, at the New Orleans Jazz Festival. I caught the crowd in my sunglasses that day.

Night and day. Most people don't realize I held a Doug Kershaw Golf Tournament for twelve years in order to raise money for charities. And I played in a lot of other tournaments, too.

Even after I appeared on shows with Ed Sullivan and Dinah Shore, my mother thought I should get a "real" job. But she loved it when David Frost invited her to join me on national TV. Here she is performing with me at the legendary Troubadour Club, in West Hollywood. That's Waylon Jennings behind me.

I had a cameo in *Zachariah,* a musical film billed as "The First Electric Western," and starring a young Don Johnson. I was wisely cast as "the Fiddler." No method acting was required.

Roger Miller and I loved to sneak onstage at a Glen Campbell show, catching Glen off-guard. This was taken during Glen's show at Harrah's, in Las Vegas. It's tough to believe that both of those amazing talents are gone. We three musicians did a lot of pub-crawling back in those days when "pub-crawling" was an art form, as well as an occupational hazard.

Roger was one of my closest friends and I have more than my share of "Miller" stories. He once said that if he could live his life over again, he wouldn't have the time. And that "old songwriters never die. They just decompose." There's not a day goes by that I don't miss that man.

To Doug Kershaw
With appreciation and best wishes,

August 27, 1972

Richard Nixon

Broadcast Music Incorporated, or BMI—this is the performance rights organization that pays royalties to musicians—asked me to take part in a political campaign for Richard Nixon. This was taken at San Clemente, when he thanked those of us involved. Later, Patricia Nixon asked me to perform at the White House, and I did.

Steamboat Springs, Colorado, 1974. I was booked to do a show there at the same time a celebrity ski slalom was being held. The place was glittering with stars. The famous Alpine skier Billy Kidd gave me a lesson and I filled in for Claudine Longet. (Yes, you read that correctly.) When I came down the slope like a gator on its belly, Clint Eastwood dug me out of the snow. From an event with Eastwood to *The Lawrence Welk Show*. That's the nature of show business.

Mary Tyler Moore was America's sweetheart and I would have been dumb not to jump at the chance to be in her TV special. It was called *Mary's Incredible Dream,* and it aired on CBS in January 1976. Mary was at the top of her game as a talented actress, but for some reason she wanted to prove her singing and dancing skills. The critics, sadly, were not kind. They called it "Mary's Incredible Nightmare." At least *my* dream came true.

Pam Eason had always imagined she would have a traditional wedding ceremony. But our big day, June 21, 1975, was anything but traditional. We were married in the Houston Astrodome, in front of 40,000 people and being filmed by television cameras from ABC and the BBC.

Pam Eason Kershaw and me after our wedding vows. This was easily the best decision I made in my lifetime. This year we will celebrate our 44th anniversary.

Jerry Lee Lewis, aka "The Killer," and me at the Palomino Club, in 1976. Jerry Lee and I are only a few months apart in age. He was born in Ferriday, Louisiana, in the northeast part of the state. And I was born and raised in Southwest Louisiana. We both became known as "wild" performers, and that was fine with me.

I wish I had a dollar for every bow hair I've destroyed during a show. When I was four years old, Uncle Abel made me a fiddle from a cigar box, a piece of hardwood, and a chunk of gator bone. My strings were wires from a window screen and my bow hairs were #50 white thread. In 2009, I was inducted into the Louisiana Hall of Fame. In 2016, I was inducted into the National Fiddler Hall of Fame. And in 2019, just after I turned eighty-three, I was inducted into the North American Country Music Association Hall of Fame. That's not bad for starting out with No. 50 white thread. I still use it in a pinch.

In my dressing room at the Palomino Club, North Hollywood, 1980. I can't remember who is with Goldie, but to my right is Richard Larsen, a good friend who was best man at my and Pam's wedding. The Palomino Club was a great place to meet up again with friends I had made in the acting community such as the talented and beautiful Goldie Hawn.

John Denver and I being interviewed at a club in Denver. John was another amazing talent we lost too soon. Who could forget "Take Me Home, Country Roads," or "Rocky Mountain High?" Not everyone knows that John wrote the classic "Leaving on a Jet Plane," made famous by Peter, Paul, and Mary. A seasoned pilot, he died at the age of fifty-three when his plane crashed into Monterey Bay, California.

They were workouts, no doubt about it. The first time I tried jumping onstage, it was spontaneous. I turned in midair and came down to face my band. The crowd loved it. So I learned to leap into the air, turn a complete circle, and land on my feet to face the audience. People soon expected this of a Kershaw show. Would you be surprised to learn that I had hip replacement surgery a few years ago?

This photo was taken by Norman Seeff, when Pam and I lived in Evergreen, Colorado. Norman is known for hundreds of iconic photographs of celebrities. It was an honor to find myself in his camera lens.

The Kershaw brothers were reunited for a day, Rusty on my right, and Pee Wee on my left. We had a Kershaw reunion in 1989, in Lake Arthur. Over 5,000 people turned up. Mama Rita sat in a wheelchair, listening to her sons make music again.

Lake Arthur, Louisiana. It looks like I'm standing in the open mouth of an alligator, doesn't it? That oak tree was growing there long before my family left our houseboat back in the swamps and came to find a better life in town.

From the swamps to Carnegie Hall. It's been one hell of a ride, folks. I want to thank those of you who came along on that ride with me. It wouldn't have been the same without you. If it were possible, I'd do it all over again. Every damn bit of it.

PART 3

THE RAGIN' CAJUN

Laissez les Bons Temps Rouler

HIGHS AND LOWS AND HIGHS

*"If you want The Ed Sullivan Show, we'll book
The Ed Sullivan Show."*
–William Morris Agency, 1971

Picture this. I'm standing in the concourse at LaGuardia airport waiting for Mama Rita to come down the ramp. I've got a bouquet of roses cradled in one arm, a small herd of television producers at my side, and a limo waiting outside to take us to *The David Frost Show*. You might say my nerves were working overtime. Mama Rita would be on national TV with David Frost as her host. It was a Cajun crapshoot as to what she might say or do. So how did this come about in the first place? On my album *The Cajun Way* I had included a song titled, "Rita, Put Your Black Shoes On." When I released *Spanish Moss* in early 1970, it had a Cajun French song I'd written called, "Mama Rita In Hollywood." On the back of that album, under credits for musicians, is written *Rita Broussard, guitar and vocals*. I had even signed her up at the Nashville Musicians Union for the gig. When *The David Frost Show* came calling for me to perform, the producers noticed those two songs among my repertoire. They decided it would be a great idea if I brought Mama Rita on the show with me. She could play guitar and we'd sing together, just like the old days back in Lake Arthur.

"She'll be quaint," one of the New York producers told me over the phone. "And that'll make for good television. A real crowd-pleaser."

I had no doubt Rita Broussard Kershaw would be a crowd-pleaser. Quaint, I wasn't so sure about. But I decided to at least feel her out about it, so I called her up. Would she like to do *The David Frost Show* with me?

"David Fross. Who da hell is dat, *cher?*" Mama Rita asked. "He some big shot?"

"Sort of," I said. This was 1970, mind you. David Frost was as hot as a bottle of Tabasco sauce. "If we do it, you have to behave, Mama Rita," I added. "Watch what you say and don't forget to bring your teeth."

There was a short silence.

"Holy *merde*," Mama Rita finally said. "He must be a big deal. Sure, I'll come."

People who work in television production have done it for so long that they come to believe real life can also be manipulated. Things aren't perfect? Just make some changes, get a better script, bring in a different actress, maybe even some stunt people. That way, all families can become a *Father Knows Best* family of *crowd-pleasers*. This is how producers think, and the David Frost people were no exception. But that's because they hadn't met the Kershaws from the swamps of Louisiana.

The bouquet of roses, true to form, was the brainchild of the show's publicity department. Since I was already in New York when Mama Rita arrived, another genius in publicity decided that a stretch limo would be the best way to pick her up and escort her to the show. On the drive out to LaGuardia in that limo with its plush, velvet seats, I looked at the fancy suits sitting around me and wondered if I should prepare them for my mother. I could tell them that our first house in town was a made-over chicken coop. Surely that would be quaint enough. A part of me felt the need to explain just how painful it is to be "quaint." And how some of us spend a good part of our lives trying to get *un*-quaint. I decided to keep my mouth shut and let them see for themselves.

Since they had flown Mama Rita in first class, I expected her among the first passengers off the plane. She wasn't. I started getting nervous. I knew that a family member had driven her to Houston and put her on the plane. But had she pulled some *Zsa Zsa Gabor* stunt at thirty thousand feet, forcing the pilot to land in St. Louis and put her off the plane? Hey, with Mama Rita your worst nightmare was possible. Just when we were certain all the passengers were off, there she was, standing in the doorway at the head of the ramp. She held the handle of her battered guitar case in one hand and a big black purse in the other. The minute she saw me with that bouquet of roses in my arms, she smiled. She had forgotten to put in her teeth.

I felt embarrassment rise up and did my best to hide it. I knew I would hate myself in a few minutes for even feeling that way. This was my mother, after all. Mama Rita must have read the look on my face because she stopped, put her guitar case down, and opened her purse. It was so shiny I knew she'd bought it for the trip. With the David Frost entourage looking on, she fished about until she found her set of teeth. She pulled them out, wiped them on her coat sleeve, and slipped them into her mouth. She smiled again.

I looked over at the producer standing next to me. I could see that a little color had drained from his face. I suppose he was thinking ahead to the actual taping of the show and how he might possibly be fired.

"Well, what do you think?" I asked him. "Is she quaint enough?"

There ain't no doubt about it. This was a first for *The David Frost Show.*

Outside the terminal Mama Rita got her first glance at the waiting limousine.

"Holy *merde,* Doug," she said. "Who died, *cher?*"

That's how Mama Rita, a small herd of New York TV producers, and I ended up in a stretch limousine, rose petals under our feet, speeding through the rush of New York City traffic. Ain't life a helluva thing?

It would make for good reading to tell you that Mama Rita cursed all through *The David Frost Show,* but I don't remember that happening. I had asked her before taping began to please, for me, mind her manners and not cuss. America would be watching.

"*Mais,* Doug, you worry too much, *cher,*" she said.

We did "Mama Rita in Hollywood." I played accordion, with Mama Rita on guitar, and both of us sang the Cajun French lyrics. And then I took the guitar and sang "Rita, Put Your Black Shoes On."

So, Rita, put your black shoes on
Rita, put your black shoes on
Rita, put your black shoes on
Come and dance with your child awhile...

She loved it, and apparently so did our host. After the show was over, David Frost told me that my mother was "charming." But that's how Mama Rita could be when she wanted to. She knew when she could push or crush the envelope. She also knew how important that show was to my career. But nowadays, judging from what I hear on television, I'd tell her to say whatever she wanted. Cuss and be damned. She'd be good for the ratings. Let me add this, however. There are many incidents I've forgotten or just don't remember clearly with the passage of years. One example is that amazing night after the Johnny Cash premiere when Dylan, Cash, and the others came to my show in Printers Alley. I have no memory due to booze and drugs. Another is the story of Melton Monceaux Jr. being eaten by an alligator. That was due to my own youthful fears of it happening to *me*. So how did Mama Rita act on *The David Frost Show*? Until I find a taping, I can't be one hundred percent sure!

True to style, what impressed Mama Rita most about her stint as a studio musician, and her appearance on *The David Frost Show*, were the two checks that arrived afterward. They were both written out in her name, and she was paid scale for her time and talent. If I remember correctly, Warner Bros. paid her more than eight hundred dollars for the session work, and the Frost show paid about five hundred. She phoned me up when each check arrived.

"They *pay* you for this, *cher?*" she asked. I think that's what finally convinced my mother that I really could make a good living as a musician and entertainer.

Later that same year I signed with the William Morris booking agency. One of the first gigs they booked for me was a television special that Al Hirt was taping down in New Orleans. Al Hirt was one of my favorite horn players, so I couldn't pass up the chance to perform with him. I decided to drive from Nashville to New Orleans, but the next morning when I woke up I was coughing and hacking. Since this was nothing unusual, I went ahead and lit my first cigarette of the day. I'd fallen into that habit when I was twenty-one years old, back at the Wheeling Jamboree. I'd start the day with a good puff of smoke and nicotine to the lungs. Then, just keep those cigarettes coming in a steady stream.

For the New Orleans trip I threw my fiddle into the back seat of my 1968 blue Mustang and took off. By the time I got to Memphis I had already emptied the ashtray a couple of times. I never needed a match or a cigarette lighter in those days since I lit one butt off the other—the eternal flame. It was sometime after I turned the Mustang south on Interstate 55 and headed into Mississippi that I noticed the ashtray was full again.

That's when I asked myself a hard question. How many packs are you smoking a day, Kershaw?

"Five packs, fool," I heard a voice in my head answer. "You need to quit." This was true. Ever since I'd gotten out of the army when I was twenty-four, I'd been smoking five packs a day.

"Your days are long ones, Doug," I heard another voice say, this one comforting. "Five packs isn't so bad. You've been under a lot of stress."

Anyone who is now a smoker, or who has been one in the past, knows these two voices very well. And any *singer* knows that five packs of cigarettes a day will eventually wreak havoc on the vocal cords. But I loved smoking so damn much that I listened to the two voices argue for another fifty miles or so. One voice reminded me that I'd always wanted to be a singer. "You'll never be Marty Robbins," the other said. "Light one up, Doug." Well, I'd never be Marty, but a lot of people seemed to enjoy my singing. "Smoking helps calm you down, Doug," the same voice added. "This is true," the other said, "but it also makes you cough and hack all day." This is the yin and yang of getting off *any* drug, and it's the voice that refers to you by your first name that you need to watch out for.

I pulled the blue Mustang off onto the edge of the road and put it in park. I looked into my open pack and saw that there were about twelve cigarettes left. More than half a pack. Damn, it's hard to crunch a pack with all those perfectly good cigarettes just staring up at you, pleading for their lives. But I did it. I crumpled it and then threw it out the window. I put the Mustang back in gear and headed due south for the Louisiana state line. By the time I saw Lake Pontchartrain unfolding like a blue dream in the distance, I'd already gotten past the first demanding cries for more nicotine. I knew then that I had it licked. I've never touched cigarettes since that day. I didn't gain any weight either, but that's because I was still doing enough pills to sink a battleship, thanks to Dr. Snapp. I've read that beating nicotine is harder than any other drug. Not for me. It was as easy as pulling the Mustang over to the side of the road that day. It would be booze and cocaine that would later almost kill me.

But I'll bet you—like Roger Miller's marijuana plants—there's tobacco growing along that road in Mississippi, and no one knows how it got there.

There was another drug back then that was taking its toll on my system. It was guilt, pure and undiluted guilt. Elsie would have made someone a good wife, but not me, for I just didn't love her. *Guilt.* And that included Rusty and Pee Wee. With every success I had, I was reminded that it was success without my brothers. And the guilt didn't end there, either, for the biggest amount I felt was over my two boys, Victor and Doug Jr. Things were going so well for me professionally that I wanted to share the experience with my sons. I even started adding them to my record-company bios, telling fans about them as if I saw them every day, when in fact I never saw them. My marriage to Elsie hadn't persuaded Donna Darlene. She still kept me at arm's length when it came to our children. It's no excuse, but whiskey was one way to smooth over the rough times I was going through. Booze, and then those smiling little pills in the palm of my hand. Back when I was a kid, Mama Rita tried to get us to mind by telling us that the devil, *le diable,* lived under our house. "If you boys ain't good, he'll jump out and grab your ass." It would be years later before I discovered that the devil really lived in bottles. Booze bottles. Pill bottles. And he's the kind of tenant that's hard to evict.

Thinking back on it, Mama Rita probably had more pills in her big, black handbag than most of my musical partying friends. But, of course, her pills were all legal.

Show business is almost always a case of taking the good with the bad, and sometimes it happens at the same time. An example of that phenomenon occurred some time later, on a day that I'll never forget as long as I live. It was January 31, 1971. At the time, William Morris was kicking butt for me. I'll say one thing for those guys. They knew how to fire up a hot streak. My agent was booking me everywhere but heaven, and I assumed we'd get that gig one day, too. As Jerry Reed once sang, "When you're hot, you're hot." My agent called me up one day and said, "Doug, let's run with this hot streak. Any show you really want to do?" I thought about it. Who in America had catapulted more performers to stardom? The answer that came back was Ed Sullivan. His show had been on television since 1948. It was an American institution, with entertainment for all walks of life and all ages. Elvis. The Beatles. Ballet dancers. Dancing bears. Plate spinners. You name it, Ed had it. It's impossible to find a show

186

on television today, what with hundreds of channels to choose from, that is comparable to the power of *The Ed Sullivan Show* back then. Stars were born in an instant.

"If you want *The Ed Sullivan Show*," my agent said, "then we'll book it."

It takes a lot to get me nervous once I hold that fiddle in my hands. But *The Ed Sullivan Show*, which was filmed in New York City at the Ed Sullivan Theater, was enough to make my knees tremble. This was live television. This was the show that hid Elvis's pelvis. It was the show that Jim Morrison defied, the night he and the Doors sang the words "we couldn't get much higher," even though Ed himself had banned the lyrics. It was the show Bob Dylan walked away from when the producers wouldn't allow him to sing "Talkin' John Birch Society Blues." And it was the show that reportedly killed comedian Jackie Mason's career for many years, all because Ed thought Jackie had given him the finger while doing his act. But it was also the show that introduced the Beatles to America as 73 million people tuned in, on February 9, 1964. If Ed Sullivan loved you, he could make the audience love you. He could make a star and break a star, no doubt about it.

It was common knowledge among entertainers that Ed Sullivan had a knack for finding the best performers for his show. He was even known to help choose their material and then carefully place the performer in just the right spot for the greatest impact. Keeping that in mind, I decided to write a special song, one that would highlight my fiddle playing as much as possible. Over the next few weeks I worked on a song that has since become one of my favorites. I called it "Play, Fiddle Play."

Tied to a tree on a river bank
not far from the place where my pirogue sank
Live in a houseboat built by hand
And I play my fiddle in a Cajun band

Play, play, play fiddle play,
Play, play, play fiddle play.

I would end up using this song as the first cut on *Doug Kershaw*, the Warner Bros. album I was working on at the time. I sent a tape of the song, along with two others from the forthcoming album, to the producers of the Sullivan show. Even though I very much wanted to perform "Play, Fiddle, Play" for the show, I decided not to tell the musical director that I'd written it with that in mind. Instead, I thought it best to give him a choice of the three songs. So, I kept my mouth shut and my fingers crossed.

I have no idea if Sullivan himself was involved in this decision, but word came back that the producers wanted me to perform all three songs. "Play, Fiddle, Play," "Colinda," and "Battle of New Orleans." The only way that was possible on a show with such a tight format was for me to do a medley. The musical director had already combined the three songs. He sent me back a tape of the medley as he heard it and asked if I approved. I did. But medleys are difficult to do—at least I always found them so. It seems you just get into a tone or feel of one song and it's time to go on to another. Cajun songs are even tougher since they each have their own unique personality. And then, it was *The Ed Sullivan Show,* broadcast live to millions of viewers around the country. No second takes and no room for mistakes.

We did rehearsals first, and I sang and played along with the tracks. That went down well. As show time crept closer, I started pacing around my dressing room. I still hadn't put a permanent band together at this point and I had come to the show alone. I had no one to talk to but strangers. And that's what I did, since talking is a release of nervous tension for me. I talked to the stagehands, the lighting people, the dressing room attendants, the cleaning lady, the makeup artists, the wall, you name it. I also made sure to open up my important-looking aluminum briefcase, with its foam enclosure, and take a slug of Chivas now and then for good measure. And pills. Well, a pill here and there could always be counted on to get the adrenalin kicked in. Good thing Ed didn't know I had pills and Chivas in my dressing room. Shit, this was the man who tried to ban the words "couldn't get much higher" by the Doors. I could hear him telling all of America, *Since that Cajun asshole can't get much higher, he won't be on our reeeely big shew tonight.*

It was just before airtime that Ed Sullivan came backstage and introduced himself, as if maybe I didn't know who he was. I was impressed. After all, he was the epitome of show business, the master. He was certainly not the stiff person he seemed to be on television, the Great Stone

Face, that guy with the jerky arm gestures that comedians loved to imitate. Nor did he seem to live up to his reputation for being high-strung and temperamental. He put me at ease instantly by asking me about Cajun food. And that's what we were talking about, gumbos and sauces, when a page came up to us and handed Mr. Sullivan a telegram. He thanked the young man, excused himself to me, then tore open the envelope. I didn't think anything was unusual until I noticed that he was visibly upset, to the point that his eyes had filled with tears. My first thought was that someone in his family had died.

"They've canceled my show," he said. "Twenty-three years, and they send me a telegram."

He handed it to me, this message from the gods at CBS. It wasn't even a standard *Dear John* letter. Nowhere did I see the word "sorry" mentioned or even an offer to talk about it. It was short and unsweet. I couldn't think of anything to say. I handed the telegram back to him.

"Good luck tonight, Doug," he said. "I'll see you on the set." In that instant, Ed Sullivan had become professional again, a man with a show to do.

My knees were still knocking when he announced me later.

And now, here tonight on are shew...the Cajun sensation...

I was wearing one of my trademark velvet suits. I remember mostly how sweaty the palms of my hands were so sweaty I was afraid I'd drop the fiddle bow. All I kept thinking was *Thirty million people are watching me right this minute.* The show had arranged for dancers to dance around me while I fiddled and sang. I did the medley and it was a long one. But it came off as if I'd been playing it all my life. The audience applauded like mad when I finished, and as fast as that it was over. All those days of preparation, all that nervous energy, over in just a few minutes. Because the show is live, you feel the immediate reaction of the house audience. But I wouldn't know until later what the reaction from the audience *out there* would be.

There was a production party after the show. For some reason Howard Cosell, the sportscaster, had dropped by. I was amazed to see Ed Sullivan talking casually with him, as if everything was fine. When Ed congratulated me on my performance, he gave no sign of what had happened earlier. As I was leaving, we shook hands.

"Take care of yourself, Doug," he said. Then he winked, as if we shared a private joke. I took it as his way of saying he'd manage.

I never saw the man again. I flew back to Nashville to begin work on my next album, *Louisiana Man*, for Warner Bros. On June 6, 1971, *The Ed Sullivan Show* aired for the last time. That night's show marked one thousand and eighty-three Sunday evenings that America had tuned in to watch the Rolling Stones, followed by a mouse named Topo Gigio, followed by an opera singer, followed by a plate spinner, followed by Sinatra, followed by Richard Pryor, followed by Rudolph Nureyev. It was the end of more than an era. That show had been a huge part of American lives. Three years later, Ed Sullivan would be dead of cancer.

The national exposure from the Sullivan show was better than I had dreamed. For the next couple of years work poured in from all over the country, including an invitation to appear in a movie. When director George Englund called in 1971 and asked me to do a cameo in his forthcoming *Zachariah*, I thought it sounded like fun. Two young actors would be co-starring, Don Johnson and John Rubinstein. It also sounded like a pretty strange movie to me since it was being billed as the "first electric Western." And it was a musical to boot. I'll tell you why it was the first. No one else was crazy enough to do it.

No one, that is, but members of Fireside Theater, who wrote it. *Zachariah* won't go down in the annals of great film moments, that's for sure. I became acquainted with a very young Don Johnson, who would later come to see my shows at the Palomino Club in North Hollywood. And I enjoyed meeting John Rubinstein, who went on to star in the TV series *Crazy Like a Fox*, among other things. I also remember a hell of a good drum solo on the soundtrack by the incredible Elvin Jones, who played the part of Job Cain. But as far as the movie itself, the ladies will probably only remember a baby-faced Don Johnson, rolling around in the sand while wearing a black leather cowboy outfit. And this on a blazing desert down in Mexico. But even early on in his career, and in that trying role, Don Johnson could act.

It took three days to film my cameo role. My character, the fiddler, was a satanic kind of wild man. How's that for good casting? I even had a small speaking role. But mostly I was to play my fiddle and sing "The

Death of Job Cain," a song I had written for the film. And I was to do this while riding a horse bareback. On the second take, the horse reared up into the air and tossed me off its back like I was just a troublesome fly. I landed flat on my ass on the sand. When I got back on my feet, I had a broken fiddle in my hand. That scene didn't make it, needless to say.

Opportunity kept knocking on my door. I was asked to appear on a CBS special hosted by John Wayne. I was thrilled to be on the same stage with a Hollywood legend like the Duke. I'd watched all those cowboy movies as a kid back in Lake Arthur, during those hungry days when I promised Mama Rita I'd take care of her. There were a ton of stars on the show, and yet the only one I can remember is Roy Clark. I do remember that one of the producers asked me to wear a coonskin cap, Davy Crockett style. This was not the first time nor the last that television producers had a hand in shaping my image. I had called myself "The Louisiana Man" up to that point. It seemed reasonable, considering the song I'd written by that title and taking into consideration other nicknames of the period. Ernest Tubb was "The Texas Troubadour," Sonny James was "The Country Gentleman," and Faron Young was "The Young Sheriff." All polite nicknames.

The press had different ideas for Doug Kershaw. By the late 1960s, when writing about my stage antics, I noticed they had begun to print things like "Kershaw's one wild, ragin' Cajun," or "Kershaw is a wild man on stage" or "the Cajun raged last night." And so on until the tag started to stick. TV producers noticed. They liked for me to appear a bit wild on their programs, dangerous, capable of doing anything. That would get the attention of the audience. Being wild and capable of doing anything, especially if I was high at the time, I was happy to oblige. I first wore a coonskin cap on that special hosted by John Wayne, and the audience lapped it up. In the years to follow, as my wild Cajun image grew, I would be asked to run down a ramp and leap off the dock onto the Staten Island Ferry, which was about a yard away by the time I reached it. I would be lifted up on a ladder, forty feet into the air, and placed in a tree. I would lie flat on my back to play fiddle, such as I did at the *Academy of Country Music Awards Show*. I would even ride in the bucket of a moving front end loader. You name it, I did it.

The Ragin' Cajun had been born.

191

In the middle of 1973, a Cajun drummer named Billy Abshire—he was no relation to Nathan—came knocking on my door in Nashville. He wanted to play drums for me. Since I had a show coming up in Seattle, I took Billy with me. It was in Seattle that we held an audition for two more musicians. I ended up hiring Max Schwennsen to play guitar and a young man named Richard—his last name escapes me—to play bass. I even picked up a roadie and sound man, Don Dodge. Now I had a band behind me. And this would begin a tradition of my getting pissed off at band members. We were only together about six months before there was a flare-up.

It was between shows at the Warehouse, which was a dinner club in Denver. After the first show I told Billy that I wasn't happy with how he was playing drums. I can't even remember now what it was I didn't like. What I do remember is the fight that followed. Billy didn't agree with me and so we got into a yelling match. When he called me a son of a bitch, I saw red and Billy saw a fist. I cold-cocked him and he went back against the wall. Out front, the audience for the second show was just coming in and getting seated. The club owner was out there and everyone could hear the fight, along with some choice swear words coming from behind the curtain. The owner hurried back stage in a huff and canceled the second show. We had to pack up and go back to the motel. Billy and I said nothing to each other that night, but the next morning I went over to his room. I was always sorry after the fact that I'd lost control. Billy had a helluva black eye. I apologized for hitting him, and that night we went back on stage at the Warehouse and did the show as if nothing had ever happened. Billy Abshire and I were friends right up until he passed away in 2014. But that fight was just the beginning of my battles with band members.

I began working the road with a vengeance, one gig after another, past exhaustion. I told myself what every entertainer says. "Make that money while you can, boy. Put it away for a rainy day." But in my heart I knew the truth. Even with booze and pills talking to me daily, clouding my brain, I knew what the constant work was all about.

I was running.

I was keeping one step ahead of everything that wasn't perfect in my life. My marriage. My inability to be a good father. My rapidly dissolving family ties. Those painful years of childhood. *Running*. I remember one night at the Palomino Club in Los Angeles that the truth came home to hit me hard. I was backstage waiting to go on when a fan approached me with a gift. She had clipped a photo of Mama Rita from a magazine and inserted it into a handmade frame. She was all smiles when she handed me the picture. I stood there high on booze and pills and stared down at my mother's face. I was living now in a world apart from her, from my whole family. It was as if I had crossed over into *The Twilight Zone* and they were all still on the houseboat back at Tiel Ridge. My eyes filled with tears, and I know that poor woman wished she hadn't given me the photo at all.

When I went back to my hotel room that night—it can be the loneliest room on earth for an entertainer—I knew that a big piece of my life was missing. I needed someone to love. I needed someone to love me. No doubt about it. What I didn't know was that a Colorado blizzard and a broken heater would throw events into action. I was about to meet that someone.

19

LOVE AT LAST

Pamela Marie, Pamela Marie
Do you love love me, me, me
Like I love you, you, you...

I met you when it was awful cold
That heater must have been awful old
But you managed well to keep me warm
In a Boulder, Colorado storm.
    —"Pamela Marie," by Doug Kershaw

It all started in 1973 when I played a concert in Denver, Colorado. A young woman was in the audience that night who would change my life. Maybe she even saved it. She was Pam Eson, a second-year nursing student who had seen my show and liked it so much that she started religiously checking the entertainment sections of the *Denver Post* and the *Rocky Mountain News* for word of return engagements. I'd been booked to appear for a whole week in early December at *Tulagi,* a club in Boulder, about twenty-five miles away. Pam read the notice. The Rocky Mountain area was just recovering from a Colorado blizzard that had paralyzed parts of the state. Cars had driven off the roads, electrical lines were down, and snow was piled to the rafters. The storm finally ended on the first day I was to appear. It was still colder than a witch's tit, but that didn't stop Pam from rounding up a group of friends.

"We're going to Boulder to see Doug Kershaw," she told them.

The storm had also hit the club where I was scheduled to appear. The heating system had stopped working, and the building was so cold that they could have stored meat in there by day. Night was something else. By the time Pam and her friends arrived at the club, the place was beyond freezing. They had come early in order to get good seats, but they needn't have worried. Not many people were crazy enough to venture out in such weather. The girls picked a table up front and sat there, shivering, to wait for the show to begin.

When I went on stage, I wasn't prepared for my damn audience to be bundled in parkas, knit hats, and warm gloves. It was about twenty degrees in the club that night. I could see puffs of breath each time someone in the audience leaned over to speak to a companion. I always try to put on the same caliber show, whether it's for fifty people or fifty thousand. And *that* night, I needed to do something to keep warm. So I poured it on as best I could, with lots of jumping and pacing on stage. Even so, by the time the first set was over, most of the crowd had realized that the heat probably wouldn't come back on. They left. I felt more like a lonely waiter in a bad café than I did a performer. Before the next set started the manager came back stage to find me.

"We got to close it up, Doug," he said. "Let's hope we've got heat for tomorrow night." That was fine with me. The band had been complaining that their fingers were so numb they couldn't feel them. So I packed my fiddle into its case and went out front to thank those pretty girls for sticking it out. It was my musical duty.

I started with the few folks at the back tables and then worked my way up to the front, to the table of young women. Even in her parka and hat, Pam Eson was red-nosed and shivering. I remember my first impression of her. She was a tall, thin, blue-eyed brunette who had a certain air that told you she was smart as hell. I was almost reluctant to talk to her. I offered Pam's table what I had offered the other tables, a rain check in the form of a free ticket for the following night. I should have called it a *snow* check. Pam quickly told me that they already had tickets for the next night. And the next and the next for the rest of the week. That news warmed me up a little.

The heating system was working again by the next day and the place had warmed back up. Pam and the girls kept their word by coming back, so I made my move that second night. For years I had to have a crowd around me a buffer, I guess, for the blues that often came after each show. That night was no different, but this time I asked Pam to come along to my hotel room with my after-the-show crowd. She did.

When we started working on this book someone asked me if I had told Pam right away that I was married. I felt sure I must have, since I had no marriage to speak of in my mind. Why hide it, right? But that's not how Pam remembered it. She says the phone rang that night in my hotel room and that I talked to someone. Pam says I pretended it was nothing important, but she knew it was a woman in my life. It was only later that she realized it must have been Elsie. She wouldn't find out about the marriage until later, in New York, and *that* could have been scripted by Hollywood.

I was impressed with Pam Eson's maturity and intelligence. I knew this was no star-struck groupie. I also knew I'd have to do something special to impress her. The next night I invited her to dinner after the show. Paul Prudhomme had opened a restaurant at that time in Boulder, and I took Pam there.

"Paul Prudhomme is going to stay open after hours and cook us some real Cajun food," I told her, "just for the band and the two of us."

Thinking back, why didn't I leave the band at the hotel? That's what drugs can do to your thinking. But I was certain this would turn Miss Eson's head.

"Who's Paul Prudhomme?" she asked. Well, maybe it wasn't time yet for Cajun food in Boulder. Paul would eventually close his restaurant and leave for warmer climes. This was a few years before his appearance on the *Today* show, with his blackened redfish creation that would make Cajun food an overnight sensation.

Pam and I spent that week getting to know each other. It wasn't all picture-perfect, I must admit. I was pretty damn broke at the time. I had left William Morris at the advice of a very bad manager I'd hired back in Nashville. At his urging, I'd gone with Buddy Lee Attractions as a booking agency. It seemed the harder I worked, the poorer I got. And I couldn't blame it all on booze and drugs. It's safe to say I wasn't the only one mismanaging Doug Kershaw. I was also without a road manager at that time. It seems I was forever firing road managers or they were forever quitting. So I asked Pam Eson if she would make some calls to deal with airlines and travel arrangements. She did it so professionally that I went ahead and asked if she'd take over that job. Pam had made friends with the band members by then. I guess they must have feared for this young woman's well-being because Max Schwennsen and Don Dodge warned her not to take the job.

"You'd have to be insane," they told her. "Don't do it."

Pam was twenty-one years old. What twenty-one year-old listens to good advice?

I had already agreed to do a television show down in Atlanta called *Music Country U.S.A.*, a summer replacement series for the *Dean Martin Show*. So I changed the airline ticket meant for my former road manager—whose name escapes me, thank God—over to Pam's name. It was set. Pam had some things to take care of in Denver and then would join us in Atlanta. By the time she drove me to the Denver airport in her 1966 Pontiac Lemans, I was hooked. I hated to admit it. How the hell could I make the relationship work with all the baggage I would bring? And then, I was almost sixteen years older than Pam. The worst part was to come. Even though my marriage had been over for a long time in theory, I still wasn't divorced. I just hadn't told Pam yet about Elsie.

I wondered what Pam's parents would think of their daughter leaving Colorado with me and my band. She was very close to her family. Her father was a mechanic for United Airlines and her mother worked in the flight kitchen, putting meals on cargo bins for the flights. Pam was the third generation on both sides to be born and raised in Denver. She had even gone to the same high school as her father and grandfather, North Denver High. That's close-knit. There was a sense of family history and support that I never had growing up. I don't think the Esons expected to see a wild Cajun fiddler staring at them from their little girl's wedding album, not unless I'd been hired to play the music. Surprisingly, no one hit the roof. Pam's mother, Shirley, knew that her daughter was unhappy at nursing school. Nonetheless, since the ticket to Atlanta was a one-way, Shirley gave Pam a credit card.

"Use this if you need to come home," Shirley told her.

Years later, Jay Leno wrote in his autobiography about the time he lost his wife, Mavis, at the airport in New Orleans. The airport cops kept telling him that she'd *run off with somebody*. Jay writes that when he finally found Mavis in the coffee shop, he took her over to the cops "just to prove my wife hadn't run off with Doug Kershaw into the Cajun Bushland."

A week later Pam joined me in Atlanta. After that, we flew to New York, where I would tape another segment of *Music Country U.S.A.* It was there that a young woman came to my trailer to take measurements for wardrobe. Believe it or not this was Elsie's daughter, Karole. That's how little I cared about my marriage. I wanted it over. I still didn't say anything to Pam, too afraid I'd lose her. But one of my band members, Billy Abshire, did. Pam could tell something was up, so she asked Billy who the wardrobe girl was.

"Doug's stepdaughter," Billy told her.

"Does that mean Doug is married?" Pam asked. Billy said it did mean that. It did, indeed.

Damn, what can I say? I wish it had been different. Chalk it up to too much booze and pills and not enough guts. That's how Pam found out about Elsie. I asked her to weigh in on this for the book, and this is what she said.

"I felt foolish, even sick to my stomach. I now realized why I was getting icy stares from the *Music Country U.S.A* crew. They all knew about Elsie. Later, as we went by bus from our hotel in New Jersey over to Manhattan, I heard one of the women refer to some *other girl* who'd been hanging around but who was now history. I understood this to mean that I was just one of many who wouldn't last too long."

There's probably a portrait of me hanging in the Hall of Shame.

By this time it was close to Christmas. Pam flew home to Colorado and I went back to Nashville. Elsie's daughter had, of course, told her mother about the tall brunette who had been with Doug at the taping of *Music Country U.S.A.* It wasn't the best way for Elsie to hear about Pam. And it wasn't a great time to celebrate Christmas. Nobody at the Kershaw residence was singing "O Come, All Ye Faithful." It hit the fan, big time, with both of us screaming and yelling. But I told Elsie exactly how I felt.

"I'm playing Vegas in January," I said. "I'm filing for divorce while I'm there."

This was a waste of breath since Elsie would beat me to it by filing first. And the Vegas gig would fall through anyway.

I was already booked for the week following Christmas at Steamboat Springs, a trendy ski resort in Colorado. My band and I flew into Denver on December 26 and Pam met us at the airport. Since we couldn't fit the entire band and all that equipment into the Pontiac Lemans, I decided to rent a car. But it was the holiday season and nothing was available, not even a horse and carriage. Added to this, it had started snowing like a son of a bitch. Then I remembered some fans in Boulder who had told me to call if I ever needed anything. I bet the Hartnagles never dreamed the phone would ring on a stormy day after Christmas and Doug Kershaw would ask, "Can you give me a ride to Steamboat Springs?" Bless them, they ventured out in that storm like St. Bernards to rescue us.

As we got up into the mountains, the snow got thicker and the wind blew harder. We turned on the radio and discovered that the storm was being called "a full force blizzard." I didn't want to think about it, so I spent the trip sitting in the back seat, drinking Coors beer and writing a song I called "Colorado."

> *Big tall pines and old gold mines,*
> *And I'm sipping on a cold Coors beer*
> *Billy, keep your eyes on the road ahead*
> *I will look at Jeanie's head*
> *Oh, it sure does snow and the wind does blow in Colorado*
> *But it's a damn good place to go.*

When we finally got to Steamboat Springs, a celebrity ski slalom was in progress. The place was glittering with stars who had flown in to do some skiing. I decided to take a ski lesson from Billy Kidd. Billy was the first great American male Alpine skier and the first American male to win an Olympic medal. I figured if anybody could teach a Cajun how to stand up on two narrow strips of fiberglass on snow, it would be Billy Kidd. Pam decided to wander around the resort until my lesson was over. When she heard that the celebrity slalom was about to begin, she found a spot in the crowd gathered at the foot of the slope and waited for the first skier. Several celebrities came down, gracefully dodging the poles, such as Ethel Kennedy and Andy Williams. An announcement then came over the loudspeaker. "Substituting for Claudine Longet is Doug Kershaw."

Pam felt panic. The first time I ever put on skis, I ended up at the emergency clinic, my back on fire. But here I come down the slope, weaving in and out, doing my best to stay vertical, arms flailing. It would be three years later that Claudine Longet would shoot and kill skier Spider Sabich, and *Saturday Night Live* would turn clips of men falling on skis into a comedy routine for a skit called *The Claudine Longet Invitational.* A strong young skier would start down the hill, a shot would ring out, and down he would go. "Uh-oh!" Chevy Chase would say. "He seems to have been accidentally shot by Claudine Longet." The next skier would go down and, "Uh, here she was just showing the gun to a friend." I did manage to make it around one pole before I, too, went down. I tasted snow between my teeth. I couldn't even get my legs untangled enough to stand up and take a bow. Clint Eastwood came over and helped me to my feet. Pam later told me that she wondered if things were always that crazy in my life.

"I knew it would mean *my* life would be crazy too," she said.

Little did Pam Eson know that she had met Doug Kershaw during a lull.

I was scheduled to play Nashville after that, at the famous Exit Inn, so Pam came with me. By now she was definitely acting as road manager for the band. Just before my show was to start that first night, I was served with divorce papers. All the usual entourage was gathered around when it happened. I was angry about it, knowing Elsie's timing was intentional. Looking back, I can't say I blame her. I went on stage anyway and did two great shows. Leon Russell was in the audience, and that helped me stay focused. It's always fun to have another performer around, and Leon was a cutup anyway. I always open "Orange Blossom Special" with a train whistle. After the show Leon came up and slapped me on the back.

"Kershaw," he said, "you're the only guy I know who can make four notes come out of his mouth at one time."

Leon and I decided on the spot that we'd go into the studio together and record some songs. It was two in the morning by then, but we jumped into a car and went over to Pete Drake's place to put down some tracks. I don't know if Leon was doing any drugs back then or not. I do remember he turned down a shot of Chivas when I offered it to him. And I remember that one of the songs we recorded that night was "Colorado," which was still so fresh in my mind. It was a long night. Pam fell asleep on the sofa at the studio. It's a wonder I didn't lose those divorce papers during the night. If my pot-smoking friends had been at the session, they might've needed some rolling paper.

When I woke up the next morning with a hangover, I was headed for my second divorce. It wouldn't be final for another year, but I could see a light at the end of the tunnel. And for once it didn't look like a train. I never did get a copy of that impromptu session with Leon Russell. But I ran into him on the road years later, and he mentioned that *he* had a copy. That's what you get for not drinking Chivas.

Up to this point I had been spending the money as fast as it came in. Since I had already bought Elsie's house for her and Pam had given up her apartment, I didn't have to worry about rent or house payments. So I spent my money on frivolous things instead. I even bought a 1961 Rolls Royce Bentley, a beauty of a car, steering wheel on the right-hand side, with an eight-track tape deck. I kept that Rolls right up until 1986 until it got too expensive to keep running right. As often as not, Pam and I flew first class and then stayed at the best hotels. I was always throwing money after something drinks for the house and dinners for everyone. I loved gambling. I didn't see any sense in a savings account. The truth is that I never really saw myself getting any older than Daddy Jack, and he died at forty. What right did his son have to live longer? The future was a hazy place to me back then, a place I never expected to visit.

I did make the mistake of investing some money once. When the Vegas gig that Buddy Lee Attractions had booked for me fell through, I fired that inept Nashville manager and left Buddy Lee for Athena, a small booking agency in Denver. My agents there approached me with an opportunity to invest five thousand dollars in a company called Crested Butte. The rocket scientists at Crested Butte had invented a Styrofoam container for mailing record albums in. That sounded like a good idea, so I forked over the five grand. My agent back then was Chet Hanson, a man who would become my future manager. Chet wanted to invest five thousand too, but he didn't have it. I loaned him the money on the condition that he'd pay me back once we were all multimillionaires. When Crested Butte went ass-up, I lost ten grand. So much for Kershaw investing.

Shortly after the Exit Inn, I was scheduled to play Grand Rapids, Michigan, with Earl Scruggs and John Hartford. As it happened I was too broke to buy the airline tickets for Pam, the band, and me. I had to sell my golf cart for nine hundred dollars to get us all to the show. I think this is when Pam and I realized that we were essentially homeless. I decided to do something about it. Since my next gig was at the Palomino Club in Los

Angeles, I sent Billy Abshire on ahead. His mission was to find us a place to live. Billy rented three shabbily furnished apartments on the Sunset Strip, just about a block from the Hyatt Hotel, a thousand bucks a month for the lot. So we all headed for Cal-a-fornie, the way Jed Clampett and his own group of ragamuffins had done. But we didn't end up in a mansion in Beverly Hills. When Pam saw what was to be her new home, I think she wanted to run back to Colorado.

"Will this do?" I asked. She just stared for a few minutes.

"It's creepy," she said. "But at least we can unpack our suitcases."

It wasn't exactly the kind of life Pam Eson might have expected, but she didn't run. She unpacked her suitcase for the first time in a month. And since she had always been the one to cook for the family while her mother worked the swing shift at United Airlines, Pam bought dishes, pots, and cooking utensils. She was a very good cook. The first thing she made was a big pot of chili. I was scheduled to play the Palomino that night, the first of a three-night gig. Pam had seemed so disappointed with the apartments that I didn't have the heart to tell her I never eat within four hours of a show. So I ate a big bowl of chili. During my show, I had to keep turning away from the microphone, my back to the audience, so I could burp.

It was only a week later that we went back out on the road, headed for another gig, then another and another. Athena had started booking me on college campuses around the country and not just the club circuit. But more and more the heavy drug use was getting in the way of my performances. I was late for the shows more often than not. Pam became a nervous wreck because of it. She was forever pointing at her watch.

"Shit, they can't start the show without me," I'd tell her. When Pam started developing the first Kershaw ulcer, she decided to quit wearing her watch altogether.

It was during this period of time on college campuses that a comedian had been hired to open for me. I rarely got to the gig in time to catch his show, but I always shook his hand as he came off stage. It was the damnedest thing. I'd be ready to go on and here would come this guy in a white suit, carrying a banjo, a balloon animal around his neck, and an arrow through his head.

"Who the hell *is* that guy?" I'd whisper to Pam.

"His name is Steve Martin," she'd whisper back.

We never did get back to Los Angeles and the apartments. Pam's parents, whom I had yet to meet, flew out to Los Angeles on their United passes, drove to the run-down apartments on the Sunset Strip, packed up all our belongings, and put them in storage for us. I wonder what they thought of Doug Kershaw at that point in time? I finally met them a month later, when I played the Warehouse in Denver. Pam's mother, father, and her two sisters joined us for dinner. I had a habit of ordering two or three entire meals just to get the things I wanted. I remember that I ordered both steak and lobster that night and ate only the meat. Pam's family probably figured it was a "Cajun thing." But we hit it off very well. I liked them, and I think they liked me, despite those apartments they had emptied on the Sunset Strip.

It would be more than a year before Pam would unpack her suitcase again. Our only home during that period was whatever hotel we happened to be staying in on the road. Our mail came to Athena. They boxed it up and sent it to wherever they could track us down. And by the way, that light I saw at the end of the tunnel? It *was* the damn train. Elsie had a good lawyer, something I was too busy on the road to stop long enough and hire. By the time the divorce became final, the judge had awarded her everything, including a life insurance policy on me listing *Elsie* as the beneficiary. And I was to pay her seven hundred and fifty dollars a month for life.

How many men would want a bitter ex-wife to have an insurance policy on their life? I should have invested in bullet-proof vests instead of Styrofoam mailers. Needless to say, even though I was smitten with Pam Eson, I wasn't ready to get married again. And Pam didn't seem to want to get married either. I think she was still stunned as to how an intelligent young college woman who had never been anything but a perfect daughter to her parents, who had never gone through any rebellious years, who had been an A student, was now on the road with Doug Kershaw and living out of a suitcase. Marriage was one thing. A good home was another. Around March 1975, I started thinking how nice it would be to have a solid foundation under me. Looking back and playing shrink, it's possible the fact that I was turning forty the next year was what motivated me. Daddy Jack's death age. Maybe I was trying to save myself from what I could sense was coming. And I saw in Pam a stable home and family. So I did what I swore I'd never do again. I proposed to another woman.

"I'm ready," I told Pam. "Will you marry me?" She had seen some wild times on the road, so I wasn't sure if she'd accept or not. But she did, and we immediately set a date for June 21, 1975. By this time Chet Hanson at my booking agency had become my manager. He talked me into having a prenuptial agreement drawn up between Pam and me. Where the hell was Chet when Elsie and I got married, when I really could have used such a contract? Chet had the prenup drawn up, and Pam and I both signed it. If we didn't stay married for five years, she would get nothing when we split. As we were writing this book I mentioned that agreement to Pam.

"Can you believe I let you sign that thing?" I said.

Pam just smiled. "Can you believe I signed it?" she asked.

Now that we'd decided to get married, it was time to find a stable home. For the first seven years of my life I had lived in a house that moved up and down the Mermentau River. Maybe that's why I was able to adjust to life on the road as a musician. But Pam had had it. She was tired of checking in and out of hotels and motels. So we found a place in Evergreen, Colorado, a rustic home that sat so high up a hill that we later had to buy a Jeep Wagoneer with four-wheel drive just to get up to it. This house caught my attention because it sat just fifty feet from the tenth green of the Hiwan Golf Club. I soon found out that this situation looked better than it was. The club members were so tight-assed and snooty that they kept reporting me for playing golf in jeans. Or for having five people in a foursome. I can hear golfers out there now saying, "A fivesome? And *jeans?*" Still, with all the big problems taking place in the world, these seemed minor to me. But the other Hiwan club members tattled on me every chance they got. Try to imagine a grown man on the telephone whispering, "Doug Kershaw is wearing jeans again!"

Later that year I was booked for a big college tour. I had no choice but to purchase a PA system and a truck to carry the equipment from show to show. I borrowed forty thousand dollars from the bank in order to do this. The third gig out, I wound up playing in the lobby of a college cafeteria while students placed their orders. *I'll have the ham and cheese on rye. I'll have the meatloaf and mashed potatoes.* In the middle of my third song, I packed up and left. But I had borrowed all that money and I was financially strapped. I ended up two months late on my Hiwan membership dues. It was only a matter of time before some of the club members spread it all over Evergreen. "Doug Kershaw hasn't paid his dues." Well, I'd paid the other kind of dues, and that's something most of those bastards at the country club had yet to do.

It was around this time, early in 1975, that a man named Jack Good was in the audience at one of my shows. It just so happened that Jack was producing a Mary Tyler Moore special called *Mary's Incredible Dream*. After the show he came backstage and asked if I'd like to be on the special. The Manhattan Transfer had already been booked, as had Arthur Fiedler. Few men alive would have turned down a chance to perform with America's Sweetheart, Mary Tyler Moore. Besides, I knew what kind of doors television could open. I'd already seen it. I was doing as many concert dates as humanly possible without a chart record. Hell, I knew guys with big radio hits who weren't being booked in the kind of venues that I was. That was the power of TV. I accepted Jack Good's offer in a heartbeat.

A couple months later, Pam, the band, and I flew out to Los Angeles, where we were met and taken to CBS studios. Apparently someone had put a lot of thought into *Mary's Incredible Dream*. Too much thought. One of the many skits was set in the Garden of Eden. All the good characters were dressed in white. I had been cast as a *good* character. Mary Tyler Moore and the other women in the skit were in white ballroom gowns. Ben Vereen, who was cast as the snake, had on a green-sequined tuxedo and a green bowler hat. Vereen sat on the limb of a big leafy tree—I guess it was the Tree of Knowledge. He convinced Mary and me to take a bite of the apple. In another skit, I played "Morning Has Broken" by Cat Stevens on my fiddle while the dancers danced around a leafless white tree I was sitting in. The critics called it "Mary's Incredible Nightmare."

But then, I don't know many critics with their own TV special.

I did get to dance with Mary, who is a very professional dancer. I'd come a long way since the time I'd jitterbugged with Little Frances back on Nightclub Row. Since Mary Tyler Moore is a diabetic, someone was always standing in the wings with a can of Tab for when she finished rehearsing a scene. "Miss Moore's Tab" was a phrase I heard a lot during the taping. If it had been *my* show, you'd have heard "Mr. Kershaw's Chivas" instead.

Mary's Incredible Dream wouldn't air until January 1976. Despite what the critics said of it, it was great publicity for Doug Kershaw. I still didn't have a hit record on the charts, but I had stopped worrying about it. The times were too damn good. I could buy all the pills and booze I wanted. Money flew, and when it flies, it talks. Trouble is, eventually even money gets tired of talking. But I was still a long way from realizing that. And I was on the path to the altar once again.

All this time, in the back of my mind, that one thought was still looming.

"Next year I'll be forty years old. Daddy Jack's age."

20

MARRIAGE

"This is the craziest thing I've ever done."
—Pam Eson Kershaw, June 21, 1975,
the Astrodome Hotel, Houston

Pam and I booked the ballroom of the historic Brown Palace Hotel in Denver for our wedding reception. Since Pam was a traditional girl, the Brown Palace would be the perfect place for a family with old Denver roots to celebrate their daughter's wedding. So we ordered the invitations. Things seemed to be on an even keel for a change. That should have made me suspicious. When I told Mama Rita I was getting married again, this time to a young woman only twenty-three years old, she shook her head.

"*Mais,* Doug," Mama Rita said. "First you marry a *putain.* Then you marry your *ma-mère.* Now you gonna marry your daughter?"

Mama Rita was like Faron Young used to be when he was drunk and on a roll. She could insult several people at one time.

I had been asked to be one of the celebrity players in the Houston Open golf tournament, so I flew down to Houston at the end of April to play some golf. My band and I would also provide the musical entertainment for the crowd that evening. It was at the tournament that I ran into Slick Johnson, who booked events at the famed Houston Astrodome.

"We got a big Cajun festival set for the twenty-first of June," Slick told me. "You could attend the festival before the game and then do a show for us after."

The Astrodome was another place I'd always wanted to play, so I told Slick that I'd love to do it. Then I remembered that June 21 was to be my wedding day. The invitations had already arrived with the venue as Brown Palace Ballroom printed on them. Pam had addressed them and was just about to send them out.

"I can't do it, Slick," I said. "I'm getting married that day."

That's when Slick Johnson made me one of the strangest offers I've ever had.

"There's never been a wedding at the Astrodome," he said. "Would you two like to be the first?"

I knew how much the Astrodome liked having "firsts" connected to its publicity, so I thought about it. Entertainers are so accustomed to playing on special occasions—Christmas, New Year's Eve, Thanksgiving—that I suppose it didn't seem like a strange request to me. Needless to say, Pam was very reluctant. After all, the Astrodome wasn't the *historic* Brown Palace. I recently asked her why she had agreed to such an untraditional church.

"Because I always went along with whatever you wanted back then, Doug," she said. "It was much easier." Man, have things changed.

Our wedding plans quickly shifted from Colorado to Texas. I told Slick Johnson that Pam and I would be there with our wedding rings and the marriage license. Our big problem now was time. There was no way we could get new invitations printed up and mailed out. Pam was close to tears. But I hail from swamp country, where you can cup your hands to your mouth and shout out an invitation in the morning. By nightfall there'd be a *fais do-do* in full swing on somebody's houseboat. In other words, I didn't give a damn about formalities. So I quickly offered Pam a solution.

"Why don't you send the Brown Palace invitations to the people we don't really like? Let them go to Denver instead of Houston." That was one idea she wasn't going for. She had no choice but to draw a line through *Brown Palace* and write *Houston Astrodome* above it. Looking back, Pam might have changed her mind about marrying me. After all, I was still up to my high jinks where pills and booze were concerned. She had already seen what being married to Doug Kershaw might hold in store. I remember one time shortly before our wedding that I was booked for two weeks at Harrah's Hotel & Casino in Reno, doing two nightly shows. Putting Kershaw in a casino back then was like putting a match in a can of gasoline. After doing two ball-busting shows every night I'd stay up gambling until dawn, just me and Chivas Regal. The casino made it damn easy for a Cajun fiddler to gamble. A hotel employee carrying a sheet of paper on a clipboard would come up to me, all smiles.

"Mr. Kershaw, would you like a thousand dollars?" he'd ask.

Does a bear shit in the woods? Of course, Mr. Kershaw wanted a thousand dollars. Hell, yes. So I'd sign his paper—it's called a marker—on the line at the bottom. And I'd take my thousand dollars worth of chips. Now, I knew the markers weren't free, but when it's chips in your hands and not real money, it's different. So I was losing a ton of chips. Big deal. This happened every night and sometimes twice a night. What encouraged this behavior was that before I lost big, I won big. Man, what a rush! One night I came upstairs to our room where Pam was sleeping, my arms full of money. I tossed it all over the bed—about fifteen thousand bucks. Pam sat up and stared. It looked like it had snowed green while she was asleep.

"We need to do something sensible with this, Doug," she said.

I agreed.

The very next day I called a dealership in Los Angeles and had them drive a new 1975 Lincoln Continental Mark IV all the way to Reno. I paid for the car in cash. That night I was back at the tables, sure I'd do it all over again. If I did, I'd do something else sensible and buy Pam her own Lincoln. And that's when I started losing. *Damn.* Talk about a loud sucking sound, all that money going down the drain. The man with the clipboard was turning up so often you'd have thought I was engaged to him instead of Pam. By the time I left Reno, I owed Harrah's Casino more than fifteen thousand dollars, more than the Lincoln had cost in the first place. It was a somber ride back to Evergreen in my new Mark IV. Pam was quiet and thoughtful in the passenger seat. I knew she wanted to kill me. She just didn't know *how much* she wanted to kill me until Harrah's tallied up my bill.

There was an irony in it, I suppose. Some of that Kershaw fate. Mama Rita and Daddy Jack had lost all their money to the river that time their houseboat sank in the Mermentau. But I had lost mine to the desert back during those two weeks in 1975. That was a lot of currency then, and it took me more than a year to pay it off. I had to agree to do my shows at Harrah's for free until my bill was cleaned up. Even that wasn't enough to cure me of my gambling habits. I lost another pile of money to Vegas before I wised up. Let me tell you something I learned from this. The river will let you win now and then and even walk away free. Vegas doesn't, not a guy like me. After that, whenever I played Vegas or Reno, I made certain the casino put a letter in my file. *Mr. Kershaw is to be given no markers.*

I think I'll get to heaven one day. And if God has a sense of humor, I'll be shown right on in. But when he opens my file, I suspect there will be a letter in it. *Don't give the Ragin' Cajun any markers.*

On the day before our wedding, Pam and I flew to Houston. I had a television interview to do later in the afternoon with Jonni Hartman, who happens to be actress Lisa Hartman's mother. That evening, the Astros were playing the Cincinnati Reds, and we were asked to throw out the ceremonial first pitch. By now it was public knowledge that we'd be getting married in the Astrodome the next day. The BBC and ABC networks were already there with plans to film the wedding, the BBC for Europe and ABC for the United States. Our spirits were high, although I'm sure Pam was feeling the same tension that would accompany any wedding, even the kind that takes place in a small church. Looking back, I'd put a lot on her shoulders. Having the wedding in Houston meant that her grandparents, aunts, uncles, and many friends wouldn't be able to make it. Pam wasn't a performer, after all, and yet we were about to get married in front of forty thousand people.

Pam and I threw out the first pitch of the game to catcher Johnny Bench while the cameras rolled. After the game, we were taken to a sprawling and elegant mansion to meet Judge Red James, who would be performing the ceremony. Judge James was one of those no-nonsense Texas types, heavyset with sensible eyeglasses and wearing a conservative suit and tie. I was all decked out in a blue polyester leisure suit that evening. I have to wonder now what that Texas judge thought of my outfit, but it was the 1970s. I do remember the advice he gave us.

"Don't you worry about getting married in front of all those people, Doug," Judge James said. He slapped me on the back. "It'll be a piece of cake."

That next morning, a Saturday, was a typically hot June day in Texas. We rehearsed the ceremony quickly and then headed back to the Astrodome Hotel. It had already been arranged that we would have one of their biggest and best suites, the kind that ran for twenty-five hundred bucks a night in 1975. When we got back from rehearsal and opened the doors to our fancy suite, it looked like a rodeo was taking place inside. The room was packed to the rafters with people. First of all, Pam's parents had flown in from Denver, along with her two sisters and brother. With them were three bridesmaids and three groomsmen. The Texas and Louisiana contingent included Mama Rita and Adam Trahan, her third husband, whom she had married a few years earlier. Pee Wee was there with his family. Little Russell Gary and his wife, Willie Mae, were also on hand. They happened to be celebrating their wedding anniversary that same day. And then scores of other friends had driven or flown from all over the country. I tell you, it was a madhouse. It was the Bucket of Blood on a Saturday night.

Rusty Kershaw, however, was a no-show. And I have to stop the wedding story right here to tell you why. A couple weeks earlier, Rusty had called and told me that he was too broke to come to the wedding. So I sent a check for five hundred dollars to his Los Angeles address, which was where he was living at the time. A couple days before the ceremony, I got another call from Rusty. This time he was somewhere in Arizona, en route to Houston.

"I'm trying like hell to get there," Rusty said, "but I haven't been able to cash your check, Doug. Can you wire me the five hundred instead?" I told him I would, and he gave me an address in Arizona where money could be transferred. Then Rusty hesitated a few seconds. "Doug," he asked. "Can I keep the check too?"

"Are you crazy?" I said. "Hell no you can't keep the check too."

So, we expected Rusty and his wife to show up at the Astrodome suite at any time, looking worn-out from the long drive but at least in attendance. They never did appear. I learned later that once Rusty picked up the money he had headed for Port Bolivar, Texas, to visit our oldest brother, Edward, and his wife, Marie. So much for sentiment.

But Pam and I were not about to let family problems keep us from having the time of our lives. Since we didn't want our guests to go hungry, we ordered several hundred dollars of room service for everyone. Waiters began filing in and out of the suite nonstop carrying dishes of food. The television crew was trying to set up lights and audio for the prewedding interview they had planned for me, Pam, and Mama Rita. Then, some genius decided we should open our wedding gifts right then and there while everyone was with us in the room. It was just good luck that the BBC or ABC weren't filming at the time, considering one of those gifts was almost obscene.

People thought that since I was a so-called celebrity I already had all the necessities to set up housekeeping, such as dishes, towels, sheets, flat-ware, a damn toaster. Whatever the reason might have been, many of the gifts we received were unusual, even outlandish. For instance, someone gave us a pair of stuffed quail, looking so real they might fly back to the bayou at any minute. But the one gift that still stands out after all these years is the large, gold, plaster-of-Paris bank. This was not a typical piggy bank, mind you, but a nude woman with her bare ass stuck up in the air. Quarters, nickels, dimes, and pennies were to be inserted in the crack of her butt. Maybe someone thought it would be an incentive for me to start saving my money.

We survived the opening of the gifts, did our interview, and then it was time to get dressed for the wedding. Pam wore a yellow, satin wedding gown with a long yellow veil. I wore a custom-made tux, also yellow. It had rhinestones and yellow satin lapels. Even my patent-leather boots were yellow. It was definitely not the traditional look. By this time the limos had lined up to take us over to the Astrodome for the ceremony. Once there, we discovered that we had to walk up several ramps to get to the locker rooms. It was during this time that Mama Rita's husband, Adam Trahan, went looking for a restroom and never came back. The staff told me not to worry, that he'd find his way eventually since the path was clearly marked with signs. But I knew better. Adam Trahan couldn't read. And while he might have been able to navigate his way through a Louisi-ana bayou with his eyes closed at midnight and three sheets to the wind, he was a goner when it came to reading directions in the belly of the Hou-ston Astrodome. Luckily, Pam's father had already become familiar with the layout of the place. He went out tracking Adam and found him wan-dering about on the opposite side of the complex from where he was sup-posed to be.

Years later when I saw the movie *Spinal Tap,* in the scene where the band gets lost backstage at a gig in Cleveland, I was reminded of my wed-ding entourage. We spent some time trying to find our way down the ramps and through the tunnels of the Astrodome. We finally arrived at the opening in back of home plate. Judge Red James was waiting for us and about as nervous as a man can be. He had been right about one thing. The ceremony would be a piece of cake for Doug Kershaw. But the good judge had no idea what it was like to stand and speak in front of forty thousand people, with all those big national and international cameras on him. Live, at that. I feared he might turn and run. He managed to pronounce us man and wife. Then our names on the Astrodome board lit up and began flashing. *Doug and Pamela!* Fireworks filled the sky. People cheered. It was over. As we walked off the field I noticed that Judge Red James seemed a bit distant.

"I need a drink," he said.

"I know where you can get one," I told him. "Follow me."

We had the most extravagant wedding reception I'd ever seen. As Pam and I entered the room we were greeted with a rousing version of "Jambalaya," played by a Scottish bagpipe band. To this day I don't know whose idea *that* was at a Cajun wedding, but we loved it anyway. The cameras and crews were waiting for us too, as the BBC and ABC continued their filming. The Astrodome had catered the wedding cake, which was actually three cakes with bridges connecting each of them. In the middle of the center cake was a full-sized fiddle. It was big enough to have fed all of Lake Arthur. For the main course there were big pots of shrimp, crawfish and gumbo. Ellis Cormier, who owns The Boudin King restaurant in Jennings, Louisiana, had brought in several hundred pounds of boudin, that famous Cajun sausage. There was just so much going on, the guests, the film crews, the excitement of getting married, that Pam never touched a bite of food at her own wedding reception. She made up for it in champagne, however.

The Astros and the Reds were playing again that night, and I was scheduled to perform after the game. Mama Rita and Pee Wee were going to join me on stage so we could kick up our heels, Cajun style, the way we used to back in the chicken coop so many ago. The whole wedding party had been given seats in the stands where we could watch the game and continue to celebrate, which we did. But the damn game went into extra innings Tenth inning. Eleventh inning. Twelfth inning. By the 14th inning and with the score still tied, the wedding party was pretty well sloshed. I was still in my wedding suit and Pam in her gown. We were drunkenly shouting out to the ballplayers, begging for somebody, *anybody,* to please just score. I had a show still to play. The Reds finally got a hit and it won them the game. But it was well after midnight when I took the stage to do my show.

In the early hours of the morning Pam and I finally unlocked the door to our beautiful honeymoon suite at the Astrodome Hotel. We were both reeling and exhausted from a day of excitement and celebration.

"This is the craziest thing I've ever done," Pam said.

And then we both promptly fell asleep.

And that's the story of The Last Time Doug Kershaw Will Ever Get Married.

The next year the Astrodome would hold what they were calling the *Doug Kershaw Cajun Festival and Gumbo Cook-off.* I wanted to call up Slick Johnson and ask, "Would you like for Pam and me to get divorced this time?" I figured that, too, would be an Astrodome first. But that was one of my ideas Pam wasn't going for.

Thankfully Pam's folks had given her a bridal shower back in Denver. That meant we had a few sensible gifts to set up housekeeping. We went back to Evergreen, Colorado, to our new home near the tenth green, where we would live for the next couple years. But we had no furniture except for a beat-up recliner that Mama Rita had given us.

"Look," I said to Pam when I showed her the chair. "It comes with its own duct tape."

We also had a lawn chair we'd gotten somewhere. And since we couldn't sit on the floor and stare at a nude woman with a slot in the crack of her butt, we had to go out and buy a television and a couch. And we also bought a new bed to sleep on. Now we were ready for married life, which was a good thing, because Pam soon discovered that she was pregnant. This was great news. I was going to be a father again, and this time I'd be there to see my child grow up. Mama Rita was also pleased to hear the news. She hadn't seen Victor and Doug, my first two sons, since they were babies. I thought it would be a great idea if we all spent Christmas 1975 together. I made arrangements for Mama Rita to fly up from Louisiana. Victor and Doug would fly in from Nashville. It would end up a visit for the books, given that Mama Rita was part of it.

Meanwhile, back at the ranch in Nashville.

Donna Darlene. By this time she was at least agreeable enough to let my sons come visit me. As a matter of fact, Pam and I had only been married for a month when Donna Darlene decided that not only could I see the boys, they should now come and live with me. She was ready to ship them out. I have no idea what was going on in her life with Shot Jackson that prompted her to do this. But Pam said she simply couldn't handle it. She was neither old enough nor experienced enough to suddenly start raising boys, one twelve, the other fourteen, while I was on the road most of the time. I'm sure Donna Darlene wasn't happy about that, so I was both surprised and relieved when she agreed to let Victor and Doug join me for Christmas.

Elsie Griffin. The divorce was over, but the aftermath wasn't. At first she had asked for more than eleven hundred dollars a month. I was shocked when I saw the list of her necessities that she wanted me to pay for. It contained, among many items, the following monthly expenses:

Cosmetics, $15
Clothes, $50
House Upkeep, $50
Maid, $60
Entertainment, $50
Car Allowance, $150
Food, $200
Misc., $100

And so on. This was in 1975. The judge decided I should pay her seven hundred and fifty dollars a month, even though she was a healthy, professional woman with a clothes-designing business that catered to country stars. She called it House of Kershaw, by the way, and was doing a brisk business until the judge awarded her that alimony check. Maybe she figured it would be enough for her to live on, seeing that I had already paid for her home. So she closed the doors to the House of Kershaw and waited for the Check of Kershaw each month. I sent them at first, even though I didn't think it was a damn bit fair. Remember that Elsie was almost fifty years old and self-employed when I married her. Shit, I was the broke one! Now, thanks to that good lawyer she hired—he was famous in Nashville—I owed her that much money every month for the rest of her life. I wish I could have afforded him first.

Needless to say, when money ran low in my own personal life, Elsie's payments were the first to get axed from my list of *must do* things. I finally quit paying her alimony altogether, and I kept a low profile when I came in and out of Nashville. It seemed fair to me. And since I heard nothing from Elsie about it, I assumed that she, too, realized it was fair. But it would turn out that Elsie, her lawyer, and the state of Tennessee didn't see the situation as I did. It eventually hit the fan. Big time. But that story comes later.

In the meantime, we had Mama Rita and the boys arriving for that Christmas visit. Since Pam and I had managed to fill our four-bedroom house with real furniture by this time, we had room for everyone. This visit would be Mama Rita's first opportunity to spend some quality time with her new daughter-in-law. I was a bit anxious about this, even though Mama Rita liked Pam, and Pam liked Mama Rita. The boys arrived first, and they seemed as happy to see me as I was to see them. They were both in school at Castle Heights Military Academy in Lebanon, Tennessee, just east of Nashville. They seemed to have adjusted well to all the problems that had taken place between their mother and father, and I was certainly thankful for that.

Mama Rita arrived next. She got off the plane in Denver with a suitcase that was so heavy I had to drag it along behind me because I couldn't lift the damn thing.

"I brung some quarts of figs, me," Mama Rita said as I was trying to hoist the damn suitcase up and into the trunk of the Mark IV. "I gonna make you a nice fig cake, *cher*."

"You're gonna break my damn back first," I told her. I could understand her bringing along all those Cajun spices she loved. She even brought figs she grew on her own trees back in Jennings. But I found out later that she had also packed a twenty-pound bag of rice, so help me God, and a big can of coffee, cans of tomatoes, and several cans of Campbell soup. One side of Mama Rita's big suitcase was reserved for food, the other side for clothes.

"Mama Rita, we got plenty of rice in Colorado," I said.

"Yeah, sure you do, *cher*," Mama Rita said. She simply didn't believe me. This would be her trademark whenever she visited us. She'd come with her own storehouse of supplies, including enough prescription medicine bottles to fill a pharmacy.

I need to mention that one wedding gift we received that we weren't embarrassed to keep was a clock given to me by my best man, Richard Larsen, who worked for Panasonic. It was a big, heavy clock about eight inches square. What made it unique was that it announced the time if you pushed a button at its base. *The time is now two-fifteen p.m.*, a very polite female voice would say. Pam had put the clock in the bedroom where Mama Rita was to sleep. That first night of my mother's visit was almost unbearable. All night long Pam and I lay in bed listening to *"The time is now eleven p.m. The time is now eleven-twenty p.m. The time is now twelve-ten a.m. The time is now one-forty a.m. The time is now two-fifteen a.m. The time is now...*

Mama Rita, pushing the damn button on the clock.

All night long.

She'd even fall asleep for an hour or two, then wake up and push the button again. I guess the clock was keeping her company, for she always had trouble sleeping when she was away from home. *The time is now four-seventeen a.m.* In the middle of the second night of this torture, Pam and I were both lying in bed with our eyes wide open, unable to sleep, wincing every time we heard the damn clock talk to Mama Rita.

"Doug, I can't take it anymore," Pam finally whispered. Neither could I. It was like one of those devices they use on prisoners of war to get them to break. The next day Pam quietly sneaked the talking clock out of Mama Rita's room. If she missed it, Mama Rita never said. I should've had a Cajun clock custom made for Mama Rita. *Mais, cher, it's almost midnight. Get off your fat ass and go to bed, you crazy fils de putain!*

Pam decided to take advantage of Mama Rita's visit by learning how to cook Cajun-style.

"What's your recipe for gumbo, Mama Rita?" Pam asked.

"First, *chère*, you gotta make a roux," Mama Rita told her.

In Southwest Louisiana and especially in Cajun cooking, if you can't make a roux you might as well not bother to turn on the stove. A roux is a mixture of flour and oil, and it takes a certain amount of patience to get it just right. Almost every Cajun recipe begins with *first you make a roux*.

"How do you make a roux?" Pam asked.

"Just brown a little oil and flour, *chère*."

"How much oil and flour?"

"Well, just enough for a gumbo."

Pam eventually gave up. But she would ask these same questions of Mama Rita and get the same answers many times over the years before she gave up for good.

The biggest problem with having Mama Rita as our guest was that she wanted no help. She was set in her ways and didn't trust anyone else's methods. Pam would have to get accustomed to such things as putting a spider web on a cut to help it heal or a dab of sugar to stop bleeding. These were home remedies that Mama Rita had learned back in the swamps. But once she lost her good friend, the talking clock, she turned her thoughts toward that fig cake she wanted to make for me. It had been a while since I had one, so I was ready. And Mama Rita really was a great cook even if she didn't give a damn about anyone's arteries.

Pam got out the utensils and the pan Mama Rita would need for the cake. Then she put out her new electric mixer and inserted the beaters.

"Do you need any help, Mama Rita?" Pam asked. Mama Rita gave her a steely stare.

"Help making a fig cake?" she asked. "You crazy, *chère?*"

Pam was six months' pregnant by this time, and baking a fig cake was the last thing on her mind. We left Mama Rita alone in the kitchen, talking to herself.

"I never needed help, me, with my fig cake before," Mama Rita was saying as Pam and I retreated to the television set. It was just a matter of minutes before we heard the loud whirring of the electric beater, followed by what sounded like *splat splat splat.*

"*Fils de putain!*" Mama Rita shouted. Then came a metallic clattering, and then a whole lot of *splat splat splats.*

Pam and I hit the floor running.

When we got to the kitchen it looked like the Pillsbury Doughboy had blown up. Batter was flung far and wide. It hung like cobwebs from the ceiling. It slid down the walls. It dotted the floor. Figs were everywhere. And there stood Mama Rita, the electric beater in her hand, still beating away and still throwing batter all over the kitchen. That's when I realized that this was a woman who mixed things by hand. She had no idea that she was supposed to keep the beaters *inside* the pan while the mixer was on. Pam quickly turned off the thing and helped clean up the batter. But Mama Rita still wanted no help baking her cake. And since she had brought a truckload of figs, she was ready to try again.

"Get outta here, *chère*," she ordered Pam. "Don't bother me no more. I'm makin' Doug this fig cake, me."

It was difficult to sit in the living room and wait, wondering what she'd do next. But soon the sweet aroma of baking fig cake was wafting through the house. Pam and I relaxed. Mama Rita came into the living room and sat down to wait. One of the things she loved was to gossip. She started telling me all about the people I knew back in Jennings and Lake Arthur. Then she criticized the Colorado weather, which she found too cool.

"You ain't got humidity here," she complained.

Now and then she'd check on her cake and then come back to gossip some more. Minutes passed. Even though Pam had never baked a fig cake, she started to suspect something was wrong.

"Mama Rita, it's been an hour and forty-five minutes," Pam said. "Shouldn't your cake be done?" Mama Rita shook her head.

"Not yet, *chère*," she said. "Your oven ain't worth a damn. That fig cake still look like a dog take a shit in my pan."

And that's when Pam knew.

"The altitude, Doug," she whispered. "Oh, Lord, *you* tell her."

Anyone who's ever moved to a high-altitude area knows that normal recipes have to be adjusted for that very altitude. Pam had grown up in Colorado. It hadn't crossed her mind that someone else might not think of making the adjustments. Not until Mama Rita came to visit. I tried to explain this altitude problem to my mother as best I could, considering science was never her long suit. She just stared at me and said nothing. We had to throw out the cake and Mama Rita had to start over. I'm not sure she ever believed that Pam didn't mess up her cake on purpose.

It was a great Christmas if you forgot about the clock, the fig cake and the twenty-pound sack of rice. I got to spend time with Doug and Victor, and so did Mama Rita. It was a visit with their grandmother that my sons would never forget. And I think Mama Rita went home to Louisiana thinking I was in good hands. And she was right. I was in good hands, maybe, considering Pam had a level head on her shoulders. But I wasn't in good shape. I was getting to that tell-tale stage where it gets harder and harder to hide it from the world. The booze and the drugs were beginning to take over.

I'd been on fairly decent behavior before Pam and I were married, at least in my opinion. I might have lost control now and then on stage, maybe screamed at a bass player, fired a drummer, got pissed off during a studio session, even missed a show entirely. But I still hadn't lost control where Pam was concerned. Something told me that this was the love of my life, for the rest of my life, and I think that held me back for a while. But drug abuse has a mind of its own. Slowly, I started losing more ground. Even sober and straight I have that quick Kershaw temper. What would set me off? Anything. Nothing. Who knows where anger lives and grows? Often, it had to do with frustration with my career. Maybe it was the ghost of Daddy Jack. Whatever it was, I began taking it out on Pam, bitching and yelling and raising hell in general. I wasn't physical with her, although I was known to shove now and then. It was an emotional roller coaster, no doubt about it.

One night in Evergreen, early in 1976, I finally went too far. I was drinking enough Chivas to have stock in the company. I can't even re-member what Pam and I were fighting about now, but we were in a heated argument. All of a sudden I felt my hand rise up to strike her. Something stopped me just in time. Maybe it was the look on Pam's face. Here was a woman who was on my side, my companion, and soon to be the mother of our first child. Maybe *that* stopped me. I stormed out of the house—I wonder if the Hiwan club members were watching *this*—and found myself a motel room. It wouldn't be the last night I spent in some motel while Pam was at home, upset and crying, thinking maybe she'd never see me alive again. I don't remember if I drank all night in that room or went to the nearest bar. I have no doubt I did whatever it took to get me through the night. That would become my standard MO. When morning came, well, things always seemed better with sunlight. It was a matter of getting through that black part of the night.

When I drove back home the next day, I went into the kitchen. With Pam watching, I dumped my bottles of pills into the sink. In they went, round ones, black ones, red ones, pink ones. I washed them down the drain with what liquor I had stocked in the house. I had made my mind up, and I wanted Pam to know it. I was on the proverbial wagon, and I would stay on it forever. I know she believed me because I believed it myself.

It was shortly after this soul-searching night and during those blustery winds of March that I flew home for a couple days before I was scheduled to play the Palomino Club in North Hollywood. Pam was very pregnant at this time, but that didn't stop her, her mom, Shirley, her sister, Terry, and me from going bowling that night. I remember we drove to the Golden Bowl, in Golden, Colorado. Shirley, Terry and I ended up doing the actual bowling while Pam sat on a bench and timed her contractions. They weren't close enough for panic, so we went home later that night and went to bed.

Sometime after midnight, and with the regularity of Mama Rita's talking clock, the contractions were coming every thirty minutes. Since the hospital was forty-five miles away, Pam and I decided it was time to head over there. This was a good thing because Zachary Douglas Kershaw, our first son, was born around 7 a.m. that morning, March 18, 1976. He weighed eight pounds and eight ounces. I was a father again. And this time I was there in the delivery room, the first time I'd ever seen a child being born. I had grown up in that generation of men who are expected to stay out in the waiting room, cigars in their shirt pockets, being patted on the back while their wives give birth alone. But times had changed since Doug Jr., and Victor came into the world. Pam and I had even taken child-birth classes together.

My heart filled with pride to see that tiny baby draw his first breath. I had missed out on so many important things with Doug Jr., and Victor. But now I was sober and with a new outlook for the future. I wanted to do things right this time. I really believed in my heart that I'd pull it off. As it would be when all three of my sons with Pam were born, it was only a fluke that I was at home for the birth and not away at some gig. When I did go on stage at the Palomino Club, the day after Zach was born, the club personnel and my fans knew about the birth. In the middle of my show I was presented with a perfect little quarter-size fiddle, in its own tiny case. I remember I played a song on it, in honor of Zach's birth, and the crowd loved it.

Pam and I were anxious for Zachary to get old enough that she could bring him on the road now and then. When he finally came with us, we noticed that some of the fans seemed to eye little Zach suspiciously. There were too many funny looks. A friend finally explained to us what was up.

"Remember how ABC filmed your wedding? Well, it just ran on TV and everybody thinks you just got married."

When the ABC special hadn't run in those weeks following our wedding ceremony, Pam and I assumed it had ended up on the cutting room floor. Not so, and now my fans thought we were newlyweds, toting about our big baby boy. Who would even comment on this today?

I had been sober for three months before Zach was born, and I stayed sober for three months after he was born. But the wagon ride kept getting bumpier and bumpier. When our first wedding anniversary rolled around, on June 21, 1976, Pam thought a glass of champagne would be a nice way to celebrate. So did I. We went out to dinner at a nice restaurant and I ordered Pam a bottle of Dom. The more I looked at that bottle, the more I convinced myself that I ought to join in the celebration. When I poured myself a glass, Pam raised her eyebrows.

"Are you sure you should drink that?" she asked.

"It's a toast to our anniversary," I said.

But I knew from the first sip that it wouldn't be long and I'd be back on the booze. It was just a matter of time. Sure enough, a few weeks later I found myself having a beer now and then in the dressing room before a show. It helped keep me calm, or so I told myself. Then, after a show, I'd have one to come down from that adrenalin rush. Pretty soon I was having a beer now and then after a game of golf with friends. Then the day came when I found myself in a liquor store, standing in the Chivas Regal section. I wasn't window shopping. My drinking was soon right back where it had always been. Somehow my career kept rolling, despite my efforts to mess it up. In fact, some of the high points of my professional life were still to come. But so were the low points. And that wagon I had promised Pam I would stay on forever? It rolled away without me. It would be another five years before it came back.

21

MAINTENANCE

*"I was trying to help Doug, to keep him from going the route
of so many musicians that are taking harder drugs, he (Dr.
Snapp) said, calling his treatment of the country music
performer a form of maintenance."*
—*Nashville Banner,* January 20, 1977

I believe it was former deejay and country music talk show host Ralph
Emery who once said that Dr. Landon Snapp should have been given half
of the songwriting awards that were passed out in Nashville. At a period
in time when many of us thought that our creativity needed a boost, Dr.
Snapp was our best friend. That's because Snapp had quickly become
known as the Nashville doctor who would write you up a prescription for
what the law called a "controlled substance." Great name for a pill doctor,
ain't it? *Snapp.* Was the Nashville music community the first to use amphetamines as a way to get high? Hell no. The history of these kinds of
stimulants goes way back.

In doing research for this chapter we learned that methamphetamine
was first synthesized in 1919 as a drug in search of a disease. As time went
by, it was used against everything from decongestion to depression. In
1930s Germany amphetamine was marketed and sold over the counter as
an inhaler to treat nasal congestion. By 1937, it had been made available
in tablet form and by prescription. Fighting men began taking amphetamine during World War II in hopes that it would keep them on their feet.
This was about the time that Mama Rita moved us into the chicken coop
and Lake Arthur was experiencing those first blackouts. When the war
finally ended and all those amphetamine supplies intended for the military
were made available to the Japanese public, abuse reached epidemic pro-
portions. And I don't think any of those users were even writing songs. It

was during the Eisenhower years in this country, the 1950s, when house-wives were being told to look and act like Donna Reed, and men were thinking of moving to that new idea of the "suburbs," that legally manu-factured tablets of Methedrine and Dexedrine became as available as TV dinners. Jazz and blues musicians discovered them, as did college kids, athletes, truck drivers and a lot of those Donna Reed housewives. They began popping pills for everything—weight loss, mild depression, or a stay-awake aid.

It was back on Nightclub Row, in 1954, that Rufus Thibodeaux gave me my first Dexedrine and I stayed in the clouds for four days. Even though I wasn't a steady user back then, I knew early on what the bad effects of amphetamines could be. I had heard from my musical colleagues about the jerky movements, anxiety, irritability, irregular heartbeat, in-somnia, dizziness, dryness of the mouth, even hot flashes. But the good side of the stuff, in even small amounts, can make the user feel euphoric, wide awake, full of strength and energy, powerful, self-assured, and moti-vated as hell. No wonder when I had to give them up, I headed straight for cocaine. It was as if I'd been in training for it all those years.

By the time Nashville musicians began using the stuff as their Muse of Choice, amphetamines were already being abused by folks from other walks of life. In Nashville, the walk led to Dr. Snapp's office, a small and inconspicuous building on Woodland Street, over in East Nashville. I got word of Snapp through the *pill-vine* all the way back in 1966, as I men-tioned earlier. This was at the time that Donna Darlene had taken me to court and gotten custody of our boys. It was when I first met Elsie Griffin. Another picker had told me that Consumers Drug Store, located on Main Street in East Nashville, was the best place to do my pill shopping. It was certainly well-named. I finally got up the courage one day to walk in the front door. I had to stand in a long line that led up to the prescription counter. I even recognized a few music business faces in the line. When it came my turn to talk to the pharmacist, I told him I needed some diet pills. I knew this was a quick way to get speed, what we called *uppers*.

"No problem," he said. "But you need a prescription first. So go on over to Dr. Landon B. Snapp's office and he'll fix you up."

I drove to the building on Woodland Street where Dr. Snapp had hung his shingle out to practice medicine. I noticed that it wasn't even a block away from Consumers Drug, and that seemed wonderfully convenient. I walked in and told the receptionist I was there to see the doctor. She didn't even ask if I had an appointment.

"Just take a seat and wait your turn," she said. It was when I sat down and got to looking around the room that I saw even more faces from the music community. "Hey, Doug, how's it goin'?" was a phrase I heard more often at Snapp's office than at the Opry. A Nashville singer-songwriter recently commented that when you sat in Dr. Snapp's waiting room, you sat there with truck drivers, prostitutes, musicians, songwriters, and so on. Nobody seemed to be sick, and that's because we weren't. We had all come to get our prescriptions. We all had, well, *needs*.

I liked Landon Snapp a lot. There's no other way to say it. He was a large, gray-haired man in his early sixties and friendly as could be. There was a fatherly air about him. The truth is that most of us would have gone to Attila the Hun to get our pills, but it helped matters that Dr. Snapp was a nice guy. When it came my turn to talk to him, he shook my hand long and hard.

"I sure love your music, Kershaw," he said. I felt a rush of relief to hear this. "Now what can I do for you?" I cleared my throat and tried to speak without letting my voice crack. I wanted to sound as sincere as I could.

"I need some diet pills," I said. Snapp looked me over. I stood five-foot-ten back then and weighed about a hundred and thirty pounds.

"Diet pills, huh?" he asked. I nodded.

"For energy," I added. This seemed to be the magic phrase. Dr. Snapp quickly wrote me up a prescription for amphetamines. Didrex. Or so I later learned that's what those round, pinkish pills—they were not much bigger than aspirins—were called. As far as I was concerned they were always just *uppers*.

"You stay off those hard drugs now, you hear?" he told me. I would have promised him anything. I went back to the drugstore and had no problem whatsoever in picking up my pills.

It took several visits to Dr. Snapp before he felt that he knew me well enough to write the prescription for two refills. It was the first time I noticed those little numbers in the upper-right corner that indicated how many times I could use that prescription to get pills. That's when I became really creative. Whenever Dr. Snapp gave me a prescription, I'd take it home first instead of to the drugstore. Then I'd do a mad search through cupboard drawers, my desk, my briefcase, you name it, until I found a pen that had the exact same color ink as the one Snapp had used. Carefully, I'd circle the highest number of refills I could—it was three if I remember correctly—then I'd head out to the drugstore to get the first one filled. One hundred pills per script. This didn't stop me from going back to Snapp for another refill when he thought the original one had been used. I'd still do that. This way, I was able to stockpile refills, my own little arsenal, so that I could be sure I'd never run out.

I didn't know until just recently that the pharmacist and owner of Consumers Drug Store was "in business" with Dr. Snapp. So many patients came directly to the drugstore to get their pills that the owner finally had a rubber stamp made up with Snapp's name on it. Apparently, their hands had begun to hurt from filling all those prescriptions. Shit, here I had spent all that time searching for a pen with the right color ink. I probably could've used an orange crayon. I doubt anyone would have noticed or cared. I should have had my own rubber stamp made up.

My visits to Snapp continued for more than eight years, and our relationship developed into a bit more than just doctor-patient. He came several times to see my shows while I was doing my stint down at the seedy Black Poodle in Printers Alley. And I remember once, high on pills he had prescribed for me, I sat on his living room rug, the Snapp family listening as I finished a song I was working on. That was "Bayou Teche," and it ended up on my album *The Cajun Way.*

Bayou Teche, Bayou Teche
Where the shrimp and the birds and the Cajuns nest
Where the turtles run and the fish won't fly
And the Cajun girl's pretty as a butterfly.

Those fish could have flown if they'd known Dr. Snapp.

As I said, I began my visits to Snapp in 1966, and they continued until I moved to California early in 1975. When I wasn't able to go get the prescriptions for myself, Elsie went for me until she and I separated. Knowing I had to head out on the road for long periods of time, Snapp sometimes wrote me up five hundred pills, or five prescriptions, during one single visit. To do that, he needed four other names to put on the scripts. I always gave him the names of my band members, unbeknownst to them.

"This will keep you away from the hard stuff, Doug," Dr. Snapp said.

I'm telling you right now that I truly believe that Dr. Snapp did think he was helping me. But there were times, in a good songwriting day and night, that I'd take as many as twenty pills. I was supposed to be taking three a day, with meals. But Didrex was and still is a pill that limits appetite because of its effects on the hypothalamus, a control center in the brain. Meals were not high on my list of essential things. Because Didrex back then led to drug abuse, pharmacologists have since tinkered with the ingredients and developed similar but safer compounds. Not in my day.

It was all bound to come to a head and explode. And eventually it did.

Pam and I were already married and living in Colorado when I heard from my manager, Mike Barnett, that I had been served a federal subpoena to come in and testify against Dr. Snapp. The authorities had had their eye on him for some time and on the cottage industry going on between his office and the Consumers Drug Store on Main Street. They had watched, they had waited, they had evidence. Literally, a *truckload* of it, since I'm told that prosecutors filled the back of a pickup with the illegal prescriptions Dr. Snapp had written in just six months and drove it up to the courthouse. I guess they wanted the judge and jury to get a glimpse at how many prescriptions this meant. It must have been a hell of a visual.

Tennessee prosecutors told me in no uncertain terms that Dr. Snapp was on his way to prison, with or without my testimony. If I would testify—remember, I'd already been served with a federal subpoena—I would not be extradited from Colorado to face charges of nonpayment of alimony.

Testify or be extradited. What a choice.

At first, I did what many people would do.

"No way in hell," I said. I wasn't going to do it. I liked Landon Snapp. I didn't know anything about his dealings with the general public until we began working on this book. Sure, I knew my songwriter and musical friends went to him. A few prescriptions here and there, as he did for me.

I hadn't yet read the old clippings of the trial. At the time of his arrest I was out in Colorado, doing a half-assed job at trying to stay clean. Now I would have to fly to Nashville, Tennessee, where so many of my fellow pill-poppers and songwriters and musicians lived. And I would have to testify against our *source*.

"No way in hell," I said to Pam. "Let 'em put me in jail."

Well, that's what you think at first. And for a while I was even pretty sure I was going to stand by it. Go to jail. It took several soul-searching talks with Pam before I realized I couldn't go to jail. I had to keep doing shows to support my wife and kids. How could I do that while locked up? And from what they were telling me, they could nail Snapp easily enough without me. *With me*, they had media and what they considered a star witness. I walked the floor a good many nights before I called my manager and told him the obvious truth.

"They've got him anyway," I said. "It's not gonna do anyone any good if both of us go to jail."

A rock and a jail cell. That's what they had me between.

It took my cowriter and me a long time to decide how to handle the Dr. Snapp trial and the role I played in it. The biggest trouble in dealing with this chapter was that I knew almost nothing about what had happened back then. The whole episode caused me such pain that I refused to read any of the Nashville newspaper articles about what was going on. This was easy since I was living in another state, a long way from the trouble. And after I came to court to testify, I wanted to shut that day away from my mind forever. Dr. Snapp and the infamous trial became a forbidden topic around the Kershaw home. We never mentioned it.

I suppose this chapter is a kind of exorcism for me. By writing it, by reliving it, I hope to rid myself of the ghost of that incident, one that has hurt me deeply all these years. There were people in the music community who were furious at me because they thought I had personally taken away their pill source. Waylon Jennings didn't speak to me for many years. I never came and went in Music City without wondering who was whispering behind my back and who still blamed me for what happened. Not since those early days of losing my father did an incident have more impact on me. I honestly believe that the trial and my unwilling role in it helped drive me over the top later on.

This is my chance to finally tell my story, and I'm taking it.

I decided the best thing to do was to present it as it was. Let the reader have the highlights of what happened at the trial of Dr. Landon B. Snapp in January 1977. The only part of the trial I saw personally was on January 14 for the two hours I was on the stand. I left Nashville the minute I was done testifying. I knew photographers had been there waiting to take my picture as I walked out of the courtroom that January day. Word gets out quickly at times like that, even back in those days before cell phones. It wasn't until we began work on this chapter that I saw for the first time a photo of me leaving the courthouse. We had sent a research assistant down to the library to spend an afternoon looking for old clippings. She came back with a tall stack about the trial. In it was a photo of me that had appeared in the *Tennessean*. I'm wearing a three-piece suit, a federal agent at my side, and the look on my face is one of pure despair. It still hurts to this day to remember.

In an amazing coincidence, the actual court transcript of the trial was destroyed at some archives down in Georgia, the very week we put in a request for a copy. So here are the highlights of the Snapp trial as re-counted in the Nashville papers. This is when I personally learned what was going on at Consumers Drug Store, by reading these clippings years after the event. And it came as a major surprise to me.

Dr. Landon B. Snapp was indicted in November 1976 by a federal grand jury on twenty-six charges of drug-related offenses. These consisted of twenty-five counts of distributing and dispensing Schedule III controlled substances without a legitimate medical purpose and one count of conspiracy to dispense and distribute controlled substances. (A *Schedule III* controlled substance means that it allows refilling up to five times during a six-month period and requires a medical examination with each refill.) Before the trial began, Snapp allowed the press to interview him at his office. He assured them he prescribed Didrex only to patients with a weight problem.

"I have a reputation of getting the job done," Snapp told the reporter. "I tell them if they don't lose weight, don't come back."

Remember, I was as skinny as the tail hanging off a cow's ass the first time I stepped into Landon Snapp's office.

The trial itself began on January 12, 1977, and ended on January 21, 1977. Before it was over, it would end up resembling a mini Greek tragedy. It had sex, drugs, and music, not to mention humiliation and the required fall from grace. A large cast of witnesses filed past Dr. Snapp to testify about the prescriptions he had given them. Reading their words as recorded by the press, they didn't sound any more anxious to convict him than I was. Again, they were from all walks of life. I remember a former detective with the Metro Police Department who had been given as many as twenty-six prescriptions in thirty days. Housewives and waitresses who didn't need to lose weight, or so they testified, were taking almost as many pills a day as the Ragin' Cajun. There was a reluctant student from Sewanee who needed some way to stay up at night and study. A skinny tree surgeon, six feet tall and weighing one hundred-forty pounds, testified about what he told Snapp his symptoms were.

"I just had the blahs," he said. "I needed some energy to work."

Another woman told the court that she had to be hospitalized because the excess pills had deprived her of the ability to sleep. Many other women testified that they *did* tell Snapp they wanted the pills to lose weight, but that they really took them "for anxiety, to stay awake, and to cope." One woman put it in more poetic terms.

"The pills give me energy and make me get up and want to do," she testified. "If I don't take them, I sit down and don't want to do."

Amen, sister. I know what you're talking about.

Then it got worse. A woman testified that she was given free prescriptions when she came to the doctor's office, often after hours, at Snapp's "request for sexual favors."

Trust me here, folks. I paid money for every damn one of my prescriptions.

Once, though, she told the court, Snapp wasn't able to "rise" to the occasion. "I was ready for you the other night," he told her, "but I'm not in the mood tonight." This female witness was quick to add, however, that Dr. Snapp never promised her free prescriptions for those sexual favors. He just did it. I suppose she thought this would help him out after such damning testimony. Even *she* liked him.

A man testified that he'd just found out his wife was getting her prescriptions from Snapp in *his* name, which was Charles, certainly not a woman's name. Others testified that the doctor's assistant gave them checkups before she phoned in the prescription to the drugstore. A waitress needed pills to get through the night shift. One housewife was taking fifteen to twenty a day, along with the tranquilizers Snapp was also giving her. Shit, I should have been co-writing with *her*.

So there you have the circus. We were all players in the game. All doped to the gills. Some of us just didn't know it. Yet I was the only one from the Nashville music community called to testify. The *only one* out of dozens and dozens. And I was living in Colorado at the time. I still don't get it. Snapp's daughters, Lana and Ginger, sat behind their father in the courtroom throughout the trial, the papers wrote.

That's right. *Ginger Snapp.*

It was a big surprise for me to read all of this. I had no idea this was going on, and that's the damn truth. My relationship with Snapp was an isolated one. Sure, I knew other musicians were getting pills from him too—he was our script doctor—but I didn't know the extent of what was taking place. I bet they didn't either. For instance, it appears that the pharmacist and owner of Consumers Drug Store, along with Snapp's assistant, became what is known as "unindicted co-conspirators." An officer from the federal Drug Enforcement Administration testified that the bookkeeping over at Consumers Drug was, well, weak to say the least. It seems they couldn't account for thousands of units of Didrex between November 1973 and July 1975.

Would anyone be surprised?

Then came a representative from Upjohn, the company that made the amphetamine. He stated that in a mere six-month period, the first six months of 1975, Consumers Drug had ordered 51 cases of Didrex. Since each case contained 24 bottles with 500 pills per bottles, this means that 612,000 Didrex pills left Memphis, where the Tennessee distributor was located. They all ended up at one tiny drugstore in East Nashville.

Imagine how many cases there would have been if I were still in town.

"Consumers Drug is Upjohn's largest Didrex customer in Nashville," he testified. "They order more than even the wholesale drug companies."

Funny that this distributor or the Upjohn Company didn't seem to mind those enormous sales and wasn't legally responsible for selling that many pills to one little drugstore. This is when it became known that many of the patients left a five-dollar fee at the drugstore. The pharmacist-owner then gave that money to Snapp. Because the drugstore was filling "40 to 45 prescriptions a day, with ninety-nine percent of them being written up by Snapp," they had that rubber stamp made with Snapp's name on it, the word *Didrex,* the instructions of *one tablet, three times daily before meals,* and the symbol for prescription. They needed it because of "the frequency" of Snapp's patients coming by for their Didrex.

I personally never left a fee at Consumers Drug Store. And if I remember correctly, Snapp charged me only three dollars for each time that I visited his office. But I realize now that the office fee was most likely added to the price of the pills—which was ten bucks per bottle—whenever Elsie or I picked them up at the drugstore.

At the trial, Snapp's assistant testified that it wasn't unusual for fifty patients a day to come by the office on Woodland Street. Then a stream of medical experts, other doctors, took their turns testifying about the dangers of Didrex. It should be used sparingly for weight loss, they said, if at all. Even a psychiatrist was sworn in and quickly pointed out that paranoia comes with misuse. I knew *that* symptom well. So did other abusers. I've read that George Jones was sitting in a barber's chair, getting his hair trimmed, when in walked another customer. George was so sure this guy was FBI that he jumped out of the chair, flushed all his pills down a commode in the back, and then flew out the front door without so much as saying goodbye to the barber.

But none of the doctors mentioned using Didrex to get high, a means to escape those blahs the young tree surgeon and I knew so well. I guess the Upjohn company didn't put *that* use in the directions on the label. Even a drug expert was called, and I don't mean the kind I used to write songs with. I mean a pharmacology expert from Vanderbilt University Medical School. He stated that a user could develop a tolerance for Didrex within two or three weeks "that would require a larger dose of the drug to satisfy the need for taking it."

Ditto.

The court case was dragged out until it was time for Doug Kershaw's command performance, although no one knew that I was coming to town. I flew in from Denver with Mike Barnett, my manager. It was a somber flight, with little said between us. I remember that January 14 was a cold winter's day in Nashville. When the plane landed at Berry Field, I felt as though I had a block of lead in the pit of my stomach. Man, oh man, but I didn't care a damn bit what Snapp had done as a doctor. I just didn't want to testify against him. And I knew how it would look to Music City, to the folks who didn't know that those government prosecutors had pushed my back to the wall.

When we began work on this chapter and I read the old clippings, I learned that Elsie Griffin, my ex-wife, had testified two hours before I did. I had absolutely no idea. She testified that she had often picked up prescriptions for me, and that Snapp often took her blood pressure and weighed her, even though he knew the pills were not for her.

"He'd fuss at me and sometimes he'd talk about Doug using so many pills," Elsie said, "but I'd get the prescriptions anyway."

She also testified that she sometimes came to Snapp's office with my band members. And that I often gave away the Didrex. Those last two statements are simply untrue. I was too greedy with those pills to give any away. And my band didn't even know their names were going on the prescriptions. They were in the dark when it came to Snapp.

Being the government's surprise witness, I was kept out of the courtroom until it was time for me to testify. When I finally walked in, you could have heard a bad check bounce from all the way across the room. And then the excited whispers began, like wind in tall grass. It was painful to actually look Landon Snapp in the eye. I remember being surprised that he didn't seem as shattered as I had imagined he might. He sat quietly watching, waiting to hear what I'd say.

"Do you swear to tell the whole truth and nothing but the truth, so help you God?"

"I do," I said, and then I lied a little.

I testified that I'd been clean of booze and pills since early in 1975. That wasn't entirely true, as you've already read in earlier chapters, but I was so used to lying to Pam Eson Kershaw about this very subject that it seemed less sinful to do so to Snapp's prosecutors. Besides, I didn't want it to appear that I had a drug problem *because of* Snapp, since I didn't. And the truth was that I really hadn't been to see him since early in 1975. So, I did my best to say everything I could to help his case. I testified that he often lectured me on taking too many pills, which was true. The irony, of course, is that he was the one giving them to me. But I was quick to offer how I had been abusing pills and "using heavily" long before I ever heard of the Nashville Pill Doctor. In her own testimony, which I would learn later, Elsie had told them that I was addicted to drugs from the age of fifteen. That's bullshit. I was twenty-five years old before pills became a problem for me, and I told them so.

I also testified that Snapp had given me vitamin shots during some of the visits and that he warned me often to stay away from hard drugs. But I had to admit that, no, he had never examined me, nor had he examined any of the band members whose names I had given him. And no, Dr. Snapp and I had never discussed weight control or diet. I also told the defense lawyer, when asked, that yes, I did have a deal with the government to avoid prosecution in return for my testimony. I wanted Dr. Snapp and everyone in Nashville to know that. I realized later that they thought the deal was drug-related, instead of about alimony.

I testified that I sometimes took ten pills a day. I was afraid the full truth would hurt the doctor even more, that I was taking nearly a pill an hour. Sometimes two. Twenty and more pills a day. And then, finally, it was over. As I left the witness stand I made a point to catch Dr. Snapp's eye as I passed the table where he was sitting. I wanted to tell him, with that one look, what was pressing on my heart. *I wanted no part of this.*

A car was waiting outside to drive Mike and me from the courthouse and back to the airport. I left the building to the glare of whatever damn camera put my picture in the local paper, that same afternoon, with a long story about my testimony. But beneath the big story, Elsie had made her own small headlines. *Kershaw's Ex-Wife Says He Owes Back Alimony. Doug Kershaw's unexpected appearance and hasty exit at the trial of Landon B. Snapp puzzled many observers, but not his ex-wife, Elsie.*

Elsie even found time to comment to the press. "If I had known Doug Kershaw was in town, I would have had his ___ arrested."

I assume she meant my *ass.*

"He owes me $20,000 in back alimony," she added.

I would one day look back on that meager amount and wish that's all I had ended up paying Elsie Griffin for the five years I'd been married to her. But that sum would multiply as the years wore away and grow, increase, and magnify until, by the time it bit me on that part of my body Elsie referred to in the press, it would be big enough to take a large chunk. But that hell was still to come. Thirteen years down the road.

Before Dr. Snapp took the stand, Assistant US Attorney Bill Farmer called a former employee of the doctor's. He asked if she had given medical examinations and phoned in prescriptions when Dr. Snapp was busy? Yes, she had. Did she have any nurse's training whatsoever, Farmer wondered? No, but she had completed high school.

Farmer: You would read the blood pressure? You would decide if it was normal. You would determine from looking at the chart whether this patient should get another prescription for Didrex?

Witness: I guess you could say I was doing the determining.

Hell, I should have quit the road and gone to work for Dr. Snapp. At least I'd learned in the army how to do eye, nose and throat exams.

On the day Dr. Snapp was to testify, according to those old newspaper clippings, his lawyers asked for an adjournment of the trial on the grounds that they hadn't had time to prepare sufficiently. The judge, L. Clure Morton, denied it. Twenty minutes later the judge returned to the bench and announced that the adjournment would be granted after all, on the grounds that it was snowing in Nashville. According to the *Tennessean*, Snapp's attorney, William C. Wilson, who was seated next to him at the defense table, spoke out loudly. "God has taken care of us!" The newspaper went on to write that "Laughter broke out in the courtroom where Snapp's daughters, Ginger and Lana, were sitting." *Ginger Snapp*. I just had to say it again.

When I read about Dr. Landon B. Snapp, age sixty-two, taking the stand to defend himself, I gotta say that I felt the old pain creep back. I liked him, I really did, no matter what he did as a doctor. On the stand, he told the court that he was a 1939 graduate of the University of Tennessee Medical School. Reading those words, all these years later, I realized that I had known very little about the man himself. And he knew very little about me, except for what he saw on television or on stage. He had graduated from medical school just a few years before Daddy Jack killed himself. And yet, somehow, Dr. Snapp and Doug Kershaw had gotten their lives tangled up together. That relationship ended in a court trial that has haunted me ever since. I wonder now if I was looking for a father in this kindly doctor with the conservative glasses and the soft voice. I do know that I liked the fact that he fussed about giving me those pills. He seemed to care whether I lived or died. His concern for me felt good. And so did the pills he gave me.

Dr. Snapp admitted that he prescribed Didrex for mild depression. "Almost everyone has some form of mild depression, and it's necessary for practitioners such as me to handle these patients so they don't have to go to a psychiatrist," he testified.

I wonder if the testifying shrink was in the courtroom to hear this.

Dr. Snapp went on to say that his assistant had given those exams and called in those prescriptions without his knowledge. He made a big point of explaining that Didrex was "a nothing drug."

"Grape juice is like wine," Snapp said, "but it doesn't have alcohol. And Didrex doesn't create adrenalin, so it's not an amphetamine-type drug."

Right. That's why those housewives and I were taking twenty of them a day.

Of course, I was most interested in reading the part where *I* was discussed.

Here's an excerpt taken from the *Tennessean*:

Snapp, again under questioning by Morton, testified he gave entertainer Doug Kershaw prescriptions under various names for as many as 600 diet pills at one time to "help Kershaw."

Dr. Snapp said he did this to avoid giving me a refillable prescription. He was afraid that "if Doug received a refill, others would find out about it and it would lead to abuse."

It was while Snapp was being questioned by his own attorney that Judge Morton interrupted.

Morton: *It was a matter of maintenance?*

Snapp: *Yes, sir. I was trying to help him.*

Morton: *How?*

Snapp: *He was going the route of so many musicians and he could end up taking other drugs that musicians can easily get hold of...*

Morton: *You prescribed Didrex not because he needed them medically but to keep him off the hard stuff? Because he'd go elsewhere?*

Snapp: *No, sir. I think he needed them medically. He was a depressive introvert. He comes on strong as an extrovert, but he's really an introvert.*

Morton: *What does being an introvert have to do with pills?*

Snapp: *They would get him out of his depressed state, cause mood elevation, keep him away from the hard drugs.*

Morton: *Are you saying that medically anyone who is introverted needs pills?*

Snapp: *No, sir. Doug was down in the dumps. He needed to be in the limelight. All these musicians do...*

Well, I sure as hell didn't need *that* kind of limelight.

One of the prosecuting attorneys, Martha Trammel, often referred to Dr. Snapp as *Mr. Snapp*. She told the jury that money was what motivated him. "Landon Snapp is not a doctor, he's a pusher." She added that the people who testified, even the ones who swore they got the pills to lose weight, were not patients, but victims. "A warm body and a five-dollar bill would get you a hundred pills of Didrex any day of the week." The jury was given 18,258 prescriptions to look over, all written by Snapp in the early months of 1975 and filled at Consumers Drug Store. Someone on the prosecution team had done the math. In his closing statement, Bill Farmer told the jury what all the fees—and the rubber stamp and the phone calls—had added up to. "At five dollars an office visit, Dr. Snapp made $50,000 in six months' time off one drug, at one drugstore. It's an insult to your intelligence to compare what he's doing to a legitimate medical practice." I looked it up. That's $238,000 today.

When Snapp's own lawyer, William C. Wilson, had his turn, the jury must have thought he'd seen too many old Perry Mason shows. Wilson told the jury that Snapp "was just gullible," that he was a great and honorable man who was doing nothing harmful. "He prescribed Didrex as a crutch or placebo for patients with diet problems and depression. He's a kindly man. It just oozes out of him. I'm sure that he's easily taken in by persons who want excessive amounts of Didrex to take for illegitimate reasons. This is a battle here between the hierarchy in the medical profession and this honored physician whom they dare not even call a doctor." Then Wilson really got dramatic. He told the jury that if he were personally choking to death he'd "want a member of the jury to give Dr. Snapp a pocket knife to do surgery right here on the floor." In the end, it must have been tough for the jury to tell who was on drugs and who wasn't.

A jury of seven women and five men took less than two and a half hours to find Dr. Landon B. Snapp guilty on twenty-three counts. Because Dr. Snapp continued to illegally write prescriptions for Didrex even after his conviction by the jury, the judge took that into consideration when it came time to sentence him. He lost his license to practice, of course, and was given twenty years in prison. He was ordered to report to the Federal Correctional Institution in Kentucky at his own expense. He did so on January 3, 1979. I told my co-writer that if there were a chance that Landon Snapp was still alive, I wanted to talk to him. That's when we found out that he had died in the facility up in Kentucky.

I cast no judgments against this man. I don't know what drove him, what pushed him to do what he did. Perhaps Landon Snapp had his own early devils to battle, just as I had my demons from those swamp days. As far as his giving me illegal scripts, I was a grown man who knew exactly what I was doing. I don't blame him one bit for that. As I said, I know he cared about my well-being. Twenty years is a long time. Child molesters, bank robbers, and rapists often don't get that kind of sentence. But I can tell you this, now that I've landed in this new world of technology and the Internet, still on my feet and gifted with some hindsight. If I found out that a doctor was giving any one of my sons a steady stream of any drug, I'd be banging on his door in a minute.

I heard that Consumers Drug Store later became a Christian bookstore. If it's true, that should help sweep away the sins of the past. Snapp's name came up the other day. I was talking to another Nashville performer who used to get his pills at Consumers Drug Store, just like me. He told me a funny story. It seems Snapp once drove up to Kingsport, in East Tennessee, just to get a look at the warehouse where all the Old Yellers were stored, waiting to be distributed throughout the South. "If Nashville musicians saw what I saw," Snapp told my friend, "their tongues would hang out."

And mine would have been the longest one.

In reliving this chapter, I've put this episode to rest. It's my way of telling everyone out there who knew me, and who also went to Dr. Snapp for their pills, that I was an unwilling player in that drama from step one. Waylon Jennings finally spoke to me years later at a show in Ohio. When I asked Pam what she remembered most about the Snapp incident, she said, "I know that people who had been your friends for years suddenly turned against you." Well, it's one way to find out who your friends are.

22

RALEIGH HILLS

I left Louisiana, I headed for L.A.
I had dreams of being famous
and be a star some day,
Well, I'm up here in California
wondering what went wrong,
and I wonder what happened to the man inside
of the real ole Cajun me.
  —Doug Kershaw "Real Ole Cajun Me,"
  (written to Doug Sahm's "Texas Me")

I always said that the radio wasn't the only invention in the world. Back in the early days of my career it was damn important, and yet I had a lasting career without it. I did have modest hit records with Rusty & Doug, and on my own. But my longevity in show business was due to television, not radio. Starting with the *Johnny Cash Show* and then *The Ed Sullivan Show*, television helped me remain a solid-selling act on Warner for years. And to this day I continue to play dates around the country at venues ranging from fairs and festivals to nightclubs.

Another television show that gave my career one hell of a boost happened in early 1977, just after the infamous Snapp trial, when producers at PBS contacted me about an idea they had. They wanted to do a show called *Fiddlers Three* and asked if I would be one of the fiddler players. I assumed this meant that they would feature my Cajun fiddling along with two country fiddlers. Maybe Johnny Gimble and Vassar Clements, two of country music's all-time greats. Imagine my surprise when the PBS representative told me that they were also inviting jazz great Jean-Luc Ponty, and classical virtuoso Itzhak Perlman. I wondered what these two accomplished musicians would think of playing their violins with a fiddler from

Louisiana, but my doubts diminished when Itzhak showed up backstage at one of my concerts in Snowmass, Colorado.

"If you do the show, I'll do the show," Itzhak said.

"I'll be there," I told him, still wondering how I could possibly hold my own with Perlman and Jean-Luc Ponty.

Each of us brought our own material to Chicago, where the taping was done. Everything was going fine until Jean-Luc brought out a new piece of music he'd written for the show. He played his part and then handed copies of the sheet music to both Itzhak and me. I looked down at those musical notes and, shit, they looked like chicken scratches. Itzhak could tell that something had rattled me. I was too embarrassed to say anything to Jean-Luc Ponty or the musical director, but there was something about Itzhak Perlman I felt I could trust.

"I can't read music," I whispered to him. He watched as I put the sheet music down by my fiddle case. Then Itzhak put his own sheet music down.

When Jean-Luc Ponty finished his part, Itzhak began playing. Needless to say, he played wonderfully. But I could tell from Jean-Luc Ponty's face that Itzhak was not playing the part that had been written for him. When he finished, Itzhak turned to me and smiled. I understood what that quick gesture meant. *Play it as you feel it.* So I played what seemed to come naturally from my own fiddle after hearing from two masters. Nothing seemed out of place to the audience. They applauded for all three of us. Afterward, Jean-Luc Ponty never mentioned it, nor did Itzhak. I often thought about what a gesture Itzhak Perlman had made that day on my behalf. It was the mark of a man who has confidence in his talent and in himself.

Television was sustaining me, no doubt about it. And I also felt it didn't hurt to have a mention of Hollywood here and there on my résumé. Regardless of what the movie critics might have said about the film itself, I had really enjoyed that stint on the set of *Zachariah*. And I had gone on to do a musical cameo with B. B. King, Alice Cooper, and others, in *Medicine Ball Caravan*, a 1971 film produced by Martin Scorsese. So when I got a call from director Terrence Malick asking if I'd do a fiddling cameo in his forthcoming *Days of Heaven*, I didn't hesitate. This was the summer of 1977, and I had no idea what a well-respected director Terry Malick already was, considering he'd done only one other film. But that one film was *Badlands,* which already had a huge cult following. When I was told that the filming would be done near Red Deer, Alberta, Pam and I threw some things in a suitcase and flew up to Canada.

Terrence Malick is famous for filming during what is known as the *magic hour* in film talk, that time between day and night, early in the morning or late in the evening. Since *Days of Heaven* was a turn-of-the-century love story set against the midwestern wheat harvests, Malick wanted no sun to appear at all in this film, just a white or a black sky. For the first couple of days Pam and I simply watched the filming. Sam Shepard was one of the stars. So was Richard Gere, who was in his late twenties back then and, at least it seemed to me, very shy. Because we were filming near miles and miles of Canadian wheat fields, Pam's allergies kicked in and nearly drove her crazy.

On the third night after we arrived in Red Deer, it was finally my turn to play the fiddle while Gere, Brook Adams, and the others danced around a huge bonfire. Malick had chosen a song I'd written called "Swamp Dance" as the tune he wanted me to play.

"Just have fun with it, Doug," he said, and that's what I did.

When the film was released later in 1978, the tag line to advertise it said, "Your eyes...Your ears...Your senses...will be overwhelmed." I rented *Days of Heaven* not long ago and damn if I don't look like I fit right into that place and time, a real turn-of-the-century fiddler. If I look a little wild, that's because I was. I had taken a few pulls from the Chivas Regal bottle I had with me, long before Malick ever thought of yelling "Action!" I guess that makes me a method actor.

It was December 1977 that Pam and I finally decided to leave the relative peace of Evergreen, Colorado, and move out to sunny California. I felt it was important for my career that I be closer to the television and film studios. I remembered well how I'd been "discovered" playing shows in Printers Alley back in Nashville. I figured Hollywood television producers would have a better chance of checking me out if I were performing more on the West Coast. Since I was already appearing often as a guest on *The Merv Griffin Show* or *The Mike Douglas Show,* it seemed like a good idea to move out there. I had done *Dinah!* the year before with fellow guests Richard Pryor, Don Knotts, and tennis player Jimmy Connors. That's an attention-getting crowd, not to mention the lovely host, Dinah Shore. Yet what I remember most about that taping was that when I walked in Richard Pryor shouted, "Hey Kershaw! Are they still hanging niggers in Louisiana?" It was his word, not mine. All I could say was, "Hell, I hope not, Richard." I was that shocked.

We sold the house in Evergreen and bought a new one in Woodland Hills, in the heart of the San Fernando Valley. As I said, it seemed like a good decision at the time. But sometimes a decision is like a car wreck. You don't know until long after it's over exactly what happened. Looking back, the move to the West Coast didn't just bring me closer to the TV studios. It also brought me closer to cocaine and all-night partying. And speaking of those all-nighters, I found a willing accomplice in Glen Campbell, who truly understood the serious art of pub crawling. Glen and I had known each other well in Nashville, but in Los Angeles we really started hanging out together. I especially liked those times when we were on the road and found ourselves partying until dawn. Man, back in those days the drugs flowed freely. Roger Miller and I loved to heckle Glen. We'd tease him by calling him the "King of Las Vegas." I remember one night that Roger and I were both playing Vegas at the same time that Glen was at Harrah's.

"Let's go see Campbell's show," Roger said. So he and I turned up unannounced. We slipped into a booth at the back, ordered drinks, and watched some of Glen's show. When we decided the time was right, we walked down to the steps that led up onto the stage. Glen didn't see us as we sneaked up the stairs, but the audience did, and they went wild. They started applauding and pointing, right in the middle of Glen's song. He knew then something had to be going on. That's when he looked over and saw us coming toward him on stage.

"Need any help, Campbell?" Roger asked.

"How about two backup singers?" I added.

"Ladies and gentlemen," Glen told his audience, "I give up!"

So, Roger and I took over his show. Since we had just one fiddle, Roger fingered the fiddle strings and I handled the bow. Then we told a few jokes, which was really a miniroast of Campbell. By the time we asked

Glen if he would join us in a song, he was laughing so hard he almost couldn't sing.

You could always count on that kind of stuff when Roger Miller was around. God, I miss him. He was the only guy I'd talk to in the middle of the night, years later, after I'd straightened up. About once a year he'd call around 3 a.m.

"Kershaw! Listen to this song I just wrote!"

If it had been anybody else I'd have said "call back tomorrow." But I always wanted to hear what was going through Roger Miller's mind, especially if it was a new song. The man had a talent that was unsurpassed.

It was in 1978, just a couple of months before our second son was born, that I had the opportunity to make music with another group of legends. It started when I played a club called Yvonne's in New Orleans, the same week the Rolling Stones played the Superdome. All through the week I heard rumors that the Stones were planning to come to one of my shows. Every evening when I walked on stage, I wondered if that might be the night. As it turned out, it was the Stones' bass player, Bill Wyman, who came to a show. Afterward, Bill came backstage and invited me to play my fiddle on a song when the band performed in Fort Worth, five days later, at the Will Rogers Memorial Center. This was July 18, 1978. I couldn't turn down an invitation like that. I went onstage and played while Mick Jagger sang "Far Away Eyes." That's one of the best perks to being a musician, this kind of camaraderie.

What Pam always remembers about that night is that she was seven months' pregnant with Tyler and had to stand next to Jerry Hall, who had on Spandex pants and spike heels and looked like, well, Jerry Hall in Spandex pants and high heels.

"I felt like a big barn," Pam says.

After the show I went back to Bill's room. To this day Pam thinks we did cocaine that night, but we didn't. Know what we did instead of cocaine? We played our favorite fiddle tunes. Bill had tapes of very old Celtic songs that he let me hear. In turn, I picked up my fiddle and played all the songs I knew by Bob Wills, the King of Western Swing. "New San Antonio Rose." "Faded Love." "Silver Dew on the Blue Grass." "Bob Wills Boogie." "Sugar Moon." "Bubbles in My Beer." "Texas Playboy Rag."

243

It wasn't cocaine, but that stuff can get you high too.

I met Keith Richards and Mick Jagger that night, but not enough to really form an opinion of the two as individuals. That's how it often happens with artists on the same show. Hell, most of the time the opening act doesn't even get to meet the headliner. Sometimes it's like that with studio sessions too. When I recorded *Hot Diggidy Doug* some years later, Hank Jr. sang on the track titled "Cajun Baby." But I never even saw Hank Jr. He came in and put his vocals on after I'd laid down the tracks. Fats Domino was on that record too, but he was there for everything. When he listened to me put my fiddle part down, he gave me a long, hard look.

"How'd you know that was gonna fit?" he asked.

Know what I remember thinking about Fats and me? That we were quite a pair, *a fat-ass and a coon-ass*. I didn't mean any disrespect to either of us. That's just the way my mind works.

It was shortly after this, on September 28, 1978, that our second son was born. And again, it was just luck that I happened to be home and not on the road. Pam and I had gone out to dinner that night with her cousin Carol Infuso and Carol's husband, Joe. Joe Infuso would later figure heavily in my life, but at that time he and Carol owned their own vacuum cleaner company. Since Pam and Carol had always been close, it was only natural that the four of us became friends. We had a pleasant dinner that night, and then Pam and I came home and went to bed. Sure enough, just like with Zachary, it was around midnight that Pam shook me awake.

"Come on, Doug, get up," she said. "My water just broke."

Water? Given that I was born and raised on a houseboat, it took me a few seconds to figure out what the hell she was talking about. Then I realized. Holy shit, the baby's coming! By the time I got up, got dressed, and drove Pam to the hospital, her contractions were two minutes apart. They wheeled her straight into the delivery room and Tyler James Kershaw, weighing eight pounds and eight ounces—the exact same weight as Zachary—was born in no time. We had already prepaid for a hospital stay of three days. Part of this package included a steak dinner with champagne that would be served to the proud parents right there in the hospital room. Pam had been in the Woodland Hills Hospital a day and a half when the nurses came and told her she had to leave.

"I'm being *evicted?*" Pam asked. She was just starting to feel great again and had been thinking about how nice that champagne and steak would be.

"We got more pregnant women than we have rooms for," the nurses explained. So they gave Pam our new baby and sent her home.

"I *still* want that steak and champagne," Pam says every time the details of Tyler's birth come up.

I played another show with Bill Wyman in the summer of 1979 when he asked if I'd do the famous telethon that Jerry Lewis did every Labor Day.

"Sounds great," I said. "Who have you got?"

"Besides me," said Bill, "there's Todd, Dave, and Ringo."

That was the band. Ringo Starr on drums. Bill Wyman on bass. Todd Rundgren and Dave Mason on guitars. Kershaw on fiddle. They even let me sing, and that night I had the greatest backup band in the world.

Pam thought meeting Bill, Todd, and Dave was exciting, but meeting Ringo Starr was the ultimate. She's been a hard-core Beatles fan since she was thirteen years old and her father took her to a Fab Four concert. So in the hopes of getting Ringo's autograph, she had brought along a record, an old 45 single of "I Want To Hold Your Hand." She also had a copy of the first Beatles magazine she had ever bought. But when Ringo pulled out a bottle of rye whiskey, I forgot all about Pam wanting his autograph. So, there we were—Bill Wyman, Ringo Starr, and me—backstage at Jerry's telethon, swilling rye whiskey out of a bottle in the corner. And there stood Pam, holding her record and magazine, waiting patiently. She finally gave up and introduced herself to Ringo Starr.

Remember how I said earlier that there's always a punch line to a Roger Miller story? It took fifteen years, but I finally heard the real reason why Roger came to my house to play me his new album. I'm talking about that time he showed up in the middle of the night back in 1964. I had had a gig canceled and drove back to Nashville, dead tired, when Roger knocked on my door. In 1979, Roger and I were both filming a television special with Dick Clark in Las Vegas. We were in my hotel suite, trading songs, fooling around on our fiddles. All of a sudden, Roger looked over at me.

"Doug," he said, "I want to apologize for sleeping with your wife."

"Oh?" I had to think. I knew for damn sure he didn't mean Pam. And I also knew he didn't mean Elsie. Then I remembered all those years ago when Roger stopped by my house in the middle of the night. I was supposed to be on the road, but I was there to open the door when he knocked. He just happened to have a tape of his new session in the car. That's when I realized what he was telling me. He hadn't come by all excited so I could hear "Dang Me." He'd been having an affair with Donna Darlene.

Dang *Me?*

Dang *HIM!*

"You know what really pisses me off, Roger?" I asked. He didn't say anything, waiting. "You never did pay back the twenty bucks you borrowed that night." His face broke into a smile. Hell, what else was there to say? It had happened a lot of years ago. Enough time had gone by that it was even funny. I laughed over it for years. After all, Roger had expected Donna Darlene to open the door in her nightgown, and instead he gets *me*, in my underwear and still smelling of road dust. So I walked over to Roger and put my arm around his shoulder.

"It took a lot of courage to tell me that," I said.

For years after that, Roger and I often ran into each other on the road. But neither of us ever mentioned Donna Darlene again. Instead, we did what we did best when we were together. We played music, we partied, we celebrated our friendship. That's how life should be.

On Christmas Day 1979, Mama Rita called me from Jennings. I was contracted to play Denver's Turn of the Century Club that week, and I was just getting ready to leave for the show. Mama Rita had some bad news. At the age of fifty-two, my oldest brother, Edward Joseph Kershaw, was dead of an aneurism. I hung up the phone and turned to Pam.

"Ed never did have good timing," I said.

Funny the things that fly into your mind at a time like that. Edward was the boy who had stood up to our father that dark night on the bayou, when Daddy Jack had threatened to throw us from the *Alice*. I felt like hell hearing that he had died, even though I had never been close to Edward.

But I was close to his wife, Marie, and his nine children, two of which were the twins, Brenda and Linda. According to Mama Rita, Ed had died in his own home and not at some hospital. I'm sure Marie was thankful for that. Since I was contracted to play the club in Denver, I missed my brother's funeral.

> *Bren and Lin are the family twins,*
> *big brother Ed is on the bayou fishing.*

I flew to Denver while the rest of the Kershaws were saying goodbye to Edward. I told myself I had a contract to fulfill, but there was more to it than that. I'd never gone to a funeral, not since Daddy Jack's. He was the only dead person I'd ever seen. I could have jumped on a plane. I could have told the Turn of the Century Club to kiss my ass. My brother was dead, for Christ's sake. I had a funeral to go to. What good did it do me to stay in Denver and perform drunk, get booed by my audience? That's what happened that night. Looking back on it, it was my way of getting out of a funeral instead of a contract. Either way, it hurt to lose a member of the family. It got me to thinking about those bayou days and that night on the *Alice*. Ed was a hero to me that night, no matter how much we grew apart in the later years. Now he was dead at fifty-two.

This is why God created Chivas Regal, for big, sad moments like that.

At least I was stupid enough to think so back then. Needless to say, I dove headfirst into a bottle. By showtime I was so drunk I could barely perform. For the first time that I could remember, the audience booed me. You will never know until it happens to you what it's like to have a whole room full of people shout "Boo!" It was *Christmas,* not Halloween. My manager at that time had the unusual name of Willie Nelson. He was Ricky Nelson's cousin and Ozzie's nephew. Both Pam and I thought a lot of Willie. He was a great guy, even though he himself tended to hit the white wine a lot after his wife left him. White wine and whiter cocaine. But he had been a damn good manager until his marriage problems started. I was always looking for Willie Nelson so I could fire his ass, but he was never around. He was that night, though, and he was as disgusted with me as he could get. Backstage, he grabbed my bottle of Chivas and threw it into the toilet. He threw it so hard that it broke the toilet in two. It cracked right down the middle and a big chunk fell off onto the floor.

It wasn't an *Ozzie & Harriet* moment. I had to pay the owner a couple hundred bucks to replace his toilet.

When I started talking to Pam about those times for this book, what she had to say broke my heart. "I knew when I went to a show with you, Doug, that it would either be the best or the worst show on earth," she said. "During that time you were out of control. You would sometimes get furious at one of the musicians. You could be so rude and mean to them, even kick their amps. Sometimes you stomped offstage after doing just a song or two. I always had pain in my stomach back then, just watching, waiting to see what would happen next." Shit. There's a lot of things I wish I could change.

I suppose there comes a time when everyone has to pay the fiddler. Even another fiddler. I was no exception. Over the course of the next two years, I started drinking Chivas and popping pills even before that cup of coffee in the morning. I always said that Chivas jump-started my day. Why not help it along with whatever drug was available? Old Yellers. Black Beauties. L.A. Turnarounds. Anything at all. The shows were still coming in hot and heavy, and I was still traveling and somehow performing through it all. Folk festivals. Bluegrass festivals. Rock festivals. Country festivals. Even the Newport Jazz Festival.

In September 1981, I was set to do a seven-week-straight run, two shows a day, six days a week at Harrah's in Reno. I was the first performer that Harrah's agreed to let do just two shows a day instead of the usual three. It was still a killer schedule. I probably wouldn't have signed on for such a grueling run, but I needed the money. Before Uncle Sam started bugging Willie Nelson about back taxes—I mean the *singer* now, not my former manager—the son of a bitch was on *my* back. I had failed to file any taxes in 1977. Who knows what I was thinking. So I had been audited. That house we sold in Evergreen? The little bit of money we got for it went to Uncle Sam. That Lincoln Mark IV I bought with the money I'd won gambling in Reno? I had to sell it in 1978 and give the money to Uncle Sam. Pam and I had also bought ten beautiful acres in Evergreen, a little aspen meadow with pine trees and a view of Mount Evans. We had to sell that acreage and give the money to Uncle Sam. Until you know how much the IRS can harass you, you'll never understand the pressure. Uncle

Sam was worse than any ex-wife could ever be. I wish I'd signed a prenup with *him* instead of Pam.

I signed the contract for seven weeks at Harrah's. Pam came with me and brought along Zach and Tyler. Harrah's provided us a two-bedroom suite, so this meant Zach and Ty had their own room. It was to be a family event. Family or not, it didn't take long for me to get my hands on a bag of Black Beauties. Speed. Something I could never handle very well. But casinos used to make me nervous as hell. I had already had a run-in with Harrah's, back around 1976, when I was playing their main room. By this time, being late for a show was a normal thing for me. My philosophy was, "Hell, they can't start without me." Harrah's felt it could do just that. I turned up late that first night back in 1976 and discovered that my name already had been taken off the marquee. "You're outta here," was Harrah's answer to "They can't start without me." I had to do a sad song-and-dance routine to get them to put *Doug Kershaw* back on the marquee. So I knew I couldn't piss off the casinos the way I might a small club owner.

It hurts just thinking about this kind of behavior. When I started out as a young musician back in Louisiana, I was always early for a gig. Always. I used to get on Rusty's back all the time about his lateness. I'm never late for a gig now, not if I can humanly help it. But I was back then. This was when Pam, who was always punctual, simply quit wearing a watch. She couldn't bear to know any more just how late I'd be. I realize now that the biggest reason for not showing up on time was simply fear. Being part of a team, as I had been with Rusty, meant having a partner there at your side, someone else to shoulder the failures as well as successes. And let's face it. Success is almost as hard to handle as failure. Sometimes it's harder. Sometimes, depending on what crap went on during those childhood years, you feel you don't *deserve* success. I'd been a solo act since 1966 and yet I was still scared to death. Booze and pills provided a warm blanket for all that fear and uncertainty. I don't like remembering things like that.

But there I was again, signed up for seven weeks at Harrah's, the casino that made me most nervous. Not only did I have to pay attention to the clock, there was all that gambling and boozing going on around me. Colorful lights. Music. Excitement. All the things that can lure an addictive personality like mine. Pam looked at the bag of Black Beauties and said nothing. During the days, she and the boys went to Circus Circus, the big indoor theme park that was part of the hotel and casino. During the nights, I did my show and often stayed out late partying and drinking. I wasn't allowed markers, but I could still buy chips. So I did a bit of gambling. All this time, Pam took care of the boys up in our suite and let it ride.

We coasted along like this for about five weeks. There were even good times. We celebrated Tyler's second birthday while in Reno. Harrah's had a big birthday cake with two candles on it sent to my dressing room so that we could have a little party to mark the event. But the boys were growing tired of clown shows, bumper cars, and arcade games. Pam was growing tired of trying to keep them entertained while I entertained myself. Life on the road, even if it's in one spot, is still tough on the most seasoned veteran. The Kershaw family was growing restless. As for me, with those nightly shows hanging over my head, with fear and addiction as my best friends, I started taking those Black Beauties every chance I got. Pam saw this. She knew something was bound to hit the fan eventually.

When it hit, I was so out of control that I can barely recall my actions. My wife remembers them well. Her word to describe my behavior this one night that I came up to our room was *psychotic*. When she ran into the bathroom and locked the door, I kicked a hole in it with my boot. She came out of the bathroom and raced across the hall to the boys' bedroom. She locked that door, too. Maybe it was the knowledge that my sons were in there asleep that kept me from kicking this door in as well. Whatever the reason, I stopped. When Pam got up the next morning she found me passed out on our bed, lying on a pile of broken glass.

"You had smashed up bottles, glasses, anything you could find that would break," she said. "I was used to you kicking in doors, Doug, but all that broken glass was more than I could handle. I had my kids to think about." So Pam took the boys and left.

I do remember waking up with glass all around me, but for the life of me, I don't remember doing it. I had a remedy for times like that. Take another Black Beauty. Pour another Chivas. For the next two weeks, I kept going at that manic pace. And it was manic, all right. In the late 60s my on-stage performances had begun to get more and more energetic and frenzied. I had always been dancing and moving about as I performed. But one night I was feeling the music so much that I jumped as far up into the air as I could and then turned in midair. When I came down on my feet, I was facing the band. The crowd loved it. After that, running, jumping, and anything else that required high, frenzied energy became a part of my act. People expected this wildness from a Doug Kershaw performance. Soon I was leaping into the air and turning a complete circle, so that when I came down I was facing the audience again, a smile on my face. I've read that Bruce Springsteen used to call his performances "three-pounders" and "five-pounders," depending on how much weight he felt he'd lost during his performance. Judging from that, a Kershaw show must have been a ten-pounder.

It's amazing what the human body will put up with, the abuse, the wear and tear. I guess the need to live is just that strong. But after eighty-two ball-busting performances at Harrah's without a major problem—at least as far as my shows were concerned—I canceled on the very last day. I was exhausted. The heavy drinking and the pill-popping had finally taken their toll. I knew down in that part of me that cares so much about survival that I *could not do one more show.* If I stepped out on the stage, I'd screw it up, some way, somehow, even if I tried my best to prevent it. So I called Pam and told her I was coming home. I asked if she would pick me up at the airport, and I was relieved when she said she would. I had no idea what her reaction might be, considering what I'd put her through. Then I called up my manager.

"I can't go another step," I told him. "I'm out of here."

The manager went down and talked to the gods that be. Even the gods agreed that if I couldn't physically do another show, best to let me ride off into the sunset. So I did. It just so happens that the sun was setting over the Raleigh Hills Rehab Center in Burbank, in the San Fernando Valley.

It was November 1981 that Joe Infuso drove Pam, the boys, and me over to Raleigh Hills. It was actually a chain of rehab centers. Doc in a box, I guess you could call it. They specialized in "addictions and behavioral problems." That sounded like me, all right. And they had great TV ads. *Are you depressed? Do you feel out of control? Do you think you have an addiction problem? Then come to Raleigh Hills!* That kind of thing. That's how we settled on Raleigh Hills. I could have been their poster boy. By this time, I was as depressed as a man could be. Pam signed me into the clinic, and then she and Joe went to a local mall to buy me pajamas and a robe. I felt like a damn kid being punished for bad behavior. But as I got out of the car, I looked back at Zach and Ty, at their innocent faces. I looked at Pam too. That's when I knew who was being most punished.

When I saw the security guard at the door, I remember thinking, "This place looks like a frigging jail." I don't think the guard would have stopped anyone from leaving, but his uniform was a discouraging sight. "What the fuck am I doing here?" I asked myself. "This place ain't fit for a wino." That's how you think when your brain is used to drugs. You tend to believe you're higher up the ladder than winos simply because they sit on street corners and beg for quarters. Trust me, it's the same ladder.

I had been assigned to a room that had four narrow bunk beds in it, dormitory-style. I would apparently share my surroundings with three other people who also fit those Raleigh Hills TV ads. My first day in, we rose early for breakfast. We were each assigned a counselor, which seemed like a nice thing. I was beginning to think Raleigh Hills might be tolerable after all, which was what I thought when I arrived at Camp Chaffee, before that army sergeant made me drop and do push-ups. When a nurse handed me a smock, I knew something was up. I mean, damn, I was out of control but I wasn't pregnant. Another nurse came to fetch me, to take me to a private room. She handed me a glass with some concoction that I had to drink. Then I was given three tall glasses of mixed booze. I mean, it was *straight* booze. It came from bottles they had left out purposely for us to see, all lined up on a table in the room. Gin, rum, whiskey, scotch, and so on. The room itself reeked the way a seedy barroom does. The smell was terrible.

"You need to drink all three glasses, Mr. Kershaw," the nurse instructed me. "And you need to do it now." The idea, of course, is to give you an aversion to booze, and let me tell you that it works damn well. Within a few minutes of drinking the last glass it all came back up. That's because the first glass I drank had a substance in it called *antabuse*, which is a drug that doesn't get along with alcohol. It makes you instantly sick to your stomach. I'm telling you, I puked until I couldn't puke any more. It made me wish I was back on the shrimp boat, out in the Gulf of Mexico. At least on the boat I could rest now and then when the sea was calm. In Raleigh Hills, that nurse rode shotgun over me the whole time. She sat on a chair in the room and waited until she saw the vomit for herself. It was the ultimate command performance.

I felt like an idiot. I tried to avoid her eyes, the way you do when you're standing next to someone in an elevator. I will say that when I started to puke, she held my head if I needed assistance.

"This is a hell of a calling you've chosen," I told her right after one of my performances. She smiled. There's been an irony in damn near everything in my life. Raleigh Hills would cost me about ten grand. I remember thinking, "Damn, I never threw up this much when I was drinking. Now here I am paying someone good money to make me puke." They earned every penny of that ten grand.

It wasn't a pretty picture in the scrapbook of my life. If it seems like I'm trying to make light of it, I'm not. It's just that humor has always carried me through the bad times. This was no exception. I was so low right then I had to stand on my tiptoes and reach up just to touch bottom. Pam came to visit me every day and sometimes brought the boys. There was a large social room at the clinic where these visits took place. It had comfortable chairs and a coffee pot. It was at Raleigh Hills that I got in the habit of drinking my coffee as strong as I could stand it. The minute I saw a fresh pot being made, I'd hold my cup under the first drippings. That's the strong stuff. And, man, I needed it. Caffeine was the only drug I was allowed. To this day I still hold my cup under the drip to catch those first drops of strong coffee. When I do, I think of Raleigh Hills. I probably will forever.

For two full weeks I had the same routine. And yet to this day, I can't remember anything about my fellow roommates. I assume this is because when you're puking you're not in a mood to socialize. Pam visited faithfully, but so did the damn nurse. She came every morning with her antabuse and her glasses of straight booze. It got to the point where I wanted to throw up even before I'd finished the third glass. Then just the smell of it was enough. By the last day all I had to do was *think* of the nurse. By the time I left, that place smelled just like the Bucket of Blood. I wouldn't have been surprised if Albert Broussard had popped his head in the door and said, "Step aside, good people, while I show this pig out."

Did it work? To this day I can't drink Chivas Regal or Jack Daniels. Just the smell turns my stomach. But I still liked the smell of beer. And I would learn to like the smell of cocaine even better. As the Steve Wariner song goes, "Some Fools Never Learn." When I left Raleigh Hills, I went back to my home in Woodland Hills. But I should have just run for the hills.

It was far from over.

23

BEVERLY GLEN

"I went from doing the two-step in the swamps,
to the twelve-step in Beverly Hills."
—Doug Kershaw

Long before the first jazz musician, the first hippie, or the first Hollywood movie star, human beings have been seeking ways to get high. They have eaten strange berries and swallowed the bark off trees. They've smoked weird-looking plants and devoured the hearts of animals. I don't care what anthropologists say. In my own version of mankind's history I see a bunch of Neanderthals sitting around a big fire, all staring forward, no one speaking. Finally, one of them asks, "Hey, anybody got any coke?"

Coke. Cocaine. Nose candy. Sherlock Holmes used to shoot it into his veins with a needle after some of his most stressful cases. And he never even met Buddy Killen. Lots of people over time have approved its use, folks such as Thomas Edison, Jules Verne, Sigmund Freud. When Coca-Cola first started putting its beverage into bottles for the American public to drink, it was laced with cocaine. Hence the name. Coke's slogan was "The drink that relieves exhaustion." Of course, Coca-Cola has now replaced the cocaine with caffeine. But there are areas of the world where cocaine is still regularly used. I recently read an article about natives down in the Andes who mix the green coca leaves with ashes and lime and then chew them. They can go for days without feeling tired or hungry. But the "habitual chewer," the guy who chews those leaves every chance he gets, staggers a bit when he walks. He has green-crusted teeth, he can't sleep, and he generally doesn't give a shit. All he really thinks about is how to get more of those coca leaves. Somebody should sign this guy to a record label.

Back when Mike Barnett was my manager, he had encouraged me to pick cocaine as my drug of choice.

"It'll help you stop drinking," Mike had said. "And drinking is gonna kill you, Doug."

Since I didn't want to die, I'd taken a snort every now and then. Sure enough, it was true. Being wild-eyed on cocaine did seem to cure my thirst for liquor. So when I left Raleigh Hills, I remembered Mike Barnett's cure for drinking. I figured I knew something my nurse didn't know. "Cocaine will keep you off the booze, Doug." With that in mind, I set about my rehabilitation in search of some good cocaine. It was all over California in those days. Hell, it was all over the country, like snow sifting down on us. And for an entertainer, it was often free. One good reason to have a road manager was to find me cocaine while I was *on the road*. I carried it most often in a glass vial, along with a little spoon that I used to measure out a nice straight line I could then snort up my nose. If I didn't have my spoon, I used my fingernail or a straw. My new philosophy was that no briefcase should be without a supply of cocaine, and mine rarely was. I also carried stashes in my boots, but this was before cocaine-sniffing dogs became customs agents.

Pam and I still don't agree on how long I was clean after Raleigh Hills before I started doing coke. It really doesn't matter. In the big picture, it wasn't long at all. How much money went up my nose? Lots. Huge amounts. A goddamn pile of money. Many times there was nothing left for Pam to pay the bills, no matter how many ball-busting concerts I was being paid for. We got behind on our second mortgage, and Pam had to ask her mother for grocery money. Pam had gone back to school by this time, studying political science at Cal State in Northridge. Along with taking classes, she was raising Zach and Tyler alone since I was almost always on the road.

I suspect Pam's family knew about the drugs, but they never brought up the subject. It was Pam's life. They would be there if she needed them. Maybe it was knowing this that kept Pam hanging in, that she had have a safe place to go if needed. But any talk of my drug problem only set off the Kershaw temper. Even a minor argument and I'd say, "That's it. We're through. I want a divorce." So it was pretty hard for Pam to approach me about the cocaine. Once, when she picked me up at the airport and we were driving home, she pointed to a bumper sticker on the vehicle ahead of us. MY OTHER CAR WENT UP MY NOSE.

"Look, Doug," said Pam. "That's you."

One good decision I made after I came out of Raleigh Hills was to hire Joe Infuso to replace Willie Nelson. Joe had already been doing my books by this time since his vacuum cleaning company had gone broke. There had been a burglary and Joe wasn't insured, so when I asked if he wanted a job as my accountant, he accepted. It wasn't long after that that Joe was handling more than accounting for me. Soon he was doing the job of manager. I finally tracked down Willie Nelson and, even though I still liked him, I fired his ass. I hired Joe Infuso instead and started giving him ten percent to manage me. Not only would Joe be a steady guy, it was obvious that he cared what happened to Doug Kershaw. He would do his best to steer me away from that cliff I was headed for. But what does a Cajun, born and raised below sea level and high on cocaine, know about cliffs?

My professional life was catching hell at this time, too. I was blowing up more and more at the band members, and it was getting hard for club owners to ignore it. That wasn't the kind of show they had hired me to do. During this time I managed to record an album for Scotti Brothers, titled *Instant Hero*. And while I might have felt like a hero back when I was a kid, the day I made my promise to Mama Rita that I'd take care of her forever, I was getting farther from a hero in the eyes of my wife, my kids, my friends, my band, and even the fans who might have been in the audience during one of my onstage temper displays. Pam had started thinking of me as Dr. Jekyll and Mr. Hyde.

"The anxiety was in never knowing which one would get out of bed in the morning or go on stage that night," she told me. "If things didn't go your way, Hyde could appear at a moment's notice." The way I was losing money in those days, Hyde was probably getting ten percent of me as well.

Again, it's nothing to laugh at. And I certainly feel no pride about those days. But humor comes to my rescue now and then. I need it these days as I go back and try to figure things out. I do know that while the boys never saw me do cocaine, they saw me drunk enough times. They heard me verbally abuse their mother. Pam says I never hit her, but I would push her around when I was mad. This was harder on Zachary than Tyler, what with Zach being the older boy. Zach and I tended to lock horns. He'd talk back to me as he got older, whereas Tyler had learned to say as little as possible. I compare this to my own brother Edward, the one who most often stood up to Daddy Jack, while the younger brothers, including me, had learned that it was best to sink into the background and become invisible. I know that during my drug days my sons both loved and were frightened of me. That's exactly how I had felt with Daddy Jack. I always made sure to follow close to Mama Rita's side at times like that for protection. My own boys stayed as close to Pam as they could.

When I wasn't around to be angry, I just wasn't around. Period. Believe it or not, I had signed up for an acting class at this time. Acting had always been interesting to me, a way to become someone else. I soon learned which of my fellow classmates were into the drug scene. When we weren't in acting class, we were either bowling or doing drugs. I always had to burn up energy some way. I never could sit still. I think it's a sign that a person just isn't comfortable with who they are. It's like you're trying to jump out of your own skin. Alcohol and drugs, especially cocaine, allow you to become another person, the guy who is sometimes the life of the party. When that other person fucks up, well, it's him doing it, not you. Everyone knows that when you're straight, you're a good guy. So that becomes a crutch in itself. You start blaming everything bad on the guy inside you who took the drugs, the guy who went down deep enough to touch all that anger that's been brewing for years. *He's* the guy who terrifies your wife, cold-cocks band members, or kicks amps off the stage. You're not *that* guy. Freud would have worn out a million pencils if Doug Kershaw had been lying on his couch.

One night as I was out bowling with "my fellow thespians," as I called them, Tyler woke up at home with a raging earache. Pam called our pediatrician, who quickly phoned in a prescription at the local drugstore. Pam didn't know where I was, but she thought of checking the bowling alley. Sure enough, my car was there. She had bundled up both boys and had them in the car with her. She came inside and told me that Tyler had a bad earache and that she needed to pick up medicine for him. I was in the middle of a game and wanted no part of a run to the drugstore.

"Take care of it," I told her. "Can't you see I'm bowling, for Christ's sake?" And Pam did take care of it. She picked up the ear medicine and then sat up all night long with Tyler. I've got a lot of those kinds of stories. A trunk full of them.

Lately, with television and talk shows telling us all about ourselves, I suppose you would say I was showing signs of manic depression. And why not? I'd come from a long line of classic symptoms, starting with Grandpa

Albert Broussard. But I was still a long way from understanding depression back in the early 1980s. Several months after my stint in rehab, I discovered that beer didn't make me sick, not the way the hard stuff did. I guess this was a loophole they didn't think about at Raleigh Hills, since they hadn't made me drink huge quantities of beer loaded with antabuse. It was a loophole I jumped at headfirst. Let me tell you how people who are addictive think. "Cocaine won't hurt me like Chivas Regal, and neither will beer, so I'll be all right. It's that damn Chivas Regal and those pills that were causing my problems."

Amazing, ain't it? But look around you, folks, and everywhere you look you'll see someone who is thinking that exact same thing. Making excuses for themselves. Addiction doesn't come hand in hand with logic and it never will. I started drinking beer sometime in 1983, and since it didn't make me sick, I added it to my list of *OK Things to Do*. And then, since tequila wasn't Chivas Regal, I figured it wouldn't hurt to put José Cuervo on the list. José seemed like a nice guy. And then peppermint schnapps. I mean, when was the last time you heard of anyone with a peppermint schnapps addiction? That went on the list, too. Yet, Pam says I was worse on schnapps than tequila. Soon I couldn't go anywhere without a six-pack of beer sitting on the seat next to me. By then it felt as if I had never stopped drinking at all. But cocaine was still the king. Cocaine ruled. When I was high on coke I had no problems.

It's sad to think of this, but I had burned out, and cocaine was what it took to get me back to that old, innocent feeling I told you about earlier in this book. The feeling I used to get from music and nothing else. The feeling I used to get every time I picked up my fiddle and heard music come out of it. *I go back into my mind and let the music flow. When I slip back into time to recapture those fleeting, childhood moments, those sounds and colors of the* fais do-dos, *I feel light. There's no other word. Light. My mind drifts upward, almost leaving my physical body behind. For a second there, it's as if I've never been judged, or criticized, or hurt. It's as if I could never do anything wrong. What I feel is pure love. Then it's over, and I'm gone from that old time and place. I'm back in the "now" time.*

In other words, cocaine had taken the place of music for me.

It had taken the place of human beings.

It had taken the place of all those old dreams.

That's how powerful the shit is.

What I couldn't know at this time was that unlike my stash of coke, Pam's patience and love were running out. But she was still there in January 1984, when I had a seizure just as I came off my last show at the Crazy Horse in Santa Ana, up in Orange County. I was certain that I was having a heart attack. I was so dizzy and weak that I couldn't get my legs to stand under me. And the pain in my chest felt like a freight train was traveling through it. I didn't pass out, but I thought for sure I was dying. Joe Infuso rushed me to the emergency room. The best the doctors could tell me was that I was hyperventilating, but I knew better.

"I wasn't hyperventilating," I said to Joe as he drove me home from the hospital. "I was hyper-cocaine-ing."

That's exactly what I was doing. I wouldn't know about the effects of cocaine on the body until later, but here's what happens. When you snort cocaine up your nose, as I always did—I never injected or freebased—at first there's a numbing effect. This happens within seconds of snorting and it lasts about five minutes. Then a feeling of pure exhilaration sweeps in slowly, sheer joy, and with it comes energy you never thought possible of yourself before. It keeps building, all this euphoria, until it peaks, anywhere from ten to twenty minutes later, and then *bam!* It's gone. The only thing you can do to get that euphoria back is more cocaine. Now the trouble is, when you snort cocaine it narrows the blood vessels, constricts them. This makes your respiration rate and body temperature go up. It can even interfere with the information that one nerve cell is trying to transmit to another. When you take a lot of the drug, as I did, there are certain areas of the brain that become more susceptible to seizures. *That's* what caused me to have a seizure that night. Hyperventilating, my ass.

I felt bad on the drive back from the hospital because I knew it hurt Joe to see me that way, just as it was hurting Pam. But the cocaine had a hold on both my heels and was dragging me down. It wasn't that I didn't care. It's that I just couldn't stop. Doctors have done loads of studies on cocaine addiction. Lab monkeys, when given all the cocaine they want, will inject themselves constantly with the stuff. They will refuse all offers of food and water. All they care about is more nose candy. That's a hell of a picture, ain't it? Now, imagine human beings doing the same damn thing. Added to this, about the only thing I *wasn't* drinking was Chivas Regal. Pam never knew it, but it was at this time that I would raid the kitchen when she was gone, looking for what I called "kitchen booze."

This means I drank the bottles of cooking sherry that I found in the cupboards.

In March 1984, I finally hit rock bottom. Joe Infuso was there when I did. And so were a lot of other people, since I was standing in the middle of the Burbank airport at the time. I don't even remember this. Nor do I remember any of the bad scenes from previous months. During the writing of this book I made a phone call to Joe Infuso. I needed to ask him about that day, the one that marked the beginning of the end of The Kershaw Drug Era. Joe obliged me with a few memories. It seems there had been an incident at Harrah's the year before that would highlight some of the events in my life that I wish I could forget. Backstage, between shows, I'd gotten into a nasty argument with Marty Vadalabene, my drummer at the time. It ended with my breaking a bottle over his head. The cut bled, someone put towels on the wound, and that might have been the end of it as far as Harrah's was concerned. It was a hell of a thing for me to do, no doubt about it. But Marty and I talked it out the next day, and I apologized to him. Shit, he ended up playing with me for a few years after that.

But, according to Joe, the other band members were now furious. To get back at me, they scattered the bloody towels all over the backstage floor, then called management to come see what I'd done. That's all it took. When my contract was up, Harrah's refused to renew it. For all these years, I didn't know the band had done this until Joe told me. And I certainly didn't know that Harrah's knew about the bottle incident. I guess I thought they just didn't want me back, period. Thinking about it now, the band should've found a better way to get back at me. After all, Harrah's represented *their* living, too. This seems like cutting off the nose to spite the face. No wonder I fired all their asses a year later. But that leads to the second part of this story.

I wanted to play Harrah's again. It had been a good, steady source of income to me. It became our plan, mine and Joe's, over that next year. We wanted to be invited back, and Joe finally set it up in March 1984. There was a junket of Cajuns flying up to Reno from Louisiana, a whole plane full of them, to gamble at the Casino. This seemed like a good time to invite Doug Kershaw back. I would be the entertainment for when the gambling was over. We even made it as far as the Burbank airport, where I got into a heated argument with my band members and promptly fired them. Every one. Joe says I then decided that I would do a solo at Harrah's

261

instead. He tried to talk me out of this, needless to say, and finally convinced me that the best thing to do was to hire a band once we got to Reno. I agreed. Joe got on the phone to Doug Bushausen, who was booking acts for Harrah's at the time, and told him the news. *Doug Kershaw is coming without his band.* But Joe assured him that I would find a pick-up band once I got there. This was agreeable to Bushausen. After all, he wanted those gambling, drinking Cajuns to be happy.

Shortly before Joe and I were to board the plane, I changed my mind again. I wasn't going, period. This is what cocaine will do to you. An idea will flash into your head. It can be as crazy as they come, but you'll grab it and hold on. Sometimes for days. When you're high on coke, a wild idea will let go of *you* before you let go of *it*.

"Fuck Harrah's," I said to Joe. "I don't need those bastards. *They* need *me*."

Well, a few angry Cajuns from Louisiana weren't going to break Harrah's. But in my brain I was the victor. I had just put it to a major casino. I stormed out of the airport. Then Joe had to call Bushausen back. He finally tracked him down in a steam bath somewhere in Reno.

"Kershaw's not coming," Joe told him. Bushausen was furious. "He called me every name in the book," Joe remembers. I know that book. I've used it myself on occasions.

From this point on, I remember very little. Joe says that he and Carol got a call from Pam, who was very upset. She had a right to be. I had come home and started raising such hell that she called the Infusos, bundled up the boys, and fled to their house to wait out the storm. Carol was more than a cousin. She was like a sister to Pam. Maybe I took it as a definite sign of abandonment. And abandonment was the one thing I feared most. If our marriage was over, then by God I'd make sure it was *really* over. A couple hours later I called Joe's house and asked to talk to Pam.

"I need you to come home and sign some papers," I told her. Pam was still furious, but this caught her interest. Just what papers might I be speaking of, she wondered.

"I've decided to sell the house," I said. "The real estate agents are here now, waiting for your signature."

This got Pam's full attention. For one thing, I was trying to sell our home. And for another, the two agents I had called were also my fans. They had come often to my shows, and Pam and had socialized with them many times over the years. Along with anger, Pam felt humiliation in front of these women who were witnessing my breakdown in person. She held her ground, though.

"Go fuck yourself, Doug," she said. And then she hung up on me.

You can't sell a house that way.

This was when Pam called Joe and told him I had finally lost it. Big time. But before Joe could drive to my house and calm me down, I took off. Knowing me, knowing how irrational I was when coked up, I probably thought, *What good is a fucking house if you can't sell it?*

While we were working on this book, I asked Pam about that night and about some of the other shaky times in our marriage. If nothing else, it's proof of what the bystanders to drug addiction have to go through. I knew she would remember well, even though it would not be pleasant. After all, she was the one who was sober through it all. And she's the one who ended up with stomach problems to this day because of the emotional roller coaster that our family life had become.

"Doug, those years were pure hell," she said. "Life with you just wasn't fun anymore."

But on that winter day in 1984, the hell still wasn't over. When I came to my senses the next morning, I was in one of the seediest motels you can imagine. I didn't even know the name of the place or where it was, but I remember thinking, "Here I am at the Chateau Shit." It wasn't the Marmont, I can tell you that. I figured I was still somewhere in Woodland Hills. How did I get there, or what did I do the night before? Your guess would be as good as mine. I'm willing to bet I hit some bars that night, did some serious drinking. And I know I must have snorted some coke. If I breathed air that night, then I did cocaine.

This is the story of Doug Kershaw at Rock Bottom.

There I was, lying flat on my back on the bed in that motel room. The curtains were dirty and the windows covered with a layer of dust. I could hear a faint *buzzing* of traffic from the street outside. Occasional voices came and went, guests from the other rooms. I turned onto my side so I could get a better look at the room. The mattress creaked beneath me. It felt like a family of prairie dogs were living in the coils. Empty beer cans were scattered everywhere. On the battered desk I saw my vial and my spoon lying where I'd obviously snorted the last of my stash. I looked down at the rug on the floor. It was covered with small black craters, holes burned there by careless cigarettes. It was a place where desperate people end up. The kind of motel where twenty-dollar prostitutes filter in and out all night long, just ghosts of the innocent girls they once were. So was I, a ghost of my old self.

I remember thinking, "What the hell am I doing here? The chicken coop back in Lake Arthur was fancier than this." I was out of control, no doubt about it. As Joe Infuso knew, being in control of myself was always so important to me. And I was more depressed than I had ever been in my life. That's when I thought of Daddy Jack, of that June morning when he woke up alone on the houseboat. I thought of my godfather, Raoul Roy, hearing what sounded like a shotgun blast. Then that second shot, the *coup de grâce*. Whether it was suicide or not, Daddy Jack died alone on that houseboat after days of drinking and too much sad thinking. And here I was, forty years later, doing the same thing. It wasn't suicide in the way you hold a gun to your head or to your heart, but I was killing myself. I had inherited that addiction from Daddy Jack. Slowly but surely it was getting the better of me. I picked up the phone and called Joe Infuso.

"Joe," I said. "I'm dying. Please find me a place where I can get help." I couldn't tell him where I was because I didn't fucking know. I told Joe that I thought I could find my way home, and that's where I was headed.

"I'll meet you there," he said. "Don't go anywhere but home, Doug."

I heard a knock on the door, two loud raps. I could barely get the phone back onto its cradle. That's how bad my hand was shaking. I opened the door and there was the maid, a woman in her sixties, the kind of tired face that has seen its own share of troubles, hands that have worked hard for a living. A cleaning lady for Le Chateau Merde. She could have been my mother. She could have been Mama Rita, who had taken in other people's dirty laundry just to put food on the table for her kids.

"You checking out?" she asked, and it startled me. In my muddled brain, I thought she really meant this. Was I in that room to *check out?* To kill myself, in other words.

"No," I said. "Joe is gonna find me a place." She looked up at me then, a funny gleam in her eye, the kind your distant kin get when they hear you've come into a bit of money.

"You're Doug Kershaw," she said. It wasn't a question, it was a statement. Entertainers often joke about this, about how sometimes a fan will tell you what your name is as if you don't know. But when you've done the cocaine I had done at that point, when you don't even know *where the fuck you are,* you appreciate a little help with your name. I nodded to her that yes, I was Doug Kershaw. She quickly pulled out the dresser drawer and fumbled around until she came out with a crumpled sheet of stationery.

"Would you write your autograph for me?" she asked. I felt a flutter of hope in my chest. See? I could still make people happy. Maybe the world wasn't such a bad place after all. So I signed my name, just barely. It looked to me like that sheet music Jean-Luc Ponty had handed me a few years earlier when we taped *Fiddlers Three*. Chicken scratches. The cleaning lady read what I'd written, then, satisfied that it was really my name, she shoved the paper into her pocket.

"Now my friends will believe Doug Kershaw really *was* in this dump," she said, pleased. She stepped past me, as if I no longer mattered, and began to change the bedsheets. Soon that awful room would look as if I'd never even been there.

As I closed the door behind me, I could only hope that the next poor bastard who checked in would also make it through the night. I found my car outside in a parking space, the keys still in the ignition, so I'd obviously driven myself to the motel. I got in, backed out, and pulled into the street. That's when I realized I was only about five blocks from my house. When I got home, Pam had already driven the boys to school. A few minutes after I arrived, Joe roared into my driveway. We sat on my sofa and talked for what seemed like an eternity, but it was probably less than an hour. Then Joe got up and walked outside. He was crying, tears running down his face.

"There was no doubt in my mind that, sooner or later, you were going to kill yourself," Joe said. "You and I had had long discussions about your father's death so many times. It was always on your mind back then."

But Joe composed himself, and he came back in to ask me if I was ready to go with him. Immediately. Not tomorrow. Not next week. *Now.* Thank God I said yes. I guess this all runs back to my sense of survival. I knew I had to do something or I was going to die. We drove first to Oxnard, California, to a facility there. Joe didn't like the looks of the place. He knew of one called Beverly Glen, in Beverly Hills, right across from the Rancho Golf Course. He thought this would be the best place for me because of their guarded policy concerning clients. Everyone checks in anonymously. No names are given out over the phone. And names are kept out of the newspaper. So we headed for Beverly Glen. Like Raleigh Hills, it would cost me more than ten grand. That was a fortune in those days. I could only pray that this time it would be money well spent.

There's often a bit of humor mixed in with the serious stuff. Joe says that as we were driving down Wilshire Boulevard, looking for the street number of the facility, I explained to him that the even numbers in an address are *always* on the right side of the street.

"I wanted to ask you about that," Joe said. "I wanted to say *doesn't it depend on what direction you're going*? But I didn't press it. You were too fragile for me to argue the point."

In March 1984, I came back to a world that still held all the same problems for me as it did when I had left it. But in my wake were new problems I had created while I was gone. And I say "gone" because I'd been having blackouts for years, and therefore no memory of the destruction I was leaving in my path. *Blackouts.* That alone should be enough to scare any us onto a straight road. But it rarely happens. There was a time in my life when blackouts meant night had come to the swamp, bringing with it the sounds of owls and frogs. On moonless nights you couldn't see your hand in front of your face. Blackouts meant those war years in Lake Arthur, when we were afraid of being bombed if we left a 40-watt bulb burning in the kitchen. Now, here was a new definition of the word for me to learn. And it scared the hell out of me.

When rock star Ozzy Osbourne checked into drug rehab, he had been told by friends who were desperate to get him there that it wouldn't be as bad as he thought. Ozzy went into the clinic gladly, since his idea of a rehab was that you would be still be allowed to drink. The staff would teach you how to do it without getting too wasted and making an ass of yourself. They would teach you how to snort cocaine like a gentleman. Ozzy was very disappointed when he unpacked and realized the truth. *You can't do drugs any more.* I found this out too, at Raleigh Hills, when I was forced to drink all that booze and then vomit it. I had to wonder if Beverly Glen would work on the same concept. I imagined the nurse coming every morning with a fresh stash of cocaine and a nice long straw. I would be encouraged to snort all I wanted to in hopes that it would make me hate the stuff. But I knew better than that. Had that been their plan, I would end up like one of those poor lab monkeys, waiting for the sound of the nurse's footsteps every thirty minutes.

When Joe first checked me in at Beverly Glen, they immediately sent me upstairs from the hospital facility to a room where I was to dry out. They gave me blood tests and monitored me. I already knew I had a hole in the inner membrane of my nose about a quarter inch round. That's often another souvenir of serious coke users. When they realized I was actually sober and not suffering any cocaine or alcohol withdrawals, they sent me back downstairs after a couple of hours. The nurses later told Pam that I was one of only a couple people who had walked through the door not falling down drunk.

I could have no visitors for the first three days. When visitors were allowed, Joe and Carol Infuso came. Pam Kershaw didn't. When I was able to make a phone call, my wife was the first person I phoned up. I asked her why she wasn't coming to visit me. As if I didn't already know. Pam wasted no words in explaining the situation.

"I don't care if you end up in the gutter, Doug," she said. "As a matter of fact, I don't care if you live or if you die. So do what you need to do. I've got kids to raise and a house to take care of only because you didn't sell it."

There was no doubt in my mind that she meant this. I knew Pam, and she was no bullshitter. Her Ragin' Cajun days were over.

"I'm done wasting precious time worrying if you're lying dead somewhere," Pam continued. "I'm putting my attention on the important things. I've got mid-term exams to worry about. My kids have to be fed and dressed properly every day. They've got to be driven to school, to gymnastics lessons, to the doctor, the dentist. But those are things you don't know about, Doug, because you've rarely been here to see them happen."

And then she said something that I'll never forget as long as I live.

"This marriage is over, Doug."

That got my attention better than anything Raleigh Hills or Beverly Glen had to throw at me, all at once.

I went about the days at Beverly Glen with a pure heart after that. I wanted to make it work. I was certain that Pam would change her mind if she saw that I was serious this time. I simply couldn't imagine life without her and the boys. So I attended all the counseling there was to attend. I talked to doctors and psychologists. I even talked to a priest who was a recovering alcoholic. I'm Catholic myself, and the priest made an impression on me. I don't remember his name, but I think it's safe to say he was Father Somebody. He'd become an alcoholic because the church had insisted that he drink the wine, the blood of Christ. Problem was, he got to drinking too much blood and he couldn't stop. But he was clean by then, and he came back often to talk to others in the hopes of helping them out. I chatted often with the priest. He was my connection to God, my long-distance carrier. If *he* could admit he had an addiction, then so could I.

Beverly Glen was a kinder, gentler rehab than Raleigh Hills had been. For one thing, I had my own private room, and that made a world of difference. I met up with other people in the music business. The one who stands out most is Jan Berry of the successful singing duo Jan & Dean. They'd had massive hits in the 1960s such as "Surf City," "Dead Man's Curve," and "The Little Old Lady from Pasadena." Then, in April 1966, Jan Berry almost met his own "Dead Man's Curve" when he ended up in a horrible car crash. When paramedics arrived at the scene, they thought Jan was already dead. But when they checked his vital signs, they realized he was still alive. They cut him out of the car and rushed him to UCLA hospital. It was there that he underwent many major brain surgeries. At first, his doctors didn't really think he'd make it. He stayed in a deep coma for weeks, and when he finally emerged he was unable to walk or talk at first. Thankfully he had good family, friends, doctors, and therapists, as well as an unbelievable drive to recover. The part of his brain where musical ability comes from was not that badly damaged. He was able to sing for many years to come.

Unfortunately, the car wreck signaled the end of Jan & Dean's recording career. That's when Jan, while recovering from his injuries caused by the auto accident, became addicted to pain killers. By the time he ended up at Beverly Glen he was, like me, at rock bottom. In one of those coincidences that happen sometimes, Jan & Dean had recorded "Louisiana Man," with an actual duck call at the beginning of their version. I liked it too. But what impressed me most was that Jan Berry, after all he'd been through, managed to kick the habit. And Dean Torrence, who never had a drug problem himself, stood by Jan during all that hard time. Later, after Beverly Glen, Jan and Dean came to our house—the one I had tried to sell—for a barbecue and to meet Pam and the kids. Sadly, after a long career, Jan suffered a seizure in 2004 and passed away.

There were about thirty of us at a time at Beverly Glen, both men and women. Some dropped out and new faces appeared to replace them. All of us were struggling to make it to our "graduation" day, when we were finally free to walk past the security guard who was stationed in uniform at the door. In another one of those odd twists that can happen only to musicians, I was scheduled to play the inaugural ball for Louisiana Governor Edwin Edwards, at a gala that had been planned for the Superdome in New Orleans. It was a big deal, and I had signed a contract to do the event. Beverly Glen agreed to let me go to the ball, like Cinderella. But it was on the condition that Tim Hauser come to New Orleans with me as my chaperone. Tim was the bass singer and founder of the New York quartet known as The Manhattan Transfer, whose biggest hit was "The Boy from New York City." It had climbed to the top of the charts in 1981. Tim himself was a graduate of Beverly Glen and, like other concerned graduates, came back now and then to help out us new pledges. I'd been in Beverly Glen about ten days by this time, so the Superdome would be the super test.

Pam wanted no part of the governor's ball, not if Doug Kershaw was attending. So Tim and I flew alone out of LAX on a flight headed east for New Orleans. A car took us to our hotel and that night I was ready to do my show. I was to perform two songs, "Diggy Liggy Lo" and, of course, "Louisiana Man" in honor of the governor of my home state. When I turned up backstage, with Tim shadowing my elbow, it looked like the same old crowd. You learn after a time to pick the drug faces from the clean faces, especially if you want to score some dope. The drug faces were there, all right. Everyone backstage was very impressed that I was hanging out with one of The Manhattan Transfer. Shit, he'd flown from California with me, or so they thought, just to hear me play two songs. They had no idea he was my chaperone. This seemed to rate me well with the hangers-on as whispers flew back and forth. Just as I was about to go on, a fellow musician pulled me aside.

"I got some real good blow, Doug," he said, sure that I'd be thrilled. "Wanna do some before your show?"

"No thanks," I said. And it wasn't because Tim Hauser was hovering at my side like someone's Aunt Margaret either. I just didn't want any of the damn stuff. It's hard for *anybody* to quit drugs, but when you're a performer, when you have to go out to clubs and arenas to make your living, strangers will appear out of a crowd to offer you free highs. That brings with it an added tension in trying to quit. So I pushed on past this guy and went out on the stage to do my show. I wasn't feeling my best, but when the adrenalin kicks in, that good ole natural high, it's amazing what the body can do to answer it.

"Congratulations, Governor Edwards," I said as I finished "Louisiana Man."

The next day I was back at Beverly Glen learning about the harmful effects cocaine has on the human body. When I wasn't in one of these classes, I was pacing the hallways. A few days later, having passed the big test in New Orleans, there was no doubt in my mind that I was ready to come home. Pam had come to visit only one time, along with Carol and Joe, for a group meeting that would include patients, family, and friends. But I could tell she did it out of guilt because she didn't seem happy to see me. I've known undertakers with bigger smiles. Nonetheless, after two weeks in the clinic, I called up Pam and told her I was cured. It was definitely time for me to come home. Her reaction stunned me.

"Doug, I don't want you to come home *period*," Pam said.

I got goose bumps I hadn't felt in years. So I asked my doctor, a pleasant woman, if she would call my wife and tell her that I was ready to graduate. The doctor was kind enough to oblige, but even this didn't sway Pam. As a matter of fact it made her angrier, since the doctor indicated that Pam wasn't being very supportive of her husband. The doctor shouldn't have said that to Pam Kershaw, a woman who was married to the Ragin' Cajun.

"I'll have you know that I've been supportive of my husband for over ten years," Pam told my doctor. "And during that time I have gone through a hell that *you* can only imagine. I have seen enough Chivas Regal, enough pills, and enough cocaine to last me a lifetime. I've seen enough doors kicked in, and I've been pushed around just one time too many. I was at Doug's side every single time he promised to change and believe me, he's promised it hundreds of times. So don't *you* tell *me* that I'm not supportive of my husband!" Then Pam bid my doctor good day.

The doctor hung up. She and I just sat there and stared at each other.

"I think you better stay with us another week," she said.

For the next week I went back to pacing the hallways when I wasn't in counseling sessions or classes. I began thinking pure thoughts for the first time in years. Drug-free thoughts. Daddy Jack. Mama Rita. Uncle Abel. The good times at the *fais do-dos* and not the bad ones. The old Cajun French tunes. My shoe shine job and how those bright, new dimes had gleamed in the palm of my hand. That first bike. There *had* been good things from my childhood, if I could just dwell on them instead of on the darker stuff. I think now that Daddy Jack's suicide overshadowed everything like a thick cloud. He was in my life for such a short time, and yet he had hardly left my side.

I remembered career times, too, as I paced the corridors or sat on the edge of my bed. The good times, the fun times. Here's one of those memories. Once, when we boys were visiting Hackberry where so many of the Kershaws lived, we were listening to *Uncle Bill's Hillbilly Show* on a Lake Charles radio station. It must have been about 1952. A song suddenly came over the airwaves by Lefty Frizzell. Our steel player, J. W. Pelsia, yelled for me to come listen. A chill ran right up my spine when I heard Lefty sing.

"Someday, I'm gonna write a song like that," I told J. W.

"Well, what's wrong with right now?" he asked and handed me a guitar.

That's when I wrote my first song in English, the language I had basically learned by listening to Ernest Tubb. It was called "All Those Dreams of Yesterday." And here I was, still just sixteen years old. Shortly after that, Lefty Frizzell played a show in Eunice, and I hitched a ride over to see him. After the show I hung around the backdoor until he came out. "How do I get to be a star, Lefty?" I asked him. Lefty just stared at me for a minute. "Son, if you want something bad enough and you work hard for it, chances are you'll get it." Good advice. But Lefty Frizzell would later drink himself and all that tremendous talent into an early grave.

Old memories like that came fluttering back to me. I thought of Rusty & Doug, of us being the youngest act booked on the Grand Ole Opry. Once, I read something Rusty told an interviewer who made a comment to him that it must be hard being Doug Kershaw. "You should try being Doug Kershaw's *brother*," Rusty answered.

I thought of some other times, too, ones I wasn't proud of. I even remembered how I'd gotten so pissed off at some bass player at the Palomino Club—what the hell was his name?—that I'd taken his bass down to the bus station and bought it a ticket to Fresno. But I did tell him the next day where he could find it.

I thought of my boys, all of them, Victor and Doug in Nashville, kids I hardly knew. Tyler and Zach in Woodland Hills, kids who were growing up with the knowledge of a father out of control. Zachary was celebrating his eighth birthday. But I was in rehab at Beverly Glen instead of at his party watching him blow out the candles on his cake.

Mostly, I thought of Pam Eson. Of that Colorado blizzard. Of the time we ran through the airport in Paris after I'd walked out on some shows I was booked to do with Herbie Mann. But shit, the audience was all Herbie Mann fans, so I had a tantrum and came home. At Orly Airport I was being paged over and over, and Pam and I were certain the gendarmes were after us. I thought of our marriage in the Astrodome. *This is the craziest thing I've ever done, Doug.* I remembered how, the night before our wedding, I had had one of my temper rages and called the whole thing off. Fuck the Astrodome. A wedding *cancellation* would be another first. It was typical Kershaw behavior by then, but Pam just went on with plans as if nothing had happened. She'd already grown used to it.

This marriage is over.

To this day Pam believes that my doctor probably thought, "What a bitch Doug's wife is. No wonder the poor man does drugs." The truth is that Pam saved my life. She let me know in plain English that the jig was up. I'd always talked my way back before, but not this time. A cocaine addict knows all about *straws,* and this was the one that had broken the camel's back. That gets you to pay attention. I did. Pam finally agreed to come to Beverly Glen and met with my doctor and me. Before I was allowed to come home, she wanted a solid plan. A contract, if you will, such as the one I'd signed for the governor's ball. Such as our prenup agreement. Such as the hundreds of contracts I'd signed over the years. Only this would be one I couldn't break.

If I came home, I would be, for lack of a better word, a *border.*

I was starting over from scratch when it came to love, trust, and re-spect.

I would never, *ever*, take another drug, no matter how little or what the situation.

No more temper tantrums, no more shoving.

One screw-up and it was over for good.

And, oh yeah, we would no longer share a bed at night.

I agreed to all of the above. Pam picked me up at the clinic and drove me home. I was a person starting over. I can remember that I was nervous, but I was also grateful at being given a second chance. When we got home the boys were overjoyed to see me, and I was sure happy to see them. To be back home. To have a family. Shit, *a house*. But something else was waiting for me at home. A living symbol, you might say, to let me know that things had changed at the Kershaw residence while I was gone. A white Samoyed puppy came bounding out to welcome the new border.

"Look, Daddy!" Zach said, all excited. "Mom gave me a puppy for my birthday!"

Pam had bought Zachary a dog?

For years I had said no when Pam or the kids asked for a dog. We were traveling too much for a pet, I always told them, using that as my excuse. But that wasn't the truth. When I was ten years old someone gave me a black cocker spaniel. I loved that little dog instantly. What was better, he loved me right back. He followed me all over Lake Arthur, staying close to my heels. I hadn't had him very long when he was hit by a car and killed. The day I buried that dog, I made myself a pledge to never own another one. "It'll just die on you," I told myself. "Besides, only a sissy would cry over his dog dying."

Absolutely no dogs. I'd made it very plain.

Pam and I locked eyes.

"Nice dog," I said to Zach and then patted its head.

It wasn't until I remembered the little black cocker spaniel for this book that I made the connection to Daddy Jack. My philosophy for a lot of years had been pretty cut and dried. *If you love something, it will die. It will abandon you. So build the walls high and guard yourself.* The dog was symbolic, no doubt about it. Things had changed.

That night, Pam left some clean sheets and blankets for me on the couch.

24

MAMA RITA

*"It was a good, simple life.
I'd like to do it again for a while before I die."*
—Mama Rita, *Newsweek*, 1974.

A good part of life is about forgiveness. Forgiveness and new beginnings. And I'm the kind of man who can start over. I've always said that if everything I own is taken from me, I can go back to a houseboat tied to a stump in Tiel Ridge and survive. Here's what else I think. If you can go back into the coils of childhood, if you can ask yourself some painful questions and give yourself some truthful answers, then you can shake up the past. You'll never be free of it, but you can learn how to live with it. Forgive and you'll endure. I was tired of sleepwalking with bad memories.

After I'd been released from Raleigh Hills in 1981, I'd gone to a couple of Alcoholics Anonymous meetings. But I simply couldn't keep it up. For one thing, many of the people in the room knew who I was. This is another time an entertainer pays for those perks. Other people, in non-public jobs, could stand up and say "I'm Jane" or "I'm John," and no one would think beyond that. But when I stood up and said "I'm Doug," well, shit, you could see the looks and hear the whispers. *That's Kershaw. You know, that Cajun fiddle player.*

A performer is trained to think in terms of building up his or her name over years of hard work, not tearing it down. You get protective of that notion. I felt humiliated those few times I did try AA. If you still feel those emotions, you're not ready to quit. It's understandable, though, since it isn't easy to admit to the whole world that you're an alcoholic asshole. I could do it at home, alone in my living room. Hell, I *knew* I was an alcoholic. I *knew* I was addicted to cocaine. And a lot of people around me knew, too. But the whole world didn't know. After Beverly Glen and

Pam's ultimatum, I was ready. No doubt about it. I got my ass into Cocaine Anonymous as well as Alcoholics Anonymous. It was time to admit my problems to the universe. I became a star of another sort. After a while I could stand right up and say "My name is Doug Kershaw and I'm an alcoholic" or "I'm a cocaine addict." And then I'd spill my guts with the best of them. I didn't even need anyone to open for me.

And that's another thing. I didn't stand up and say, "My name is Doug." I decided that if this was really about honesty, about the heart of the matter, then I would use my full name. So when it came my turn, I stood, stated my full name, and then listed some of the things I'd done during my drug and alcohol reign. Doors kicked in. Wife shoved. Blackouts. Verbal abuse. Tons of money wasted. Band members conked with bottles or fists. I owned up to it all, brothers and sisters. Amen.

I often saw other faces who had been at Beverly Glen turn up at the CA and AA meetings. And it was good to know that some of them were still hanging in. After all, I had made solid friends while I was in rehab, Jan Berry and Dean Torrence being only two of them. Some of those folks kept in touch even after we *graduated*. Later, during a show I was doing at the Palomino Club, I looked up and saw a whole table of my fellow Beverly Glennites beaming up at me.

Over the next two and a half years, I attended meetings at both AA and CA. And by CA, I don't mean *Cajuns* Anonymous. I mean *Cocaine* Anonymous. Alcoholics Anonymous always got a good turnout, but it was nothing compared to CA. Let me remind you that the postal code for California is *CA*. At one meeting the irony hit me.

"Shit," I thought. "How'd I go from RCA to CA?"

You almost needed a reservation to get into a CA meeting. Two or three hundred people at a time was nothing. I've played for crowds in clubs that were smaller than some of those meetings. They even had to rent extra halls. Just looking around the room, hell, it could have been a television special. The Grammys. The Academy Awards. A lot of famous faces. I had done shows with many of them. *The Midnight Special. Don Kirshner's Rock Concert.* When I saw Richard Pryor's ex-wife, I almost shouted, "Where's Richard? Tell him we got our shit together down in Louisiana!"

But, of course, I didn't. She wouldn't have known what I was talking about anyway.

I learned a lot about myself at those meetings. Drug addiction affects the whole family, not just the addicted person. In my case, Pam and the boys were living proof of that. Mama Rita must have known about my drug problems, but she never said anything to me. I suppose, like Pam's family, she figured I was a grown man calling my own shots, no matter how bad they were. There's no doubt Mama Rita knew that Rusty and I took all those pills back in our Nashville days. But she loved pills herself, even if she was supposedly taking them for her health. Shit, Rusty would find Mama Rita's purse, which was always bulging with prescription bottles, and he'd take as many of her pills as he dared. Pills for a bad heart, pills for high blood pressure, pills for low blood pressure, diet pills, you name it. But Mama Rita was of that generation that associated pills with doctors, and doctors wouldn't give you bad things.

Mama Rita would have loved Dr. Snapp.

I attended tons of meetings even while I was on the road: Las Vegas, New York, Atlanta, Reno, Chicago, Tahoe. Any place big enough to have a chapter. I sometimes went two and three times a day. After a while, I found myself sponsoring people with a bad addiction who had asked for my help. Again, *they* had to approach *me*. That's the only way it will work. You can't drag people to a cure, just as I couldn't be dragged. They need to know they're ready. One person who comes to mind still hurts my heart to this day, and that's Paul Butterfield. Paul was a Chicago bluesman who had learned his harmonica skills, amplified style, by listening to the likes of Junior Wells, Little Walter, and Big Walter Horton. Paul had attended classes at the University of Chicago by day. By night, he was one of the first young white musicians to perform in the black clubs on the city's South and West sides. He later teamed up with slide guitarist Elvin Bishop and guitarist Michael Bloomfield to form the Paul Butterfield Blues Band, which can be credited with bringing blues to a generation of rock fans during the 1960s. When the band split up in 1972, the three men went on to their own successes.

I met Paul early in 1987 in upstate New York, when he and Rick Danko, of the well-known group The Band, came to see my show. I told the audience a little bit of what I was going through as a recovering addict before I did a song I'd written and recorded called "Just Like You."

I did drugs and I did booze,
It was there for me to do,
And it was up to me to choose...

This got Paul Butterfield's attention. He was higher than a kite at the time, and I suspect he was taking and doing anything he could. But he wanted badly to get off the roller coaster, to go straight. I'm sure many things were weighing on Paul's mind by this time. For one, Michael Bloomfield, that incredibly talented guitarist and Paul's former band member, had already died of a drug overdose in 1981. They had buried Bloomfield in Culver City, not far from where Paul and I were both living. Paul and Rick Danko even came to my hotel room that night so that Paul and I could talk. I told him what I knew to be true. "It's all up to you, Paul." We exchanged phone numbers, and he promised he'd call me if things got bad and he needed to talk. And Paul did this, too, a couple of times, catching me at home in Woodland Hills. It was always very late at night that he called, and he was depressed as hell. We talked a couple hours, and I listened as he told me how much he wanted off the drugs. "If *I* can do it, Paul, *you* can do it," I assured him. But even though I offered to drive him to rehab myself, he didn't want to go. "Hang in there, buddy," I said. I could tell his whole soul was crying out, but he still wasn't ready to take the final step toward treatment. "I'm trying, Doug," Paul said each time before he hung up the phone. And he was, too. But a couple months later, on May 4, 1987, Paul Butterfield was found dead in his Los Angeles home, another victim of a drug overdose. He was only forty-four years old.

Imagine a large, lonely field somewhere, a place where all the musicians who have died on drugs could be laid to rest, side by side. This field would put Arlington Cemetery to shame. Then imagine how many fields it would take to bury the truck drivers, the schoolteachers, the mixed-up teenagers, the doctors, waitresses, lawyers, secretaries. The sons and daughters, mothers and fathers, who have ended up on the streets because of drugs. Imagine *that* cemetery.

The sadness is in the ones who died before they knew how to get help. And Paul Butterfield was one of them.

I know that some people reading this will say it was their own fault. They shouldn't have started on drugs in the first place. They were weak. And maybe that's true for those people who remain safe. But no one, *no one*, would go headfirst into that nightmare if they knew what it was all about. The majority of us didn't realize what the dangers of drugs were back in the 1960s and 1970s. And I don't think anyone who knows Doug Kershaw well would describe me as a weak person. To this day I'm thankful, down-on-my-knees grateful, that one of those stones in that field of musicians doesn't say, *Douglas James Kershaw, Born Tiel Ridge, Louisiana.*

So, Pam and I went about our new lives. As is typical of us, we can't quite agree on just how long what I called the "couch clause" was in effect. Pam even remembers that *she* was the one who slept on the couch. I remember it was *me*. Chances are we switched off. Wherever I was sleeping at this time, I do know one thing. I set about my rehabilitation in earnest. I wasn't perfect but I was trying hard, and I think Pam knew that. We still had our moments, though. One day, as Pam was on her way to the store, I asked her if we had any bologna. I couldn't believe her response to this simple question. She started shaking all over, her purse dropped to the floor, and before I could say anything she was in tears. Later, she told me why. During one of my blackouts, I came home in the middle of the night, shit-faced drunk, and got Pam out of bed. I was furious that there was no bologna in the fridge, so I screamed at her for hours, saying some pretty nasty things. Pam remembered it as one of the worst times she'd gone through with me. And it was over bologna.

I stuck to those meetings. I kept on sponsoring others who needed help, and I'm living a good life today. While I don't miss cocaine, I still think of alcohol in a way that will always make me fear it. It's when I'm around people in a social situation or when I'm trying to relax and come down after a show that I still think of how nice it would be to have a drink. Something to help me rise above the anxiety. Then I think of sitting in my smock at Raleigh Hills, waiting for the nurse to come with her glasses of booze and antabuse, and even that desire goes away.

Well, almost. I would dance again with the devil in the bottle.

Amazing, ain't it? It's true. But I'll tell you about all that when the time is right.

What this means, I suppose, is that life rarely runs by the book. And human beings are only human. I'm a work in progress. I always will be.

Back on the career front, things settled down to an even keel. I'm still amazed at how so many people welcomed me back from the brink as if I'd never even been there, teetering like a fool. Club owners knew I could still draw a crowd, so they booked me back into their establishments. Bookers knew it too, and so my tour dates filled up with fairs and festivals. It wasn't too long after Beverly Glen, in summer 1984, that I was scheduled to play the Mid-California State Fair in Pasa Robles. Jerry Lee Lewis, although he was recovering from a broken leg, would also be on the bill. The Killer and I had crossed paths a couple times on the road, even chatted a bit, but we had never shared the bill before. I had a soft spot in my heart at the time for Jerry Lee, a memory that I keep to this day. A few years after the infamous Dr. Snapp trial, I had run into Jerry at Yvonne's club down in New Orleans. He brought up Snapp.

"I understand what happened," Jerry Lee said. "They didn't give you any choice, did they?"

It meant a lot to me that a fellow musician understood. But beyond this "sensitivity" of his, I'd certainly heard a lot of wild things about Jerry Lee Lewis. And I'm sure he'd heard some wild things about me. The truth is, I had always had a secret ambition to perform on the same stage with Jerry Lee Lewis *at the same time.* I think we two Louisiana boys could tear up a crowd, me on fiddle and Jerry Lee on piano. So I was anxious to see what would happen at Pasa Robles. Jerry Lee would be closing the show and I'd be the middle act. Opening for us was an amazingly talented young man from Texas who was shaking up country music big time. He'd already had several No. 1 hits by this time, and he would have a damn lot more before becoming Entertainer of the Year. His name was George Strait.

I wasn't worried about the crowd that night since I was already one of the mainstays of the Mid-Cal State Fair. I was quite confident that I'd be welcomed back with open arms and loud cheers. Maybe Jerry Lee knew this and that's what prompted him to do what he did, though he's not known to be a man who needs any prompting. I mean, shit, he got drunk one night and tried to scale the walls at Graceland so he could shoot Elvis

Presley. *Elvis.* The Killer also torched his own piano once to make it impossible for Chuck Berry to follow him on stage.

But I never thought the son of a bitch would pull one of his stunts on a fellow Louisianan.

We were scheduled for two shows, and the first of those went very well. It was easy to see that George Strait was going to be a superstar. Hell, all he had to do was walk out on stage and the crowd fell in love with him. When he sang in that pure, stylist way it was a cinch. I'm surprised Jerry Lee didn't try to sabotage George Strait, too. After George's act, I went out with my usual manic, full-tilt energy. That legal drug I mentioned before, good ole adrenalin, kicked in, and when it does I always know I'm gonna be fine. The adrenalin was pumping in full thrust. I came off to a rousing applause. Jerry Lee, leg cast and all, did the same. He came out on crutches, hobbled on over to his piano chair, got his leg cast all situated, and then he pounded hell out of that piano. The crowd ate it up. It was reasonable to expect that the second show, with a fresh audience, would be just as successful for all three of us.

I was in my dressing room with Pam, waiting for the second show to begin, when Bob Moore, Jerry Lee's manager, knocked on the door. He had an unusual request. Jerry Lee wanted to know if he could please go on after George Strait for the second show, in my slot. That way, I could close the show. It appears that the Killer's leg was, well, *killing* him.

"He's in a lot of pain," Bob explained to us. I told Bob that while I was sorry to hear that Jerry Lee was having a hard time with his leg, it would be best to stick to the lineup that the crowd expected. When Moore left I turned to Pam, who already knew what I was thinking.

"Jerry Lee is up to no good," I told her. "I can feel it in my bones."

A few minutes later another knock sounded on my door. This time it was the guy who managed talent for the fair. He had a problem. Jerry Lee needed a big favor. He was in even greater pain now and wanted to leave the fairgrounds early. Therefore, would I let Jerry Lee go on second and close the show myself? I decided to witness in person just what kind of shape Jerry Lee Lewis was in. So Pam and I went over to the Killer's dressing room to talk to him. His pain and misery would have made him a perfect pilgrim for Lourdes. He grimaced now and then as he situated that broken leg in front of him.

"Doug," he said. "I worked my leg too hard on that first show and now it's really hurting me. I doubt I can do more than twenty minutes. That'll give you extra time. I'd sure be grateful." I looked over the situation, the grimace on his face as he talked, the heavy cast. Anyone with eyes could see how that leg seemed to be causing him anguish.

I still didn't trust him. But what could I do?

"I want you to promise me something, Jerry Lee," I said. I had played the Mid-State Fair at Paso Robles enough times to know that by midnight everything was over. Equipment was broken down, people were ushered out the gate, and the whole shebang was locked up tight. Kaput. The fair-grounds kept to that strict policy. "Promise me you won't take longer than an hour to do your show."

The Killer seemed amazed that I would even ask this of a man in such pain as he was.

"Hell, I won't be able to do but twenty minutes the way my leg hurts," Jerry Lee said, agony etched all over his face. "I promise Doug."

Pam and I went back to my dressing room.

"He's definitely up to something," I told her. But I would've looked like a certified jerk in front of everyone if I hadn't agreed to let him go on first. That's what happened. The Killer went on after George Strait and guess what? It must have been an act of God, because after twenty minutes of banging wild-man style on his piano, that bad leg flailing all over the place, Jerry Lee seemed to have healed miraculously. At least all the pain had left his body because at that point he stood up on his bad leg and began *really* pounding the keys. A half hour passed. Forty-five minutes. An hour. An hour and twenty minutes. There was no sign that his leg was giving him any discomfort at all. Nor was there any sign of Jerry Lee letting up. Pam and I stood in the wings, watching, and I tell you what. Mad as I was, I had to smile at the son of a bitch.

It's a good thing for Jerry Lee that I was fresh out of rehab.

A few months earlier, I'd have gone on stage and broken his other leg.

It was close to eleven-thirty before Jerry Lee saw fit to cease and desist. I was all ready to confront him when he hobbled offstage, but damned if he hadn't already thought about that too. Rather than come back to his dressing room, Jerry Lee had arranged for his limo driver to park the car right at the bottom of the stage stairs, door open. Before I realized what was happening, the last I saw of Jerry Lee Lewis was a crutch disappearing into the back of his limo. Red taillights smirked at me as the big, long limo hauled ass out of the fairgrounds. By this time the roadies were ready to start breaking down the equipment. The management announced to the audience that, due to lack of time, Doug Kershaw would not be performing. As I said, I had built up a faithful following at the Mid-Cal State Fair, and I hated to think that fans who had come to hear Doug Kershaw that night wouldn't get their money's worth. Some of those fans drove a long way. But they sure got a double dose of Jerry Lee Lewis.

"At least he didn't set fire to anything," I told Pam as I put my fiddle in its case.

Why do I imagine Jerry Lee Lewis, his leg in a cast, being denied entrance at the Pearly Gates one day and saying to St. Peter, "Well, could I at least come inside and sit down for a spell? I got this broken leg, see..."

In spring 1986 a wonderful thing happened again for the Kershaw family, and it would be proof that "the couch clause" had long since expired. Pam discovered she was pregnant again. This prompted us to think of moving. We had often talked of going back to Colorado, to a more peaceful life in the mountains than LA could offer us. But Pam wanted to finish her political science degree first, which she finally did in December 1985. With a new baby on the way, we both agreed that it was time for the Kershaws to put down roots in the breathtaking Rockies. In March 1986, Pam flew to Denver and began house hunting while I went back on the road. We knew we wanted to live in the country and were hoping to find a house with some history under its roof. So Pam directed her search north of Denver, near Greeley. That's where she found us a place where we could raise the boys: a Queen Anne house built in 1898 and sitting nicely on seven beautiful acres.

Our new house had been built within the city limits of Greeley, where it sat patiently until 1979. When town officials decided that a new recreation center would be erected on the same block, the Queen Anne house and other older buildings were marked for demolition. They didn't stand a chance in the path of progress. But along came a man and a woman, a happily married couple, who decided they wanted to save the house. So they bought it dirt cheap and began the process of moving it out to the country. This turned into a living hell for them. They even had to slice off the third floor and move that part separately. Added to this, all electrical lines along the way had to be cut so that the truck pulling the house could get through. This poor couple was just beginning to breathe when, a half mile from the final destination, an axle broke on the truck. The house sat there in the middle of the road for two months. The town of Greeley sued the couple, but they eventually got the house situated on its new foundation. By this time, they'd undergone such stress that they decided to get a divorce instead of a welcome mat.

When the house went up for sale, Pam found us a future home. In August 1986, the Kershaws left California behind and moved back to Colorado. Now remember how I told you my life is filled with irony? While this house sat in Greeley, it was the local Alcohol Rehab Center.

Something else had happened to the Kershaws back in spring 1986, one of those dreaded human events. I got a call from my sister-in-law Marie Kershaw, Ed's widow, back home in Jennings, Louisiana. Mama Rita was on a downhill spiral. Marie was doing all she could to take care of her, but things were getting out of control. In 1984, Mama Rita had been diagnosed with arteriosclerosis, better known as hardening of the arteries. She'd had an angioplasty done, and she seemed to be on the mend. But not any more.

"I can't keep track of what medicines she's taking, Doug," Marie told me.

Marie promised to do as she had always done, and that was to keep a watchful eye on Mama Rita. But hardly a month had passed before things got out of hand again. Mama Rita had always been somewhat difficult, but now she was acting downright crazy. She went so far as to lock all her doors so that Marie couldn't get inside the house. Nor could anyone else for that matter. After three weeks of this irrational behavior, Marie felt she had no choice but to call an ambulance for assistance. Someone needed to get into Mama Rita's home and find out what was going on.

A sheriff came along with the ambulance, and Marie was waiting at Mama Rita's when they arrived. The attendants came up to the front door and knocked loudly. For some reason, Mama Rita didn't hesitate a second in opening the door to them. Marie was stunned at the scene that followed.

Mama Rita hadn't bothered to dress, not even to put on a nightgown or underwear. There she stood, stark naked in the doorway for all the world to see. It was later, after she had been admitted to the hospital and the doctor had examined her, that we discovered what was causing this wild thinking. As Marie feared, Mama Rita had no idea how much medication she'd been taking or how often. She loved all her pills anyway, and so she'd been popping them as fast as she could. The excess medicine had put her in a psychotic state of mind. Her doctor immediately took her off everything, cold turkey, and in a week or so Mama Rita was back to normal. The only difference was that the doctor would now release her only to a nursing home.

"She's no longer capable of taking care of herself," he told us.

He went on to say that it would be virtually impossible for anyone but professionals to care for her properly. It's typical today that most American families aren't able to tend to our loved ones at home, not when they require medication and nursing. I was on the road most of the time, making a living for my family. Mama Rita wouldn't have lived in Colorado anyway, not that place where they "have no humidity." And Marie had her own home to run, her children and grandchildren to care for. And Mama Rita, well, my mother was a handful even in her prime. Still, what a damn dilemma.

It was early summer when I flew back to Jennings to make the arrangements. Pee Wee came over from Galveston and together we drove Mama Rita to the nursing home in Lake Charles. Her sister Victoria— Mama Rita always called her *Vic*—had been in that same home for several years, and so it seemed like a good idea for Mama Rita to go there. She and Vic would be roommates. As girls, those two had been through hell together thanks to a couple of inconsiderate parents. From pillar to post, as Mama Rita always said. Maybe now they would find a consolation in being together once again. Still, I felt this was the worse kind of betrayal. After all, I had promised to always take care of Mama Rita. Guilt is never your friend, especially at a time like that. Mama Rita wasn't happy about having to leave her little house behind, no doubt about it. But I think my being there helped ease the situation for her. I know she believed that if there was any other way out, we'd have taken it. And then she had Vic to keep her company. "Life should leave us some better options." That's what I kept thinking on the flight back to Denver.

We had been back in Colorado about a month when, on September 16, 1986, our last son, Elijah Duncan Kershaw, was born. He weighed seven pounds, six ounces. I was booked for two weeks at the 4 Queens in Vegas at this time. Since I had Mondays off, I used to fly home early Monday morning to spend time with the family. It wasn't a long flight from Denver to Vegas. I'd fly back Tuesday in time for my show that night. So it was again by accident that I happened to be home when Eli made his intentions known to us during Monday Night Football. It would take something like labor contractions to get me away from a Broncos game, and that's what happened. Since Pam had been in labor for only four hours with Tyler, her doctors had warned her that this new baby would also come quickly. When her contractions started in earnest, I turned off the Broncos game and we headed to the hospital in Greeley. Eli ended up taking ten long hours before he made his debut. Again, I was there for my last child's birth. I even called the 4 Queens and took a day off so that I could bring Pam and the baby home. That's something I might not have done if I'd still been on drugs and booze.

Eli was barely two months old when Pam and I took the three boys and flew to Lake Charles. We wanted Mama Rita to meet her new grandson. She held the baby in her arms and made a big fuss over him. We had a great visit with her, and again it was thanks to Marie. We had gotten two rooms at the Downtown Inn in Lake Charles for Pam, the boys, and me. Marie and her daughter Rachel made up a ton of food and carted it all over to the hotel. A lot of the Kershaw nieces and nephews came along to visit. So did Pee Wee, driving over again from Galveston. For some reason or other, Rusty didn't make it. We picked up Mama Rita at the nursing home and brought her to the Downtown Inn, and there we had a nice family gathering.

But Mama Rita was slipping downhill faster with each day. Along with that bad heart she was also overweight. By this time she needed a walker to help her get around. When her legs were bothering her, it was difficult for her to go anywhere easily. But we all remembered the time we gathered at Uncle Abel's for a little *fais do-do* and some of his famous duck gumbo. Mama Rita's legs were giving her such a hard time that we damn near had to carry her into the house. An hour later, when she had to use the restroom, she stood up and strolled across the floor like she was twenty years old. It was hard to know what was going on with Mama Rita. Of course it's possible the Cajun French music had healing powers.

Mama Rita soon grew weary of the nursing home in Lake Charles. For one thing, her sister had become senile and wasn't providing good company after all. Mama Rita didn't realize just how senile until she moved into the same room. It turned out to be more upsetting than comforting for her to be around Vic. Mama Rita wanted a change of scene. She missed Jennings. She wanted to be nearer to her home. The following summer, Marie—a saint on earth to everyone who knew her—packed up Mama Rita and moved her to the Jeff Davis Nursing Home in Jennings. Rachel was there again to help get her grandmother into a more comfortable place. Mama Rita settled into her new home, closer to Marie and the grandkids, and she seemed content there. She had another angioplasty in 1987, so her doctors were doing what they could to stay on top of her deteriorating health. Over the next two years I called her often. And I visited her three or four times a year. It's never enough, I know that, but it was the best I could manage with my outrageous tour schedule. Then I thought of something that would be a nice tribute to Mama Rita Kershaw, a family reunion to be held at Lake Arthur the following summer.

I doubt the Kennedys could have rallied up a bigger family reunion faster than we Kershaws. The first thing we did was to make up a ton of fliers to mail out.

KERSHAW FAMILY REUNION

If you're a Kershaw,
if you're related to a Kershaw,
or if you want to be "a Kershaw for a day,"
you're invited to the Kershaw Family Reunion!

You would reasonably expect that maybe two hundred or more people would turn up. By the time it was over, Kershaws who couldn't even trace their roots to our family came from Kansas, South Carolina, and North

Carolina. This was before the Internet. Kershaws came out from under rocks as far away as London, England, when a deejay who worked for the BBC, also named Kershaw, flew over the big pond to attend the reunion. By the time it was over, the little town of Lake Arthur—its population is only about three thousand—saw five thousand visitors pour in. They arrived in cars pulling campers, in pickup trucks, in vans, anything with wheels. They slept wherever they could find a spot. The town collected a buck or two per car to pay for parking and other services they were providing. Pam and I had asked our friend George Rodrigue, the artist, if he would design the logo for our T-shirts. George happily obliged us for free. The T-shirts had the signature Rodrigue live oak on the front. My fan club president, Ray McCarty, had the shirts printed up for sale to visitors. The town wheeled out its make-ready bandstand and situated it in front of moss-draped oak trees. We had arranged for several Cajun French bands to entertain throughout the day, so festive music soon filled the air. Vendors were well stocked with all kinds of Cajun foods, soft drinks, and even souvenirs. My son Doug Jr. had managed to drive in from Nashville, making the day even more special. But Victor was working and couldn't make it.

Man, oh man, it was hot that day, with heat waves rising up in little corkscrews off the pavement. Even in May, in Southwest Louisiana, the heat finds you. It engulfs you and damn near smothers you. Lake Arthur is only thirty degrees north of the equator. That day of the family reunion, May 29, 1989, you could stand dead still under the shade of a tree and feel the sweat run in small rivers down your back. Mama Rita was in her wheelchair by this time. Someone had parked it under the shade of a spreading tree, close enough to the stage where she would have a good view. Sitting with her back to Mama Rita and in her own wheelchair was Daddy Jack's sister Ozite Kershaw Babineaux, or "Tante Ozite." Whoever put those two wheelchairs so close together that day made a social blunder without realizing it. Mama Rita and Tante Ozite were never on friendly terms. Their two wheelchairs sat back to back all that day, yet they never spoke a word to each other. Family feuds. They come in all shapes and sizes, and some of them last a lifetime.

At two o'clock came the special event that we knew would please Mama Rita most. Her three sons would play music together again. Pee Wee, Rusty, and I took the stage with my band backing us and did a show by ourselves. It was our own personal reunion. It had been forty-six years since Mama Rita and her boys had come off the river to that very town.

Forty-six years.

My son Tyler, who was almost twelve by then, played drums on one song as a special tribute to Mama Rita. Then Ty and Zachary, who had just turned thirteen, sang harmony on a couple songs, proof that the Kershaw musical tradition will go on. I thought it would be a good time to sing "Rita, Put Your Black Shoes On" for the guest of honor. And so I did.

I'm going back, I'm going back,
I'm going back to Louisianne,
I can't stay long, no I can't stay long
But I'm going back to my Louisiana home.

Mama's gonna meet me at the door
It's sad but Dad ain't there no more
Have plenty coffee, Mama, that will be nice
Have plenty gumbo and have plenty rice.

It was a *fais do-do* like no other. And it came off without a hitch, except that Zach actually collapsed from sunstroke after the show and paramedics had to tend to him.

I can't say what went through Mama Rita's mind as the hours wore away. Did she think of the day she brought four young sons into Lake Arthur, penniless, her husband dead and buried. Were the memories that flooded over her that day good or bad? Is it wise to rake up the past as we humans tend to do? I kept expecting Mama Rita to jump up out of that chair and dance, kicking her feet up high, the way she had always loved to do. But she didn't. She sat quietly listening, her back to Tante Ozite.

On July 1, 1989, I was on the road when Pam called my motel room. She had something very important to tell me.

"Doug," she said. "Mama Rita passed away."

It wasn't that I was surprised. But as everyone says, you're never prepared for it. After the first wave of sadness, I remember thinking how good it was that we held the family reunion a month earlier. At least Mama Rita had seen her sons back together again, playing music, the way it had been in the beginning. I quickly booked an airplane ticket to Lake Charles with the intentions of meeting Pam there. She and Tyler were flying in from Denver. Since all I had on the road with me were stage clothes, Pam picked an appropriate suit out of my closet back home. She and Tyler brought it with them. As it had been for the reunion, the weather in Louisiana was sweltering. I needed a short-sleeved shirt to wear under the suit and I had no necktie. We went to Marceaux's Clothing Store in Jennings, where I bought a shirt and tie.

It rained all that first day I arrived in Louisiana, a steady, drumming rain. Steam rose up off the pavement of the Holiday Inn in Jennings, where Pam had booked us a room. There would be no church service before the funeral, but a rosary would be said that night. The three of us, Pam, Tyler and I, got dressed and went over to the funeral home to see Mama Rita and tell her goodbye.

This was the hard part. This was the part I didn't think I could do. As I said, ever since that day I saw Daddy Jack lying in his cypress coffin I have avoided funerals, caskets, wakes, and everything else that comes with them. When I have had to attend a funeral out of respect for the departed, I've gritted my teeth and done it. But I've never walked up to a casket and looked down at the face lying there. I know this is because of what happened that day when I was seven years old, the day I looked into my father's coffin expecting to see him and saw instead that pillowcase stuffed with Spanish moss.

The second dead person I have ever looked at in my lifetime was Mama Rita. I felt I owed her that. When I got to the funeral home, I walked over to her coffin and forced my eyes to look down at her. Know what? She looked good. Pretty, even, her features soft and peaceful. My niece Rachel had done her hair and makeup. And now Mama Rita was ready for her last night out, her last big dance. *Mama Rita.* I finally reached down and touched her forehead. It was cold, even in the muggy heat of Southwest Louisiana. My eyes filled instantly with tears. "Be a man," I told myself. But it wasn't easy when it came to Mama Rita. What can I say about this woman except that I loved her with all my heart. A lot of years had come and gone since that day in Lake Arthur when I came home from the cowboy show excited to tell her of my decision. *Mama Rita, I'm gonna take care of you for the rest of your life.* I not only meant it, I stuck by my promise. *C'est bon, cher.* That's good, dear. I remember how she had once told me, "Doug, you're my right arm."

I stood looking down at her as if waiting for one of her sarcastic remarks. *Whatsa matter, Doug? You look like somebody pissed in your gumbo. Smile a little bit, cher.* I thought of the gray suit I had bought for my high-school prom, which I never even attended because I was working at some club. What had Mama Rita said about that suit? *It's nice, Doug. Now you can go to funerals.*

I had always run the gamut of emotions when it came to my mother. I went from being nervous about what she *might* say and then embarrassed over what she *did* say. And yet, I'd turn right around and agree to let her be interviewed or appear on some television show. I was always proud of her. I admired her wit, her *joie de vivre*, her sheer staying power. I guess, like all those TV producers who had helped create Doug Kershaw, I had helped create Mama Rita, too. I never failed to tell the stories of her wild antics at each and every chance I got. Hell, *I* was the one who agreed to let her appear on *The David Frost Show*. But I knew she liked it. It made her feel important, needed, interesting to people. And she was certainly all of those things.

By the way, did I tell you the story about Mama Rita and the Cocktail? Not long after we came off the Mermentau River, Mama Rita was in a dance club having a good time. A man came up to her and asked "Can I buy you a cocktail?" Now, in her whole life Mama Rita had never heard of a *cocktail*. It sounded kind of dirty to her, a sexual remark. So she let this man have it right across the face, a hard slap. "I'll cock your tail, you!" Mama Rita told him.

See what I mean? I knew about Mama Rita what television knew about me. You can't invent something that's not there to begin with.

I remember thinking as I stood and said my goodbyes to Rita Anna Broussard Kershaw that I could do so without feeling one ounce of guilt. I'd never once denied her. I'd done all I could by her. Blood of my blood. And she had done all she could by me. Now, the dance was over. The priest said a rosary. He made mention of how much everyone loved Mama Rita, her family, the nuns, the folks who stopped by to visit her. He added that even though she "liked to cuss," Mama Rita was still a very religious woman. I guess the priest wanted to remind the Big Guy Upstairs that cussing ain't the worse thing in the world, at least not in Southwest Louisiana.

The custom we had always grown up with is that someone should stay with the departed through the night, an act of courtesy. So my sister-in-law Marie, my nieces Mona and Rachel, and Rachel's husband, Glen, all spent the night at the funeral home, sitting up with Mama Rita.

The morning of the funeral, I woke to hear rain still beating down in long, gray sheets. I dressed in my proper suit, although I knew Mama Rita would have preferred the wilder outfits I wear on stage. We managed to eat a bit of breakfast, and then we were ready for the ride to Bertrand Cemetery in Hathaway, where Mama Rita would be laid to rest. Our shoes made squishing sounds as we walked toward the tent that had been erected over the grave site to shelter us from the rain. Mama Rita had always asked if I'd play "Jolie Blon" at her funeral. I never really thought seriously about it because she was always joking around. Now, here we were at her funeral and there was no music at all.

There should have been accordions and fiddles at a time like this, I thought. *Some of those old Cajun French songs that made her feet move.*

I noticed that Pam kept bending down to swat at her legs and wondered what the hell was going on. Then I knew. I felt it too. Red fire ants had come swarming up out of the wet earth, afraid of drowning, I guess. They'd come up to feast on the feet and ankles of the mourners. I had to smile. I knew Mama Rita would have liked this idea. There we all were, dressed in our funeral best and having the shit eaten out of us by ants.

Mama Rita had already paid for her funeral. And she had paid for her coffin. She had also made sure that everyone knew she wanted to be buried next to her first-born son. So, as she requested, Mama Rita was laid to rest next to Edward Joseph Kershaw. But she was also buried in the same plot as her mother, Ophelia Benoit Broussard. As a matter of fact, Mama Rita's coffin was placed on top of Ophelia's, with a foot or so of dirt separating them. It's not uncommon in Louisiana to share grave plots in this way. I'm not sure how the practice started, but I was told that one reason was simply to save money. Nowadays, since we're running out of land too, it's probably not a bad idea. Mama Rita once told me that Daddy Jack had been buried on top of his brother in the cemetery over in Hays, Louisiana. Mama Rita couldn't remember which brother it was. I hope it was one of the ones Daddy Jack got along with.

When you're a musician, you go back on the road, you smile, you sing, you play for the people. You go on. The morning after the funeral Pam, Tyler and I got on an airplane and flew back to Denver. As the plane banked, I looked down at rice fields, crawfish farms, and wet, steamy swamplands stretching out toward rolling fogs and mist. There are parts of Louisiana as much as eight feet below sea level. But I was on my way home to Denver, the Mile-High City, with its lofty elevation and snow-capped peaks. An important chapter in my life had just ended.

25

CONTEMPT

To the Sheriff of Davidson County—Greeting:
You are hereby commanded to take the body of Douglas James Kershaw
if to be found in your County, and him safely keep,
so that you have him before the judge of our First Circuit Court...
...in the city of Nashville...
...then and there to answer the State for contempt.

Arrest Warrant, Issued January 14, 1975,
by the State of Tennessee

Reply from Claude Key, Sheriff of Davidson County:
"Defendant not to be found in my county."

Damn straight I wasn't in his county. I wasn't even in his *state*.

Before I get to *Kershaw, Doug, Arrest of,*...let me say that 1990 had opened in a big way for me, much like the cork popping out of a champagne bottle. I was asked to play halftime at the Super Bowl, which would be a salute to the city of New Orleans. Seemed logical to bring a Cajun down there to the Astrodome to sing for the folks. Appearing with me would be a gospel singer named Irma Thomas, known as the "Soul Queen of New Orleans." And the characters from Charles Schulz's cartoon strip *Peanuts,* since Snoopy had just turned forty years old. Now think of this. Some executive genius behind a desk somewhere scratched his head at a board meeting and then said, "By God, I've got it! Let's have Snoopy, a gospel singer, and the Ragin' Cajun!"

Hell, it didn't matter to me. I've been such a football fan all of my life that being asked to play halftime at the Super Bowl was one of the greatest honors ever to fall on my plate. Plus, the Denver Broncos, my favorite team on the planet, would be playing. And to have it all happen in my home state made it even more special. So off Pam and I went to New Orleans and Super Bowl XXIV, where the Broncos would collide with the San Francisco 49ers. I got to tell you that it was a rush to play for that crowd. I read later that 72,919 people turned up to see the Broncos get their asses kicked 55 to 10 by the 49ers. Joe Montana came away as Most Valuable Player. And I came away with a big lesson in economics. During rehearsal the television producers of the halftime show told me that I had a limited amount of time to do my song. After all, there was also Snoopy and Irma Thomas. So I came up with a version of "Diggy Liggy Lo" that was ten seconds longer than the time they had allowed me.

"I'm still over," I told the scheduling people, "but it's only ten seconds."

They smiled to hear this, big corporate smiles.

"Doug," one of them said, "ten seconds is a half million dollars of ad time."

I quickly took ten seconds off "Diggy Liggy Lo."

In a photo of the entertainment at Super Bowl XXIV that I saw not long ago, Snoopy commands the foreground while I'm fiddling away in the background. Second fiddle to a cartoon dog. Yet that Super Bowl gig had gone so well and gotten me so much press that I was all primed to come back to Nashville in June to play at country music's famous Fan Fair. This is where thousands and thousands of fans from around the country and the world gather to meet many of their favorite stars and hear them perform. Pam and the boys would come with me from Colorado. We would join up with Doug Jr. and Victor in Nashville. It would be a family affair. It turned into pure hell.

In the early 1980s, I had decided it was time to work out a settlement with Elsie so that I wouldn't have to worry about coming to Nashville on business. Joe Infuso, who was still my manager at that time, negotiated a deal with her lawyer, Jack Norman. Elsie agreed to settle for $50,000. Joe sent her a check as down payment—I can't remember now how much it was made out for—but by the time the check was deposited, it bounced. What can I say? My own family was having a hard time with finances. My good intentions couldn't hold up against actual bank deposits. This apparently hurt Elsie's lawyer more than anyone else because when I tried to contact him again in the mid-'80s, at a time when I had a little money in the bank and might actually pay her some of the alimony she expected, he wouldn't accept my phone calls. I dialed Nashville information, hoping I could talk to Elsie in person, leaving that lawyer out of it. But there was no listing for her. And I also couldn't find a listing for her daughter, Karole. Remember that this was all precomputer days, let alone the Internet and social media.

Then I asked my son Victor if he would call around town and see if he could find where Elsie was living. Victor didn't have any luck either. So I kept coming and going in and out of Music City when I had the occasional need to be there. For all I knew, Elsie had married some other starving fiddle player. That's why I agreed to come to Nashville, on June 8, 1990, to perform as part of the Cajun show that Fan Fair was presenting. Since I would already be in town and since the show was on a Friday afternoon, it seemed like a good idea to book me on the Friday night Opry as well. So, after all the years I'd come in and out of Nashville to make records unheralded, there was a huge flurry of publicity. I didn't think a thing about it since Elsie seemed to have moved to Mars. But I was dead wrong. Regular people might move to Mars but their lawyers don't.

On Thursday night Pam and I and our three boys flew into town and got motel rooms close to Music Row. It would be a quick visit to Music City because I was also booked to play that Saturday and Sunday at Mickey Gilley's Family Theater in Branson, Missouri. The plan was to meet up with Victor and Doug the next day so that we could all go out to the Nashville fairgrounds together. We had my fan club president, Gail Delmonico, and her husband, Tony, along with us. And so was a gentleman named Bob Hoffman, a friend to Gail and Tony. Bob had formed a partnership with the Delmonicos involving merchandising for my shows. He had bought himself a huge recreational vehicle, one that teetered around the hundred-thousand-plus price range, and that's what he used to travel to my shows when he had the opportunity. So we were happy campers until we arrived backstage for the Cajun show. It wasn't the Welcome Wagon waiting out there for me, I can tell you that. All of a sudden I found myself surrounded by four big, burly, serious-faced cops. Since they were all dressed in plain clothes, I didn't realize at first what was happening.

"Mr. Kershaw," one of them said. "We got a warrant for your arrest."

"What the hell for?" I asked.

I was stunned and as embarrassed as a man can be. I had my wife and sons with me, and Eli was not quite four years old. It must have scared the hell out of him to see this happening to his father. To top it all off, the backstage area was crowded with music business folks. But everything grew quiet in a hurry so that one of the cops could read me my rights. From what Pam and I could understand, it was all pertaining to the warrant Elsie had filed on me all those years earlier. I asked the cops just one thing—that I be allowed to do my show first. They refused. Folks from the Country Music Association started showing up, everyone from Helen Farmer to Jo Walker. I believe it was Jerry Flower of Acuff-Rose who talked either the cops or their superiors into letting me perform before carting me off to jail.

It was a hell of a way to go on and do forty-five minutes, I can tell you that. But the fans out front in the bleachers didn't suspect a thing. Every now and then I'd glance over to see two of the cops guarding each of the exits from the stage. The other two stood at the rear of the stage, watching every move I made. What did they think? That I was going to jump on my fiddle and ride it like a broom up, up, and away from the fairgrounds? It was almost funny, if it hadn't been so pathetic. There they were, dark glasses hiding their eyes, arms thrust stiffly behind their backs. You'd have thought they were there to take in Capone or Dillinger, not *Kershaw,* for Christ's sake.

The most pathetic part of it was that my wife and my sons had to stand there too and watch this unfold as I did my show. My heart broke for them, just seeing their pained faces. When it was all over, I was led to the open door of a police car. I had no choice but to pile into the back seat. One of the cops gave Bob Hoffman the name of a bail bondsman, and Bob took off to find the guy and try to work out something with him. As for me, I was driven down to the station where I was promptly fingerprinted. I kept thinking, "Where the hell are all the *real* criminals right now? What are the murderers, rapists, and bank robbers doing at this minute? Shouldn't all these busy cops and all this tax money be put to work looking for *them?*" And that's when I learned something that stunned me almost as much as the arrest did. By the time that old warrant finally caught up with me, the alimony Elsie Griffin was expecting—she and her faithful sidekick, the lawyer—had reached the astronomical sum of $132,225!

Yet, what I remember most about those awful few hours was that I was booked to play the Grand Ole Opry that night. Funny how those things never leave you. After years on the road they become ingrained, as much a part of you as breathing, eating, smiling. I know musicians from the old school who still dream at night of being late for the Opry, thirty years since they've done their last show.

"Call the Opry and tell them I might be late," I told my road manager, Jimbo Byram. "Tell them the truth about what's going down."

As I was being led through the jail, through that area known as the holding tank, something happened that I can laugh about today, although I didn't back then. There I was, the new Doug Kershaw. I mean, it had been more than thirteen years since the Snapp trial. I'd pretty much cleaned up my act except for a short dance with the bottle here and there. But those were dances that most folks never even knew about. So I was pretty much hoping no one would recognize me. All of a sudden I heard a woman's shrill voice.

"Hey, Doug Kershaw!" she shouted. "I was the one on the couch!"

I looked around to see who had shouted that. The scene was getting more *Twilight Zone* by the minute. Lo and behold, what do I see behind bars but a woman who looked as if life kicked her in the gut every damn day. I've no idea what she was in for, but I suspect it had to do with drugs. Maybe even some disorderly conduct.

"What did you say?" I asked. Her words didn't make any sense.

"I was the one sitting on the couch at that picking party you were at!" she yelled, a bleary smile on her face. What picking party? I thought. We went on through the room and left her in that cell. I finally realized that she meant one of the old picking parties I used to frequent in Nashville. Those wild Roger Miller-Kris Kristofferson songwriting, drug-taking, booze-drinking parties. My God, that had been twenty-five years ago.

I was the one sitting on the couch.

I had worse things to think about than past parties. The future held for me a very bleak picture. I knew I'd have to come up with at least ten percent of that huge sum or I'd see jail bars. Lots of them. And I could tell by Pam's face as I was carted off from the fairgrounds that she thought the same thing. She told me later that she was already thinking about how she'd have to fly back to Denver and start begging for bond money.

I had yet another surprise waiting for me. Because I was scheduled to leave town the next day for Mickey Gilley's theater in Branson, the bondsman wouldn't accept ten percent as sufficient collateral. No dice. He wanted it all secured, every penny of it. Someone at CMA managed to find me a lawyer, Carol Solomon, and she did her best to contact the judge who would be handling the case. Now as it turns out, the judge was a woman who at that time was married to a Nashville booking agent named Tandy Rice. No one at CMA could reach her by phone that weekend to see if she might lower the bond so I could leave town. No one at Acuff-Rose could reach her. But sometimes good luck travels with me, and it was traveling with me on that day. Bob Hoffman decided on the spot that he'd go bail for me in the full amount. He wrote out a check for $13,225 and gave it to a bail bondsman. Then Bob put up his big, expensive RV and some other belongings of his as collateral for the rest. That done, I was set free for the time being, let loose back into polite society. I made it out to the Grand Ole Opry just in time to do my show.

It had already been arranged that my band would leave right after the Opry show and drive to Missouri with Bob Hoffman in his RV, that big motor home that had managed almost single-handedly to keep me out of the clink. The next morning Jimbo Byram and I left Nashville on a plane headed for Springfield, where a promoter met us and drove us to Branson. Pam and the boys flew home to Colorado, and I suspect that was a pretty awful time for them. Mickey Gilley's Theater paid me $9,000 for those two shows I did, and it was a damn good thing. Jimbo and I flew back to Nashville bright and early on Monday morning in order to make an 11 a.m. court appearance. But first, my new lawyer, Carol Solomon, the one CMA had found for me, wanted her fee in cash. I had to turn $7,500 of the money I'd made in Branson over to her.

When I appeared before the judge that Monday, I was pretty damn tired. I had done a lot of shows in just a few days and under the most intense pressure. And I'd seen a lot of travel miles pass in front of me in the process. The judge looked at my lawyer and asked, "Does your client understand the seriousness of this litigation?"

Is the Pope *Catholic?* You're damn right I knew how serious it was.

She set a trial date for later on, which would give me time to come up with the money. I had to hire yet *another* lawyer—he would get $25,000 for *his* marriage to Doug Kershaw before it was all over—and we worked out a deal in which I would pay the money over the next few months. Bless Bob Hoffman's heart. He stood by me all the way. I later managed to come up with $60,000, but Bob came up with the rest.

It was only later that we learned Elsie was in a nursing home, at Metropolitan Bordeaux Hospital, which was a city-owned, long-term-care facility. On top of the huge alimony fee I had to fork over, I was also required to pay that hospital $750 a month to maintain Elsie until she died. I had to wonder where her children and blood family were all this time. Where were the friends who cared about her? I have no idea how much of all that money Elsie actually held in her own hands. I do know that the state of Tennessee got a nice portion of it. And I also know that her lawyer, Jack Norman, got a third. Imagine that. I suspect I paid for a lot of golf games.

Here's how I see it. One day, gathered in hell, there will be a whole lot of lawyers sitting on top of a huge pile of green money. They'll be sorting through it one buck at a time, saying "And this little piggy is when Doug divorced the first wife. And this little piggy is for that fight with the IRS. And this little piggy is for the second wife. And this was when Billy Deaton stole half of 'Louisiana Man.' And this little piggy is for..." And that's just for me. Imagine all the others.

There was no way of my knowing back during that humid summer of 1968 that my short, loveless marriage to Elsie Griffin would haunt me as long as it did and cost me as much grief as it did. But I'll tell you this much.

Life doesn't play fair with most of us.

The very next day after my court appearance I left Nashville, as the newspapers were only too happy to report. I didn't make the front page but I came close. And I'm sure that Jack Norman, the lawyer, puffed up a bit to see his name in print as the fearless lawman who had finally brought in the renegade Cajun. Just days ago, I read that newspaper article for the first time. It said this, among other things:

"Her lawyer, Jack Norman, stated that he didn't know the nature of her (Ms. Griffin's) illness, but he did state that she was destitute and penniless."

That's nice. He didn't know the state of his client's physical health, but he knew the state of her bank account. Or at least what he *wanted* it to be. How could he not know Elsie's condition when the two of them had to have laid plans together to nab me at Fan Fair? Well, I can tell you the nature of *his* illness. Greed.

After all those years, it was finally over. I flew out of Nashville and on westward to Denver. I was scheduled to perform again in two days in Los Angeles. And that was fine with me. There was nothing else I *could do* but to go back on the road, make some more money, start paying off that enormous debt. And I did that. I kept up my payments of $750 a month to Elsie's hospital until she died there in 1998. I felt nothing but sadness when I heard the news that Elsie Griffin had passed away.

There are no winners in situations like this. No winners at all.

It took me five years to pay back Bob Hoffman's kindness to me, including the $13,225 he'd given the bondsman and the interest that had accumulated on the loan. But I did that too. And while I haven't seen or heard from Bob Hoffman in some time, he remains high on my list of caring people. I will put in a good word for him if I should reach the Pearly Gates before he does. But if I end up going in the opposite direction from heaven, then I'm gonna take back my pile of money that those damn lawyers are sitting on down there. It represents a lot of rosin dust flying from my fiddle bow. I could buy myself an island off the coast of Greece.

Irony. Remember how it follows me around like a pet dog? It was while we were at work on this book, at Cathie Pelletier's house in Nashville, that I came face to face with the past once again. On one of the visits I made to to collaborate on the book Cathie and her husband invited a few folks over to say hello. My manager at that time was Paul Mascioli, and Paul was there with us. Devon O'Day, a renowned local radio personality, was there as well as next-door neighbor Joe Mansfield, who was at that time president of Asylum Records and the man responsible for launching Garth Brooks. With Joe had come a lovely lady friend, Muriel Robinson. We all had a nice visit that evening. As Joe and Muriel were leaving, I told them goodbye.

"Goodbye," Muriel said. "It was nice to see you again."

I just nodded, figuring we'd met somewhere before in Nashville. That's how it is in the music business. Lots of functions over the years.

Lots of music business parties. After they left, Paul Mascioli said to me, "Did you know that Muriel's a judge?"

No, I didn't know.

"At least she's not the judge who was married to Tandy Rice," I said, thinking back to that embarrassing court day ten years earlier.

"Oh, but that *is* the judge who was married to Tandy Rice," Paul said. "They're divorced now."

Nice to see you *again,* she had said.

I just smiled. You've got to love it or it'll kill you. Muriel Robinson seemed like a nice woman in those friendly circumstances. But that's how irony works.

Back to money. You know what? The only time I think about money is when I need it. And that's how it was back in those early days of shining shoes on the streets of Lake Arthur. Survival is always first and foremost to me. I know that money plays an important role in the modern world. Some people build big houses, buy fancy cars, and wear imported suits. Me? Money buys me peace of mind.

And peace of mind came to me after the Fan Fair arrest, but I had to pay more money to get it. Remember Billy Deaton? The little son of a bitch who took half of my song "Louisiana Man" before he'd give me the measly $1,800 to bail Rusty out of that Dallas jail? Well, it had been eating at my insides to know his name was on my song, and that he was still receiving money from it. So in the summer of 1991, I decided I had to get my song back. I asked Chuck Glaser—of the Glaser Brothers trio—if he would accompany me to Deaton's office. Michael Martin Murphy and I had just done a fund-raiser in Las Vegas that Chuck produced, and so he was willing to come along as a witness and do what he could to help out. I seriously think the real reason I wanted Chuck Glaser along was that I wanted someone to stop me if I suddenly decided to beat the shit out of Billy Deaton.

There Billy was that day at his office, perched like a little crow behind his desk. It was all I could do to keep my hands off his feathers.

"Billy," I said. "I want to buy back that percentage you have of 'Louisiana Man.' I'll give you ten thousand dollars for it."

His eyes lit up.

"I'll take it Doug," Billy said. "The song is yours again."

I walked out of that office feeling damn good that I'd just gotten a part of my soul back where it belonged. Billy got his ten grand from Doug Kershaw. Know what I found out later from Acuff-Rose? Those rights to the song that were in Billy's name had already reverted to me. When Acuff-Rose renewed the copyright, Billy's claim was null. Billy had to have known this when he jumped on my offer like a swamp frog on a mosquito. And there was another piece of information Mr. Deaton failed to tell me. He had borrowed against the royalties from BMI. It took me years to pay back BMI what that little bastard spent. I called him up and asked for my $10,000 back.

"No, Doug," said Billy, "I'm afraid I can't do that. I already spent the money." This is why I don't carry a gun.

But I do return sometimes to the scene of the ambush.

It was at Fan Fair again, in June 1998, that Charlie Daniels asked if I'd come play fiddle with him during his own portion of the show. I had just finished mine, and I couldn't think of anything I'd rather do than join Daniels onstage. And I tell you what. The rosin was flying while the two of us fiddled up a storm. Afterward, I asked Charlie if he remembered that Toronto Festival all those years ago when Yoko Ono had squirmed all over the stage under a sheet while John Lennon sang his song. Charlie *did* remember. And he got the same look on his face as he did back then.

"What the hell *was* that?" I asked.

Charlie shrugged. "Damned if I know," he said.

I'd bid my goodbyes to Charlie and was just putting my fiddle in its case when I looked up to see none other than Billy Deaton walking by. My first impulse was to take him out behind the bleachers and kick his ass. But then I noticed that he was walking like he could use some help. He went right on by, not realizing how close he was strutting to me. I let him be and I'm glad I did. It was about a decade later that I heard Billy had passed away. I guess I could say that this is one of those times to forgive and forget. But it isn't. I still haven't done either.

As the song goes, time marches on. It was on October 25, 1992, that Pam and I, along with Porter Wagoner and others, were on our way back from a show in Japan. I remember we were at the airport in Detroit when Pam heard a television announcement. *Singer-songwriter Roger Miller died today of cancer at the age of fifty-six.* After Pam told me the sad news, I went into the men's room, tears filling my eyes, and I stayed there until I felt enough composure to come back out. I didn't know what to say or what to think. Roger had just had tremendous success on Broadway with *Big River,* and his creativity was still going full blast. He had built a good life with his wife, Mary, and his children. He'd even put the cocaine and booze behind him. But fate doesn't care about stuff like that. What a loss to music. And what a loss to those of us who loved him.

"Old songwriters never die," Roger said once. "They just decompose." He also predicted that if he had to live his life over again, "I wouldn't have time."

As for Doug Kershaw, you'd think that after Raleigh Hills and Beverly Glen, my own demons would have quenched their thirst. End of the addiction story. But it wasn't so. That's how powerful booze can be. But I *had* gone eleven years after Beverly Glen before I had a bit of a relapse, enough to get my full attention, and Pam's too. It was sometime after I decided I would write a book about this crazy life I've led. That meant I had to start digging up all the bones of my past. Old ghosts. Stuff that hurts. Since it had been such a long time that I'd had a drink, I started feeling pretty safe about the whole idea. A beer now and then couldn't hurt me, could it?

Then, one day, I saw some wine coolers at a 7-Eleven convenience store. They looked so innocent sitting there on the cooler shelf, almost like soda pop or Kool-Aid. This was in Las Vegas, of course, the Land of Big Enticement. After my show one night, I went on down to the 7-Eleven and bought myself one of those innocent-looking wine coolers. Damn, it tasted good. Soon I was having a beer now and then after a golf game. After a concert show. Before a show. While watching a Broncos game on TV. I never really went on a Big Drunk, mind you, or did any raging. But the more beer I'd have, the shorter my temper was getting with Pam. I started fighting with her again, arguing, being the kind of jerk I can be when I'm on booze.

"Doug," Pam said to me one night. "You're drinking again, and I'm not going to put up with it." This snapped my head back. I remembered that room at the seedy motel. I thought of Raleigh Hills, of AA, CA, every damn "A" in my life. I thought of those days at Beverly Glen when Pam refused to come visit me. I knew she meant it back then, and I knew she meant it now. I started drinking O'Doul's, a nonalcoholic beer. It tasted so good my immediate impulse was to hide it from Pam.

The famous Kershaw temper? I've had to work very hard at that. It's a slow process. But today it's rare that I lose my temper. I walk away so that I can think out the trouble, let myself simmer down. I'm almost a damn diplomat these days.

Unless you piss me off.

Remember how I told you many times already that my life has been filled with ironies? Well, it has. They keep popping up in the strangest places. It was a few years ago when Pam and I were driving down to Louisiana from Colorado that another one popped up. You talk to most musicians about the road, and they'll be able to tell you where restaurants and motels are in damn near any major city in the world. That even goes for the small towns in this country that are big enough to put on a music show. Chances are we've probably been there. You cover a lot of miles in more than sixty years on the road like I've been. When Pam and I pulled up to a small motel in Childress, Texas, I got that old feeling that I'd been there before, a long time ago. It wasn't the best place to stay, but it was the only place we could find that late at night. We were both tired and ready to stop driving. The sign outside the motel said VACANCY, so we pulled in.

"This place looks familiar," I said to Pam. It did. But it was such a nondescript little motel that I couldn't remember when or how I had ended up there. It just felt as if I *had*. It was later, after we'd checked in and Pam was in the shower. I sat down on the edge of the bed. I have no idea what made me do it, but I pulled open the top drawer of the night stand next to the bed. I turned it over and looked down at the runner. I smiled at what I saw.

"Pam," I said, even though I knew she couldn't hear me with the water running. "I was here."

Let me explain.

Richard Larsen, who was the best man at our wedding, worked for Panasonic. This was the friend who gave us the talking clock that so fascinated Mama Rita that she stayed up all night long, making it tell her the time. Richard's job in those early years kept him on the road a lot all over the country. He often told me that the first thing he did after he checked into a hotel room, plain or fancy, was to pull out the dresser drawer and flip it over.

"Just to see if Kershaw's been there," Richard always said.

That's because for all of my life, whenever I was on the road and found myself without a peg for my fiddle, I would pull open one of the dresser drawers in some motel room and shave off a piece of the runner on the bottom with my pocket knife. I always had a sure supply of pegs while on the road. When Pam came out of the shower, I was sitting on the side of the bed, the drawer still in my hands. I held it up so that she could see the little chunk gone from the runner. We both smiled. We didn't have to say a word to each other. By that time, we'd been together too many years. Pam had seen a lot of pegs being made with my pocket knife. I put the drawer back in its place.

Once, when Roger Miller was asked how he wanted to be remembered, he said, "I just don't want to be *forgotten.*"

I think there is something very primitive in all of us that makes us want to leave a mark, a sign that will tell others we have passed this way before. Like the cut of an ax on a tree along some wooded trail, we want to leave proof that we existed. We want people to remember that we lived. That we laughed, cried, hated, loved. Most of all, we survived.

I was here.

PART 4

THE
RETURN

Dear Friends

26

FULL CIRCLE

"I liked the swamps better when there was nothing here but us."

—Mama Rita, *Newsweek*, 1974

I'll say it again. Some things you have to leave home to do. Other things draw you back. I had to travel a long way to make my mark in rock 'n' roll and in country music, but I never forgot how Cajun music got me there. Or that my Cajun heritage defined me. All those years ago when I started writing this book, I pulled out boxes of old newspapers and magazines. I searched through dusty files I'd had in storage for years. I pored over scrapbooks of photographs, some of people I'd forgotten in the swirl of time. I even found a Bible among those souvenirs. On the cover, in gold lettering, were written these words: *To Doug Kershaw from Little Richard*. It was a gift from the architect of rock 'n' roll. I found a newspaper clipping of Dolly Parton and me, an announcement that we were appearing at Harrah's. I remembered when the management asked who I wanted to open for me back in the mid-seventies. I said "Dolly Parton." She was much more country then, and it was with reluctance that they agreed to let her open the show. But she was magnificent, and soon to be a superstar.

Another clipping of me performing at a club in Denver had in small letters beneath my name, "Also Appearing, Comic Jay Leno." It was a lot of years ago that Jay Leno opened the show for me in Denver. Even then he was funny as hell, and he always turned up with chocolate chip cookies for anyone who had a sweet tooth. Old memories. I found a tattered flyer for when Willie Nelson opened for me in Galveston, Texas, and again in Louisiana before he got bigger than God.

I went headfirst into the past. I opened my mind to incidents I did not particularly want to recall. Sometimes during the first long nights I would dream of the places I'd been and the stages I'd performed on around the world, from the narrow sidewalk in front of the Red & White Café to Carnegie Hall and Madison Square Garden. Did I forget to mention those last two? I played in the worst and the best venues on the planet. For some of them, I was so high on booze and pills I hardly remember having been there. But now that I have a chance to look back, I'll be dammed if I could say one was better than another. They were all places along the road I had to travel. But I will say this. There was something wonderful about that street in front of the Red & White Cafe. It held something that Carnegie Hall couldn't give me, something that was still waiting up ahead: that exciting future.

During the nights, familiar faces appeared in my dreams, people who had passed through my life. People who shaped me, whether good or bad.

Grandma Ophelia Broussard. She certainly wasn't the best mother. She wasn't even close, for Mama Rita suffered greatly as a child. But Grandma Ophelia went on to live a life full of imaginary ailments. She had everything wrong with her, from heart trouble to varicose veins—what Cajuns call *very close veins*. Ophelia even envied and stole other people's illnesses, hoarding them to herself. One time I told her a lie, just to stir her up. "Grandma Ophelia," I said. "I got syphilis." I had no doubt that she'd never even heard of syphilis. She thought about it for a couple seconds. "I got that too, me," she said. Ophelia Benoit Broussard died on February 20, 1964. She's buried in Hathaway, Louisiana, in that same grave with Mama Rita, just a foot or so below where her daughter is resting.

Grandpa Albert Broussard. He died in Big Lake, Louisiana, on July 31, 1972. I suppose Grandpa Albert was what we called a *bon à rien*, a good for nothing. But before he died he had some big moments in his life. Or *maybe* he did. A cousin was recently telling Pam all about Grandpa Albert, about his wild drinking and wilder carousing. According to Broussard family history, Albert lit out one time for Port Arthur, Texas, on a serious binge. He got so drunk that he ended up joining the Texas National Guard and fighting Pancho Villa on the Mexican border. I don't even care if the story is true or not. It's just good to think that at least for a short time Grandpa Albert had a job.

Aldous Crip Cormier. I saw Crip several times after he and Mama Rita parted back in 1950. I was told he died of spinal cancer in the 1970s. I hope that life dealt the man a fair deal. I know he certainly deserved it. In the short time that Crip Cormier spent with Mama Rita, he became the closest thing I ever knew to having a father in my life. I'll always thank him for that. Just as I'll always thank him for the memory of that rainy night in Port Neches, Texas, as Crip screamed and peed, electricity coursing through his dick. *"Boys, that felt good!"*

Zenis and Marie Lacombe. I visited them both in the early 1970s. We laughed a lot about the old days and how Zenis wanted to name us *Zenis Lacombe & the White Shirt Band,* which didn't fly since he was the only one who could afford a white shirt. I never brought up the time he fired me, though. And neither did he. We talked over the best times instead. Zenis and Marie are both buried in Lake Arthur.

Uncle Abel. This was the man who took a cigar box on that day so long ago and made my first fiddle. Believe it or not, for many years after I was playing fiddle professionally I still used No. 50 white thread if I needed hairs for my bow. It worked fine once I rosined it. Nobody seemed to notice that I was using plain old thread. I never did this but what I thought of the man who taught me that. Uncle Abel Kershaw not only made a small boy happy, he opened up my young mind and heart by putting a piece of music into my hands. Uncle Abel went on to marry a woman named Irene Istre, with whom he raised a family of three children. I'm thankful he attended the Kershaw Family Reunion to hear his nephews make music again. In 1991, Abel Kershaw died of cancer in Hackberry, Louisiana, where he and Edward had gone so many years earlier to work in the oil fields.

J. D. Miller. It was in 1996 that J. D. Miller left this planet. I suspect he's writing and producing records in heaven, paying the angels hamburgers to sing. Things really do seem to come around in my life. In 1999, I ended up at Master-Trak Studio back in Crowley, Louisiana, rice capital of America, recording with another Miller. This time it was with J. D.'s son, Mark, who was the engineer and also played bass. He's a fine musician. I had started out with Mark's dad at a time when I was doing my best to learn English. Now I was in the studio to do something Pam had wanted for a long time. I recorded an entire album of Cajun French songs. It's called *Fièvre de Deux Étapes,* or *Two-Step Fever.* I made sure I included "Fe Fe Foncheaux," Daddy Jack's favorite accordion song. One of the reasons I wanted to work with Mark Miller on this session was so that I could put the past with J. D. to rest. I think I've done that.

Marie Hebert Kershaw. She was my big brother Edward's wife and the only sister I ever really knew. Marie had had six children with her first husband before she married my brother. She and Ed had four more of their own. Marie died at the house in Jennings where she and Edward lived. She had been bothered by a bad heart for some time. In October 1998, she passed away in her sleep. Marie was the one who told me about Mama Rita climbing up into the cypress tree with her moss dolls. Pam and I will miss the woman more than we can say. Along with her children, who all loved her dearly, we hold Marie's memory close to our hearts.

Russell Lee Kershaw. Well, we had us quite a time, Rusty and I did. We kicked up our heels. We raised some dust and we raised more hell. We made a mark. Rusty went on to play on a lot of recordings for Neil Young. He moved to New Orleans and kept playing music around town, and he even did his own album. I still think the duo breaking up back in 1965 was for the best. As a result, Rusty and I stayed friends. Better yet, we stayed brothers right up until the day he died of a heart attack in January 2002. A part of me is now missing.

Nelson Kershaw. Pee Wee passed away in July 2018. While we three were brothers by blood, I never felt that Pee Wee allowed me to be his friend, whereas Rusty did. I hope I'm wrong and that my brother thought differently. Maybe the Kershaws will play music again one day.

When we began work on this book, we started looking for Kershaw stories from anyone who had one to tell. We heard some pretty incredible things. Some of them were true, like the time my little bottle of cocaine came flying out of my boot on stage. I was jumping around during a performance at the Palomino Club in North Hollywood and didn't even notice it. But Mike Simon, who was a roadie for me at the time, saw it happen and quickly grabbed it. The audience probably thought it was part of the performance.

But other stories weren't true, like the one that Roger Miller and I used to turn up at the Opry with wild, spiky hair, wearing black capes and looking like vampires. Roger would have loved that one. Or the story of how he and I would rent a plane and fly to Georgia for hot dogs. Now that story is almost true. Roger *did* rent a Lear jet once when we were hanging out together in Los Angeles. We flew up to Vegas to hear our friend Judy

Lynn, a former Miss Idaho, sing at the Golden Nugget. But vampires? Flying jets to Atlanta for hot dogs? I think they mixed us up with Elvis.

But I kinda like those stories. After all, myths don't spring up around boring people. But I wish that folks wouldn't just talk about my wild days, my ragin' pills-booze-cocaine days. It'd be nice if someone mentioned now and then that I did my part to help this planet along. I did a lot of benefits for children. After all, our future rests with them. And I often worked with charities such as the United Way over the years. I played a lot of golf tournaments that raised money. I even held my own tournament for twelve years to benefit charities. But I guess those tame stories aren't as interesting, and that's all right. At least the Ragin' Cajun is alive to hear them.

I'm still performing and loving every minute of it. I've had hip replacement surgery. But when you've jumped and danced all over a stage as I have for all these years, you're lucky a hip can *be* replaced. Since then I've worked in the studio in Nashville with Marty Stuart as my producer. Along with concert dates around the country, Pam, the band and I traveled in the past years to South Korea, Norway, Ireland, England, and France. I just headlined a rockabilly concert in London, and now I'm booked in Spain. One of my most heartfelt accomplishments was when the University of Northern Colorado awarded me an honorary doctorate of letters. That means I'm Dr. Ragin' Cajun now. Added to this honor, I performed with the University of Northern Colorado Symphony Orchestra, with Tyler playing drums. *Classical Cajun Gumbo,* as the evening was called, was recorded for DVD release and aired on PBS. It ain't over yet.

I need to share this story because it's so important. Way back in June 1998 I got a notice in the mail that my life insurance policy had lapsed. I immediately called up my insurance agent down in Louisiana. He told me the insurance company would renew the policy with one stipulation. I had to get a physical. A nurse came to the house and gave me a checkup, which included taking samples of blood. That July, I received a letter from the insurance company informing me that something was amiss with my blood work. Therefore, they would not renew my insurance policy. Instead, they suggested that I get my ass to a doctor. Immediately.

Only those of you who have also been through this know just how helpless and scared you can feel at a time like that. After many tests and a biopsy, doctors discovered that I had cancer of the prostate, a fate that befalls far too many men. For me, it was another swamp I had to get across. The following February, I decided which treatments I would undergo. I had ruled out surgery right away. Hell, I couldn't let my ass lie in bed for three months when I had all those shows to perform and a family to support. So I chose external radiation, along with brachytherapy, a method by which radioactive seeds are implanted directly into the prostate gland using needles and a specialized "gun." I wouldn't have to be hospitalized, so that was good news. I had 83 seeds implanted in my prostate. I looked at Pam when it was over.

"I can probably piss iron right now," I told her. I might have joked about it, but I had my fingers crossed and my knees were shaky.

When I started treatment, my PSA reading—that stands for prostate-specific antigen—was 5, which is not too high. That's because the cancer hadn't spread beyond my prostate. Three months later, it was time for me to get tested again and see if the treatment had worked. I felt my knees really knocking then. I didn't want to seem too concerned in front of Pam. I knew she was scared too. I swear a hundred years went by as we waited for the phone to ring with the results. Finally, the nurse was on the line. The results weren't all that good. My PSA reading was still 3.7. When I hung up the phone, I was certain that I would soon need to start getting things in order to make it as easy on Pam and the kids as I could. Later that same day, the nurse called back again.

"I'm so sorry, Mr. Kershaw, but there's been a mistake," she said. "I gave you someone else's test results. Your PSA reading is 0.97."

I hung up the phone and danced around my kitchen like it was the stage at Harrah's and I was high on Black Beauties. That's what the adrenalin of *life* can do for you.

Now, here's something important I want to say to those of you reading this book who might fit the picture. If you're a male over fifty-five years old, *run*, don't walk to get yourself a prostate exam. It's just too important to ignore, and it affects nearly 200,000 men a year, the second largest killer after lung cancer. Call your doctor and set up an appointment. Or you can find answers on the internet. Don't wait until it's too late. If there are wives and girlfriends and mothers and sisters reading this, *make him go!* Better yet, let me say this to all men out there who should be think-ing about an exam. "Hey, buddy, the prostate is the male sex gland!" That ought to get their attention.

When I started *remembering* for this book, the faces that came to visit me most often in the late hours of the night or in the early hours before dawn, the faces that most spurred me on were those of Mama Rita and Daddy Jack.

Mama Rita. Like I said, she was one of a kind. I remember her in many ways, but I think it's the smell of coffee that can bring her memory back to me faster than lightning. I never open the canister and dip into those rich, dark grounds without thinking of my mother. Sometimes when the smell of coffee rises up, I'll even reach for the phone to call her, invite her to come have a cup like I used to do. And then I remember.

When Mama Rita died, she was just twenty-two days short of her seventy-eighth birthday. Folks who knew her well still talk of her in Southwest Louisiana. What was it A. J. Bertrand told me once? *Everybody loved Mama Rita. Even when she called them a fils de putain.* Someone re-cently asked me if I had heard a certain story about Mama Rita. Heard it? Hell, I'd told it a million times.

This is the story of Mama Rita and the Speeding Ticket:

She'd just bought herself a newer model car and wanted to really try it out. So she barreled down Highway 26 at eighty miles an hour. She never noticed that a police car was chasing her until it pulled up alongside with sirens blaring and lights flashing.

"Holy *merde*," Mama Rita told herself. "I'm in big trouble now!"

I can guarantee you this police officer thought he had heard every excuse in the book until he stopped Mama Rita for speeding. But he hadn't. Mama Rita lowered her window and looked up at him.

"Do you know how fast you were going?" he asked.

"*Écoutez, toi*," Mama Rita shot back. "Listen, you. If you gonna give me a ticket, you better hurry up, *cher*. I just took a big bunch of laxative. If I don't get home soon, me, I'm gonna shit all over my new car."

The policeman stood there, amazed, and weighed his options. I guess he just couldn't risk it.

"All right, ma'am," he finally said. "But please slow down."

When that story first started circulating around Jeff Davis Parish, I asked Mama Rita if it was true.

"Sure it's true, *cher*," she said. "What you think? I'm gonna pay a ticket jus' for drivin' my new car fast?"

"Had you really taken laxatives?" I asked.

"Hell no," she said. Then her face broke into that Mama Rita smile.

The smell of coffee might conjure up Mama Rita, but she's soon followed by Daddy Jack. She always kept one step ahead of him in life too.

Daddy Jack. I can still see him sitting at the table, his gun resting between his legs as he waited for the coffee beans to roast, sleep still in his eyes, dawn not yet come to the bayou. In his scrapbook picture, Daddy Jack is a handsome man. But by the time he died at the age of forty, he had lost all of his teeth. His face had sunk in some, giving him a gaunt look. Life presses down hard on some folks, presses down until they've got nothing left to give. Daddy Jack never went to school long enough to learn how to read and write. For the short time he was alive, he signed his name with an X. He was just another poor fisherman, hands smelling of fish and muskrat, waiting for the few dollars he'd earned for his catch. Not many people remember now how hard Jack Kershaw worked to survive in the harsh world he lived in or what he had to do to provide for his family. Few people remember that he raised his little brother, Abel. Or that he helped care for his own father. For the most part, Daddy Jack will be remembered as a mean-drinking son of a bitch. Sometimes, life just doesn't cut any slack, and I think this was true of Jack Kershaw.

Daddy Jack died when I was seven and a half years old, but "Louisiana Man," the biggest song I ever wrote, was my tribute to the father I hardly knew. Life may have beaten down Jack Kershaw, but he could still shine when he picked up his accordion, nestled it just so on his knees, and pumped out "Fe Fe Foncheaux." This was during those nights when he steered the *Alice* with his feet, bringing us home from a *fais do-do*. That is the greatest gift my father left me. Music has been my salvation.

A few years ago, I found this poem in an old notebook where I kept song ideas. I don't even remember writing it, but I obviously did. The date at the bottom is 1970.

A Peace to Mr. Jack Kershaw

Jack, today I have earned the right to say to you
that I have worn your name
brought pride to your name
shamed your name.
But today, Jack, January 4th, the year nineteen-seventy,
twenty-seven years after you left me
with only your name, your wife, my mother,
your boys, my brothers, your fears, your courage,
your weakness and mind, three memories
and one picture,
Your wife has said, not to me, but to others,
that I am your image, both in body and in mind.
I'm taller than you, Jack,
but I'll never be as big a man as you are,
because you have been weighed by my scale,
and measured by my ruler,
and my sons, my offspring
cannot possibly know your size.
It's only known through my eyes.
But your face they will know
cause I carry it well,
And your name they will wear
and wear without shame.
Mister Kershaw, today I claim,
I have earned you the right
to be proud of your name.

From your son, Doug Kershaw.

27

EPILOGUE: THE SECRET

Greely, Colorado

Digging into those old boxes of clippings and files, I read everything about Doug Kershaw I could find. Which critics liked my music, which critics didn't, which critics didn't know what to make of me, which ones did. In the end, they all sounded alike. In the same *Newsweek* article I mentioned earlier, Pete Axthelm wrote this:

> *Doug Kershaw is a star. He wears bright velvet suits and drinks Chivas Regal from the bottle while he drives his Rolls between lucrative concert dates.*

A Cajun dressed in a velvet Edwardian suit, riding around in a Rolls, and singing "Natural Man." Funny, isn't it, how we invent ourselves? How, like gods, we even *create* ourselves. It was an older model Rolls, but I never let Mama Rita see me in it. I wanted to avoid what she might have said about it. When she thought someone wasn't being real, Mama Rita would say of them, *frou-frou*, that they liked to wear frills. I even wondered what Daddy Jack might think. Yet that was how I was back then. It's who I had become. And let me tell you something. For a while, before the spotlight gets too hot, while it's still warm and soothing, it's a wonderful place for some of us to be. I read on.

> *As we moved out onto the choppy waters of Grand Lake, boat owner Russell Gary opened the throttle and pointed us toward a long, flat island. A few yards off the shore, the upper half of a twisted cypress jutted from the water. "That's it!" Mama Rita called in triumph. "That's the tree where our houseboat was tied when Doug was born."*

It's a dangerous thing to write a book about your life, to start asking yourself and other folks a whole lot of questions. What happens is that you move old stones, most of them covered with moss and wanting to stay that way.

"Speak to me Lake Arthur," I said when I began writing this book. That's when I saw the rainbow, what we Cajuns call *une arc-enciel,* hanging in the sky over Tiel Ridge. "Talk to me Mama Rita. Talk to me Daddy Jack."

I got what I asked for. Just when I thought I had said all I could about my past, I received a phone call from someone in Lake Arthur. This person knew I was writing a book about my life and wanted to hear the truth, nothing but the truth. I had put the word out around town. Maybe most folks didn't want to rile the waters or move the old stones. I promised the caller that I wouldn't print his or her name. And I'll keep that promise. But that was the day I learned the truth about why Mama Rita left Daddy Jack and took us kids to Grandma Ophelia's house in Bell City. It was one of those swamp secrets. I was right. They can bite like deerflies, hard enough to draw blood. This one hurts. On January 24, 2019, I turned eighty-three years old. What the hell do I have to hide now? So here's the last story I'll tell you.

It's the story of Mama Rita and Her Lover:

She was having an affair with a man Daddy Jack knew well. Everyone knew him, and the whole damn bayou knew about the affair. I grew up liking Mama Rita's lover. I called him by his first name. I shook his hand on many occasions. I knew all of his children. But I didn't know *this.*

"The minute Jack went out the front door of the houseboat," my caller told me, "*he* came in the backdoor. Everybody knew about it, even Jack."

"*Quand même je léntends, je le crois pas,*" I said. Even though I hear it, I don't believe it. But I did. Down in my heart I believed every word. It suddenly made sense to me after all these years. That's why Daddy Jack had been threatening to kill himself during those days and nights alone on the houseboat. And it was probably what set him off during his *I'm-gonna-kill-you* drunks, especially that night we were going up the bayou from the *fais do-do* when he threatened to throw us from the *Alice.* I'm willing to bet he had just found out the truth about this other man. It still doesn't excuse what he did, but at least I can understand him better. Love can make you crazy. Jealousy can turn you inside out. Alcohol can set it all on fire.

I've lived my whole life puzzled and shaped by an event that happened one morning in the swamps, June 30, 1943. "Why'd you do it Daddy Jack?" That's what I kept asking his memory. There wasn't a single good reason I could come up with. And so I believed until not so long ago that Daddy Jack's death was an accident. I believed it because it was all I had to live by. Mama Rita never once told me about this affair, never came close, not even when I pressed her for details about the suicide. And she let me grow up with a picture of my father as a violent man who went crazy over her leaving for a few days. So he blew his brains out. It just didn't add up. Now I understand, at least more than I did before. I also know how too much alcohol can leave a person depressed. Now I wonder if Mama Rita told my father she was leaving him for good to live with this man. I would ask her lover this question, but he's gone too.

Sounds like a damn country song, don't it? Hell, I've written hundreds of *You Done Me Wrong* songs. I just didn't know it was Daddy Jack's theme song.

Mama Rita and Her Lover.

At first, this new information made me angry at my mother. I figured she could have told me after I became a grown man. And she might have placed Daddy Jack in a better light. Hearing about this old affair forced me to replay every little event in my memory. I even thought back to the funeral, the open casket. *What was Mama Rita doing?* I wondered. *Was she crying? Did her lover come to the funeral?* The truth is that I can't recall. All I do remember of that day is *me*, my sorrow, how it ate at my heart when I looked at what was left of Daddy Jack in his cypress casket. *Ti gâteau. Laisse ça tranquille, ti bébé.*

The anger was natural. It went away. Mama Rita probably carried around more than her share of guilt all those years. I think of her sometimes as she must have been in the early days, barely thirteen years old, her first child dead. I think of her sitting up in the arms of a tree, playing with her Spanish moss dolls and waiting for Daddy Jack to come home with that day's catch. My parents. Blood of my blood. What was it Mama Rita told the journalist from *Newsweek* back in 1974?

"*When you live on the water, you spend your life doing a lot of things you shouldn't have to do.*"

She was right. So I forgive her. Let the dead rest. Leave the moss alone. These days, I remember only the good things when I find myself back in Southwest Louisiana. And that's Cajun friends, Cajun food, and Cajun music. That's how I started out, after all.

I live a long way from Lake Arthur now, in Greely, Colorado. But I bet there's a moon over the water tonight. I can imagine it. The lake is splattered with silver moonlight. Everything is just a reflection of its own truth when you think about it. I can almost hear the foghorns from the tugboats out on the lake as they push oil barges toward the Gulf of Mexico. Once, when I was a boy fresh from the Mermentau, I thought Lake Arthur was a noisy place. The swamp had been quiet, with its frogs and crickets. Off in the distance across the lake, I bet the oil rigs are pumping right now. The big companies have their drills running deep as roots.

When we first moved to town, I had to learn how to fall asleep at night without waiting for the slap of water in my ears like a soothing lullaby. I know now there's a safety in houses that stay put. But sometimes I miss that old excitement of just picking up and heading out into open water, to a new place where the fish are biting. A new place to tether our lives. That's the kind of philosophy that a road musician knows well. *Chuk. Chuk. Chuk.*

I wish I had sung "Jolie Blon" at Mama Rita's funeral.

Quoi Ta fai? Tu ma quité, pour t'en aller.
What did you do? You left me, to go away.
Jolie blon, Cajun angel,
let me tell you once again that I love you.

I could feel sorry about a lot of things in my past. But the past is just a boat that carries us here to the present. And it carried me through one hell of a life. In that same *Newsweek* story that I found among my souvenirs, I read this paragraph.

There was something in the swamp that Kershaw couldn't quite leave behind. "If my daddy hadn't died, and Mama Rita hadn't moved to land," he said, "I might still be living on that island."

321

Go outside some night and look up at the full moon. It was from the black space around it, in 1969, that the song I wrote about Daddy Jack was broadcast back to earth. That's two hundred and fifty thousand miles. Yet there was a time when I thought Clovis Bailey's radio station in Jennings, KJEF, with its little 500 watts, was as big as it would get for me. These days, especially since I've acquired twenty-twenty hindsight, I think back to all those people I've known in my life. I know they did the best they could with the cards they were dealt. Hell, we'd all like to hold aces over kings or four of a kind. But you gotta play your own hand, not dream about someone else's.

Considering that, I guess I can cut myself the same kind of slack. I'd like to think that I, too, did the best job I could.

So, here's my own take of the Doug Kershaw Story.

No apologies.

What you see is what you get.

DOUG KERSHAW

RUSTY & DOUG

RECORD DISCOGRAPHY

By

Kent Heineman

IN CHRONOLOGICAL ORDER

STORY

Douglas James KershaW:Born 24 January, 1936 in Tiel Ridge, Louisiana.
Russell Lee Kershaw:Born February 2, 1938 died October 23, 2001

RECORD DISCOGRAPHY

45 Singles

FEATURE

1081	When Will I Learn/My Heart Is Broken	1953

Note: As The Bewley Gang (Vcl. Doug Kershaw)

45-2003 It's Better To Be A Has Been (Than A Never Was)/
No, No, It's Not So   1954

Note: As Rusty & Doug

HICKORY   **As Rusty & Doug**

1027	So Lovely Baby (1)/Why Cry For You	July 1955

Note: (1) With Wiley Barkdull

1036   Look Around (Take A Look At Me)(1)/Can I Be Dreaming October 1955

Note: (1) With Wiley Barkdull

1042   Let's Stay Together/Honey Honey   January 1956

1048   Your Crazy, Crazy Heart/Hey You There (1)   April 1956

Note: (1) With Wiley Barkdull

1055   Mister Love (1)/I'll Understand   October 1956

Note: (1) With Wiley Barkdull

1061   Money(2)/ If I Win I Win (3)   March 1957

Note: (2) Al Terry With Rusty & Doug/(3) Al Terry, Only

1063   Going Down The Road (4)/You'll See   April 1957

Note: (4) With Carolee Cooper

1068   I Never Had The Blues/Love Me To Pieces   August 1957

1072   Dream Queen/Take My Love   November 1957

1077   Why Don't You Love Me/Hey Mae   April 1958

1083   Sweet Thing (Tell Me That You Love Me)/Hey Sheriff   August 1958

1091	It's Too Late (4)/We'll Do It Anyway	December 1958
	Note: (4) With Carolee Cooper/(1) With Wiley Barkdull	
1095	Kaw-Liga (1)/I Never Love Again	April 1959
	Note: (1) With Wiley Barkdull	
1101	Dancing Shoes (1)/I Like You (Like This)	July 1959
	Note: (1) With Wiley Barkdull	
1110	Oh Love/The Love I Want (1)	November 1959
	Note: (1) With Wiley Barkdull	
1137	Louisiana Man/Make Me Realize	January 1961
1151	Hey May/Diggy Liggy Lo	July 1961
1163	Cheated To/(So Lovely Baby #2	January 1962
1177	Cajun Joe (The Bully Of The Bayou)/	July 1962
	Sweet Sweet Girl To Me	
1575	Louisiana Man/(Our Own) Jole Blon	May 1970

RCA VICTOR   As Rusty & Doug

47-8182	My Uncle Abel/Pirouge	May 1963
47-8266	Cajun Stripper/Half The Time	April 1963
47-8362	Cleopatra/Malinda	May1964
47-8415	St. Louis Blues/I Can't See Myself	August 1964

MERCURY   As Rusty & Doug

| 72451 | I'd Walk A Country Mile (For A Country Girl)/ | August 1965 |
| | I Haven't Found It Yet | |

PRINCESS   As Rusty & Doug

4045	The Sooner You Go (I Can Cry)/It Takes	?
	All Day (Just To Get Over Nite)	
4054	Little Papoose/Sweet Genevieve	?

CRAZY CAJUN   As Rusty & Doug

| 9025 | Sweet Genevieve/? | ? |

D-TON **As Rusty & Doug The Louisiana Men**

DT-101	A Mighty Big Love/Contract For Misery/	
	The Only Hurt Left Is You/Go Right On/	?
	I'm Keeping Me All To Myself/Two Empty Arms	

K-ARK   As Doug Kershaw The Louisana Man
754   Ain't Gonna Get Me Down/Fa-Do-Do   1968

WARNER BROS. As Doug Kershaw
7304   Feed It To The Fish/ You Fight Your   June 1969
         Fight And I'll Fight Me
7329   Diggy Liggy Lo/Papa And Mama Had Love   September 1969
7413   Orange Blossom Special/Swamp Rat   June 1970
7432   Natural Man/You'll Never Catch Me   October 1970
         Walking In Your Tracks
7463   Play, Fiddle, Play/That Don't Make   January 1971
         You No Better Than Me
7494   Mama Said Yeah/Natural Man   June 1971
7590   Sally Jo/Swamp Grass   April 1972
7648   Devil's Elbow/Jamestown Ferry   October 1972
7763   Hippy Ti Yo/Mama's Got The Know How   November 1973
7813   Nickel In My Pocket/Swamp Dance   June 1974
8033   All You Want To Do Is Make Kids/What 'Cha   October 1974
         Gonna Do When You Can't
8195   It Takes All Day To Get Over Night/Mon Chapeau   April 1976
8257   House Husband/I'm Just a Nobody   August 1976
8374   I'm Walkin'/Kershaw's Two Step   March 1977
8424   Mamou Two Step/You Won't Let Me   July 1977
8594   Marie/Louisiana Sun   June 1978
PRO 346 An Autobiography In The Oral Tradition-   ?
         Part One/Part Two

SCOTTI BROTHERS As Doug Kershaw
02137   Hello Woman/Sing Along   1981
02508   Instant Hero/Don't We Make Music   1981
02957   Ballad Of The General Lee/Flash (5)   1982
Note: *(5) Vocal & Narration James Best*
03065   Keep Between Them Ditches/Ballad Of The General Lee 1982
BGM   As Doug Kershaw
70889   Cajun Stripper (Short Version)/Cajun Stripper (Long Version)
81588   Cajun Baby (6)/I Wanna Hold You   1988
Note: *(6) With Hank Williams Jr*

012989   Boogie Queen/Jambalaya   1989

TOOT TOOT   As Doug Kershaw & Fats Domino
1 & 2   My Toot Toot/Don't Mess With My Popeye's   ?
001   My Toot Toot-One (Country)/My Toot toot-Three (Rock)   1985

GOLDBAND RECORDS By Pee Wee Kershaw (Dougs brother)
1118   That's How It's Been/You're So Fine
              By Ed Kershaw & His French Accordian (Dougs brother)
1155   Grand Pa And Grand Ma Waltz/La' Lake Arthur

LONG PLAY ALBUMS

Crown (Jay Miller Cuts)
CST 331 "Guest Stars Of The Grand Ole Opry,   ?
              Rusty & Doug, Jerry & Glenn"
              Do You Remember/Let's Do It Anyway (1)/Mr. Love (1)/Let's Not Put It Off
Anymore (1), I Wanna
Note: *(1) With Wiley Barkdull, remaining tracks by Jerry & Glenn.*

Flyright (Jay Miller Cuts)
Fly 571   "Rusty & Doug kershaw with wiley barkdull"   1981
              Rusty – Kary-On Boogie /Doug & Little Sunshine -Nothing Matters
Dear/Rusty & Doug - I Wanna Wanna/Rusty & Doug - I'm Gonna Leave Adieu/Rusty
& Doug & Wiley - So Lovely Baby/Rusty - Stop Look And Listen/Rusty & Doug –
What Will You Do /Doug – Let's Get Married Tonight
Note: *Remaining tracks by Wiley Barkdull*

FLY 619 "RUSTY & DOUG & WILEY & FRIENDS"   1989
              Rusty & Doug & Wiley – Let's Stay Together/Wiley with Rusty & Doug –
Knock Knock/Wiley with Rusty & Doug –
              Rattelsnake/Rusty – You Ain't No Buddy Of Mine/Rusty & Doug – I Under-
stand/Rusty & Doug & Wiley –Let's Do It
              Anyway/Rusty & Doug – Please Make Up Your Mind/Rusty – Heartbreak
Hotel/Rusty – John Henry/Wilfwood Flower
Note: *Remaining tracks by other artists*

HICKORY

LPM 103   "RUSTY & DOUG SING LOUISIANA MAN
              AND OTHER FAVORITES"   ?

     Louisiana Man/Diggy Liggy Lou/(Our Own) Jole Blon/So Lovely Baby/Why Don't You Love Me/Look Around

     (Take A Look At Me)(1)/Hey Mae/Kaw-Liga(1)/Hey Sheriff/I Never Had The Blues/Never Love Again/Love Me To Pieces

Note: *(1) With Wiley Barkdull*

LPS 163   "KERSHAW (GENUS CAMBARUS)"   ?

     Louisiana Man/Kaw-Liga(1)/Sweet Thing(Tell Me That You Love Me)/Look Around(Take A Look At Me)(1)/Diggy Liggy Lo/(Our Own) Jole Blon/We'll Do It Anyway(1)/I Never Had The Blues/Going Down The Road(4)/Never Love Again/Cajun Joe(The Bully Of The Bayou)/I'll Understand/Hey Sheriff/Mister Love(1)/Make Me Realize/Cheated Too/Love Me To Pieces/You'll See/Hey, You There(1)/Money(2)/So Lovely Baby

Note: (1) With Wiley Barkdull, (2) With Al Terry, (4) With Carolee Cooper

HR-4506   "LOUISIANA MAN"   1974

     Louisiana Man/Diggy Liggy Lo/Cheated Too/Cajun Joe/We'll Do It Anyway(1)/Jole Blon/So Lovely Baby/Look Around(1)/Mister Love(1)/Going Down The Road(4)/I Never Love Again/Kaw-Liga(1)

Note: (1) With Wiley Barkdull, (4) With Carolee Cooper

BEAR FAMILY (HICKORY CUTS)

BFX 15036   "RUSTY & DOUG KERSHAW THE   1979
              CAJUN-COUNTRY ROCKERS"

     Sweet sweet Girl (To Me)/Cheated Too/Cajun Joe (The Bully Of The Bayou)/So Lovely, Baby/Diggy Liggy Lo/

     Louisiana Man/Hey Mae/Sweet Thing (Tell Me That You Love Me)/Why Don't you Love Me/It's Too Late (4)/

     Going Down The Road (4)/Hey Sheriff

Note: *(4) With Carolee Cooper*

BFX 15143 "RUSTY & DOUG MORE CAJUN COUNTRY ROCK"   1984

328

(I'm Gonna, Gonna, Gonna) See My Baby/Hey You There (1)/Kaw-Liga
(1)/Our Own (Jole Blon)/Look Around
(Take A Look At Me)/Your Crazy, Crazy Heart/Can I Be Dreaming/Money
(2)/You'll See/Love Me To Pieces/
Never Love Again/I Never Had The Blues/Mister Love (1)/I'll Under-
stand/We'll Do It Anyway (1)/Make Me Realize
Note: *(1) With Wiley Barkdull/(2) With Al Terry*

STARFLITE (CRAZY CAJUN CUTS)   ?
2003   ""LOUISIANA CAJUN COUNTRY VOLUME 1"
It Takes All Day (To Get Over Night)/The Sooner You Go
I Can Cry/Mistakes By The Numbers/Town's Romeo/
Wichita Wildcat/Louisiana Sun/Cash On Hand/Hip A Tayo/
Big Ed Special (7)/Mama&Papa Waltz(7)
Note.   *(7) By Ed Kershaw*

51 WEST RECORDS   ?
Q 16035   "WICHITA WILDCAT"
Same tracks as Starflite 2003

WARNER BROS.   1969
1820   "THE CAJUN WAY"
Diggy Liggy Lo/If We Don't Stop Rushing(We'll Never Get There)/Bayou
Teche/Come Kiss Your Man/Papa Died Old/
Feed it To The Fish/You Fight Your Fight And I'll Fight Me/Papa And
Mama Had Love/When I'm Fully Grown/
Rita, Put Your Black Shoes On/   Sweet Jole Blon/Louisiana Man

1861   "SPANISH MOSS"   1970
Cajun Joe(The Bully Of The Bayou)/Fais Do Do/Dans La Louisianne/
Cajun Stripper(8)/Spanish Moss/Orange Blossom Special/My Uncle Abel/
Pirogue/Swamp Rat/I've Got Mine/Mama Rita In Hollywood (8)
Note: *(8) Mama Rita Kershaw sings and plays rhythm guitar and triangle.*

1906   "DOUG KERSHAW"   1971
Play, Fiddle Play/Trying To Live/Who Needs That Kind Of Friend/My
Books And Julie/Mama Said Yeah/Colinda/

Battle Of New Orleans/That Don't Make You No Better Than Me/Natural Man/Son Of A Louisiana Man/You'll Never Catch Me Walking In Your Tracks

BS 2581 "SWAMP GRASS"   1972
Louisiana Woman/Louisiana Man/Isn't That About The Same/Can't It Wait Till To-morrow/Swamp Grass/From A Little Flirt Comes A Big Hurt/Take Me Back To Mama/Zacharia/Vicki Brown/(Ain't Gonna Get Me Down) Till I Hit The Ground/Cajun Funk

BS 2649 "DEVIL'S ELBOW"   1972
Super Cowboy/Devil's Elbow/Get A Little Dirt On Your Hands/Jamestown Ferry/Billy Bayou/Lou'siana Sun/You Don't Want My Love/Honky Tonk Wine/Fisherman's Luck/Sally Was A Good Girl/I Like Babies/(Had Not Been For) My Sally Jo

BS 2725 "DOUGLAS JAMES KERSHAW"   1973
The Best Years Of My Life/Mardi Gras/Willie's Shades/Play That Old Sweet Song Again/You're Gonna Be Impressed/Tricks/You'd Best Believe You've Heard/A Song Called Jeannie/I Had A Good Woman But She Married Lawrence/Louisiana Love Song

BS 2793 "MAMA KERSHAW'S BOY"   1974
Nickel In My Pocket/Hi Lady/Lady Ann/Whatcha Gonna Do When You Can't/Cajun Grass/I Just Remember Just Enough/Can't Be All Bad/Swamp Dance/Colorado/Mama's Got The Know How/Hippie Ti Yo

BS 2851 "ALIVE & PICKIN' RECORDED LIVE IN ATLANTA"   1975
Diggy Liggy Lo/Battle Of New Orleans/Medley:Orange Blossom Special-You Are My Sunshine/Natural Man/Alive & Pickin'/Cajun Joe (The Bully Of The Bayou)/The Cajun Stripper/Dixie Creole/Louisiana Man/Uncle Pen

BS 2910 "RAGIN' CAJUN"   1976
It Takes All Day (To Get Over Night)/I'm Not Strong Enough/You Won't Let Me/Mamou Two-Step/House Husband/Bayou Girl/I'm Just a Nobody/Sweetest Man Around/Mon Chapeau (My Hat)/Pamela Marie/I'd Live Anywhere/Blow Your Horn
BS 3025 "FLIP, FLOP & FLY"   1977
Rag Mama Rag/Louisiana Blues/Flip, Flop & Fly/Twenty-Three/You Won't Let Me/I'm Walkin'/Bad News/Black Rose/I'm A Loser/Kershaw's Two Step/Roly Poly

BSK 3166   "THE LOUISIANA MAN"   1978
Jambalaya (On The Bayou)/Louisiana Man/Marie/Pourquoi M'Aimes-Tu Pas?/Subter-
ranean Homesick Blues/I Just Want To Feel The Magic/Hardly Anymore/The French
Waltz/If You Don't, Somebody Else Will/The Sooner I Go/ Louisiana Sun

SCOTTI BROTHERS
37428   "INSTANT HERO"   1981
It's All Your Fault/Hello Woman/Don't We Make Music/It's The Best I Can Do/Sing
Along/Instant Hero/I Might Cry/Mr. Jones/I'm a Rock & Roll Cajun (Singin' Funky
Country Rock & Roll)

ABC RECORDS   1970
ABCS-OC-13   "ZACHARIA – SOUNDTRACK"
            Ballad Of Job Cain
Note: *Remaining tracks by other artists*

U.S. AIR FORCE RECORDS   ?
#205   "COUNTRY MUSIC TIME"
Theme: Diggy Liggy Lo/Who Needs That Kind Of Friend/Rita Put Your Black Shoes
On/Louisiana Man/Theme: Orange Blossom Special

FILMWAYS RADIO INC. RECORDS   November 1978
CC9-12577   "COUNTRY CONCERT"
Diggy Liggy Lo/Battle Of New Orleans/Chicken Reel (Fade Out)/Chicken Reel (Fade
In)/Flip Flop And Fly/Jambalaya/Momma Rita In Hollywood/Cajun Stripper
Queen/Interview/Natural Man/Rita Put Your Black Shoes On/Cajun Joe/Mama's Got
The Know How/Louisiana Man/Vamp-Louisiana Man

ARMY RESERVE RECORDS   1974
#143   "PRESENTS COUNTRY COOKIN' WITH LEE ARNOLD
GUEST ARTIST DOUG KERSHAW"
Louisiana Man/Tricks/Honky Tonk Wine/Jamestown Ferry/Mama's Got The Know
How/Outro-You Fight Your Fight And I'll Fight Me

COTTILION RECORDS 1970

SD 9030 "RUSTY KERSHAW RUSTY...CAJUN IN THE BLUES COUNTRY"

That Don't Leave Much Time Too Fool Around/This Day And Time/Fisherman's Luck/Keep On Trying/Sweet Peace Of Mind/The Country Boy/Love City/The Country Singer/I'm Going To Louisiana/What'd I Say/Bad Luck Blues/Do Me Right Now

Note: *Doug Kershaw produced and plays fiddle on this album*

UNITED ARTISTS RECORDS 1969

UAS 6711 "BILLY ED WHEELER -NASHVILLE ZODIAC"

My Uncle Abel*/ Sweet Jole Blon*

Note: * Doug Kershaw plays Cajun fiddle on those tracks, remaining tracks by Billy Edd Wheeler

COMPACT DISCS

FLYRIGHT (Jay Miller Cuts)

FLY CD 35 "RUSTY AND DOUG WITH WILEY BARKDULL-THE LEGENDARY JAY MILLER SESSIONS" 1991

Rusty&Doug&Wiley-Let's Stay Together/Wiley&Rusty&Doug-Knock Knock/Rusty-Kary-On Boogie/Wiley&Rusty&Doug-Rattelsnake/Doug&Little Sunshine-Nothing Matters Dear/Rusty&Doug-I Wanna Wanna/

Rusty&Doug&Wiley-So Lovely Baby/Rusty-Stop Look And Listen/Rusty&Doug-What Will You Do/Rusty-You Ain't No Buddy Of Mine/Rusty&Doug-I Understand/Rusty&Doug&Wiley-Let's Do It Anyway/Rusty&Doug-Please Make Up Your Mind/Rusty&Doug-Can I Be Dreaming/Rusty-Wildwood Flower

Note: *Remaining tracks by Wiley Barkdull*

CURB (HICKORY CUTS)

D2-77465 "THE BEST OF DOUG KERSHAW 1991
& RUSTY KERSHAW"

Louisiana Man/Kaw-Liga(1)/Diggy Liggy Lo/(Our Own) Jole Blon/Cajun Joe (The Bully Of The Bayou)/The Love I Want(1)/Oh Love/Why Don't You Love Me/Hey Mae/Your Crazy, Crazy Heart/Sweet Thing (Tell Me That You Love Me)/I Like You Like This

Note: (1) With Wiley Barkdull

SUNDOWN (HICKORY CUTS) 1991
CDSD 022 "RUSTY&DOUG KERSHAW - LOUISIANA MAN"
Louisiana Man/Diggy Liggy Lo/Cheated Too/Cajun Joe/We'll Do It Anyway(1)/Jole
Blon/So Lovely Baby(1)/Look Around(1)/Mister Love(1)/Going Down The
Road(4)/Never Love Again/Kaw-Liga(1)
Note: (1) With Wiley Barkdull, (4) With Carolee Cooper

KANGAROO RECORDS (Jay Miller & Hickory Cuts) 1995
RDW-CD 001 "RUSTY & DOUG KERSHAW WITH WILEY BARKDULL"
Louisiana Man/Diggy Liggy Lo/Cheated Too/Cajun Jo/We'll Do It Anyway(1)/So
Lovely Baby(1)/Look Around (Take A Look At Me)/Going Down The Road(4)/Kaw-
Liga(1)/Rattlesnake(1)/I'm Gonna Leave Adieu/Rusty-Stop Look And Listen/(I'm
Gonna, Gonna, Gonna) See My Baby/Hey You There(1)/You'll See/Love Me To
Pieces/I Never Had The Blues/I'll Understand/Knock Knock(1)/Sweet Thing/Hey Sher-
iff/Sweet Sweet Girl/Let's Stay Together/Honey Honey/
It's Too Late(4)/Hey Mae/Take My Love
*Note: (1) With Wiley Barkdull, (4) With Carolee Cooper remainnig tracks by Wiley Bark-
dull*

OH BOY RECORDS (HICKORY CUTS)
OBR-410 "OH BOY CLASSICS PRESENTS RUSTY ?
& DOUG KERSHAW"
Cajun Joe (Bully Of The Bayou)/Diggy Liggy Lo/Hey Mae/I Like You Like
This/(Our Own) Jole Blon/Look Around(1)/
Louisiana Man/The Love I Want(1)/Sweet Thing (Tell Me That You Love Me)/Why
Don't You Love Me/Your Crazy Crazy Heart
Note: (1) With Wiley Barkdull

VARÈSE SARABANDE RECORDS (HICKORY CUTS) 2002
302 066 347 2 "RUSTY & DOUG KERSHAW GREATEST HITS"
Louisiana Man/So Lovely Baby/Can I Be Dreaming/Honey Honey/Going Down The
Road(4)/You'll See/I Never Had The Blues/Love Me To Pieces/Take My Love/Hey
Mae/Why Don't You Love Me/Sweet Thing/Hey, Sheriff/We'll Do It Anyway(1)/Never
Love Again/Diggy Liggy Lo/Cheated Too/Cajun Joe (Bully Of The Bayou)/Sweet
Sweet Girl To Me/
(Our Own) Jole Blon

Note: (1) With Wiley Barkdull, (4) With Carolee Cooper

ACE RECORDS (HICKORY CUTS) 2004
CDCH2 992 "RUSTY & DOUG WITH WILEY BARKDULL LOUISIANA MEN"
So Lovely Baby #1(1)/Why Cry For You/Look Around (Take A Look At Me)(1)/Can I Be Dreaming/Honey, Honey/
Your Crazy, Crazy Heart/Let's Stay Togheter/Mister Love(1)/Hey You There(1)/I'll Understand (alt.)/Going Down The Road(4)/You'll See/I Never Had The Blues/Love Me To Pieces/Take My Love/Dream Queen/Hey Mae/Why Don't You Love Me/Hey Sheriff/It's Too Late(4)/Sweet Thing (Tell Me That You Love Me)/We'll Do It Anyway(1)/Never Love Again/Kaw-Liga(1)/I Like You (Like This)/Dancing Shoes(1)/Oh Love/The Love I Want(1)/Louisiana Man/Make Me Realize/Diggy Liggy Lo/Cheated Too/So Lovely Baby #2/Cajun Joe (Bully Of The Bayou)/Sweet, Sweet Girl To Me/ (Our Own) Jole Blon/(I'm Gonna, Gonna, Gonna) See My Baby/Money(2)
Note: (1) With Wiley Barkdull, (2) With Al Terry, (4) With Carolee Cooper, I'll Understand (alt.) is not the Hickory 1055 version. Remaining tracks by Wiley Barkdull

WOUNDED BIRD RECORDS (HICKORY CUTS) 2006
WOU 163 "KERSHAW (GENUS CAMBARUS)"
Same tracks as Hickory LPS 163

EDSEL RECORDS (CRAZY CAJUN CUTS) 1998
EDCD 584 "DOUG KERSHAW THE CRAZY CAJUN RECORDINGS"
Hey Mae/It Takes All Day To Get Over Night*/Down South In New Orleans/Hold Me Tight/Mendocino/Cash On Hand*/Mama And Papa Waltz(7)/Juke Box Songs/Hippy Tie-O*/You Done Me Wrong/Bad Moon Rising/Real Ole Cajun Me/Sweet Genevieve/The Rains Came/The Town's Romeo*/We'll Take Our Last Walk Tonight/Wichita Wildcat Man*/Louisiana Sun*/Mistakes By The Numbers*/The Sooner You Go I Can Cry*/Slow Cajun Waltz
Note: * By Rusty & Doug, (7) By Ed Kershaw

LASERLIGHT RECORDS (BGM & HICKORY CUTS) 1995
12 474 "CAJUN GREATS – DOUG KERSHAW"
Cajun Baby (6)/Don't Mess With My Toot Toot (8)/Jambalaya (On The Bayou)/Cajun Boogie Queen/Fiddlin' Man/

Diggy Liggy Lo*/Our Own Jole Blon*/Cajun Joe The Bully Of The Bayou*/Cheated Too*

Note: (6) With Hank Williams Jr., (8) With Fats Domino, * As Rusty & Doug

WARNER BROS. RECORDS   1989
9 25964-2   "THE BEST OF DOUG KERSHAW"

Diggy Liggy Lo/You Don't Want My Love/Louisiana Man/It Takes All Day (To Get Over Night)/Mamou Two-Step/

Jambalaya (On The Bayou)/Hippy Ti Yo/Mama's Got The Know How/(Had It Not Been For) My Sally Jo/ I'm Walkin'

WARNER BROS. RECORDS   1993
9 45257-2   "MARK O'CONNOR HEROES"

Diggy Diggy Lo –Mark O'Connor, Doug Kershaw, Lionel Cartwright and Clinton Gregory/Jole Blon – Mark O'Connor & Doug Kershaw

VOLCANO RECORDS   ?
32035-2   "THE DUKES OF HAZZARD-VARIOUS ARTISTS"

Cover Girl Eyes**/Keep Between Them Ditches**/Ballad Of The General Lee

Note: ** *By Doug Kershaw & The Hazzard*

VOO DOO RECORDS (BGM CUTS)   1989
VD 101 CD   "HOT DIGGIDY DOUG – DOUG KERSHAW"

Cajun Baby(6)/Louisiana/Jambalaya/I Wanna Hold You/Calling Baton Rouge/Toot Toot(8)/Boogie Queen/Just Like You/Louisiana Man/Mansion In Spain/Cajun Stripper/Fiddlin' Man

Note: (6) With Hank williams Jr., (8) With Fats Domino

COLLECTABLES RECORDS (WARNER BROS. CUTS)
COL-CD-6563   "THE CAJUN WAY"   2005
        Same tracks as Warner Bros. 1820
COL-CD-6564   "SPANISH MOSS"   2005
        Same tracks as Warner Bros. 1861
COL-CD-6565   "RAGIN' CAJUN"   2005
        Same tracks as Warner Bros. BS 2910
COL-CD-6566   "FLIP, FLOP AND FLY"   2005
        Same tracks as Warner Bros. BS 3025

WOUNDE BIRD RECORDS (WARNER BROS. CUTS)

WOU 1906   "DOUG KERSHAW" "MAMA KERSHAW'S BOY"   2007
  Same tracks as Warner Bros. WS 1906 and BS 2793
WOU 2581   "SWAMP GRASS" "DOUGLAS JAMES KERHAW"   2007
  Same tracks as Warner Bros. BS 2581 and BS 2725
WOU 2851   "ALIVE & PICKIN'" "THE LOUISIANA MAN"   2005
  Same tracks as Warner Bros. BS 2851 and BSK 3166

CRYSTAL RECORDS   1997

RRCD 8004   "THE UNRELEASED PERFORMNCES RECORDED LIVE
AT GILLEY'S"
  Diggy Diggy Lo/Ballad Of New Orleans/Instrumental/Natural Man/It's All
Your Fault/Mama's Got The Know How/
  Jambalaya/When I Get The Blues-Mississippi Bull Frog*/Sing Along/Louisi-
ana Man
Note: *Flip, Flop And Fly*

SUSIE Q RECORDS   1999

SQCD 9105   "TWO STEP FEVER"
Intro: Fe Fe Foncho/Midland Two-Step/Crowley Two-Step/I Went To The
Dance/Back Door/Johnny Can't Dance/Mamou Two Step/Bosco Stomp/Saturday Two-
Step/My Hat/Let's Go To Lafayette/Step It Fast/Lake Arthur Two-Step/Outro: Fe Fe
Foncho

ERA RECORDS   2001

5047-2   "STILL CAJUN AFTER ALL THIS YEARS DOUG KER-
SHAW LIVE!"
  Diggy Liggy Lo/Mama's Got The Know How/Louisiana Saturday Night/Ca-
jun Baby/Colinda/Jambalaya/Cajun Stripper/
  Toot Toot/Orange Blossom Special/Louisiana Man/Uncle Pen

COOKING VINYL RECORDS   2001

GUMBO CD 020 "CAJUN-SWEET HOME LOUISIANA"
  Johnny Can't Dance**/Jole Blon/Back Door/On The Bayou
Note: ** *By Doug Kershaw, Michael Doucet & Lee Benoit*

COOKING VINYL RECORDS   2002
SPART 111   "EASY"
Make It Easy On Yourself/On The Bayou/Cajun Capers/Go Right On/The Country
Singer/Sing Along/I Care/Do What You Gotta Do/Love City/I Might Cry

BESSETTE/WELCH PRODUCTIONS   2002
"RAGIN' CAJUN DOUG KERSHAW IN CONCERT"
Same tracks as ERA 5047-2 + When Will I Learn/Except

COLLECTOR'S CHOICE MUSIC   2001
CCM 239-2   "RUSTY KERSHAW RUSTY...CAJUN IN THE BLUES
COUNTRY"
Same tracks as COTTILION SD 9030

DOMINO RECORDS   1992
DOMINO 8002-2 "RUSTY KERSHAW NOW AND THEN"
New Orleans Rag/Don't Make An Outlaw Outta Me/Boys In The Band/I Like To Live
On The Bayou/Musician's Woman/The Circle Song/This Is Rock & Roll/I Don't Like
The Feeling/Married Man/In The Backroom/Goin' Down To Louisiana/Stop Kicking
My Dog Around/Future Song

INDEX

AUTHORS

DOUG KERSHAW has enjoyed a prolific career in television entertainment and as a musician and songwriter, recording over 400 songs with such labels as Hickory Records, RCA, Columbia, and Warner Brothers Records. A friend and mentor to many stars, he was a longtime member of the Grand Ole Opry along with his brother, Rusty. Kershaw is a 2009 inductee into the Colorado Country Music Hall of Fame and was honored in 2007 as the first inductee into the Cajun Zydeco Hall of Fame in Louisiana.

CATHIE PELLETIER is the critically acclaimed author of twelve novels, including *The Funeral Makers* and *The One-Way Bridge*. Several of her books have been translated into numerous languages and two have become films. She has co-written *Proving Einstein Right* with physicist S. James Gates Jr. With Tanya Tucker, she has co-written *100 Ways to Beat the Blues*. She lives in the house she was born in, on the banks of the St. John River in Allagash, Maine.